RUANDA-URUNDI

1884–1919

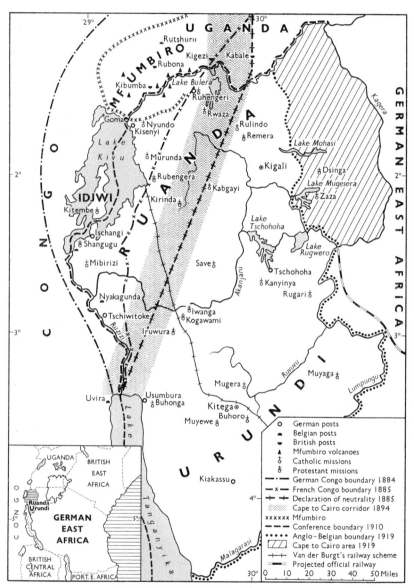

German posts
Belgian posts
British posts
Mfumbiro volcanoes
Catholic missions
Protestant missions
German Congo boundary 1884
French Congo boundary 1885
Declaration of neutrality 1885
Cape to Cairo corridor 1894
Mfumbiro
Conference boundary 1910
Anglo–Belgian boundary 1919
Cape to Cairo area 1919
Van der Burgt's railway scheme
Projected official railway

0 10 20 30 40 50 Miles

RUANDA-URUNDI 1884–1919

RUANDA-URUNDI
1884–1919

BY

WM. ROGER LOUIS

CLARENDON PRESS · OXFORD
1963

© *Oxford University Press 1963*

PRINTED AND BOUND IN ENGLAND BY
HAZELL WATSON AND VINEY LTD
AYLESBURY, BUCKS

PREFACE

RUANDA and Urundi are not a duality, though they have often been considered as one. The term 'Ruanda-Urundi' in the following pages sometimes refers merely to the geographical region of the two countries. I have intentionally used 'Ruanda' and 'Urundi' (the traditional European names of the two countries) rather than 'Rwanda' and 'Burundi' (the traditional African names) because Ruanda and Urundi were the terms used by Europeans during the time with which this book is concerned.

Place names have been standardized in accordance with the official Belgian map attached to the annual reports submitted by Belgium to the United Nations. The only major exception is that the term 'Mfumbiro' has been used instead of 'Virunga'. I have used Mfumbiro in preference to the more orthographically correct Mufúmbiro, because it was Mfumbiro to which Speke referred in his *Journal*, because Mfumbiro was the term used in the Anglo-German agreement of 1890, and because Mfumbiro was the consistent usage in British diplomatic despatches.

Names of Africans follow the most common usage in the German documents.

I have sometimes slightly altered grammar, punctuation, and spelling in quotations.

Prefixes of German and Belgian names have usually been dropped after the first reference.

For African terms I have used the shortest forms—for instance, the Rundi, rather than the Barundi.

TABLE OF CONTENTS

PART THREE: RUANDA-URUNDI, THE FIRST WORLD WAR
AND THE PEACE SETTLEMENT

ACKNOWLEDGEMENTS

I WAS given the chance to undertake this study when I received a Marshall Scholarship to St. Antony's College, Oxford. In Oxford I profited from E. M. Chilver's knowledge of German colonial history, and from her suggestions on how to improve my manuscript. During the course of my research in Belgium I benefited from the friendship and help on central African history of Professor J. Stengers of the Université Libre de Bruxelles. A grant from the Ford Foundation took me to Ruanda-Urundi, where I enjoyed the hospitality and provocative conversation of C. B. Cuenod of the U.S. Foreign Service. In England H. B. Thomas generously applied his encyclopaedic knowledge of east Africa to my work, and enabled me to make substantial improvements by his meticulous criticism; similarly, I have benefited from the suggestions of Professor Ernest R. May of Harvard, and from the father of African colonial history in America, Professor Harry R. Rudin of Yale. The administrative part of the book has been scrutinized by Margery Perham, who first directed my attention to the rich topic of Ruanda-Urundi. Other sections have been read by Sir John Gray and Professor Kenneth Kirkwood. I am also indebted to my examiners, Agatha Ramm (to whom I owe more than she will permit me to express) and Professor John Gallagher; to Dr. Hans-Peter Schwarz of the University of Freiburg; to Professor J. Vansina of the University of Wisconsin; to the ungentle criticism of my friends, W. B. Cook, M. P. K. Sorrenson, and Alison Smith, all of Oxford, and Robert Hennemeyer of the U.S. Foreign Service; to Kenneth Timings of the Public Record Office (I must thank the Public Record Office for allowing me to quote from the unpublished British documents); and, of course, to my wife, Patricia. But above all I am grateful for the stimulating guidance of my supervisor, A. J. P. Taylor, who has carefully followed the project from its beginning, and who, perhaps, has learned more about Ruanda-Urundi than he ever wanted to know.

Yale University
Thanksgiving, 1962

ABBREVIATIONS

A.A.	Records of the Politisches Archiv des Auswärtigen Amtes (Bonn), Abteilung A, Kongo Kolonie.
A.G.R.	Archives Générales du Royaume, Brussels.
C.O.	Colonial Office records, Public Record Office, London.
E.S.	Entebbe Secretariat records, Entebbe.
F.O.	Foreign Office records, Public Record Office, London. When reference is to a Confidential Print, the number of the original despatch is given in parenthesis.
I.D.	Intelligence Division of the War Office.
M.A.E.	Records of the Ministère des Affaires Etrangères (Brussels), Service des Archives, Afrique.
RU.	Ruanda Residency records, Usumbura.
UR.	Urundi Residency records, Usumbura.
USU.	Usumbura District records, Usumbura.

INTRODUCTION

THE novelty of this book is that it is a diplomatic as well as an administrative history of two African countries: Ruanda and Urundi. Before the First World War, Germany, Belgium (or rather, the Congo State), and Britain struggled for possession of the region north of Lake Tanganyika. Ruanda-Urundi was the strategic junction of three empires, seen by the German colonial jingoes as part of a German central African empire, by King Leopold II as a stepping stone toward Lake Victoria and the Indian Ocean, and by the Cape to Cairo enthusiasts as the link between the British possessions in the north and south.

When the Congo State was founded in 1884–5, and when Britain and Germany divided the interior of east Africa in 1890, Ruanda-Urundi was still unexplored. Yet the partition of Africa was to have a profound impact on the two countries, determining whether they would eventually fall under German, Congolese, or British administration, and establishing them as the centre of an international controversy which lasted until 1910.

Ruanda-Urundi was insignificant in the negotiations of 1884–5, but of paramount importance in 1890. In 1884–5 diplomats discussed lines on vague and inaccurate maps as King Leopold delimited his Congo State. Whether one line was better than another no one could tell. In ignorance of the geography of the region, the diplomats took their boundaries geometrically from the heavens; the result was 'astronomical' boundaries, a convenient means of postponing decisions of how a region should be 'correctly' partitioned. The origin of the controversy over Ruanda-Urundi in 1884–5 was no more than the accident of selecting one arbitrary line rather than another. In 1890, however, Ruanda-Urundi (along with the international waters of Lake Tanganyika) was viewed as the link connecting the British possessions in the north and south of Africa. The British in 1890, and again in 1894, were forced to yield their corridor through Ruanda-Urundi because of the inflexible position assumed by the Germans that German East Africa could not be cut off from the Congo; but the British reserved rights to a 'mountain' in northern Ruanda called 'Mfumbiro'. Exactly what was 'Mfumbiro' was debated for the next two decades. The British claimed that it was the entire mountainous region in northern Ruanda; the Germans claimed that it was non-existent.

These controversies which originated in 1884–5 and in 1890, together with the important question of the Cape to Cairo route, form an interesting chapter in the history of Africa. In some ways the story reads like a farce, including a fraudulent treaty concluded by H. M. Stanley, German efforts to prove that Belgian claims were based on a bogus map, and the blunders of the British government during the Kivu expedition of 1909. Yet the controversy produced statesmanship also: in 1910 the representatives of the three powers decided that the Ruanda-Urundi settlement should be based on natural frontiers rather than 'astronomical' boundaries.

The diplomatic history of Ruanda-Urundi is closely related to its administrative history. For although Ruanda and Urundi were administered almost entirely by Germany (the first German post was established at Usumbura in 1896), parts were claimed by other empires. Fear always lurked in the minds of the local German officials that the two countries might be handed over to the Congo State or Britain.

The amount of research that has been done on German colonial administration is minute; the history of German East Africa remains to be written. The second section of this book is intended to fill part of this gap (although it does not attempt to discuss all aspects of the German administration in Ruanda-Urundi in relation to the government of German East Africa and the German Colonial Office), and is based on one of the very few extant collections of German colonial documents in Africa. On a few topics, such as the Urundi Residency, the documentation is thin; but in general the records are full, giving detailed accounts of all aspects of administration. The Germans invented a system of indirect rule; they conducted punitive expeditions; they tried to introduce 'law and commerce'. The history of the German administration shows its successes and failures in Ruanda-Urundi, the hopes and frustrations of German colonialism.

There is no major part of this book which has been dealt with in detail by any other historian. In part this is no doubt due to the difficulty of collecting material from three diplomatic archives, not to mention the necessary trip to Ruanda-Urundi itself to read the almost forgotten German administrative documents. The research for the last part of this book raised the problem of how to write history when the necessary archives are closed; the British and Belgian documents after 1912 are not open to public inspection. I was able to solve this problem to some extent when I received permission to study certain confidential records, on which my account (in Part Three) of the Anglo-Belgian partition of east Africa in 1919 is mainly based; a condition attached to my use of these valuable papers was that I would not reveal my source.

The aura of romanticism about Ruanda and Urundi—the picturesque mountainous countries inhabited by the Tutsi, the Hutu, and the Twa—explains in large part the importance which the imperial powers attached to them. Germany lost Ruanda-Urundi through the First World War and the peace settlement of 1919. Belgium claimed 'the pearl of German East Africa' as the spoils of victory.

Only through skilful negotiation, however, were the Belgian claims realized. Belgium was almost excluded from the east African peace settlement; Ruanda-Urundi was nearly handed over to Britain, along with the rest of German East Africa. Belgium's acquisition of the two countries is ironic, because her statesmen had intended to use them merely as a pawn to obtain the southern bank of the Congo river from Portugal. These negotiations foundered, and Belgium was left with Ruanda-Urundi, which was severed from east Africa and established as a separate international entity. This history relates in detail the diplomatic and administrative events of over a quarter of a century which culminated in 1919; and it attempts to show how an African territory was created and ruled by European powers.

PART ONE

RUANDA-URUNDI AND IMPERIAL DIPLOMACY

I. THE ORIGIN OF THE KIVU DISPUTE

. . . The exact delimitation of a future state in unoccupied country in large part unknown is a task in which the difficulties and the consequences escape all foreknowledge. (Bismarck, 1884)[1]

RUANDA and Urundi are located slightly south of the equator between east and central Africa. They are beautiful mountainous countries, often compared to Norway; Lake Kivu resembles a fiord. Rounded, rolling, brown and green mountains are inhabited by slender, giant Tutsi, stocky Hutu, and dwarf-like Twa. Ruanda and Urundi are delimited in the west and north by the central African great rift valley, in the east and south by rivers and swamps. The political frontiers, however, were determined in Europe in almost complete ignorance of both the inhabitants and the geography. The result was the 'Kivu-Mfumbiro' controversy.

Few African colonial disputes were so irksome or complicated as the Kivu-Mfumbiro controversy. Even fewer lasted so long. The dispute involved two problems. The first was the western frontier of German East Africa north of Lake Tanganyika. The question was whether Ruanda and Urundi were to be divided between Germany and the Congo State, in accordance with the diagonal line drawn across the area by the Congolese Declaration of Neutrality of 1885, or whether the natural frontier of the Ruzizi river and Lake Kivu was to be established.

The second was the mythical—or, at least, hotly disputed— mountain or region which the British called 'Mfumbiro', and claimed to inherit from Stanley. This was reserved to Britain through the Anglo-German agreement of 1890. The problem consisted of what 'Mfumbiro' was, and how the British were to occupy their possession.

Complicating the seemingly commonplace problems involving lakes, mountains, and frontiers was the grand scheme of the Cape to Cairo route. It would have run through Ruanda-

---

[1] Bismarck to Leopold, 4 September 1884, 'Der Kiwusee-Grenzstreit mit dem Kongostaat', *Deutches Kolonialblatt*, XVII, July 1916 (pp. 172–85), p. 173.

Urundi. The problems concerning the Cape to Cairo route and Mfumbiro had their origin in the Anglo-German agreement of 1890.[2] The Kivu dispute originated in the diplomacy which created the Congo State.

Leopold II was able to realize his enormous ambitions in central Africa only because of Bismarck's support during the years 1884–5.[3] But even Bismarck balked at Leopold's original territorial designs. In June 1884 Leopold sent to Bismarck through the German Minister in Brussels a draft of the proposed treaty between the International Association of the Congo and Germany. The Congo 'would stretch from the Atlantic toward the possessions of the Sultan of Zanzibar'.[4] Bismarck flatly rejected the scheme, probably more because he thought that the other European powers would never recognize these grandiose claims than because of his own objections to Leopold's territorial pretensions. On 8 August 1884 Leopold wrote to his confidant, Bleichröder,[5] the Berlin banker, asking him to urge Bismarck to accept the boundaries sketched on another map.[6] His proposals were now more modest. The eastern boundary followed the west shore of Lake Tanganyika; the real goal was the 'Muta Nzige',[7] which the boundary of the Congo enclosed. The frontier from the north end of Lake Tanganyika arched to the west, then curved gradually back to the thirtieth meridian east longitude. This was the origin of the curved line on the map attached to the Congolese-German agreement of 1884.

Bismarck's response to Leopold's boundary proposals was cautious. There did not appear to be any difficulties, but he observed that a boundary demarcation through unexplored territory could result in unforeseen problems. Bismarck preferred to speak in a general way about the territories of the Association. This would obviate criticism from the other powers.[8]

---

[2] See below, chapters II and III.
[3] See R. S. Thomson, *Fondation de l'Etat Indépendant du Congo* (Brussels, 1933); and S. E. Crowe, *The Berlin West African Conference* (London, 1942).
[4] See note A, p. 272.
[5] See M. E. Townsend, *The Origins of Modern German Colonialism* (New York, 1921), p. 110.
[6] 'Kiwusee-Grenzstreit', p. 172.
[7] Lake Edward, which was greatly exaggerated in size on the early maps.
[8] Bismarck to Leopold, 4 September 1884, 'Kiwusee-Grenzstreit', p. 173.

Bismarck clearly foresaw the dangers of drawing definite boundaries through unknown territory.[9] But Leopold was persuasive and Bismarck indifferent; on 8 November 1884 Germany recognized the International Association of the Congo—with definite boundaries.[1] Leopold was sure that France would follow shortly with identical recognition of Congolese claims.[2]

The Congo boundaries on the map accompanying the Congolese-French agreement of 5 February 1885,[3] however, differed in some important respects—which seemed insignificant at the time—from the boundaries of the Congolese-German agreement. The boundary from the north end of Lake Tanganyika, for instance, in contrast to the western sweep of the one of the Congolese-German agreement, was now drawn northwards, following the hypothetical course of the unexplored Ruzizi river, to the second degree south latitude, where it then gradually curved eastwards to the intersection of the first degree south latitude with the thirtieth meridian east longitude. Lake Kivu was drawn to the east of the Congolese frontier.[4]

Still more differences appeared in Leopold's Declaration of Neutrality of 1 August 1885.[5] A draft of the Declaration had been read to Bismarck while he was convalescing in Kissingen the previous June. He was concerned, of course, to see whether the boundaries of the Congo corresponded to the Congolese-German agreement. According to the draft Declaration, the frontier in the east ran: 'The 30th degree of longitude east of Greenwich up to 1° 20′ of south latitude; a straight line drawn from the intersection of the 30th degree of longitude by the

[9] Cf. Crowe, pp. 177–8.
[1] See Sir Edward Hertslet, *The Map of Africa by Treaty* (3 vols.; London, 1909 edition), III, pp. 572–3. Article VI: 'The German Empire is ready on its part to recognize the frontiers of the territory of the Association and of the new State which is to be created, as they are shown on the annexed map.' The map, however, was not published with the Convention. The boundary north of Lake Tanganyika corresponded with the one marked on the map sent to Bismarck on 8 August 1884. The United States Declaration had not mentioned territorial delimitation.
[2] Leopold to Bismarck, 11 September 1884, in Thomson, pp. 323–4.
[3] See Hertslet, III, pp. 564–5.
[4] The Belgian government recognized the International Association on 23 February 1885. The boundaries on the map annexed to this agreement approximated roughly those on the Congolese-French map. See Hertslet, III, p. 544.
[5] A map was not annexed to the Declaration; the subsequent controversies were based exclusively on the text of the Declaration.
See Hertslet, III, pp. 552–3. The different boundaries are illustrated on the map facing p. 604.

parallel of 1° 20′ south latitude, as far as the northern extremity of Lake Tanganyika.'[6]

This was in contrast to both the Congolese-German and Congolese-French agreements; a frontier following a straight line had been substituted for the curved boundaries.

Bismarck referred the draft to the German Foreign Office, requesting that the boundaries be examined against the previous agreements.[7] An expert did not examine the document; instead the Director of the *Geheime Kanzlei*, Wolman, who had been present at the Berlin African Conference as a protocol officer, gave his perfunctory approval. The Germans later claimed that no one had studied the Belgian note closely. But if the document was not examined with German 'Gründlichkeit', the German Foreign Office was at least aware of the discrepancies.

On 21 July 1885 Germany approved the draft:

According to the wish of His Majesty the King of the Belgians, the draft declaration of His Majesty's inauguration as 'Souverain de l'Etat Indépendant du Congo' and the draft declaring the neutrality of the new state have been transmitted to Prince von Bismarck through the offices of the imperial representative, Graf von Brandenburg. An examination of the Congo boundaries reported to the treaty powers indicated that they on the whole correspond with those arrived at in the previous treaties of the 'Association Internationale du Congo', with Germany, France, and Portugal. His Excellency makes no objection to such further concession which the French treaty extends to the Association in comparison with the German draft. His Excellency likewise acknowledges that the Declaration of Neutrality draws the east boundary of the new state through Lake Tanganyika and Lake Moero, although according to the French treaty the west banks of each lake would form the boundary. The indication of the northwest boundary is possibly in error. The declaration states, page two, paragraph 3: 'la rivère Chiloango depuis l'océan jusqu'à

---

[6] The draft was identical with the Declaration in its final form; see Hertslet, III, p. 553. On the translation, see Arthur R. Hinks, 'Notes on the Technique of Boundary Delimitation', *Geographical Journal*, LVIII, December 1921, p. 418.

[7] 'The Reichs Chancellor asks whether the Belgian documents submitted by Graf von Brandenburg are in agreement with the specifications of the Conference, specifically with reference to the boundaries of the Congo. If this is the case, please answer that the Reichs Chancellor is in agreement. His Excellency himself is not interested in dealing with the matter any further.' Bismarck to A.A., 9 June 1885 (A. 4557 I 8066/85), in 'Denkschrift über deutsch-ostafrikanisch-kongolesische Streitfragen', undated (1909), A.A. 3/3.

sa source la plus septentrionale.' Instead, according to the above citation, the Chiloango should form the northwest boundary of the Congo at the point where the Luculla opens into it, in accordance with the treaties with France and Portugal. His Excellency believes he ought to draw attention to this contradiction, lest it give rise to possible disputes. Otherwise the Reichs Chancellor declares himself in agreement. . . .[8]

Clearly the German Foreign Office was aware that the Congo boundary was now drawn through Lake Tanganyika, that a straight line north of the lake had been substituted for a curved one. Germany made no objection. Why?

In 1885 German colonialism in east Africa had hardly begun; only the most rabid imperialists could foresee the possibility that one day German East Africa might border the Congo. The territory was unexplored: who was to say that a straight line might prove less satisfactory than one following the supposed course of an unknown river or an even more indefinite line curving westward? One arbitrary line was as good as another; in any case the boundaries did not directly affect German claims. In contrast to the Chiloango, which involved Portuguese and French claims, the region north of Lake Tanganyika was in darkest Africa. Perhaps the modification was merely to simplify the form of the Declaration. Bismarck was in poor health; he had neither a colonial office nor a group of experts upon which to rely. Wolman had examined the document, if not superficially, at least without foreseeing possible consequences. Anyway the various maps were on such a small scale that it was impossible to be exact. The Germans simply did not care.

Leopold did care. The differences between the boundaries appeared slight when they were compared: 'these [boundaries] . . . on the whole correspond.'[9] In fact, the Congo had grown 490,000 square kilometres.[1]

On 25 August 1885 Germany ratified the boundaries described in the Declaration of Neutrality. The ratification had two parts, one recognizing the neutrality of the Congo State,

---

[8] Beust to Caraman-Chimay, 21 July 1885, 'Kiwusee-Grenzstreit', pp. 175–6; see also 'Note sur le territoire contesté de la Ruzizi et du Kivu', undated (1908), M.A.E. 1/38/5.

[9] This was the crucial phrase: 'In der Hauptsache übereinstimmen', which the Belgians translated as 'en général'.

[1] See the 'Kiwusee-Grenzstreit', p. 174. 13,000 square kilometres affected Ruanda-Urundi; see also 'Denkschrift'.

the other recognizing its boundaries. With this the matter seemed closed. It was not until years later when the territory north of Lake Tanganyika was opened up that the question was raised whether the boundary, or which boundary, had been correctly drawn. The Belgians in 1910 argued that the German ratification in 1885 of the straight line boundary was 'explicit and precise'; the Germans pointed out that their acceptance was based on previously concluded treaties, as was stated in the Declaration.[2]

These attempts to determine political boundaries in unexplored country could only result in difficulties, mistakes and confusion. Eventual adjustment was necessary, if only to agree on which was the legal frontier. Leopold, however, refused to cooperate; by 1910 the Germans were convinced that he was, moreover, guilty of fraud.

[2] See Hertslet, III, p. 552.

II. THE SCRAMBLE FOR RUANDA-URUNDI

. . . The territory we think essential to the future development of British territorial influence in central Africa. . . . (Sir William Mackinnon, Director of the Imperial British East Africa Company, 1890)[1]

WITHIN five years after the founding of the Congo State the region north of Lake Tanganyika became highly coveted; the battle for it was fought both in Europe and in Africa.

As Britain and Germany divided east Africa they invoked two principles[2] to defend their claims. The first was the 'hinterland doctrine'.[3] In 1886 the two powers had delimited their spheres of influence east of Lake Victoria;[4] in 1887 they agreed to 'discourage annexation' in the rear of each other's sphere—where one power occupied the coast the other could not, 'without consent, occupy unclaimed regions in its rear.'[5] The Germans were free to colonize to the south of Lake Victoria, and, as the German colonial enthusiasts interpreted the theory, to the west of the lake also[6]—which would have included Ruanda-Urundi. The British would confine themselves to the north of the lake; this was similarly interpreted by the British jingoes to include the west.[7] Had the hinterland agreement

[1] Mackinnon to Nicol, 1 August 1889, forwarded to Stanley 5 November 1889, F.O. 84/2036.
[2] Both are discussed in Salisbury to Malet, no. 223 Africa, 14 June 1890, F.O. 84/2030; see also: Lady Gwendolen Cecil, *The Life of Lord Salisbury* (4 vols.; London, 1931), IV, pp. 283–4; J. S. Keltie, *The Partition of Africa* (London, 1895), pp. 245–6; F. D. Lugard, *The Rise of Our East African Empire* (2 vols.; London, 1893), II, pp. 599 600; and *The Times* editorial of 5 June 1890.
[3] See especially *The Times*, 10 April 1890; and Hatzfeldt to Marschall, 14 May 1890, *Die Grosse Politik*, VIII, no. 1676.
[4] Hertslet, III, pp. 882–7. The line ran to the point of intersection of 1° south latitude with the east shore of Lake Victoria.
[5] Salisbury to Malet, no. 223 Africa, 14 June 1890, F.O. 84/2030.
[6] But seldom north of the 1st parallel. Even the 'bellicose and defiant' *Kölnische Zeitung*, as *The Times* dubbed it, usually regarded Uganda and Equatoria as out of bounds. (*The Times*, 5 April 1890; also 12 April 1890). The German jingoes, however, left no room for a link connecting the British possessions in the north and south, but insisted on all the region from Lake Victoria to the Congo. See *The Times*, 24 May 1890.
[7] And even the southwest; see Kemball to Anderson, 2 June 1890, F.O. 84/2083.

extended definitely the line of demarcation, the boundary would probably have been the first degree south latitude to the eastern frontier(s) of the Congo.[8] But the hinterland agreement was vague. As *The Times* commented in 1890, it 'left considerable room for misunderstanding in the future'.[9]

Although the first principle was 'not entirely destitute of support from international usage',[1] the second, according to Salisbury, was more valid. It was the theory of 'effective occupation'. The discovery of a region and the establishment of missions and stations were far stronger claims than the coincidence that certain territories lay within the same parallels of latitude as possessions further to the east. Even questionable treaties with African chiefs were a stronger claim than the vague hinterland doctrine. The question in 1890 was whether there were any treaties affecting Ruanda-Urundi which could be used to support British or German claims north of Lake Tanganyika.

In the late 1880s nationals of both powers were competing for the region between Lake Tanganyika and Lake Victoria, pressing their governments for annexation.[2] Two entirely different ideas of empire clashed in central Africa. The one was a British Cape to Cairo route, spanning the continent from north to south; the other, a German central African empire,[3] stretching from east to west. While Stanley merely urged annexation of what he considered valuable territory, William

---

[8] In September 1888 Mackinnon, the Director of the Imperial British East Africa Company, fearing German annexation west of Lake Victoria, had written to Salisbury about the necessity for delimitation. According to Mackinnon, the understanding of 2 July 1887 'expressly stated that Germany desired a free hand only in the territories south of the Victoria Nyanza Lake and eastwards from Lakes Tanganyika and Nyasa', leaving the west of the lake for the British. Mackinnon then said that the boundary should run west from Lake Victoria along the second parallel south latitude—which would not have given the British Company access to Lake Tanganyika. (Mackinnon to Salisbury, 24 September 1888, F.O. 84/1928.) H. Percy Anderson, the Africa expert in the British Foreign Office, however—in 1888—interpreted the agreement to mean that the division should be along the first parallel south latitude. (Anderson's minute on Mackinnon's letter of 24 September.)

[9] 5 June 1890.

[1] Earlier Salisbury had denied the hinterland principle any validity at all in international law. Hatzfeldt to Marschall, 14 May 1890.

[2] See especially R. Coupland, *The Exploitation of East Africa, 1856–90* (London, 1939), p. 319.

[3] See the map in F. M. Müller, *Deutschland-Zanzibar-Ostafrika* (East Berlin, 1959), p. 481. This work contains a fully documented account of the Peters and Emin expeditions based on the German colonial archives in Potsdam.

Mackinnon and Harry Johnston were committed definitely to the Cape to Cairo notion. Karl Peters and Emin Pasha tried to extend Germany's influence to the sources of the Nile, and Emin even aimed to link German East Africa with the Cameroons. All these schemes would have entailed acquisition of Ruanda-Urundi.[4]

Stanley's was the only exploit that directly influenced the Anglo-German settlement in 1890. The rest were either frustrated from the outset, or were ineffective because their results became known after the negotiations and agreement had been concluded. The Mfumbiro controversy was a product of Stanley's treaties.

Stanley arrived—with the rescued Emin—at Mackay's mission station on the south end of Lake Victoria in August 1889, after having travelled from Lake Edward on one of the 'most peaceful and happy marches ever made in Africa'. 'Four hundred miles of an absolutely new region, untravelled and unvisited by any white man . . . were travelled by us without meeting a single instance of tribal hostility.'[5]

Stanley had concluded six treaties on the way.[6] As Sir John Gray has correctly pointed out,[7] most of the documents were vague and inaccurate. Even whether they were ever concluded is highly questionable. Stanley wrote to Mackinnon in February 1890: 'I have made several verbally [sic] but no written

---

[4] These adventures have been the subject of much comment and research. It lies beyond the scope of this study to deal with them in detail; what is necessary is to show the background and part they played in the Anglo-German delimitation of 1890 and what the consequences might have been for Ruanda-Urundi. Rivalry for Uganda will be considered only to the extent that it influenced the 1890 negotiations; British acquisition of Uganda would not necessarily have meant a British Ruanda-Urundi—as was shown; a German central African empire would have included a German Ruanda-Urundi.

[5] Stanley to Euan-Smith, 19 December 1899, *Accounts and Papers*, LI, Africa no. 4, 1890, c. 5906. After crossing the Semliki river, Stanley and his group skirted the western edge of the 'splendid range of snowy mountains called Ruwenzori', and camped on the southern shore of Lake Edward. From there he marched through Ankole and crossed the Kagera river into Karagwe.

[6] See note B, p. 272.

[7] 'Early Treaties in Uganda, 1888–1891', *Uganda Journal*, XII, March 1948, pp. 25–42. 'As I have said in my article . . ., I believe that in the majority of cases the persons named in those documents did in all probability go through a ceremony of blood brotherhood either with Stanley himself or else with one of his officers, but at the same time I do not believe that any one of those chiefs understood that he was giving away "all rights of government . . . and the sovereign right and right of government over our country for ever." . . . I think I can confidently say that the idea of cession of sovereignty and rights of government never entered the heads of any of them.' Sir John Gray, in a letter to me of 8 June 1961.

[treaties]—as the Pasha and Casati were there . . .'[8] Stanley nevertheless claimed to have acquired treaty rights to 'Mount Mfumbiro'. Yet in none of the six documents is the word 'Mfumbiro' to be found; nor is there any other documentary proof that Mfumbiro was 'ceded' to Stanley.[9]

The question of Stanley's mountain in central Africa, however, was insignificant compared to Mackinnon's grandiose ambitions. Mackinnon wrote in August 1889:

It is of the greatest possible importance in British interests that Mackay [the missionary] or some one else should promptly make treaties on the line drawn from Msalala to the north end of Tanganyika, as I hear the Germans are pressing our Foreign Office to agree to a line of delimitation as regards these territories, drawn right across the lake and straight from there to the boundaries of the Congo Free State. This would altogether exclude us from the territory we think essential to the future development of British territorial influence in central Africa, as it would absolutely prevent us from getting access to the Lake Tanganyika and there joining with the new South Africa Company which is now being formed in London and for which a royal Charter on the same lines as ours will be obtained. I cannot urge too strongly the importance to British commerce and to our Company of securing all the territories north of the line drawn from the south end of Victoria Nyanza—Msalala or other point—to another point on Lake Tanganyika about 30 miles from the north of that lake.[1]

Mackay did not, however, conclude the treaties, nor did Stanley's fulfill all Mackinnon's expectations. To make matters worse, some of Mackinnon's letters to Stanley fell into the hands of the Germans. Mackinnon, as Salisbury expressed it, had 'an

[8] Stanley to Mackinnon, 6 February 1890, Mackinnon papers; see Margery Perham, *Lugard, The Years of Adventure, 1858–1898* (2 vols.; London, 1956-60), I, pp. 258-9.

[9] Sir John Gray has kindly answered my queries on this point; he knows of no foundation of Stanley's claim to Mfumbiro. To my knowledge there is no record at the Public Record Office, in the Mackinnon papers, or in the Salisbury papers which throws light on Stanley and Mfumbiro.

H. B. Thomas comments: 'The *bona fides* of these treaties is the more suspect since all alike are dated "May 1888" at which date Stanley had not been within 200 miles of Mfumbiro. He had just met Emin for the first time and was on the point of returning to the Congo in search of the Rear Column. He claimed to have caught sight of Ruwenzori for the first time on 24 May 1888. Four of the six treaties purport to be with chiefs through whose territory he did not pass until over twelve months later. None of them except possibly the chief of Ankole can ever have seen or heard of Mfumbiro.' In a letter to me of 11 May 1962.

[1] Mackinnon to Nicol, 1 August 1889, forwarded to Stanley 5 November 1889, F.O. 84/2036.

intensely hostile animus' toward the Germans; the letters were blunt and outspoken about his suspicions of German aims in east Africa.[2] Salisbury observed that the importance of the letters was that they clearly revealed Mackinnon's 'designs on what the Germans would call their "Hinterland" ' and might even explain the German Emin expedition.[3] Mackinnon's sentiment about the Germans, Salisbury said, was probably no news to them; but it was 'much to be regretted that such compromising documents were not sent in cypher'.[4] Probably more distressing to Mackinnon than the capture of his letters was his failure to get the strip of land connecting Lakes Victoria and Tanganyika.

As Mackinnon tried to secure the corridor from the north, Harry Johnston approached from the south. One of the goals of Johnston's Nyasa–Tanganyika expedition in 1889 was to conclude treaties in the Ruzizi valley, north of Lake Tanganyika, to acquire the passageway to the north, 'carrying the British flag (with the necessary treaties) to Uganda.'[5] He was not able to carry out his plans because of Anglo-Portuguese complications in Nyasaland. Johnston had, however, met Alfred Swann, of the London Missionary Society, to whom he broached 'the grand idea of embarking in his repaired steamer and going the full length of Tanganyika, there to secure by treaty the north end of the Lake.'[6] To Swann this posed a dilemma: he was tempted 'with hoisting our flag over a people for whom so much had been spent'; but on the other hand he was forbidden by the London Missionary Society to participate in political affairs,[7] and his colleagues refused to have anything to do with the project.[8] Swann's reluctance to accept the charge was illustrated in a letter in August 1890 to Johnston, in which he

[2] Copies of the letters may be found in F.O. 84/2086.
[3] Stanley thought so also. Anderson's memorandum of a conversation with Hatzfeldt, no. 1, 29 April 1890, F.O. 403/142. For the Emin expedition, see below, pp. 14–16.
[4] Salisbury to Malet, no. 139 Africa secret, 6 May 1890, F.O. 84/2030.
[5] Johnston's introduction to A. J. Swann, *Fighting the Slave-Hunters* (London, 1910), p. vii.
[6] Harry H. Johnston, *The Story of My Life* (London, 1923), p. 275.
[7] Roland Oliver, *Sir Harry Johnston and the Scramble for Africa* (London, 1959), p. 168. Oliver gives a full account of the episode (pp. 168–72), as does A. J. Hanna, in *The Beginnings of Nyasaland and North-Eastern Rhodesia* (London, 1956), pp. 161–3.
[8] Swann, pp. 203–4.

asked Johnston to write the directors of the mission, from whom he feared censure.[9] Johnston wrote in reply: 'The north end is the highway to the equatorial regions, and the Germans have despatched Emin Pasha to take it over and so close the door to Britain. Go at once.'[1]

Swann succumbed to Johnston's entreaties. Sailing from Ujiji, he concluded treaties at the north end of the lake in late July and early August. Swann's treaties, however, did not arrive in London until December 1890—several months too late to influence the Anglo-German negotiations. Johnston commented later that the treaties would have done little good even had they arrived before the signing of the agreement because it was an *idée fixe* of the German emperor to break the uninterrupted chain of British influence.[2]

Meanwhile the Germans were also active. Karl Peters embarked upon the German Emin Pasha relief expedition in 1889 to win Uganda and the sources of the Nile for Germany.[3] When he arrived in Uganda, however, he found that Emin had already been 'rescued' by Stanley. This did not deter him from negotiating a treaty of friendship with the Kabaka, Mwanga, on 28 February 1890. Peters had no doubt that he had outwitted the British. He wrote from Uganda in March: '. . . I have saved for Germany the commercial territory of Uganda . . . with King Mwanga I have concluded a treaty of commerce and friendship which will tear the country from the grasp of the English . . .'[4] Having learned of Stanley's 'rescue', however, he gave up his plans to proceed to the north[5] and marched with all speed to the coast. He arrived to find that his extraordinary feat had been matched by another: the Heligoland agreement, which bartered, as Peters put it, three kingdoms for a bathtub in the North Sea.

Emin was also actively trying to secure the hinterland for Germany. After losing his Equatorial Province and entering the German service, he concentrated his efforts on the lake country.

[9] Hanna, p. 161.
[1] Swann to Thompson, 2 August 1890, cited in Hanna, pp. 161–2.
[2] *Story*, p. 277.
[3] Peters, *New Light on Dark Africa* (English translation; London, 1891), chapter X; see also Müller, chapter XV.
[4] *The Times*, 28 June 1890.
[5] Müller, p. 475.

On 24 April 1890 Emin left for the interior.[6] *The Times* correspondent in Zanzibar reported that he would 'probably visit the north end of Lake Tanganyika'.[7] The Pasha was under instructions from Wissmann, the German Imperial Commissioner for east Africa, 'to secure on behalf of Germany the territories situated south of and along the Victoria Nyanza Lake and Tanganyika up to the Muta Nzige and Albert Nyanza, so as to frustrate England's attempts at gaining an influence in those territories.'[8] Emin apparently entertained hopes that he would be able to administer this part of Germany's east African possession.[9]

The hinterland delimitation of the Heligoland agreement in July 1890 sharply circumscribed Emin's ambitions for Germany in central Africa. Wissmann recalled the Pasha during the winter of 1890–1. Apparently the order was so vague and loosely worded that Emin might have misunderstood it; more probably he ignored it. His plans became known to Wissmann in an extremely interesting letter of 4 February 1891.[1]

Emin proposed to rescue Germany's 'natural hinterland' in central Africa. This stretch of territory (the eastern Congo and western Uganda) had been discovered and explored by Germans; it was one of the richest and most productive in Africa. He was quite frank—in 1891—about his hope of eventual German annexation.

Ruanda was to play an important role in his scheme. By using Ruanda as his point of departure he would be able to link German East Africa with the Cameroons, without, he submitted, injuring British or Congolese interests. A glance at the map would prove his point. After establishing a station in

[6] The purpose of the expedition was quickly guessed: 'It is assumed, indeed, in some quarters here [Berlin] that the real objective of Emin Pasha's new expedition must be the Equatorial Province, as there is nothing in particular for it to do about the lakes.' (*The Times*, 3 April 1890; see also 4 April.) The discussion in the press is especially interesting because the same ideas appeared in a different form in the 1890 negotiations and the 1894 crisis. On 30 April *The Times* reported: 'It is rumoured that Emin Pasha has pledged himself to endeavour to monopolize all the trade of central Africa for the Germans, so that none shall henceforth reach the British sphere.' Emin intended 'to spoil the English scheme of gaining complete possession of the waterway routes connecting the sources of the Zambezi with the sources of the Nile'.

[7] 26 April 1890.

[8] George Schweitzer, *Emin Pasha* (2 vols.; London, 1898), II, p. 41.

[9] Ibid., p. 41; see also Sir John Gray, 'Anglo-German Relations in Uganda, 1890–92', *Journal of African History*, I, 1960, pp. 281–97.

[1] A copy may be found in Müller, pp. 542–4.

Ruanda he would reconsolidate his old adherents on the shores of Lake Albert.[2]

Emin's letter to Wissmann was disingenuous. One look at the map showed, above all, that the early dreams of a German empire in central Africa were ended by the 1890 settlement. Emin must have known that his actions would be repudiated by the German government, which had, in fact, been cool from the beginning toward efforts to win a German central African empire.

Bismarck had refused to interfere with Stanley's expedition in 1887 to rescue Emin, commenting at the time that Germany already had more African possessions than she could manage, and also more than enough friction with Britain.[3] In 1889 Bismarck stated that the German government 'would regret any attempt to penetrate into England's sphere of influence . . . and that English friendship was worth much more than the results which the [Peters's] expedition into the upper Nile might secure.'[4]

Bismarck's attitude was firm, shaped by domestic as well as international considerations:[5] he assured Salisbury privately that the German government had nothing to do with the Peters's expedition while he publicly disowned it. An officially supported Peters's venture would have inflamed Anglo-German relations, and if it had miscarried would not have helped Bismarck's problems of gaining support for his colonial policy in the Reichstag and from the public. Peters's treaties made as a private citizen, however, would have strengthened Germany's claims in central Africa; they would have created an opportunity upon which a German government more inclined toward colonial enterprise might have acted.

Caprivi, Bismarck's successor, ended the possibility of a German central African empire based on the work of Peters and Emin by concluding the Anglo-German negotiations in

---

[2] Emin and Stuhlmann did not in fact go through Ruanda, but, by passing through Karagwe and Mpororo, skirted its northeast corner; they then proceeded north of the Mfumbiro region. See Franz Stuhlmann, *Mit Emin Pascha ins Herz von Afrika* (Berlin, 1894), chapters XI and XII and the annexed maps.

[3] Müller, p. 460.

[4] 14 August 1889, cited in M. E. Townsend, *The Rise and Fall of Germany's Colonial Empire* (New York, 1930), p. 138; also in Alfred Zimmermann, *Geschichte der deutschen Kolonialpolitik* (Berlin, 1914), p. 157.

[5] See Müller, pp. 465–6.

June 1890. Caprivi was, if possible, even less enthusiastic about colonies than Bismarck; and he preferred a European settlement on friendly terms with Britain to an African empire that would satisfy the German colonial jingoes.

To reach a settlement at all both governments had to act quickly. In 1890 the scramble for east Africa threatened to become uncontrollable, which might make any solution impossible. Claims were becoming increasingly entangled.[6] Stanley especially aggravated the situation.

Both the British and German governments could not but observe Stanley (who arrived in England on 26 April 1890) making inflammatory speeches about the disputed territory in the African lake country. Yet how far south were his treaties valid? All the way to Lake Tanganyika?

Stanley's adventures influenced the negotiations in a way that Swann's, Emin's and Peters's did not. Peters's exploit created a sensation in Germany and Britain; in both countries there was speculation about what the consequences might be. But the negotiations were concluded in spite of him. The Germans repudiated the work of their agents. The British used Stanley's treaties for all they were worth, and perhaps much more.

[6] Salisbury had suggested in 1889 that the two powers should define their spheres in the hinterland. Hatzfeldt, the German Ambassador in Britain, remarked to Anderson in late April 1890 that the situation was becoming urgent; Stanley's return to England and Emin's recent departure for the interior had attracted the attention of the press; this would probably cause new and more serious difficulties. (Hatzfeldt to Bismarck, 22 December 1889, *Grosse Politik*, VIII, no. 1674; Anderson's memorandum of 30 April 1890, no. 1, confid., F.O. 403/142; Hatzfeldt to Caprivi, 30 April 1890, *Grosse Politik*, VIII, no. 1675.)

Salisbury, as well as the British public, feared a German bid for control of the source of the Nile; since the Nile could not be secured by way of the Sudan, 'Salisbury tried to close the backdoor of Egypt by diplomacy . . .' (A. J. P. Taylor, *The Struggle for the Mastery of Europe*, Oxford, 1957 edition, p. 329.) Caprivi and Marschall were conciliatory, anxious for a friendly settlement—and not especially interested in Africa. If the German claims in Africa overlapped with the British, there was room for negotiation and compromise. There were few points on which they were absolutely adamant. This was the background to the 1890 negotiations.

III. THE ANGLO-GERMAN
HINTERLAND SETTLEMENT OF 1890

The agreement may be summed up by saying that Germany accords to England the primary place in east Africa, while England, on the other hand, cedes Heligoland to Germany. (*Freisinnige Zeitung*, 1890)[1]

. . . the most abject and ignominious surrender of British interests since England abandoned the virgin continent now known as the United States of America. (*Daily Chronicle*, 1890)[2]

ON the eve of the negotiations which were to partition east Africa—and to give Ruanda-Urundi to Germany—rumours reached Berlin that treaties had been concluded by representatives of the Imperial British East Africa Company with the sovereign of Uganda.[3] The British Ambassador in Germany, Sir Edward Malet, commented to the German Foreign Secretary, Baron von Marschall, that the reputed treaties had been made many months before, and that as far as he could see 'Uganda was within the geographical hinterland of the British sphere'. 'Baron Marschall replied that there was no agreement as to the sphere of interest west of Lake Victoria Nyanza and that with regard to popular pretensions German maps embraced all the territory between the Lake and the Congo State in the German sphere, whereas English maps represent it all in the British sphere.'[4]

This conflict of views became immediately apparent at the outset of the Anglo-German negotiations, which began in Berlin on 5 May. H. Percy Anderson,[5] the British negotiator, in accordance with Salisbury's instructions, claimed all the hinter-

---

[1] Translated in *The Times*, 19 June 1890.
[2] Clipping in F.O. 84/2083.   [3] See *The Times*, 1 May 1890.
[4] Malet to Salisbury, no. 44 Africa, 3 May 1890, F.O. 84/2031; also no. 140 Africa, 5 May 1890, F.O. 84/2030. D. A. Low covers some of this same material in his unpublished Oxford D.Phil. thesis, 'The British and Uganda' (1957), as does D. R. Gillard in 'Salisbury's African Policy and the Heligoland Offer of 1890', *English Historical Review*, LXXV, 1960, pp. 631-53.
[5] H. Percy Anderson is of especial interest because of his role in the 1890 and 1894 agreements. Anderson was the British Africa expert; since 1883 he had been head of the Africa Department of the Foreign Office and had participated in the Berlin Conference of 1885. Lugard commented in 1895: 'After all *the* great and only African power is Percy Anderson.' Perham, I, p. 556.

land west of Lake Victoria. Dr. Krauel, Anderson's German counterpart, was 'both startled and alarmed'.[6] Since there was total disagreement about the hinterland they decided to begin with points which were not contended; the interior would be dealt with later.

The region north of Lake Tanganyika played an important role in the negotiations; the reason is commonly assumed to be that it was the link connecting the British spheres in the north and south (the waters of Lake Tanganyika being international). Anderson's despatches from Berlin, however, show that he did not expect Krauel to accept his initial hinterland claim. Even at the beginning of the negotiations Anderson considered the uninterrupted British sphere impossible to achieve.[7] Three days after his original bid for the whole area west of Victoria he agreed with Krauel that the German sphere should abut on to the Congo; the Anglo-German boundary was to be drawn along the first parallel south latitude.[8] Anderson was, above all, interested in securing Uganda. Had he thought the Germans might concede the corridor, or even had he been attracted to the Cape to Cairo idea (there is no evidence that he was), it is highly improbable that he would have conceded the crucial link so easily or quickly. Krauel's acceptance of the first degree boundary was equally revealing: the Germans had no serious hopes of acquiring Uganda.[9]

Salisbury objected to Anderson's first parallel proposal. The British government could not regard this as a compromise, because the hinterland doctrine, as Salisbury understood it, would give Britain at least as much. Anderson was to put aside for the present the question of the hinterland.[1]

At this point in the negotiations Stanley's treaties became

[6] Malet to Salisbury, no. 10 (no. 14 Africa tel.), 8 May 1890, F.O. 403/142.

[7] '. . . this idea was already impracticable when the negotiations commenced . . .' *Accounts and Papers*, Africa no. 6, LI, 1890 (Anderson to Malet, 28 June 1890). Anderson wrote this as he was winding up the negotiations; there is no reason to believe that it was not his attitude from the beginning.

[8] Anderson argued that the limits of Uganda were not defined, but that the British government held that with its tributary states it comprised the whole of the west of Victoria, and even to the south (including Ruanda and Urundi). Anderson admitted that this was disputed, but that there was no disagreement that Uganda extended at least to the first degree south latitude; it should be taken as a settled point that Uganda to the first degree was within the British sphere and outside the German. Malet to Salisbury, no. 10 (no. 14 Africa tel.), 8 May 1890; and Anderson to Malet, no. 4, incl. in Malet to Salisbury, no. 53 Africa, 9 May 1890, F.O. 84/2031.   [9] Malet to Salisbury, 8 May 1890.

[1] Salisbury to Malet, no. 12 (no. 27 Africa tel.), 9 May 1890, F.O. 403/142.

important. Salisbury thought that Stanley had concluded treaties in the districts 'lying between the northern point of Lake Tanganyika and the Victoria Nyanza.' If this were true, then Britain's claim to the disputed territory would be strengthened, and it would 'be scarcely permissible for Her Majesty's Government to transfer them [the treaties] to Germany, even though they have not yet been adopted by this country'.[2]

Anderson knew about the treaties; he had talked to Stanley about them before leaving for Berlin.[3] The question was how far south they extended. Stanley himself was energetically demanding before large audiences British annexation of the valuable territory between Lakes Tanganyika and Victoria.[4] Yet he had told Anderson that he had made no treaties south of Mfumbiro, estimated to be on the first parallel of south latitude or some twenty minutes beyond.[5]

Stanley confused and exasperated both governments. Salisbury was misled and Anderson puzzled.[6] Dr. Krauel pointed out to Anderson that Stanley in a speech in the Albert Hall had claimed 'vast territories between the lake and the Congo State'; Anderson replied that he had only seen an outline of the speech and that Stanley was not a British official.[7]

In reply to Salisbury's telegram of 9 May to drop the hinterland question, Anderson requested on 10 May that a map be obtained from Stanley showing the territories affected by his treaties; then the whole matter might be cleared up. He

---

[2] Ibid. *The Times* on 29 May reported that Peters had entered Uganda. On 30 May a leading editorial commented that the Germans would have difficulty in maintaining any claims to territories in which the chiefs had recently entered into treaties with Stanley. According to *The Times* the area secured by Stanley included 'the north and west of the Victoria Nyanza and thence southwards to the upper end of Lake Tanganyika, thus "marching" for a long distance with the Congo Free State.'   [3] Anderson's memorandum of 29 April 1890, F.O. 403/142.

[4] To Stanley's credit, he advocated annexation on grounds of the hinterland principle rather than on the treaties which he was reputed to have concluded. (See *The Times*, 3 June 1890.) Stanley's letter to Mackinnon of 11 June shows that he thought the first parallel division fulfilled all the claims to which the British Company was entitled. Mackinnon papers, 55/219.

[5] Anderson to Currie, no. 14, private, 19 May 1890; Malet to Salisbury, no. 13 (no. 17 Africa tel.), 10 May 1890, F.O. 403/142.

[6] 'If there is a liar about (and there must be one), I should be surprised to learn that it is Stanley, though of course, it may be. It seems to me more likely that the Company is bragging, as usual.' Anderson to Currie, no. 14 private, 10 May 1890, F.O. 403/142.

[7] Anderson to Malet, no. 4, 9 May 1890, incl. in Malet to Salisbury, no. 53 Africa, F.O. 84/2031.

emphasized the advantage of his understanding with Krauel: none of the British claims were prejudiced by the first parallel settlement: 'it covers Jackson's treaties, if they exist, and, I believe, the whole of Stanley's; . . . it secures Uganda as beyond present controversy.'[8] In accordance with his instructions, however, he informed Krauel that the British claimed the whole area west and southwest of Lake Victoria as hinterland. The question was dropped for the present.

Mackinnon sent Stanley's map to Salisbury on 14 May.[9] Salisbury had told Hatzfeldt the day before (13 May—before Salisbury could have seen Stanley's map) that the theory of the hinterland, which he said the Germans had invented, was not recognized by international law.[1] Salisbury also told the German Ambassador that Stanley had concluded treaties in the interior which the British government could not ignore because of public opinion. Hatzfeldt thought Stanley's inflammatory speeches made Salisbury's position difficult; they deceived the British public about the justice of German claims in east Africa.

At this point the negotiations reached deadlock. There was, above all, no agreement about the region north of Lake Tanganyika, 'the most important and most difficult' problem, the one over which there was the most 'sharp fighting'.[2] Salisbury confidentially made a number of proposals to Hatzfeldt on 13 May; he maintained his position that the line of demarcation should be drawn from Lake Victoria to the north end of Lake Tanganyika. Germany, in return for African concessions, however, was to receive Heligoland, which the German statesmen thought had great strategic value in the North Sea.[3]

Even before the Heligoland proposal Krauel was becoming increasingly uneasy about Caprivi's and Marschall's expressions of friendship to Britain and their disavowal of a 'policy of annexation for the sake of annexation'.[4] Anderson was optimistic, under the impression that Krauel had a free hand to get as much as he could but that he would not be allowed to

---

[8] Malet to Salisbury, no. 17 Africa tel., 10 May 1890, F.O. 84/2035.
[9] Mackinnon to Salisbury, 14 May 1890, Salisbury papers, unbound.
[1] Hatzfeldt to Marschall, 14 May 1890, *Grosse Politik*, VIII, no. 1676.
[2] Anderson to Currie, no. 14 private, 10 May 1890, F.O. 403/142.
[3] Marschall to Hatzfeldt, 25 May 1890, *Grosse Politik*, VIII, no. 1680.
[4] See *The Times*, 12 May 1890, and Caprivi's speech in the Reichstag of 12 May, *Stenographische Berichte über die Verhandlungen des Reichstags*, 4 Sitzung, I Session, pp. 39–42.

go too far—Germany wanted a friendly settlement.[5] Heligoland provided the way out of deadlock to a settlement satisfactory to both sides.

The acquisition of Heligoland became the most important goal; on almost all else Germany was prepared to compromise. Africa was of secondary importance to the North Sea.[6] The Germans, however, did not appear to swallow the Heligoland bait immediately, and Hatzfeldt's skilful diplomacy salvaged African territory that Marschall might have given away.

There was one point on which Marschall was especially firm. The boundary must run from Lake Victoria to the Congo; the British must not be allowed to drive a 'wedge' to Lake Tanganyika behind the German sphere. Salisbury's Lake Tanganyika proposal was flatly rejected. This was expressed in forceful language.[7] As Marschall explained to Anderson, it was impossible to permit Britain 'to close up behind the German sphere'.[8] The British attempt to reach Lake Tanganyika contradicted the hinterland agreement of 1887; the German public would never accept being 'cut off' from the Congo. It is extraordinary that four years later Anderson appeared to have forgotten how strongly the Germans put their case.

By 21 May Salisbury apparently was convinced that the Germans could not be persuaded to abandon their claims to the region north of Lake Tanganyika. Moreover, the British claims to the disputed area had been destroyed by Stanley's map. It was clear that Stanley had made no treaties south of Mfumbiro. Salisbury's principle of 'effective occupation' was irrelevant; the territory was unexplored and there were no treaties. He yielded.[9] On 21 May Salisbury told Hatzfeldt confidentially that he would consent to the demand that the German sphere touch the Congo.[1] There was to be freedom of trade, however, between Lake Tanganyika and the British sphere.[2]

Hatzfeldt had been under instructions to make every effort to

---

[5] Anderson to Currie, no. 24 private, 15 May 1890, F.O. 403/142.
[6] Marschall to Hatzfeldt, 25 May 1890, *Grosse Politik*, VIII, no. 1680.
[7] Marschall to Hatzfeldt, 17 May 1890, *Grosse Politik*, VIII, no. 1677.
[8] Anderson to Malet, no. 10, 16 May 1890, incl. in Malet to Salisbury, no. 30 (no. 64 Africa), F.O. 403/142.
[9] See especially *The Times* of 14 June 1890.
[1] Salisbury to Malet, no. 186A, 21 May 1890, F.O. 84/2030.
[2] See the agreement between Salisbury and Hatzfeldt, no. 48, 17 June 1890, F.O. 403/142; also *The Times*, 14 June 1890.

secure Heligoland. The next priority was the acquisition of the territory north of Lake Tanganyika. The Germans were willing to make concessions south of Lake Tanganyika, if the British would agree to a straight line drawn from the mouth of the Kagera river to the Congo State (along the first parallel).[3] If Salisbury insisted on the Kagera boundary (south of the first parallel), and if the whole of the agreement depended on this point, Hatzfeldt was to telegraph for further instructions.[4] Hatzfeldt knew the value which his superiors attached to Heligoland; but he also saw that if the Germans appeared too eager the result would be an abandonment of all African claims in order to acquire the island. In his conversations with Salisbury he let Salisbury broach the question of Heligoland. Perhaps Hatzfeldt's tactic of restraint was decisive in Salisbury's acceptance of the first parallel rather than insistence on the Kagera boundary, which the Germans probably would have yielded.[5]

Salisbury, of course, knew nothing of Hatzfeldt's instruction to telegraph for further orders; he did know the determination of the Germans to secure the area north of Lake Tanganyika. Lady Gwendolen Cecil, Salisbury's daughter and biographer, comments that he concurred because 'hard bargains make bad diplomacy'.[6] Yet for an unexplored territory to which Britain had no claim, Salisbury had put up a hard fight. Why? The answer usually given is that he was trying to acquire a corridor for the Cape to Cairo route.[7] The correct explanation lies in the relation between Salisbury and the British Company.

Salisbury's famous comment in early April ran: the 'difficulty here [in the east African problem] is the character of Mackinnon. . . . Any terms we might get for him from the Germans by negotiations he would denounce as a base truckling to the Emperor.'[8] Salisbury had a difficult task: to wrench as much as possible from the Germans in the hope that it would meet not only the British public's but also Mackinnon's minimum demands. Salisbury was arbitrator as well as Prime Minister.

[3] Marschall to Hatzfeldt, 25 May 1890.
[4] Marschall to Hatzfeldt, 31 May 1890, *Grosse Politik*, VIII, no. 1683.
[5] Ibid.; also Hatzfeldt to Marschall, 30 May 1890, *Grosse Politik*, VIII, no. 1682.
[6] Cecil, IV, p. 296.
[7] William L. Langer, *The Diplomacy of Imperialism* (New York, 1956 edition), p. 119.
[8] Cecil, IV, p. 281,

If there was any point on which the Germans were adamant it was the boundary west of Lake Victoria. Yet Mackinnon wanted his corridor. As *The Times* put it: 'The full satisfaction of both desires is geographically impossible.'[9] Salisbury knew through his conversations with Hatzfeldt that the Germans would never accept the British 'wedge'.[1] Could Mackinnon, then, be induced to acquiesce?

Mackinnon's position was weak; after Mackay's failure to acquire treaties north of Lake Tanganyika, Mackinnon's claim to the disputed area could only be based on Stanley's six alleged agreements, which did not extend south of Mfumbiro. Nor was there complete agreement in the Company itself about the corridor. Sir Francis de Winton, one of the directors of the Company, told Salisbury in mid-May[2] that, in his opinion, 'all the claims of that Company would be fully satisfied by a line of demarcation which would correspond with the first degree south latitude'.[3]

The proposition was put before Mackinnon and a committee of the Company's directors. They objected. The proposed boundary violated the hinterland agreement of 1887—as they interpreted it. Their stockholders, who had subscribed money for the development of the British sphere, would object to a settlement at variance with the original goals of the Company, which presumably included the colonization of the disputed region. The most important objection was that 'the effect of the suggested line of demarcation would be to debar the Company from access to Lake Tanganyika and from the free navigation of that lake in virtue of the possession of a port on its shores'.[4]

[9] 5 June 1890.
[1] 'Germany gave way to us in the south of Lake Tanganyika and we admitted her claims on the north of Lake Tanganyika. We had nothing to advance in answer to the argument which she based on the possession of the coast. We had no settlement, no experience of missionaries, or of merchants, and therefore, the argument advanced by Germany was not refuted, and we could not have resisted it without abandoning the agreement altogether.' Salisbury, *Parliamentary Debates*, third series, CCCXLVI, c. 127.
[2] The date of the conversation is not clear. On 28 May Salisbury noted: 'I had an interview last week'; this appears to be when Salisbury learned that Mackinnon did not have the unanimous support behind his Lake Tanganyika demand. The debatable point is whether the division in the Company influenced Salisbury's decision to yield the area north of Lake Tanganyika on 21 May.
[3] Salisbury to Malet, no. 208A Africa, 28 May 1890, F.O. 84/2030.
[4] A. Kemball to Anderson, no. 35, 2 June 1890, F.O. 403/142.

Salisbury finally persuaded Mackinnon in early June.[5] In a letter to Salisbury dated 7 June Mackinnon reluctantly but explicitly consented to the proposed boundary. '. . . although the concessions required by them are of a character calculated materially to curtail our legitimate claims to the territory which is required to give us free access to Lake Tanganyika, and the advantages which such access would afford to national interests and the development of British trade. . . . I am prepared on behalf of the Board of Directors, if more satisfactory terms cannot be secured, to agree to the line of delimitation arrogated by Germany.' The Company 'ardently and confidently' hoped, however, that Salisbury would be able to secure as a boundary the second degree of south latitude instead of the first.[6]

Even Stanley urged Mackinnon to be happy with the arrangement. In a letter to Mackinnon of 11 June he told him that the Company 'may very well accept it and be grateful. . . .' The Company would receive 'Mfumbiro' and 'the best part of Ruanda'.[7]

By bartering Heligoland Salisbury had accomplished the remarkable feat of satisfying the minimum demands of both the German statesmen and the Company, which had British jingo opinion behind it.[8] For the latter Salisbury had utilized conscientiously and literally every treaty or agreement which could conceivably be interpreted as 'effective occupation'. An example may be found in a peculiar article of the agreement. The boundary running from Lake Victoria to the Congo State was to swing around the mountain Mfumbiro (if it was found later to be in the German sphere), enclosing it in British territory. On 21 May Salisbury had emphasized to Hatzfeldt the value which the British Company placed on Mfumbiro.[9] A few days later, however, Sir Francis de Winton told Salisbury that he 'attached no importance to the possession of the mountain Mfumbiro,

<hr />

[5] At an interview with Mackinnon and Kemball, at which Anderson (who had returned from Berlin for instructions) was also present. 'To the surprise of Sir Arnold [Kemball], Sir William, who had assured him he never would yield, gave way and accepted the 1st degree line.' Anderson's memorandum of 17 November 1892, F.O. 84/2263. The date of the interview is not clear.

[6] Mackinnon to Salisbury, 7 June 1890, F.O. 84/2083.

[7] Stanley to Mackinnon, 11 June 1890, Mackinnon papers, 55/219.

[8] See, for example, the letters from a 'British Patriot', 21 May 1890, and 30 May 1890, F.O. 84/2082.

[9] Salisbury to Malet, no. 186A Africa, 21 May 1890, F.O. 84/2030.

because, though it would be valuable as a sanatorium undoubtedly to the Germans, it was not required by the English, who already had one of superior value a little to the north in Ruwenzori.'[1] Nonetheless the 'mountain' was ceded explicitly to the British in the agreement.[2] The seed of controversy was planted; it was Mfumbiro which eventually determined Ruanda's northern frontier.[3]

One month after the signing of the agreement, an interesting article appeared in the *Deutsche Kolonialzeitung*. It was concerned with Mfumbiro, and discussed the exploration which led to the discovery of the mountain and its possible significance for the future. Weichmann, the German African authority who wrote the article, expressed surprise that such a little known mountain played such a prominent part in the treaty. So little about it was known, indeed, that it was impossible to be certain whether the term 'Mfumbiro' applied to one mountain, a range of mountains, or a whole territory. Was it possible that a series of lakes, rivers, and mountains designated 'Mfumbiro' might extend all the way to Lake Tanganyika? If this were true then the British might yet attempt to push their 'wedge' between German East Africa and the Congo; perhaps this was the motive for reserving British rights to Mfumbiro.[4]

Weichmann's speculation was not true; the idea did occur to the British—but ten years later.[5] The mountain was mentioned in the 1890 agreement because Stanley supposedly had a treaty which ceded it to the British Company and because Salisbury thought it would be 'scarcely permissible' to 'transfer' to Germany anything to which Britain had a claim.[6] The German government accepted the British claim, including Mfumbiro, because Salisbury said the area was covered by Stanley's treaties indicated on a map: the treaties themselves were not questioned.

[1] Salisbury to Malet, no. 208A Africa, 28 May 1890, F.O. 84/2030.
[2] See the Cabinet Memorandum of 14 June 1890, F.O. 84/2030.
[3] In a memorandum in 1892 Anderson smugly noted that he had known from the beginning of the negotiations that the first degree was the line of demarcation which the British would be able to get, and that it was, 'with a slight modification . . . finally adopted.' (17 November 1892, F.O. 84/2263.) The modification was Mfumbiro.
[4] E. Weichmann, 'Der Nordwesten Deutsch-Ostafrika', *Kolonialzeitung*, August 1890, pp. 203–5.
[5] See Gibbons to Salisbury, 1 October 1900, F.O. 2/800.
[6] Salisbury to Malet, no. 12 (no. 27 Africa tel.), 9 May 1890, F.O. 403/142.

German suspicions, however, were well founded. Mackinnon had let go of his plan very reluctantly. Salisbury could not secure the corridor through negotiations with Germany; there were other ways. Mackinnon had not agreed until early June to give up hope of attaining access to Lake Tanganyika through the German negotiations. In the meantime he had made other arrangements for his road with King Leopold.

On 14 May Mackinnon wrote Salisbury that 'The King of the Belgians . . . most generously expresses his desire to help us in every way to facilitate our access to [Lake] Tanganyika'. 'In a day or two I should like to communicate to you for your approval full particulars of what is proposed.'[7] A draft was prepared of an agreement between the British Company and the Congo State. The main object of one part of the agreement was a delimitation of Congolese and British spheres; the other section ceded to the British Company a road five miles in width from the centre of the south shore of Lake Edward to Lake Tanganyika (with sovereign rights over the territory through which the road would pass) and a port on Lake Tanganyika with a district of ten miles around it.[8] Salisbury thought that this would form the basis of an arrangement between the Congo State and the Company; he refused to comment further, and asked that he be shown the draft when it was completed in more detail. Salisbury wrote to Leopold on 21 May: 'I have satisfied myself that no objections will be raised on the part of the Foreign Office. . . .'[9]

The agreement was signed on 24 May by the representatives of the Company and the Congo State; in a letter of 7 June Mackinnon informed Salisbury that the agreement had been ratified by the two parties. Salisbury, however, now had second thoughts. In a draft letter to Leopold of 9 June he mentioned that 'the line which the German government have taken in recent negotiations has left in my mind the impression that it would view with objection the concession of territory at the back of their sphere without their knowledge and consent'.[1]

---

[7] Mackinnon to Salisbury, 14 May 1890, Salisbury papers, unbound.
[8] An agreement was also drafted with the British South Africa Company, which granted to them 'should . . . [they] desire it' a road five miles wide from Lake Banguelo to Lake Tanganyika. See F.O. 84/2082.
[9] Salisbury to Leopold, 21 May 1890, F.O. 84/2082.
[1] Salisbury to Leopold, no. 77 Africa confid., 9 June 1890, F.O. 84/2082.

The Mackinnon agreement was never ratified by the British government. Nothing further took place. The negotiations were dropped; the agreement was inchoate only and never completed; it never became a valid international instrument, as ratification by the British government was a condition of its validity.[2] The Company received no port on Lake Tanganyika, no road between that lake and Lake Edward. The matter was forgotten until two years later when Leopold despatched an expedition to the Nile and justified his action by the Mackinnon agreement. Percy Anderson commented in 1892 that Mackinnon 'found out he had made a mistake and went no further.'[3]

The corridor to Lake Tanganyika had been blocked by the 1890 Anglo-German delimitation. Salisbury, defending the Heligoland agreement, stated that 'there has been only one strong criticism adverse to that agreement'. 'It has arisen from a curious idea which has become prevalent in this country, that there is some special advantage in handling a stretch of territory extending all the way from Cape Town to the sources of the Nile. . . . It could not have been obtained without absolutely breaking off the agreement altogether.'[4] The partition was so advantageous to Britain, however, that the few dissident voices objecting to the surrender of the corridor were lost in the general exultation.

Salisbury had concerned himself with the scheme only in relation to the practical problems of negotiating with the Germans and satisfying the Mackinnon clan; he was not enraptured by the idea itself.[5] He did not hesitate to push British claims as far as possible (as in the Mfumbiro matter); he was sceptical about German acceptance of the passageway which might have been secured by the Mackinnon agreement. It is

[2] See Anderson's memorandum of 4 June 1890, F.O. 84/2082, with minutes by Anderson and Salisbury.
[3] See Anderson's memorandum of 3 March 1892, F.O. 84/2200; Salisbury to Gosselin, no. 35 Africa, 19 March 1892, F.O. 84/2200 (Salisbury's reconstruction); and Anderson's memorandum of 17 November 1892, F.O. 84/2265. For a few more details on the Mackinnon Treaty, see the version of this chapter to appear in the *Uganda Journal*. I hope to consider this problem further in an article about Sir Percy Anderson and British Congo policy.
[4] *Parliamentary Debates*, third series, CCCXLVI, c. 1267–8.
[5] 'The Nile valley was a tangible interest; the Cape to Cairo route was not. Salisbury did not mix sentiment with diplomacy.' Ronald Robinson and John Gallagher, *Africa and the Victorians* (London, 1961), p. 293.
[6] In contrast to the frequent discussions in, for example, *The Times* about the uninterrupted chain. See the editorial of 5 June 1890.

remarkable how very seldom the project was mentioned at all during the negotiations.[6] Salisbury's decision to accept the first parallel as the division between the German and British spheres was shaped by the German determination to acquire the region north of Lake Tanganyika, the failure of Stanley's alleged treaties to cover the region, and, perhaps, the division in the Company itself regarding the necessity to have access to Lake Tanganyika.

All in all it was a clear cut agreement which pleased almost everyone in both countries; there were only a few small points like Mfumbiro which remained to be settled.

IV. THE CAPE TO CAIRO CORRIDOR AND THE ANGLO-CONGOLESE AGREEMENT OF 1894

The value of this fatal strip must really be very small to us . . .
(Sir Edward Malet, British Ambassador in Germany, 1894)[1]

THE objectives of the Anglo-Congolese agreement of 1894 were almost identical with those of the one concluded by the Imperial British East Africa Company and the Congo State.[2] Both agreements were concerned with the upper Nile; both provided a British corridor to Lake Tanganyika through Ruanda-Urundi. In contrast to the 1890 agreement, however, the main purpose of the 1894 arrangement was to prevent a French advance to the Nile.[3] And a significant difference also distinguished the parts of the two agreements concerned with the corridor. In 1890 the passageway was a main object of Mackinnon's negotiations because of his persistent aim to link the British possessions in the north and south. In 1894 the corridor was clearly subordinate to the other part of the agreement and was included (Article III) almost accidentally. No one in the British government pondered the possible consequence for European diplomatic relations. Article III turned out to be an 'extraordinary and almost incredible blunder'.[4]

Cecil Rhodes was responsible more than any other person for the popularization of the Cape to Cairo notion between 1890–4.[5] In October 1892 Rhodes had offered to construct a telegraph from British Central Africa to Uganda at his own expense; the 'ultimate object', as he expressed it, was to connect the Cape to Cairo by a line of British communication.[6] The

---

[1] Malet to Kimberley, private, 16 June 1894, F.O. 343/13, Malet papers. A much expanded version of this chapter is to appear in St. Antony's Papers.

[2] See above, pp. 27–28.

[3] See A. J. P. Taylor, 'Prelude to Fashoda: The Question of the Upper Nile, 1894–5', in Rumours of Wars (London, 1952), (pp. 81–113) (reprinted from the English Historical Review, LXV, 1950, pp. 52–80).   [4] The Times, 23 June 1894.

[5] See especially Harry Johnston, 'My Story of the Cape-to-Cairo Scheme', in Leo Weinthal, ed., The Story of the Cape to Cairo Railway and River Route, 1887–1922 (4 vols.; London, 1923).

[6] Rhodes to Rosebery, dated October 1892 (received 31 October), Accounts and Papers, LXII, Africa no. 1 1893.

difficulty, of course, was that the telegraph would have to pass through German East Africa. Rhodes's proposal eventually was politely refused by the German government.[7] And despite his great enthusiasm for the Cape to Cairo route, the influence he exerted on the 1894 Anglo-Congolese negotiations was little, if any.

H. Percy Anderson is the key to understanding what happened. In the spring of 1894 Rosebery had left the Foreign Office to assume his responsibilities as Prime Minister. Kimberley had just begun his work as Foreign Secretary. Philip Currie, the Permanent Under-Secretary, had left for another assignment, and Thomas Sanderson, his successor, was still unfamiliar with his new position. The result of this transition was that Anderson, as the Africa expert in the Foreign Office, virtually determined British African policy.[8]

In the margin of the typewritten instructions to Rennell Rodd, who conducted the preliminary negotiations[9] at Brussels in mid-March with van Eetvelde, the Congolese Minister of the Interior, Anderson had commented in handwriting, as if by afterthought: 'A further condition should be a concession of powers of telegraphic communication in the [Congo] State territory between the British spheres.'[1] Eetvelde told Rodd that there would be no problem about the telegraph, although the Congolese authorities preferred communications to complement their Central African Telegraph scheme.[2]

The preliminary negotiations were successful. Rodd's impression was that Leopold was anxious to come to terms; for the King there were a 'number of bargains wholly advantageous to himself which at the same time he barely expects to realize'.[3]

---

[7] Rosebery to Trench, no. 38 Africa, 29 March 1893, F.O. 84/2213.

[8] Anderson was appointed Assistant Under-Secretary of State on 1 January 1894. See *Foreign Office List*, 1895. As A. J. P. Taylor has expressed it, Anderson was more interested in 'any scrap of African territory' than in friendship with France; he wore blinkers as far as general policy was concerned. 'Prelude to Fashoda', pp. 90–91.

[9] A quarter of a century later Rodd retold the incident. 'I was to go to Brussels and there endeavour to see the King of the Belgians, with the object of obtaining from the Congo Free State the lease of a corridor or strip of territory connecting Lake Tanganyika with Uganda. This would ensure an eventual exclusively British highway connecting the Cape with the Nile and the road to Cairo . . .' James Rennell Rodd, *Social and Diplomatic Memories* (London, 1922), pp. 345–8. This account does not agree with the British documents; there was nothing in Rodd's instructions which mentioned the corridor, only the telegraph.

[1] Rosebery to Rodd, secret, 5 March 1894, F.O. 10/625. This became Article V.

[2] Rodd's 'Report of the Proceedings at Brussels', 19 March 1894, F.O. 10/625.

[3] Rodd to F.O., private, 17 March 1894, F.O. 10/625.

Leopold, through Eetvelde, made a minor counter proposal, nevertheless, which the British had not anticipated. Rodd called it a 'startling request'; a port on Lake Nyasa and a concession for a railway to join Lakes Nyasa and Tanganyika, as well as a port on Lake Albert.[4] The King was willing to send a confidential agent to London to conclude the arrangement.

Anderson, reading Rodd's report, thought that the King's proposals afforded 'a fair basis for negotiation'. The duration of the lease in the Nile valley was the main problem, which he discussed at length in a memorandum of 25 March. He also discussed Leopold's proposal for Britain to concede to the Congo State ports on Lake Albert and Nyasa. If Leopold was to administer the upper Nile, Anderson commented, he should be entitled to a port on Lake Albert; as for Lake Nyasa, the British had already ceded the Portuguese a port there, and Germany was already established on the lake also. '. . . but we should stipulate on our side for one in the north end of Lake Tanganyika.'[5]

This was the origin of Article III—Leopold's greed and Anderson's willingness to bargain.[6]

The final negotiations took place in London between Anderson and Eetvelde; the talks proceeded without difficulty. On 10 April Anderson 'broached the question of the lease to us [Britain] of a port on Tanganyika with a road from Lake Albert Edward'. Anderson, who feared that Eetvelde would parry by proposing the Congolese port on Lake Nyasa, said that the Tanganyika port was a 'natural equivalent of a port on Lake Albert'. This point was not covered in Eetvelde's full-powers; he would telegraph for instructions. Anderson then replied 'that the whole arrangement depended on its acceptance'.[7]

Anderson's bluff worked. On the morning of 12 April Eetvelde said that 'he was authorized to give way as regards the Tanganyika port and road'. The agreement was signed on the

---

[4] Rodd's report of 19 March.

[5] 'Memo. by Sir Percy Anderson respecting the Negotiations with the King of the Belgians', 25 March 1894, F.O. 10/625.

[6] According to a note in the *Grosse Politik*, Rosebery asked Anderson whether German rights might be involved. Anderson is said to have replied no. VIII, pp. 473–4.

[7] Anderson's 'Notes on the Belgian Negotiations', 13 April 1894, F.O. 10/625.

same day, and laid before the British Parliament on 21 May. Copies reached Berlin on 26 May.[8]

Public and official opinion in Germany was hostile from the time of announcement of the treaty; it increased in stridency and intensity until the British were finally forced to withdraw the corridor article. There were two reasons.

The first was the diplomacy peculiar to European relations in 1894, which were ripe for an Anglo-German colonial quarrel. A. J. P. Taylor describes the main causes of the German protests against Article III as 'principally an attempt to blackmail the British into renewing their support of Austria-Hungary and Italy in the Mediterranean; it had perhaps a secondary motive of improving German relations with France.'[9] The Anglo-German friction in Samoa increased German suspicions of British plans in Africa. The idea of a Germany surrounded by hostile powers in Europe was transplanted to Africa: the All-Red-Route would encircle German East Africa by British possessions. The Cape to Cairo route was a symbol of British domination of the massive continent, to be prevented at any cost by Germany. Rosebery failed to confer with the German government before the conclusion of the treaty, which made the Germans indignant and, as Malet expressed it, gave rise to the 'feeling that we [Britain] have stolen an unfair march upon Germany in general'.[1] Anderson pinned the blame on Kayser, the German Colonial Director, who was 'going through an anti-English phase'. Marschall had no trouble convincing himself that the German government was being 'jockeyed'. These elements crystallized in May–June 1894 into a squeeze policy toward Britain.

The second was a reason associated not with Europe, but with Africa, and was consistent with German African policy in 1890. The All-Red-Route was more than a symbol of imperial grandeur: the heart of the great continent was to be

[8] Gosselin to Kimberley, no. 63 Africa confid., 28 May 1894, F.O. 64/1333. The Anglo-Congolese agreement signed on 12 April was secret; shortly afterwards Leopold was confronted with a French proposal for a settlement favourable to the Congo State on the Ubangi frontier, if he would allow France 'son chemin libre' to the Nile. To enable Leopold to escape from the embarrassing position of negotiating with the French after he had already concluded an agreement with the British, the date of the agreement was altered to 12 May. See Taylor, 'Prelude to Fashoda', pp. 87–88.

[9] Taylor, 'Prelude', p. 92.

[1] Malet to Kimberley, 16 June 1894, Malet papers, F.O. 343/13.

opened to commerce and civilization. If communications were established from north to south, the lucrative commercial profit would accrue to the British. The German idea was in contrast, expressed most fully in the notion of a German central African empire, but also in the hope of a flourishing German trade from east to west, across German East Africa and through the Congo to the Atlantic. 'Instead of having a back door opening on to a small, neutral state which could never be her rival politically, and whose economic conditions are favourable to the development of trade in central Africa, Germany finds herself cut off from all direct access to the Congo State by the interposition of a first-class colonial Power, which is at the same time her foremost competitor in the world.'[2] This was why in 1890 and 1894 the Germans protested so vigorously against the British corridor—even though European trade in the corridor area, Ruanda-Urundi, did not exist.

There were two main legal arguments marshalled by the Germans to give force to these political and commercial objections. The first was that the Germans thought Leopold had violated the neutrality of the Berlin Act (Article X) by 'granting one state privileges and rights at the expense of other states. . . .'[3] More emphasis was placed on the second: the boundary fixed by the Congolese-German agreement of 8 November 1884 could not be altered without the consent of the German government.[4] In short, German treaty rights had been violated.

On 25 May Marschall, on Kayser's recommendation, telegraphed Alvensleben, the German Minister in Brussels, to notify the Congo government that the road must be kept at least 20 kilometres from the German frontier. Two days later Marschall stated bluntly that Leopold had violated the neutrality of the Congo State by aiding the British 'policy of aggression' in Africa; Germany had no interest in the existence of the Congo State and would prefer the French as neighbours.[5] On 28 May Caprivi observed that the basic German policy of German-Italian friendship should not be changed, but that there could be no objection to drawing closer to France and

[2] *The Times*, 13 June 1894.
[3] Marschall's memorandum of 13 June 1894, *Grosse Politik*, VIII, no. 2049.
[4] See Hatzfeldt to Kimberley, 3 June 1894, F.O. 403/201.
[5] Marschall to Alvensleben, 27 May 1894, *Grosse Politik*, VIII, no. 2034.

turning more away from Britain; Samoa and the Anglo-Congolese agreement were the reasons.[6] Hatzfeldt commented on 1 June that the treaty gave the Germans a good opportunity to make clear to the British Cabinet the disadvantages of annoying Germany.[7]

Toward the end of May, Plunkett, the British Minister in Belgium, began his series of long reports about Leopold's apprehension concerning the unfavourable German reception of the treaty. Leopold was anxious to appease the Germans: 'the German government did not ask for much of a concession, and he [Leopold] considered it would be good policy to satisfy Germany as soon as possible, in order thereby to detach the German press from making common cause on this question with that of France.' Perhaps a declaration could be made that the strip would remain neutral. More important was the simple matter of moving the road 20 kilometres to the west; Plunkett thought it did not matter greatly 'whether our [the British] tract of communication touched the German territory or not'.[8]

Anderson's reaction to Plunkett's report was incredulous: 'This is unnecessary bullying if it is correct, but we have some reason for thinking that the Congo authorities occasionally exaggerate the language used to them.'[9] Anderson commented, however, that 'if we are pressed we must admit that as it is still Congo territory it remains neutralized'; but since the chances of having to send troops along the road in case of war were remote, it made no difference. Anderson also thought that the British government could meet the German request that the road should be kept 20 kilometres from the German frontier.[1]

Kimberley had accepted Anderson's initiative to include the corridor in the agreement without question; he was puzzled when he learned of German objections. Moreover, the language in which the Germans worded their protest was, Kimberley thought, highly discourteous, which made a reply difficult.

Upon Anderson's advice, however, Kimberley wired Plunkett: 'You may assure the Congo government that no disturb-

[6] Caprivi to Hatzfeldt, 28 May 1894, ibid., VIII, no. 2035.
[7] Hatzfeldt to Caprivi, 1 June 1894, ibid., VIII, no. 2039.
[8] Plunkett to Kimberley, no. 86 Africa very confid., 28 May 1894, F.O. 10/615.
[9] Anderson's minute of 29 May, on Plunkett to Salisbury, no. 86 Africa, 28 May 1894, F.O. 10/618.
[1] Ibid.

ance of the existing frontier arrangement between Germany and the Congo State was ever contemplated by Her Majesty's Government, who will ask, as a matter of course, for an interior road to run behind the frontier.'[2]

The German protests had begun in late May after Kayser contemplated Leopold's violation of Congo neutrality and after the German request for 20 kilometres distance. Supposedly the small British concession of keeping the road away from the German frontier would appease the Germans. By mid-June, however, Marschall was forcefully presenting ultimata which could have led to a scramble for the Congo. The Germans remembered that a main goal of the negotiations in 1890 had been to secure a land frontier with the Congo State. Marschall said that in 1890 he had flatly refused the request for a British corridor. The 'English girdle' around a German possession, and the possible injuries to German trade in central Africa, became emotionally charged issues, which the British were apparently ignoring.[3]

The British problem, as well as the Belgian, was to determine exactly what the Germans wanted. It was not until 15 June that the British were certain that the Germans were demanding unreserved abandonment of Article III. In the meantime Kimberley found himself bombarded with increasingly hostile, though not arrogant, notes from the German government, and reports from Brussels and Berlin about the severity of the crisis.

For Kimberley the revelation of the German attitude came as a series of unpleasant surprises. When he first heard of the German objections he noted: 'If I believed the Belgian account of the language of the German Minister, I should feel much hesitation, whether we could quietly acquiesce in this demand, but it is probably grossly exaggerated. . . .'[4] By 11 June—Hatzfeldt's note of protest—Kimberley was deeply alarmed. He found the German attitude 'even less friendly than I had supposed'. Kimberley, however, hardly knew what to do: 'with regard to the satisfaction which Germany required he [Hatzfeldt] had no instruction.'[5] Did the German government want

[2] Kimberley to Plunkett, no. 5 Africa tel., 29 May 1894, F.O. 10/618.
[3] Malet to Kimberley, no. 9 Africa secret tel., 11 June 1894, F.O. 64/1355.
[4] Kimberley's memorandum of 29 May 1894, F.O. 10/615. Rosebery's minute: 'I agree'.
[5] Kimberley to Malet, no. 86 Africa, 11 June 1894, F.O. 64/1332.

compensation? Apparently not: 'The Imperial Secretary of State for Foreign Affairs said to me [Malet] today that a report had been circulated that Germany would be contented with compensations with regard to the Congo agreement, but that this was not the case. The Imperial Government . . . took their stand upon treaty engagement only . . .'[6] Finally Kimberley pondered: would the German government be satisfied only by the complete withdrawal of Article III? But this would create enormous difficulties; the withdrawal of one article could set a precedent for the withdrawal of others. The alternative was just as sobering: 'Unless satisfaction is given to Germany in this matter, it is quite clear that Her Majesty's Government must be prepared to meet with an unfriendly attitude in all directions on the part of the Imperial Government'; this might even mean another Congo conference and a battle for central Africa.[7]

June 15 was decisive. Two days previously Alvensleben, the German Minister, had called on one of the Congolese authorities and had 'spoken to him about the Anglo-Congolese agreement in terms so peculiar' that Leopold, dissatisfied with the report of the conversation, requested Alvensleben to call on him 'to explain what it was precisely that the Germans wanted.'[8] The interview lasted over an hour; it was unsatisfactory. On 15 June Alvensleben requested another conference.[9] The King agreed to see Alvensleben, but ordered that the official answer of the Congo government to Marschall's note of 9 June should reach the German legation before the audience. The Congolese note was drawn up 'in the most courteous form'.[1] Alvensleben during his interview pressed the King in urgent language to withdraw his signature from the whole agreement. That evening he returned to the palace with the Congolese note; Alvensleben told the King that to send it to Berlin would be useless; it by no means would satisfy the German government. Alvensleben 'declared in plain terms that Germany considered that the Congo State had exceeded its powers by making common cause with England, and that Germany would no longer respect

[6] Malet to Kimberley, no. 12 Africa tel., 15 June 1894, F.O. 64/1335.
[7] Malet to Kimberley, no. 11 Africa tel., 14 June 1894; and no. 13 Africa tel., 15 June 1894, F.O. 64/1335.
[8] Plunkett to Kimberley, no. 201 (no. 131 Africa), 15 June 1894, F.O. 403/201.
[9] See the footnote to number 2057, Alvensleben to A.A. 15 June 1894, *Grosse Politik*, VIII.
[1] Plunkett to Kimberley, no. 130 Africa, 15 June 1894, F.O. 10/616.

the neutrality of the Congo, unless the King withdrew his signature from the agreement'.[2] This was the German ultimatum.

In Berlin, Malet, having learned of the German demand for annulment of the treaty, pleaded with Marschall that 'this would be too much, as it would affect the whole agreement, whereas the German objection . . . applied to the strip of land only'. Marschall eventually agreed; the damage would be repaired if Article III were abandoned. Marschall said 'that the feeling that Germany had been jockeyed in the matter was really the foundation of all the trouble, but that she was willing to recognize that we [the British] had no deliberate intention of doing this when we made the agreement'. 'This would be proved if we consented to abandon Article III, and the impression which has been created in Germany would thereby be removed.'[3]

Rosebery and Kimberley had already come to this conclusion. On 16 June Kimberley had wired Plunkett: 'You may tell the King that if he likes to ask for withdrawal of Article III we shall consent in view of pressure put upon him.'[4]

The crisis had passed. The rest was anticlimax, concerned with the form in which the annulment should occur. The article was 'withdrawn' on 22 June.[5]

The German objections to Article III, which culminated in mid-June in the unconditional demand for surrender of the corridor, were consistent with the German colonial objectives in 1890: the prevention of a British passageway behind the German sphere. The intensity of the demand corresponded to the tense European diplomatic relations in 1894: the Germans felt justified, even compelled, to teach the British a lesson.

The German reaction to the corridor in 1894 was immediately negative, but also uncertain. The transformation during the two- to three-week period from uncertainty to inflexibility took the British by complete surprise. For two reasons. First, because the Germans chose to direct their principal attacks on the

[2] Ibid.
[3] Malet to Kimberley, no. 13 Africa tel., 16 June 1894. '. . . explain frankly that H.M.'s Government have no intention of jockeying the German government.' Kimberley to Malet, no. 19 Africa confid. tel., F.O. 64/1335.
[4] F.O. to Plunkett, 16 June 1894, F.O. 10/618.
[5] Plunkett to Kimberley, no. 140 Africa, 22 June 1894, F.O. 10/616.

weaker partner: Leopold, on whom the British had to rely for information during the early part of the crisis. This was unfortunate, because of the Foreign Office's past experiences with the King. They immediately discounted part of what he said as exaggeration. This was why Anderson, with some justification, could talk of 'coloured language', and why Kimberley referred to the reports of the Congolese authorities in Brussels as probably 'grossly exaggerated'. The second reason that the British were caught off guard was that it was not until mid-June that the Germans decided what they wanted: cancellation of the article. This was why Kimberley, who was receiving his information from Hatzfeldt as well as Plunkett and Malet, was baffled by the German behaviour. He knew that the German demands were becoming more harsh, but what exactly did they want? When Kimberley asked the German Ambassador as late as 11 June what satisfaction the Germans required, Hatzfeldt still had no instructions. Plunkett, and especially Malet, were very good about providing explanations of why the Germans were behaving in this extraordinary way, but were no better than Hatzfeldt about providing information about what they wanted. The British government yielded immediately when it was definitely ascertained through both Plunkett and Malet that the Germans demanded cancellation of the article and threatened to cease to recognize the neutrality of the Congo State.

Could the crisis have led to a scramble for the territory of the Congo? Perhaps. But German diplomacy, when it finally found its target, aimed at the withdrawal of Article III instead. The Germans demanded satisfaction for injuries to their political, commercial, and treaty rights. This was accomplished by the cancellation of the article, and talk of a new scramble for the Congo consequently ceased. The German problem was to exploit the British blunder without losing control of the sequence of events. By mid-June the danger point had been reached; this can be seen in the alarm of both the German and British despatches and the German effort to curtail the crisis by convincing the British that only the excision of Article III would satisfy the German indignation. The crisis would never have arisen, of course, had there been more foresight in the British Foreign Office. The inclusion of the corridor occurred because of Anderson's whim; it was not even mentioned until a few days before the close of the negotiations, and was not questioned by Rosebery or Kimberley. The whole agreement, product in large part of Anderson's draftsmanship, was redundantly framed: the provision for a telegraph in Article V was duplicated by the strip in Article III.[6] Poor Percy Anderson! He could not believe the Germans were serious. Throughout the crisis he showed no comprehension of the forces he had released and suggested as late as 15 June that the German language was 'highly coloured'[7] 'for the sake of Her Majesty's Government'.[8]

The folly of the idea had been exposed by Malet when he said that 'a road in this region is certain to be made along with the opening up of the country, the use of which we should enjoy to the full extent that we could if it were on land we had leased'.[9] But the notion of the Cape to Cairo route—the opening up of central Africa to trade and civilization and the Union Jack spanning the great continent from north to south—was an idea which caught and fired men's imaginations.

Kimberley was honest when he said that it simply 'did not . . . occur' to the British government what the consequences of Article III would be.[1] Yet there could not have been results of 'wider importance—as have been clearly seen by the alarm of the other parties to the Triple Alliance'.[2] Surely there have been few caprices of 'forgotten imperialists'[3] which had such far-reaching consequences.

[6] The result was an unintentional redundancy which was assumed by the public to be purposeful: 'Mr. Rhodes's Transcontinental Telegraph will not necessarily be confined to the strip of territory leased to and administered by Great Britain.' *The Times*, 24 May 1894.

[7] Anderson's minute on Plunkett to Kimberley, no. 130 Africa, 15 June 1894, F.O. 10/616.

[8] Plunkett to Anderson, private confid., 24 June 1894, F.O. 10/616; also Plunkett to Anderson, private confid., 15 June 1894, F.O. 10/616.

[9] Malet to Kimberley, private, 16 June 1894, F.O. 343/13, Malet papers. Cf. Lugard's comment about the Cape to Cairo route in 'The New African Crisis with France and Germany', *Blackwood's Magazine*, XLVI, July 1894, pp. 145–58.

[1] Kimberley to Malet, no. 104 Africa, 2 July 1894, F.O. 64/1332.

[2] Kimberley to Malet, private, 19 June 1894, F.O. 343/13, Malet papers.

[3] The phrase is D. H. Simpson's, describing Anderson. 'Royal Commonwealth Society Library Notes', New Series, no. 44, August 1960,

V. THE RIVALRY FOR KIVU AND THE PUZZLE OF MFUMBIRO

My government may disavow my action, they may punish me, hang
me, if they like; but I shall get Lake Kivu and the Ruzizi valley for
my country. (Von Bethe, Commander of the Usumbura Military
Station, as reported by Lionel Decle, 1900)[1]

Mfumbiro is a myth. (Salisbury, 1900)[2]

LEOPOLD, ironically, was leasing to the British in 1894 a
corridor through territory to which he had a questionable
claim.[3] This was not challenged by any of the European powers
in 1894; not until that summer did the first European travel
through Ruanda.[4] It is remarkable, perhaps, that on 16 June,
when the European crisis reached its climax, the German
explorer—and later Governor of German East Africa—G. A.
von Götzen discovered Lake Kivu.[5]

Before Götzen's expedition, all debate about Ruanda-Urundi
had been theoretical. The boundaries were vague; European
claims overlapped. Götzen's expedition compelled the imperial
powers to ask whether this corner of Africa had been partitioned
correctly, and how the conflicting claims could be adjusted. He
raised this issue in two ways.

First, he explored Ruanda's northern volcanic region—
Mfumbiro. 'At long last the long-looked-for Virunga mountains became visible . . . the whole group has previously been
called Mfumbiro, although only the easternmost cone above is
called Ufumbiro. The Ruanda call them "Virunga".'[6]

[1] Decle to Barrington, 16 May 1900, F.O. 2/800.
[2] Salisbury's minute on Sharpe to Salisbury, no. 17, confid. tel., 1 May 1900,
F.O. 2/800.
[3] 'If the geographical data as at present are exact, it would appear that the strip
of territory referred to in Article III of the agreement of 12 May 1894 does fall
within the tract to which Germany lays claim.' Phipps to Lansdowne, no. 10
Africa, 18 February 1901, F.O. 2/800.
[4] Oskar Baumann had passed through Urundi in 1892. 'It is possible that Lake
Oso [Kivu], indicated by the Arabs and Stanley, is the source of the Ruzizi river.
To the north of Lake Oso, at the bottom of the fault, rises the massive volcano,
"Fumbiro".' See Baumann's *Durch Massailand zur Nilquelle* (Berlin, 1894),
chapter IV.
For the exploration of Ruanda-Urundi, see below, chapter X.
[5] G. A. Graf von Götzen, *Durch Afrika von Ost nach West* (Berlin, 1895), pp. 218–20.
[6] Ibid., p. 163.

Second, he noticed that Lake Kivu lay farther to the west than was indicated on the early maps, and that the boundary of the Congolese Declaration of Neutrality (the straight line) did not coincide with the course of the Ruzizi river. Therefore, according to Götzen, the Congo State would have to be persuaded to accept the reasonable solution: natural boundaries.[7]

The German Foreign Office instructed Alvensleben in January 1895 to inform the Congolese authorities that Germany desired a boundary adjustment in Ruanda-Urundi. Eetvelde in response observed that in principle a natural boundary was preferable to an astronomical one.[8] But Leopold was at present reluctant to negotiate a new frontier because of the pending transfer of the Congo State to Belgium; Alvensleben was assured in March 1895 that the Congo State would be glad to deal with the matter later.[9]

Leopold's real attitude—which determined the policy of the Congo government—was different. He had no intention of meeting the German request.[1] In a memorandum concerning Alvensleben's proposal, Eetvelde, who 'reflects his Royal master's opinions',[2] noted three points. First, that the Belgians should hold out for a mountain, and not a river boundary. Second, that possession of the territory in question should be secured definitely, because the mountainous area was favourable for European settlement. Third, that the region was needed for a Congolese telegraph and railway connection between the lakes.[3] Leopold regarded Ruanda-Urundi as a valuable piece of real estate.

In June 1896 the proposed bill for annexation of the Congo State was withdrawn from the Belgian parliament. Now Leopold, according to his own assurances to the Germans, should have been ready to discuss the Ruanda-Urundi boundary. Instead, Congolese troops appeared in the Kivu

---

[7] 'Denkschrift über deutsch-ostafrikanisch-kongolesische Streitfragen', undated (1909), A.A. 3/3.
[8] See especially 'Note sur le territoire contesté'. Most of the original correspondence may be found in M.A.E. 1/38/5.
[9] Ibid.
[1] See the letter in the 'Kiwusee-Grenzstreit mit dem Kongostaat', *Deutsches Kolonialblatt*, XVII, 1916 (pp. 172–85), p. 177: de Burlet to de Borchgrave.
[2] Plunkett to Kimberley, no. 98 Africa confid., 3 June 1894, F.O. 10/615.
[3] 'Kiwusee-Grenzstreit', p. 177.

area[4] and established a station at Uvira; the Congolese army controlled Lake Kivu and the western part of Ruanda-Urundi. Their attempts at permanent occupation, however, were unsuccessful. In 1897 the Congolese troops mutinied. One post east of Lake Kivu managed to hold out, with 52 Africans and one European, until 27 December 1897. Lt. Dubois, who attempted to restore order, was massacred along with his 60 men. The remaining Congolese authorities with their loyal troops were twice forced to seek refuge at the German station at Usumbura. Finally they had to withdraw completely from the area leaving anarchy in the Kivu region.[5]

This provided the Germans with the opportunity for which they were waiting. Captain von Bethe, under instructions from the German Foreign Office, occupied in October 1898 the disputed territory around Lake Kivu, to the Ruzizi and the Mfumbiro mountains, 'in the interest of peace and security'.

Not until a year later was the Congolese Commandant Hecq, after two victories over the rebels, prepared to reoccupy the turbulent Kivu region. He found German troops already in occupation in part of what he considered Congolese territory. The dispute between the local Congolese and German forces over who was entitled to occupy the region east of Lake Kivu led to the Bethe-Hecq agreement of 23 November 1899.

The main point of this provisional agreement was the recognition of the status quo as it existed on Hecq's arrival. The Congolese could establish two posts in the disputed zone, but they were only to be regarded as evidence of Congolese claims. The Congolese posts were not to be considered as an occupation, and were to be 'without any political, administrative rights'. The conflict was not to be settled in Ruanda and Urundi by force, but in Europe by diplomacy.

Upon concluding this arrangement and after establishing two stations, Hecq and his colleague, Lt. Hennebert, left the Kivu region. According to one Belgian account, Bethe intimidated

---

[4] The first Belgian to reach the Ruzizi was Lt. Lange in 1894. See 'La frontière orientale de notre colonie', *Mouvement Géographique*, XXVI, November 1909, pp. 535–8.

[5] See 'Historique de l'occupation Belge dans les territoires contestés de la Ruzizi et du Kivu', 27 January 1910, M.A.E. 1/38/5. This document summarizes in detail the local events in Ruanda-Urundi which are not to be found in the German documents. The Congolese agents had established two posts east of Lake Kivu called Luahilimte and Lubugo; their exact locations are not clear.

the African heads of the two Congolese posts, and also prevented the local Africans from providing them with supplies. This forced Congolese evacuation. When Hennebert returned with reinforcements Bethe refused to let them enter the disputed zone. The Congolese authorities pointed out, not without justification, that this made a farce of the Bethe-Hecq agreement of November 1899. Only after instructions reached Bethe from the German government on 7 May 1900 did Bethe permit the Congolese forces to establish their two protest posts: Shangugu and Nyakagunda. These posts were maintained until the final settlement of 1910.[6]

The British had not been unaware of this activity. Lionel Decle,[7] a French explorer on a Cape to Cairo venture for the *Daily Telegraph*, passed through Ruanda-Urundi shortly after the time of the Bethe-Hecq incident. He reported the clash to Commissioner Sharpe, who in turn wired Salisbury that the Germans had seized Congolese territory up to the Ruzizi river and Lake Kivu, and that the German commander had given notice to the Congolese commandant that unless Congolese troops withdrew they would be considered as an enemy. 'Germany is establishing a line of posts north of the lake, having concentrated 1,000 men, 15 officers. . . . Do you desire me to take any steps regarding British interests?'[8]

It was at this time that the British remembered they had received a mountain named Mfumbiro through the 1890 negotiations. Sharpe's telegram created a stir in the Foreign Office. A letter from Decle arrived shortly after; so did reports from Major A. St. H. Gibbons, who had just returned from the Zambezi by way of Lake Tanganyika, and Harry Johnston, then Special Commissioner in Uganda.

Three points were raised by their reports. The first was the question of the Congolese-German frontier. E. A. W. Clarke in the Foreign Office noted that it was difficult to say what the

[6] Ibid.; see also Lionel Decle, 'The Development of our British African Empire', in *Proceedings of the Royal Colonial Institute*, XXXVII, 1905–6, pp. 311–40.

[7] On Decle's background, see his *Three Years in Savage Africa* (London, 1898), and Perham, I, pp. 373–4.

[8] Sharpe to Salisbury, no. 17 confid., 1 May 1900, F.O. 2/800. It was on this telegram that Salisbury noted 'Mfumbiro is a myth'. Salisbury replied: 'Question between Germany and Congo. Take no action.' Salisbury to Sharpe, no. 16 tel., 10 May 1900, F.O. 2/800. See also Hardinge to Salisbury, no. 50 (no. 28), 29 January 1900, F.O. 403/298.

legal boundary was; the Congo State claimed it was a straight line according to the Declaration of Neutrality of 1885, but the Germans based their claim on the Congolese-German agreement of 1884, which showed a curved line to the west. Whatever it was, the quarrel did not concern Britain. The second point was the rumour Decle reported that the 'German forces are marching on Lake Albert Edward'. If true, this would be a serious violation of the 1890 agreement. The third was the question of Mfumbiro. To Mfumbiro the British had 'indefeasible rights' through the treaty of 1890. Furthermore, it was suspected to be of some value. Major Gibbons had written that the 'Mfumbiro district together with all the country contiguous to Lake Kivu, surpasses any country I have passed through in Africa'. There was also a far more important point than the small question of a mountain in central Africa. It was raised by Harry Johnston, who was still beating the drum for the Cape to Cairo route. Gibbons had the same idea. Occupation of the Mfumbiro district would give Britain 'access to Lake Kivu and a direct line of trade communication from the south of that lake to Egypt and within 60 or 70 miles of Tanganyika, which would be the only break in a direct communication between the Cape and Egypt'.[9]

Mfumbiro had suddenly acquired a new importance. Could the Germans have forgotten that it was a British possession?

Lansdowne, now Foreign Secretary, wrote to Salisbury: 'It seems clear that the Germans have no business with Mfumbiro, which is ours whatever it is.'[1] There was also the lurking suspicion that Germany might 'intrude herself beyond that line ["the admitted boundary line"] thereby securing for herself access to the head waters of the Nile'.[2] An assurance should be obtained from Germany, Lansdowne said, 'as to [their] intentions'.[3]

While the British pondered Stanley's enigmatic legacy of Mfumbiro, the Germans and Belgians tried to settle the problem of Ruanda-Urundi. The German occupation of the Kivu region in 1898 had followed a remarkable change in their

[9] See note C, p. 273.
[1] Lansdowne to Salisbury, 13 December 1900, F.O. 2/800.
[2] Ibid., Salisbury's minute: 'Mfumbiro is certainly ours if it is not Congolese.'
[3] Ibid., Britain received 'assurances' from the German Embassy in London on 9 January 1901. Lansdowne to Lascelles, no. 7 Africa confid., F.O. 2/800.

diplomacy. The Germans as early as 1895 had requested a 'boundary modification'; but not until 1899 did they claim that the German-Congolese agreement of 1884 rather than the Declaration of Neutrality of 1885 established the western frontier of Ruanda-Urundi.[4]

Beernaert, the distinguished Belgian statesman, made an abortive trip to Berlin in January 1900. He submitted to Baron von Richthofen at the German Foreign Office a memorandum summarizing the course of events leading to the discussions, as well as the Belgian plan for a settlement.[5]

In February 1895, Beernaert said, Alvensleben had expressed the wish to substitute a natural frontier for the astronomical one of the Declaration of Neutrality. Alvensleben had also stated that the German government desired no territorial aggrandizement. On 6 October 1899, however, the Germans had notified the Congolese authorities that they had discovered 'contradictions' in the Declaration of Neutrality: it stated that the boundary was established in the earlier treaties, but the boundary described in the Declaration was different. The Germans claimed that the true boundary was the one established by the Congolese-German agreement of 1884. The German letter of 6 October 1899, Beernaert observed, was significant; it was the first time that the Germans refused to recognize that the Declaration of Neutrality established the true legal frontier. Beernaert explained that the Congo government was willing to recognize in principle that a natural frontier was more desirable than an astronomical, but that there could be no question that the Declaration established the legal frontier, and that all discussion must begin by recognizing this fact. The Congolese authorities were ready to agree that there was a need to send a mixed commission to survey the region, but negotiations must proceed on the basis that if the Congo government were to renounce her claims to Ruanda-Urundi, the Germans must provide just compensation. Beernaert suggested that the Germans should cede to the Congo govern-

---

[4] Professor Stengers comments that the new line of argument first appeared in a despatch from Richthofen to Alvensleben of 4 June 1898; but that the new boundary demands were not presented to the Congo government until 1899. In a letter to me of 25 August 1962.

[5] Beernaert to Richthofen, 27 January 1900, M.A.E. 1/38/5; cf. Pierre van Zuylen, *L'Echiquier Congolais* (Brussels, 1959), pp. 389–90.

ment a strip of land running from the Congo north of Ruanda (through the Mfumbiro region) to Lake Victoria. This was the Congolese condition of negotiation.[6]

Beernaert received a flat no in reply to his Lake Victoria suggestion. He left Berlin on 28 January 1900; the negotiations were to be continued in Brussels.

Even if the two parties had been eager to compromise, there were no detailed geographical surveys on which to base a settlement, only vague, inaccurate maps. The negotiations were not entirely fruitless; on 10 April 1900 Germany and the Congo State accepted the Bethe-Hecq status quo agreement as binding, and agreed to send a mixed geographical expedition to Ruanda-Urundi to survey the Kivu region.[7]

In December 1900 the German contingent, led by Captain Herrmann, reached Usumbura; there they joined the Congolese group, under the leadership of Captain Bastien. The work progressed slowly; finally the German group reached Kisenyi in January 1902. Herrmann surveyed the islands in the lake and the volcanic region independently. The result was the first reliable large scale map of western Urundi and Ruanda, which confirmed the reports that Lake Kivu lay further to the west than had been indicated on the early maps; based on Leopold's straight line boundary, this meant that Ruanda-Urundi was divided between the Congo State and German East Africa.

The Congolese and German groups had difficulty in coordinating their work. After waiting several months for the Congolese contingent at the north end of Lake Kivu, Herrmann decided in March 1902 that he could wait no longer; the expedition had to be reorganized, fresh supplies and new recruits procured, for the Anglo-German delimitation in the north, which had been planned after the decision to send out the Congolese-German expedition.[8]

The British Foreign Office and War Office had begun to talk about an Anglo-German delimitation shortly after news reached

---

[6] See especially Chevalier de Cuvelier to Alvensleben, 22 April 1899, and 2 November 1899, M.A.E. 1/38/5, and 'Note sur le territoire contesté'. The Belgian documents (in M.A.E. 1/38/5) are more enlightening than the German, but see Alvensleben to A.A., 24 January 1900, A.A. 3/1.

[7] See note D, p. 273.

[8] 'Denkschrift'.

London in May 1900 that there was a Congolese-German frontier controversy. The Germans suggested that the work should be postponed until the end of 1901 so that the German officers who had started the survey of the Congolese-German boundary could continue their work with a British team.[9] This proposal was accepted.[1]

A report of gold and other valuable minerals in the disputed region from a Special Commissioner in Uganda increased British anxiety about the Anglo-German frontier westwards from Lake Victoria. Sir William Nicholson, Director of the Intelligence Division of the War Office,[2] wrote that 'it is most important that the whole settlement of this boundary should be completed with the least delay . . . British representatives should be on the spot in good time, and if they arrived there before the German party, any spare time might be advantageously spent in surveying the neighbourhood country and collecting information as to the whereabouts of Mfumbiro'.[3]

Harry Johnston, convinced that the Germans aimed 'to get access to the south shore of Lake Albert Edward', noted in December 1901 that the British should stick to the first degree south latitude because 'the desirable boundary would be the Kagera river', but the Germans would never grant this without 'marked compensation'; the only thing Britain had to offer was Mfumbiro. Nevertheless the attempt should be made to barter Mfumbiro for the Kagera boundary. 'Failing this improbably good arrangement it would be better to stick resolutely to the first degree of south latitude, as the instant we begin to waver, the Germans will make a hundred insidious proposals.'[4]

Clarke disagreed. Johnston had 'light-heartedly'[5] changed his mind about the value of Mfumbiro. His idea of an exchange of Mfumbiro for the natural boundary of the Kagera was, Clarke said, impracticable. 'I do not believe myself that the

[9] I.D. to F.O., confid., 13 November 1900, F.O. 2/800.
[1] Lansdowne to Lascelles, no. 7 Africa confid., 9 January 1901, F.O. 2/800.
[2] The War Office, more precisely the Geographical Section of the General Staff, played an important role in the Mfumbiro negotiations; Col. Close explains the organization of the Geographical Section and the intelligence branches in 'A Fifty Years Retrospect', *Empire Survey Review*, II, April 1933, p. 71.
[3] I.D. to F.O., no. 13, 26 November 1901, F.O. 2/800.
[4] 'Notes by Sir H. Johnston on the Delimitation of the Anglo-German Boundary West of the Victoria Nyanza', 5 December 1901, F.O. 2/800.
[5] Clarke's memorandum of 29 December 1901, F.O. 2/800.

Germans would agree to such a buying and selling of pigs in pokes, unless, indeed, they possess information which we do not as to the relative merits of the two objects of the proposed bargain; but in any case it would, I submit, be unwise for us to make such an offer until we know something of the two countries. So far as we know anything at all of Mfumbiro . . . it ought to prove a valuable possession . . . in the event of such an exchange as that suggested taking place, we should eventually discover that we had surrendered a really valuable territory for a large tract of uninhabitable marsh.'[6]

Nicholson pointed out that Johnston's proposal deserved consideration; but for a different reason from the one Johnston had stated. The German claim against the Congo State could result in a frontier which would push the boundary to the west of the 30th meridian, especially if the dispute were settled on the basis of the Congolese-German agreement of 1884, which showed the German boundary sweeping to the west. The British in 1894, however, had explicitly accepted the 30th meridian as a boundary between Uganda and the Congo State. A problem might therefore arise which was not contemplated when the Anglo-German agreement of 1890 (or the Anglo-Congolese treaty of 1894) was drafted. Mfumbiro might lie to the west of the 30th meridian. The agreement of 1890 stated that the boundary was to be deflected around Mfumbiro and 'return so as to terminate at the above named point.' (The point where the parallel of 1° south latitude met the Congo frontier.) The problem was more complicated, however, than simply going beyond the 30th meridian—to which the Congo State would in any case object; 'a strict adherence to the letter of the agreement would result in the frontier making a loop from and returning to this point, so as to include Mfumbiro, which would give rise to a very awkward, if not impossible boundary line'.[7]

Perhaps Johnston's suggestion about exchanging Mfumbiro for the Kagera boundary was not a bad one. The leader of the British expedition, Delmé-Radcliffe, was instructed in June 1902 to form 'an opinion as to the relative value of the two districts which would be affected by such an exchange. . . .'[8]

[6] Ibid.   [7] I.D. to F.O., 23 December 1901, F.O. 2/800.
[8] Bertie to Delmé-Radcliffe, confid., 20 June 1902, F.O. 2/800.

The British fears of Mfumbiro lying to the west of the 30th meridian were realized. The boundary commissioner wired in September 1903: 'The region to any part of which the name Mfumbiro can be applied appears to lie to the west of the 30th meridian . . . [is] the survey of the British commission . . . to be extended to the southwest of the point of intersection of the 30th meridian with the first parallel south latitude . . . ?'[9] The German commissioner had no authority to extend the survey beyond the 30th meridian.

'It would really be too absurd,' commented Clarke, 'if just as it becomes possible to ascertain once and for all exactly where Mt. Mfumbiro lies we were to allow our chance of doing so to escape us.' How could the Germans, in view of their repeated assurances that Mfumbiro belonged to Britain, 'refuse to assist us in ascertaining precisely where it was'. Lascelles, the British Ambassador in Germany, was instructed to inform the German government that the British considered it highly important to find the exact location of Mfumbiro; this was one of the original objects of the commission.[1]

Three weeks later no answer had yet been received from the Germans. Lascelles was telegraphed: 'urgent . . . press Germany for early reply.'[2]

At first sight Johnston seemed wrong: apparently he had mistaken the comments of local zealous German officers for extensive central African ambitions of the German government. The Germans were not even interested in what this curious British possession in Ruanda was. In late October 1903 the Germans informed the British that 'geographical determinations, however valuable and desirable they might be from a purely scientific point of view, lie outside the duties of the Anglo-German boundary commission'. Even if it were decided that this might be desirable, any work done to the west of the 30th meridian 'could only be justified if the Congolese commissioner were present during and took part in this further work'.[3]

Delmé-Radcliffe, however, tended to agree with Johnston:

[9] Sadler to F.O., no. 57, 16 September 1903, F.O. 2/801.
[1] Clarke's memorandum of 16 September 1903, F.O. 2/801.
[2] Clarke to Campbell, 6 October 1903, F.O. 2/801.
[3] Mühlberg to F.O., 24 October 1903, incl. in Lascelles to Lansdowne, 26 October 1903, F.O. 2/801.

the real reason why the Germans seemed uninterested in Mfumbiro was because they had no intention of sharing it with the British. 'The Germans refused to go there on grounds that it was Congo territory and the Belgian commissioner was not cooperating. The Germans evidently expect to get a large portion of the Mfumbiro region from the Belgians.'[4]

The positions of the Mfumbiro mountains had been fixed by the Congolese-German Kivu boundary commission. Delmé-Radcliffe therefore assumed that it was not intended that the British commission should go beyond the 30th meridian.[5] The most he could do was to agree formally with Schlobach, the German commissioner, that 'Mfumbiro' lay southwest of the point of intersection of 1° south latitude with the 30th meridian.

On 21 January 1904 Delmé-Radcliffe received a telegram from the Foreign Office that the boundary commission was not expected to go to Mfumbiro.[6] The problem of Mfumbiro was left 'for decision by the two governments when report of commissioners is received'. Mfumbiro seemed 'hopelessly lost'.[7]

[4] Delmé-Radcliffe to Trotter, 1 November 1903, F.O. 2/898. 'Schlobach, the German commissioner, insists . . . that the 1st parallel is the boundary all the way . . . and tried to ignore Mfumbiro and our claims in that direction entirely. I think his directions were to this effect.'

[5] Delmé-Radcliffe to F.O., no. 1 tel., 18 December 1903, F.O. 2/898; Wilson to Lansdowne, no. 63 (no. 1 tel.), 5 January 1904, F.O. 2/898. A curious minute appears in F.O. 2/898 (by Clement Hill?): 'It still remains to be ascertained whether the mountain was, under the Congolesese-German treaty, in German territory at the time Germany undertook to give the mountain to us. It is possible that Germany has since given that territory to the Congo State; but we do not know how the diplomatic ground lies because the German-Congolese treaty merely says that the frontier is shown on a map, which has never been published. We shall eventually have to ask Germany whether the mountain was at any time hers under that treaty; if it was she ought not to have given it to the Congo.' 5 January 1904, F.O. 2/898.

[6] 'Extracts from Lt.-Col. C. Delmé-Radcliffe's Typescript Diary Report on the Delimitation of the Anglo-German Boundary, Uganda, 1902–04', *Uganda Journal*, XI, March 1947, p. 28.

[7] Sadler's remark, 7 October 1904, no. 74, memorandum, Foreign Office Confidential Print 8416.
Clarke commented: '. . . I think we had better not press too much at this stage on our right to Mfumbiro. If we do and they are prepared to give way to us, we might very possibly put them off bargaining with the Congo government for it, as they would naturally not care about securing a property merely to hand it over to us. And, in the event of the place remaining Congolese, it is, of course, lost to us for good. If, on the other hand, the Germans are not prepared to surrender the place—supposing they get it—except under stress of arbitral decision, we shall be no worse off by saying nothing now. We made our reservations on the subject as long ago as January 1901, so, far as that goes, we are all right.' Clarke's memorandum, 8 November 1904, Foreign Office Confidential Print 8614.

VI. THE ANGLO-GERMAN MFUMBIRO
NEGOTIATIONS OF 1906–9

... we have no reason for making ourselves pleasant to Belgium.
(J. A. C. Tilley, British Foreign Office, 1909)[1]

ALTHOUGH 'Mfumbiro' was not occupied by Britain, the British persistently refused to waive their rights to it. The work of the Anglo-German boundary commission resulted in a protocol of 18 June 1906. Article IX stated that Germany recognized the British right to Mfumbiro. The protocol eventually was not ratified because of this article.

In 1904 Delmé-Radcliffe had reported: 'There can be no doubt that if the Mfumbiro area or a portion of it could be retained within the British sphere a considerable step would be made towards securing a line along which the Great Trunk Railway from the Cape to Cairo might run.'[2] T. T. Behrens, who worked with Delmé-Radcliffe on the boundary commission, confirmed Major Gibbons's report that the region itself was valuable: 'The whole of the area is exceedingly well-watered, and contains an abundant supply of timber. The luxuriant vegetation which covers the country, the ample water supply and cool climate, combined with a fertile soil, makes it a most suitable area for European occupation.'[3] C. F. Close (of the Geographical Section of the General Staff), who was instrumental in the Ruanda-Urundi settlement of 1910, later attributed the revival of British interest in Mfumbiro to the reports of the British boundary commission: 'We were allowing our claims to a valuable upland region to go by default . . . meanwhile the Congo State had occupied the greater part of it.'[4]

The British Foreign Office requested a map of the Mfumbiro

[1] Tilley's minute of 22 May 1909 (18999), F.O. 367/127.
[2] Delmé-Radcliffe to Lansdowne, confid., 31 October 1904, F.O. 2/898.
[3] T. T. Behrens, 'Notes on Mt. Mfumbiro in relation to the treaties between Britain, Germany and the Congo Free State', 25 April 1906, incl. in Director of Military Operations to F.O., 1 June 1906, F.O. 367/10. The Director commented: 'There would appear to be no doubt of the validity as regards Germany, of the British claim to this region. . . . Such a frontier would give us access to Lake Kivu, and would include in British territory a healthy and fertile upland country.'
[4] Close's 'Memorandum . . . on the agreement signed in Brussels on May 14, 1910' (25 May, 1910), F.O. 367/174.

region from the German government.[5] On the basis of this map, which had been prepared by the German section of the German-Congolese boundary commission, the British reformulated their claims to Mfumbiro. Discussions about the Anglo-German boundary took place in Berlin in July 1906.[6] 'The German commissioner admitted without hesitation our claim to it [Mfumbiro].' If Germany should receive the territory which was in dispute with the Congo State, she would recognize her obligation to hand it over to Britain. The only objection to the British proposal made by the Germans was that 'Mt. Mfumbiro' had been changed to 'Mfumbiro'. Since 'Mt. Mfumbiro' was the phrase used in the 1890 treaty, the British had to agree that 'Mt. Mfumbiro' should be used in the 1906 protocol.[7] The Germans also 'lay much weight on obtaining a declaration in the protocol to the effect that the British government will raise no objection to any future regulation of boundary between German East Africa and the Congo State south of 1° 20' south latitude'.[8] The British refused to include the declaration itself, but Sir Edward Grey, the British Foreign Secretary, was willing to make the assurance, provided the Germans would keep the British informed about the Congolese-German negotiations.[9] Apart from this minor skirmishing, there was no problem about the German recognition of the British right to Mfumbiro. Grey was satisfied; there could be further negotiations 'when it has been ascertained exactly what and where it is'.[1]

[5] The British were able to obtain the map 'owing to the friendly relations which have always existed between British and German officers who have been employed on boundary commissions . . .' Ibid.

[6] G. Pearson in the Foreign Office noted in preparation for the Anglo-German discussions: 'I have marked the treaty line as running round Mfumbiro in the way it theoretically should, but of course we do not really want such a curious enclave.' 10 April 1906, F.O. 367/10.

[7] 'In order to secure access to Mt. Mfumbiro we proposed the cession of a strip of German territory one kilometre in width to connect the mountain with the Uganda Protectorate. To this the German commissioners demurred on the ground that it might cut their German territory in two and would involve both administrations in the numerous difficulties inseparable from an extended frontier. After some discussion, the best solution appeared to be the grant by Germany to Great Britain of the right of free access to Mt. Mfumbiro.' Erskine to Whitehead, 10 July 1906; also Erskine to Grey, 19 July 1906, F.O. 367/10.

[8] Whitehead to Grey, no. 6 Africa, 13 July 1906, F.O. 367/10.

[9] Grey to Lascelles, no. 130 Africa, 14 August 1906; see also Clarke's minute of 14 July 1906, F.O. 367/10.

[1] Grey to Whitehead, no. 7 Africa tel., 13 July 1906, F.O. 367/10. This telegram was drafted by Clarke, who commented: 'The Germans have shown themselves very conciliatory.' (23614.)

Despite the efforts of British explorers, however, Mfumbiro remained a puzzle. Ewart Grogan reported in 1900: 'I made a rapid tour to establish the identity of Mfumbiro, which is conspicuously marked on most maps with the height added, and I ascertained for certain what I had been led by the Germans to suspect, namely, that Mfumbiro has never existed outside the imagination of the British statesmen.'[2]

Geographical explorations after the turn of the century had shown that the Virunga[3] mountains—the term preferred by the Belgians and Germans to Mfumbiro—were a series of eight volcanoes, most of which lay south of 1° south latitude and west of the 30th meridian.[4] None could properly be called Mfumbiro; but the British zoologist J. E. S. Moore, who travelled through the region after Grogan, argued that the term applied to the whole area.[5]

The problem of Mfumbiro, as the British had foreseen in 1900, was complicated by the confirmation that the 30th meridian on the early maps had been drawn about 12 miles too far west. This meant that not only Mfumbiro but also approximately 4,500 square miles of Uganda might belong to the Congo State instead of Britain. It also meant an increase of territory for Leopold in Ruanda-Urundi, since the diagonal line of 1885 was to be drawn to the 30th meridian. The new position of the meridian also gave Leopold grounds to claim the Mfumbiro volcanic region.

Dernburg, the German Colonial Secretary, observed in October 1906 that the British Foreign Office had the same attitude as the Germans toward the 30th meridian: for both

---

[2] Ewart S. Grogan, 'Through Africa from the Cape to Cairo', *Geographical Journal*, XVI, August 1900, p. 172. See also Grogan and Sharp, *From the Cape to Cairo* (London, 1900), pp. 134–7. Cf. J. E. S. Moore, *To the Mountains of the Moon* (London, 1901), p. 188. Grogan renamed some of the volcanoes. Moore observed: 'It is . . . somewhat superfluous and misleading for Mr. Grogan to apply the names of his sisters and cousins and his aunts to these peaks, as if he had discovered them in 1899.' (Mountains, p. 188.) Moore describes Mfumbiro as 'perhaps the most interesting range in the whole African continent.' See his article 'Tanganyika and the Countries North of it', *Geographical Journal*, XVII, January 1901, pp. 1–39, with an appendix by Malcolm Fergusson, 'Methods Used in Surveying and General Notes'.

[3] See E. M. Jack, 'The Mufúmbiro Mountains', *Geographical Journal*, XLI, June 1913, pp. 535–6.

[4] Ibid.; see also *Report of the British Section of the Anglo-German-Belgian Boundary Commission, 1911* (H.M.S.O., 1912).

[5] Moore, *Mountains*, p. 189. On the origin of the term 'Mfumbiro', see especially E. M. Jack, *On the Congo Frontier* (London, 1914), pp. 200–1.

Germany and Britain a more satisfactory frontier could be obtained if the dispute with the Congo State were settled on the basis of the assumed location of the meridian at the time of the early exploration rather than its actual location. If the British would not press their Mfumbiro claims south of 1° 20' south latitude (the natural boundary, Dernburg said, because of the volcanic ridge), and not support the Congo State in their claims to the Kivu region, then Britain and Germany might be able to come to a mutually advantageous understanding about their 30th meridian claims.[6]

By February 1907 Grey was willing to assure Germany that Britain would not interfere with the boundary between the Congo State and German East Africa south of 1° 20' south latitude. Apparently the Foreign Office had forgotten about the War Office's proposed boundary, which extended to the north shore of Lake Kivu. The Foreign Office was unwilling, however, to state explicitly for the sake of the German government that Mfumbiro was a district and not a mountain: the British boundary commissioners in 1906 had wanted to substitute the term 'Mfumbiro' for 'Mount Mfumbiro'; but the Germans had insisted on the latter, as the treaty of 1890 referred to a single mountain. Now the Germans, for no apparent reason, had changed their minds.[7]

Discussions about Mfumbiro were held by the British and German governments at the British Foreign Office in May 1908;[8] the two groups were immediately at loggerheads. Victor Wellesley, one of the African experts in the British Foreign

[6] Dernburg to A.A., 24 October 1906, A.A. 3/1. Cf. W. Erskine's minute of 1 August 1906: 'When in Berlin I was approached privately by several members of the Colonial Department with the suggestion that England and Germany should act together in attempting to get the rectifications which they respectively desire in this district, on the ground that the Congo would be far more amenable to the combined pressure of two powers than to that of each acting separately. The Germans are evidently afraid that we intend to place obstacles in the way of their negotiations respecting Lake Kivu, and if they find that far from wishing to do so we are willing to help them they will be the more ready to assist us to get what we want west of the 30th meridian, and also in any negotiations with the Congo respecting Mfumbiro. A settlement of this latter question would be much facilitated by joint negotiation between the two powers and the Congo. . . . I gather in general that the Germans are prepared to bully the Congo to any extent and that what they really like would be a partition of the country between England, Germany, and France.' (24926; cf. the minutes on 32974), F.O. 367/5.
[7] Grey to Lascelles, no. 21 Africa, 12 February 1907; cf. Erskine's minute of 4 December 1906, F.O. 367/10.
[8] The British were represented by C. F. Close, Head of the Geographical Section of the General Staff; Victor Wellesley of the F.O.; T. T. Behrens, Royal

Office, presented the British Mfumbiro claims, which included the German station of Kisenyi on the north end of Lake Kivu. Dr. Baron von Danckelmann, the Geographer and African expert of the German Colonial Office, asked the inconvenient but anticipated question of how the British planned to go about this without contradicting Grey's 1° 20′ assurance. Wellesley replied that the point of British insistence on Mfumbiro was to secure British access to Lake Kivu. Close displayed maps, on which he indicated the area Britain claimed as Mfumbiro. Mfumbiro meant 'land that smokes'. The eastern volcanoes were no longer active, but those in the west (Nyamlagira and Tshanina Gongo) were; they therefore belonged to Mfumbiro. Close argued that Speke and Stanley had sighted the highest mountain—Karisimbi.[9]

The discussions were merely exploratory. Neither side was authorized to negotiate a settlement, but only to hear the other's views. Danckelmann remarked, however, that the British claims seemed to him extravagant. It was unthinkable, he said, that Germany, in view of the native population, should renounce the eastern volcanoes, the vegetable products, the German station at Kisenyi, and the excellent natural boundary of the volcanic ridge in favour of a British 'artistic boundary'.[1]

Such a divergence of views made discussion impossible. The groups adjourned without agreement about Mfumbiro. Wellesley had pointed out at the conference, however, that despite

Engineers, of the General Staff; C. Strachey, Head of the West Africa Division of the C.O.; G. R. Warner of the F.O.; and H. M. Hull, formerly of the Gold Coast Government Service. The Germans: Wilhelm zu Stolberg Wernigerode; *Geh.* von Danckelmann; Captain von Seefried.

The conference was primarily designed to discuss the Aka boundary in west Africa; Grey thought that the opportunity might be further utilized to discuss Mfumbiro, but was uncertain how strong the British legal claims to Mfumbiro were. On receiving a favourable report from the Law Officers, Grey decided to proceed with the Mfumbiro discussions with Germany. See F.O. to Law Officers of the Crown, no. 26, 7 June 1907, F.O. 403/391: 'Opinion of the Law Officers of the Crown', no. 35, 2 September 1907, F.O. 403/391; 'Memorandum respecting the Congo-Uganda Boundary and Mfumbiro', 9 October 1907, F.O. 403/391; and Dernburg's 'Instruktion für den Wirklichen Legationsrat Dr. von Jacobs, geheim', 6 February 1908, A.A. 3/1.

[9] 'Bericht über die im Mai 1908 in London stattgehabten Besprechungen betreffend die Aka-Grenzfrage in Togo, sowie die deutsch-kongolesisch-englischen Grenzverhältnisse im Norden des Kivu-Sees', undated (1908), A.A. 3/2. See also 'Report by Mr. Wellesley respecting the Aka-Mfumbiro Conference', 26 May 1908, Foreign Office Confidential Print 9267. The German report is more illuminating than the British.

[1] 'Bericht über die im Mai 1908 in London stattgehabten Besprechungen.'

their disagreement over Mfumbiro, Britain and Germany held similar views about the treaties of 1884–5, 1890, and 1894. It might still be possible for the two governments to work together against the Congo State. 'Subsequently this suggestion bore fruit.'[2]

After the conference Lindequist, one of the German colonial secretaries, observed in a series of memoranda that if nothing else was accomplished in the London discussions, it was at least clear that the British intended to use Mfumbiro to try to gain access to Lake Kivu.[3] It would be pointless for Germany to quarrel over this non-existent mountain, especially since the Germans had no interest in the western group of volcanoes. But what was important was that Kisenyi as well as the southern slopes of the volcanoes, which formed the north of Ruanda, were included in British claims.[4] The Duke of Mecklenburg was soon to return from his expedition across Africa; he had passed through the volcanic region and would be able to furnish information and advice as to the wisest German course.[5] In any case said Lindequist, the unratified protocol with Britain, which mentioned Mfumbiro, should be handled in a dilatory way unless an exact definition could be agreed upon.[6]

The British uneasily watched Mecklenburg's actions. In 1908 the War Office learned that the German Colonial Office planned to obtain from him an accurate survey of the volcanoes and a report on the economic value of the region. The Duke was an advocate of a 'forward' colonial policy: he had no doubt that the Germans would be able to obtain their maximum demands—the Ruzizi, Lake Kivu, and the whole of the volcanic region of Mfumbiro.[7]

As the Anglo-German discussions in 1908 had been fruitless, the British feared the Germans might attempt to negotiate with Leopold. Grey said in August 1908: 'It appears to me not unlikely that an attempt may be made by the German government to obtain concessions south of Lake Kivu (i.e. the line of the river Ruzizi), by abandoning Mt. Mfumbiro to the Congo State.'[8]

[2] Close's memorandum of 25 May 1910, F.O. 367/174.
[3] Lindequist to A.A., 4 June 1908; 3 July 1908; 21 July 1908; A.A. 3/1–2.
[4] Ibid., 3 July.   [5] Ibid., 4 June.   [6] Ibid., 21 July.
[7] See note E, p. 273.
[8] Grey to Wyndham, no. 23 (no. 97 Africa), 7 August 1908, F.O. 403/403.

Congolese-German cooperation had been discussed, in fact, by the German Chancellor, Bülow, in July 1906: 'It seems to me that a recommended fundamental principle of our general policy might be that as friendly as possible relations with the Congo State should be maintained. . . . Its existence for [German] East Africa is valuable in so far as it is for us, no doubt, a much friendlier neighbour than the English would be, if they succeeded either partially or wholly in taking its place.'[9]

Dernburg disagreed, and foresaw in 1906 that any attempt to settle the Kivu problem with Leopold would be futile. The Congo State had not been a good neighbour; the Congolese authorities had been completely adamant in maintaining their claims to the astronomical boundary dividing Ruanda-Urundi; and, Dernburg observed, their heavy military occupation of the region did not augur well for the future.[1]

As early as 1899 Leopold had hinted that he might accept compensation for recognition of the German Ruzizi-Kivu boundary. In December 1906 Wallwitz, the German Minister in Belgium, wrote that Leopold had shown an eagerness to come to terms with Germany, either by receiving monetary compensation or by an exchange of territory.[2] The Germans, however, always considered Leopold's hints of compensation exorbitant,[3] and his proposals for territorial exchange impracticable. In the meantime both the Congolese and German forces entrenched themselves further in the Kivu region.

The provisional Bethe-Hecq agreement of 1899 was designed to prevent local clashes by maintaining the status quo. Ironically this understanding proved as vague and unsatisfactory as the earlier agreement. No precise definition of the contested region was to be found in the text of the agreement. The Germans considered it unquestionable that the 'contested territory' included all the region up to the Ruzizi and Lake Kivu, including the island in the lake, Idjwi. The German Captain von Grawert had raised a flag over Idjwi in October 1899; this meant, according to the Germans, that the island

[9] 24 July 1906, in Dernburg to A.A., 24 October 1906, A.A. 3/1.
[1] Ibid., see also Maj. z. D. Max Schlagintweit, 'Nochmals die Nordwestgrenze von Deutsch-Ostafrika', *Kolonialzeitung*, XXV, April 1908, p. 295.
[2] Wallwitz to A.A., 22 December 1906, A.A. 3/1.
[3] Leopold demanded at least 80 million marks, a sum which the Reichstag would never have appropriated. See 'Kiwusee-Grenzstreit', p. 178.

was included in the contested territory of the Bethe-Hecq agreement of November 1899. In December 1900 the Congolese Captain Milz, Commandant of the Kivu-Ruzizi district, however, tried to establish Congolese sovereignty over Idjwi. Both sides were willing to agree that the median of the lake would divide the Congolese and German spheres (this did not mean, of course, renunciation of the Congolese claim to Ruanda-Urundi based on the Declaration of Neutrality, but only recognition of the limits of the 'contested territory'). The problem was what was the median of the lake. Herrmann's departure in March 1902 had prevented any agreement about the geography of Lake Kivu. According to Herrmann, the median of the lake was a line which included the large island of Idjwi in German territory; according to Bastien the median included the island in Congo territory. This meant that not only the island in the lake, but also the region on the north shore was disputed. Thus, there was no agreement about the diagonal line from the north of Lake Kivu to 1° 20′ south latitude. If it were drawn from the Congolese median, Lake Bulera would be included in Congolese territory.

The years 1902–4 for the Kivu controversy were quiet; the Congolese authorities observed that the Germans were diverted because of unrest in German East Africa. The problem arose again in January 1905, however, when Grawert protested against the Congolese officials raising a flag over Idjwi.

The resolution of these local conflicts was the object of Baron Joostens's mission to Berlin in July 1906. Joostens explained to the German Foreign Office that the Congolese authorities had never raised flags on islands east of the median of the lake; the Congolese survey showed that all of the island Idjwi lay in Congolese territory. The Germans replied that this was debatable, and, moreover, that the cartographic group which had determined this was causing 'disturbances among the indigenous population'. The Germans demanded that the cartographic mission be withdrawn; the Congolese authorities complied. On 29 July 1906 the Congo government wired Joostens that they would not attempt to exercise sovereignty over the islands in the lake—on three conditions. First, that this would not prejudice the Congolese claim to Ruanda-Urundi based on the Declaration of Neutrality; second, that the Germans would not raise any more flags over the islands in the lake than were already there; third, that Germany would enter into negotiations to settle the Ruanda-Urundi question before the end of 1906. This was the substance of the understanding reached between the Congo State and Germany in 1906; it was only a small step toward the solution of a large problem. During the next two years there were various exchanges of notes between the two governments, but no progress resulted. On 12 March 1908 Dernburg instructed the German Foreign Office that talks with the Congo State about Kivu should be conducted desultorily, in view of the impending Mfumbiro negotiations with Britain and because Leopold's condition of negotiation— the stretch of territory to Lake Victoria in return for a German Ruanda-Urundi—was infeasible.[4]

Just as Grey feared the possibility of Congolese-German negotiations at Britain's expense,[5] so Dernburg saw that Leopold might try to barter Mfumbiro for British support in the Kivu dispute. In February 1909 Dernburg stated flatly that there was 'no hope that a direct understanding between Germany and Belgium in this affair [Kivu] could be reached'. In view of the 'threatening danger' of an Anglo-Congolese agreement, which would be much to Germany's disadvantage in the Kivu quarrel, Dernburg favoured an understanding with Britain—even if it meant renunciation of German claims to Mfumbiro, and British access to Lake Kivu. The Mfumbiro question, after all, was not so important. Both countries had similar grounds for complaint against the Congo State about more important problems. They both had received no satisfaction from Leopold; both preferred a settlement based on old maps (so the 30th meridian would appear farther west); both declared they favoured natural frontiers.[6]

[4] The Belgian documents are more illuminating than the German, and are found in M.A.E. 1/38/5. The details are conveniently summarized in 'Note sur le territoire contesté' and 'Historique de l'occupation belge'; see also the Congo government's aide-mémoire of 4 July 1906 and 7 March 1907, A.A. 3/1; Wallwitz to Chevalier de Cuvelier, 8 November 1907, M.A.E. 1/38/5; Dernburg to A.A., 24 October 1906, A.A. 3/1; Dernburg to A.A., 6 January 1908, A.A. 3/1; and Dernburg to A.A., 12 March 1909, A.A. 3/2.

[5] The British overtures to the Congolese authorities, like the German, were fruitless. The Congo State refused to recognize any validity to British claims west of the 30th meridian. See Grey to Hardinge, no. 19 (no. 24 Africa), 12 February 1907, F.O. 403/391. See also van Zuylen, L'Echiquier Congolais, pp. 405–10.

[6] Dernburg to A.A., 8 March 1909, A.A. 3/2.

The Germans, as a lengthy memorandum later explained, had no choice other than to negotiate with the British. There were only three possibilities. The first was to negotiate with the Congo State. This was impossible because of Leopold's adamancy. The second was to do nothing. This was impracticable because of the administrative problem in Ruanda-Urundi and because the Congo State and Britain might come to an agreement to support each other's claims against Germany. The third was to negotiate with Britain, with whom Germany had common complaints against the Congo State and no seriously contested issues other than Mfumbiro. The third was the only sensible solution.[7]

The British had come to a similar conclusion. Grey thought that 'the German government are more likely to accept a reasonable definition [of Mfumbiro] while their negotiations with Belgium are still unfinished'.[8] After the German hint that they would concur in the British demand for access to Lake Kivu the Foreign Office eagerly accepted the German invitation to a conference.[9]

The delegates[1] to the Anglo-German Mfumbiro conference assembled in Berlin on 26 April 1909.[2] The instructions to the British members of the conference were simple: 'to come to an agreement . . . as to the meaning of the territory "Mt. Mfumbiro".'[3] Then the area to which it applied should be marked

---

[7] 'Denkschrift'.

[8] See F.O. to C.O., no. 37, 7 December 1908, F.O. 403/403; also F.O. to C.O., no. 38, 7 October 1908, F.O. 403/403.

[9] To insure coordination, Grey suggested that as a preliminary step to intergovernmental negotiation, there should be a meeting between representatives of the Foreign Office, Colonial Office, and War Office to decide on a definite British policy toward Mfumbiro. In the selection of delegates the C.O. deferred to the W.O.; Crewe, the Colonial Secretary, thought that Close, as Head of the Geographical Section of the General Staff, and Behrens, who had personal knowledge of Mfumbiro, were 'eminently fitted' to represent the C.O. In Germany the delegates represented the C.O. and the F.O.; but while the W.O. and F.O. ran the show in Britain, it was the C.O. in Germany that determined the German policy. See F.O. to C.O., no 37, 7 December 1908, F.O. 403/403; and C.O. to F.O., 6 April 1909, F.O. 367/127.

[1] The German delegates: Geh. von Ebermaier and Dr. Baron von Danckelmann, of the Colonial Office; and Captain von Grawert, Resident of Ruanda-Urundi. Captain Herrmann was in attendance, while at some of the sittings von Griesinger or von Eckert were also present on behalf of the F.O. The British delegates: Count de Salis, the Chargé d'Affaires in Berlin; Close; Behrens.

[2] Negotiations began on the 28th.

[3] 'Instructions to the British Members of the Mfumbiro Conference at Berlin', 22 April 1909, F.O. 367/127. '. . . the first thing to do is obviously to approach the Germans with some definite proposal as to what Mfumbiro really embraces

on two maps and signed by members of both delegations. It proved easier to mark the maps than to agree about the meaning of 'Mfumbiro'.

The British began by explaining the grounds on which they based their claims. The presentation was divided into three topics: what Mfumbiro meant to (1) Africans; (2) the treaty-makers in 1890; and (3) travellers. These three parts corresponded with the British attempt to prove that Mfumbiro included the western, central, and eastern groups of volcanoes.

First was the evidence from the name itself, which was the same argument as that used at the 1908 conference. 'Mfumbiro', as used by the Africans in the region, meant 'place where there is fire'. Since the active volcanoes, Nyamlagira and Tshanina-Gongo, were in the extreme west of the group, the term 'Mfumbiro' must apply to the region of the western peaks.

The second was evidence attached to 'Mfumbiro' by those who drafted the treaty in 1890. De Salis argued that apart from Stanley's 1888–9 expedition, the only information available about Mfumbiro in 1890 was derived from the geographical descriptions of Speke in 1863 and Stanley in 1878; Speke's sketch in particular must have had some bearing on the 1890 negotiations.[4] In an article in the *Geographical Journal* in 1907,[5] Behrens had identified the position of the principal peaks—Karissimbi, Muhavura, and Mikeno—illustrated in Speke's sketch. Therefore 'Mfumbiro' included at least these three; in other words, the central and eastern groups.

As for evidence from travellers Speke was the first to place Mfumbiro on the map, when he saw its peaks from Karagwe in 1861. In his *Journal* he alluded to 'some bold sky scraping cones situated in the country Ruanda'.[6] Stanley next saw Mfumbiro, again from Karagwe. Stuhlmann, however, during

making our claim as preposterous as we reasonably can.' Walter Langley's minute of 6 April 1909 (13174), F.O. 363/127. Langley was Assistant Under-Secretary of State for Foreign Affairs, and drafted many of Grey's despatches concerning Mfumbiro.

[4] There is no evidence that either Speke's *Journal of the Discovery of the Source of the Nile* (London and Edinburgh, 1863), or Stanley's *Through the Dark Continent* (2 vols.; London, 1878) was consulted in 1890. Speke's sketch is on page 214 of the *Journal*. Stanley 'obtained a tolerably distinct view of the triple cone of Ufumbiro'. *Dark Continent*, I, p. 465.

[5] T. T. Behrens, 'The Most Reliable Values of the Heights of Central African Lakes and Mountains', *Geographical Journal*, XXIX, March 1907, pp. 307–26.

[6] p. 213.

Emin's expedition of 1890–2, was the first explorer to set the location of Mfumbiro with precision.[7] 'Stuhlmann's route took him along in the sight of the peaks for some distance, so that he was able to fix them by cross-bearing from his line of march.'[8] And then, of course, Götzen in 1894, who mentioned 'Ufumbiro' as the eastern cone. From all this the British delegates concluded that ' "Mfumbiro" as intended by the treaty of 1890 applies to the whole group of mountains . . .'[9]

The Germans were not impressed. 'Mfumbiro' meant the 'land of potter's clay', not 'land of fire'. Furthermore, they argued, according to the researches of German officers on the spot, the name Mfumbiro simply was not applied locally to the group of mountains north of Lake Kivu. The British countered by saying that this was not surprising, since European explorers had often used names which were unknown locally. Neither the Semliki, nor Ruwenzori, nor Kilimanjaro were known as such by the Africans in those areas.

And so the discussion went round and round. The British observed that on no occasion did the Germans 'oppose to our definition of the term any counter-definition which they considered to be in conformity with the intention of the framers of the treaty'.[1] The German delegates, however, had not seen the possibility of agreement about Mfumbiro. The point was theoretical; they wanted a practical solution. The Germans submitted a memorandum summarizing their proposals.

Both governments, said the Germans, should agree that the old maps should be used as a basis for adjusting boundary difficulties with the Congo. Natural frontiers might thus be obtained. Germany would then be in a position to come to a definite agreement with the British concerning the southern slopes of the volcanoes claimed as part of Mfumbiro. These slopes, the Germans pointed out, belonged politically and economically to Ruanda. Since both Britain and Germany had declared that it was undesirable to break up political and economic units, Germany would be prepared to offer Britain

---

[7] 'Far in the west rises high over the plateau a mighty mountain cone, the much talked of Mt. Mfumbiro, as the people of Uganda and Karagwe call it.' F. Stuhlmann, *Mit Emin Pascha ins Herz von Africa* (Berlin, 1894), pp. 227–8.

[8] 'British Delegates to the Mfumbiro Conference to Sir Edward Grey', 19 May 1909, incl. in Goschen to Grey, no. 30 Africa, 20 May 1909, F.O. 367/127.

[9] Ibid.   [1] Ibid.

compensation at some other point along the Anglo-German boundary west of Lake Victoria. On two conditions: first, if her Ruzizi boundary was established satisfactorily with the Congo State; second, if Britain would renounce her Mfumbiro claims to the southern slopes of the volcanoes.

The British delegates thought the proposals feasible—a 'very reasonable arrangement'[2]—if the Germans would provide Britain access to Lake Kivu. The Germans concurred. The territory to be ceded to the British for Mfumbiro losses was a portion of Mpororo. Britain was to occupy Mfumbiro. The bargain was to become effective when the Congolese authorities evacuated their 'protest' posts east of the Ruzizi frontier. An agreement was drafted and signed on 19 May 1909. The British and Germans were 'convinced that the government of the Congo State cannot but recognize the justice of the above mentioned views, and will not therefore maintain an attitude of opposition . . . '

Whether the Congo government would, in fact, be convinced of the justice of British and German claims was highly questionable. The problem remained of how to bludgeon Leopold into accepting the Anglo-German demands. A supplementary secret agreement was drawn up and signed. The point of this secret diplomacy was to ensure definite agreement about common action against the Congo State. Britain was to occupy her part of Mfumbiro immediately, so that the treaty would not be 'disregarded' by the Congo government.[3]

Leopold's obstinacy had led to disaster. Britain and Germany had ganged up against the Congo State.[4]

[2] 'We have not been able to get the Germans to agree in theory, as a preliminary to the settlement of the frontier, to a definition of Mfumbiro which is anything like in accordance with our views. But you will observe that in the course of the agreement they agree not to object to our marking it on the map in accordance with our ideas. . . . We hand over to Germany the southern slopes of the mountains. The line of the summits forms a very good boundary, while the ceded territory is more or less in their occupation but not in ours.' De Salis to Langley, 8 May 1909, F.O. 367/127.

[3] Exactly when and how the British occupation and the notification of the Congolese authorities were to take place was neither stated nor discussed. De Salis wrote on 8 May: 'As a practical means of securing the execution of the agreement it is proposed that we should take common action in the matter as regards the Congo, while Germany agrees to a provisional frontier which will enable us to get into the Mfumbiro country and occupy it now. We could not do this before. These last provisions are beyond the letter of our instructions but . . . I gather from co-delegates that we shall hardly reach a practical solution of the question without some such arrangement.' De Salis to Langley, 8 May 1909, F.O. 367/127.

[4] The Congo State was annexed by Belgium on 15 November 1908; further references will be to the Belgian rather than the Congo government.

VII. THE KIVU EXPEDITION AND THE DESBUISSONS MAP

Not knowing the policy which dictates these orders, I can but obey them, although the ultimate object of His Majesty's Government is not clear to me. (J. M. Coote, Commander of the Kivu Expedition, 1909)[1]

. . . the possibility cannot be excluded that in 1885 the Congolese authorities purposely deceived the Imperial [German] Government. (Dernburg, German Colonial Secretary, 1909)[2]

ON the conclusion of the Anglo-German treaty of May 1909, the British immediately made plans for 'pouncing'[3] on their lost territory of Mfumbiro. After consultation with the War Office and Foreign Office, the Colonial Secretary, the Earl of Crewe, on 22 May instructed by telegraph the Acting Governor of Uganda, Stanley Tomkins, to select 'a suitable officer[4] for this somewhat delicate task' of securing Mfumbiro before the Belgians pushed their posts further to the east.[5] The expedition, not to exceed one company,[6] was to establish a chain of posts

---

[1] Coote to Boyle, 28 June 1909, incl. 4 in no. 101, C.O. to F.O., 25 August 1909, F.O. 403/411. For convenience and consistency I have referred throughout this chapter to the Foreign Office Confidential Prints (which in general accurately reproduce the most important correspondence of the Foreign Office, Colonial Office, and War Office), and have referred to the original documents only when despatches or minutes did not appear in the Confidential Prints, or when they appeared in modified form.

[2] Dernburg to A.A., geheim, 11 January 1910, A.A. 3/4.

[3] '. . . occupation would no doubt be very useful . . .' Minute by J. A. C. Tilley of 22 May 1909 (18999), F.O. 367/127. Sir Charles Hardinge, the Permanent Under-Secretary (and cousin of Sir Arthur Hardinge), noted: 'The danger of collision is not great and with a tactful officer in command should easily be avoided.' (19316.) Grey: 'I agree.' F.O. 367/128.

[4] 'I have selected as political officer Mr. J. M. Coote, who is, in my opinion, the most suitable available officer for this delicate undertaking . . . assisted by [Captain de Courcey] Ireland, a thoroughly reliable and experienced officer.' Coote was the political officer in charge of the expedition; Ireland was the military officer in command of the troops. Tomkins to Crewe, secret, 7 June 1909, incl no. 3 in no. 54, C.O. to F.O., no 54, 9 July 1909, F.O. 403/411.

[5] Crewe to the Officer administering the Government of the Uganda Protectorate, 22 May 1909, incl in no. 28, C.O. to F.O., 28 May 1909, F.O. 403/411.

[6] One company was the size of the expedition prescribed by Crewe's first telegram of 22 May. On 28 May Crewe wired: 'There is reason to suppose that the Congolese post . . . has strength of 9 Europeans, 150 askaris and 2 machine guns.' This telegram was sent at the suggestion of Col. Close. (Crewe to Tomkins, no. 101, 28 May 1909, incl. 1 in no. 35, C.O. to F.O., 11 June 1909, F.O. 403/411.) Tomkins added to the Mbarara force of one company, 50 sikh troops, under the command of Captain Ireland, and 2 maxim guns. Crewe's telegram of 5 June was

as far as Lake Kivu—with a British station on the north shore
of the lake—but no post was to be within 20 miles of the Belgian
camp at Rutshuru.[7]
J. M. Coote, the political officer in charge of the expedition,
thought that 'speed is imperative'.[8] He left Entebbe on 7 June;
the expedition left Mbarara on 11 June; all necessary posts had
been established, with the exception of the Kivu station, by 28
June. The expedition had covered almost 300 miles in 17 days.
The first post was formed on 21 June at Kibumba Hill,
'which completely dominates the only exit from Mfumbiro to
Lake Kivu.' The other post was established at Rubona, 22 miles
northeast of Kibumba, 18 miles from Rutshuru. Rubona
'commands the whole [Mfumbiro] valley . . . has three separate
water supplies, looks down into five separate richly cultivated
subsidiary valleys . . . no movement from Rutshuru could be
made unobserved.' Both Kibumba and Rubona were 'positions
of exceptional strength . . .'[9]
The Belgians at Rutshuru had no suspicion of the British
expedition; but neither had the Germans at Kisenyi. Krauss,
the German officer in charge of the Kisenyi post, was astonished[1] when Coote and his force appeared on 24 June. This was

the go ahead signal; this was 'most opportune, as Mr. Coote arrived at Entebbe . . .
by one of the Uganda railway steamers . . . yesterday.' (Tomkins to Crewe, secret,
7 June 1909, incl. no. 3 in no. 54, C.O. to F.O., 9 July 1909, F.O. 403/411). The
original despatches are in C.O. 536/29.
    [7] A few days after these initial orders, Grey instructed Arthur Hardinge, the
British Minister in Belgium, that the British would take immediate steps to occupy
Mfumbiro 'in accordance with the terms of the recent supplementary agreement
with Germany'. Hardinge was to 'refrain in the meantime from saying anything
to the Belgian government on the subject of the agreement'. Grey to Hardinge,
tel., no. 26 (no. 7 Africa), 27 May 1909, F.O. 403/411. See Tilley's and Langley's
minutes of 1 June, F.O. 367/127.
    [8] '. . . any Congolese post in this neighbourhood cannot fail to get news of the
movement of so large a body of men. I shall therefore push on without delay, and
hope to reach Lake Kivu without encountering any Congolese officials.' Coote to
Acting Chief Secretary, Entebbe, 14 June 1909, incl. no. 2 in no. 75, C.O. to
F.O., 21 July 1909, 403/411.
    [9] On the route taken by the expedition, see H. B. Thomas's note to J. M. Coote's
'The Kivu Mission, 1909-10', Uganda Journal, XX, September 1956, p. 112.
    [1] As was Coote at Krauss's lack of instructions from his government. Kisenyi
and Kigali were, of course, cut off from Tabora by several weeks; but it is clear
from the German despatches that the Kivu expedition took the German Colonial
Office by complete surprise. See 'Resident of Ruanda to Mr. Coote', 29 June 1909,
F.O. 403/411.
    Krauss was more disturbed, however, at the news of the Belgian 'working parties'
constructing a road from Goma to Rutshuru than he was at the British expedition.
'H. Krauss's wrath was very freely expressed. The Germans and Belgians in this
district are constantly quarrelling, the Germans claiming the whole north shore
of the lake.'

a novelty which Krauss had not foreseen. He had received no instructions from his government; therefore he could not permit the British to establish a post on Lake Kivu. Krauss promised, however, to prevent Belgian occupation.

What was the 'Mfumbiro' that the British had finally occupied? As Captain Ireland described it, it fell into three distinct sections. The first was from Ihunga to Kigezi (89 miles, the eastern part of the Mfumbiro district), which was 'by far the worst', without life. The second, from Kigezi to Kibumba (55 miles) was the Mfumbiro valley, 'exceedingly rich in crops and cattle, and . . . most desirable territory'. The third, Kibumba to the north end of Kivu, was 'absolutely waterless . . . uninhabited lava country'.[2] One of the main objects of the expedition was to establish a post on Lake Kivu, where the British would be able to profit from the flourishing trade; to their disappointment they learned that the 'Belgian and German accounts of Lake Kivu do not give a very favourable impression of its importance as a trading centre'.[3]

The occupation of Mfumbiro proved easy; the Africans were split into 'innumerable tribes and clans' which were 'unwarlike', united only by hatred toward the Belgians. The Belgians themselves learned of the expedition when Coote wrote to the commandant at Rutshuru on 28 June to inform him of the British occupation. 'I should love to have been present when he got the letter. The effect was instantaneous.'[4]

About 12 noon on the 28th of June the picquets gave warning of the approach of a large party and presently two Europeans and 107 askaris filed onto a hill 1,100 yards from Rubona. Their obvious intention was to impress us with their numbers. They advanced some 100 yards and formed up. I [Ireland] had meanwhile caused the Sikhs to file round the top of a knoll at Rubona in full sight of the Belgians. As the Sikhs were lost to the Belgians' sight they doubled round joining their own rear, thus presenting to the Belgians' view a continuous stream of Sikhs. The ruse apparently succeeded. The Belgians withdrew into a nullah out of sight and reconnoitred for half-an-hour. Eventually the two Europeans, Captain Wangermée and Lt. Brochard, and one askari (with a

[2] Ireland to Jenkins, 9 July 1909, incl. 6 in no. 108, C.O. to F.O., secret, 3 September 1909, F.O. 403/411.
[3] Close's memorandum of 25 May 1910.
[4] Coote, 'The Kivu Mission', p. 106.

white handkerchief tied to his bayonet), approached. Wangermée's first remark was 'You have rearmed your Indians'. Our mobility certainly confused the Belgian officers, who seldom march more than 10 to 12 miles apparently. We had marched some 67 miles in three days and they imagined several points besides Rubona and Kibumba were occupied, though these points had only been visited. The political officer did not undeceive them, and Captain Wangermée was much disgusted at this ignorance of the presence of the mission, nor did he know part of the mission had camped on Lake Kivu, which he described fairly accurately for our benefit.[5]

The Belgians described the Kivu expedition as a 'Jameson raid' on Congo territory, and threatened violence if the British did not retire. 'He [Wangermée] demanded our withdrawal, etc., etc. I [Coote] asked him up to lunch to discuss it over a bottle. He astonished me by accepting.'[6] Coote and Wangermée managed to reach an amicable agreement, subject to instructions from their governments, by which neither side was to establish more posts. Since the British had already established their line of strategic posts, this was, from the British point of view, a good arrangement which conceded nothing. But on the same day that Coote concluded this agreement, he received two telegrams from London, by way of Entebbe. The first, dated 9 June, ordered Coote to defer action; the troops should remain in Mbarara. The second, dated 16 June, urgently commanded Coote to evacuate Mfumbiro.

'It was heartbreaking from a soldier's point of view to, three distinct times, let off the Belgians. Throughout they gave us every tactical opportunity.'[7] Through a peculiar set of circumstances the British Colonial Office had botched the success of the Kivu expedition.

The Governor of Uganda, Sir H. Hesketh Bell, had arrived in London; alarmed at the dangers of an Anglo-Belgian clash, he advised the Colonial Office to telegraph instructions to Uganda that the Mfumbiro expedition should be deferred (the telegram of 9 June). When it was learned that the force had already departed on the 11th from Mbarara, urgent orders

[5] Ireland to Jenkins, 9 July 1909.
[6] Coote, 'The Kivu Mission', p. 107.
[7] Ireland, 'Diary of the Kivu Mission between 11 June and 14 July 1909', confid., 15 July, incl. 11 in no. 108, C.O. to F.O., secret, 3 September 1909, F.O. 403/411.

for withdrawal were wired (the telegram of 16 June). Coote did not receive these orders until 28 June, the date of the agreement with the Belgians at Rubona.[8]

'The order for withdrawal has come at a very unfortunate moment. . . . Owing to the urgency of your orders to retire my hands are tied, and my withdrawal at the present juncture naturally bears the appearance of running away. . . . I regret exceedingly the necessity for withdrawal, as I have already got in touch with the natives of the district, who will naturally not understand our retiring and will be slow to trust us in the future.'[9]

Under these circumstances Coote did the best he could: he told Wangermée that since the Belgians promised to remain at Rutshuru, the British, pending instructions from their government, would withdraw. The territory was to be considered as disputed, and no Belgian was to enter until the issue was settled by the two governments. Wangermée agreed. Coote hoped that this would 'prevent the Belgians from at once occupying the fort [Rubona] I had established, and so leave the road open for some future occupation of the district'.[1] After the British evacuation, however, Wangermée immediately broke his promise, and descended on Rubona 'with bugles blowing', capturing '2 Nubi askaris, one Muganda headman, and 4 porters', who had stayed at Rubona after the evacuation to purchase food.[2]

All the Africans who had helped the British expedition with food supplies and information were punished by the Belgians, either by appropriation of cattle or imprisonment. Coote was

[8] When Tomkins received on 10 June the 'defer action' telegram of 9 June, he immediately despatched special runners by two different roads 'to stop the forward movement of the troops'. Coote's letter from Ihunga of 14 June showed that the runners had not been able to catch the expedition, and that Coote was still advancing full speed toward Lake Kivu. 'Owing to the difficulties of the country between Ankole and Lake Kivu, which in parts is uninhabited and foodless, and in one district the natives being hostile, communication with the expedition is not by any means easy, as a large escort is required to carry letters to and fro. As Your Lordship is already aware, a great proportion of the 4th King's African Rifles is at present in Somaliland, and consequently the troops at my disposal are limited to such an extent that delay is caused on account of the scarcity of men for this duty.' Tomkins to Crewe, secret, 5 July 1909, incl. 1 in no. 94, C.O. to F.O., 14 August 1909, F.O. 403/411.
[9] Coote to Boyle, 28 June 1909, incl. 3 in no. 101, C.O. to F.O., 25 August 1909, F.O. 403/411.
[1] Ibid.
[2] See note F, p. 274.

'left in the unpleasant position of being unable to fulfill the promises made to these people when I assured them that they were British subjects and under the protection of my government'.[3]

The policy of the British government was much less skilful than the manoeuvres of the Kivu expedition. On 5 June Crewe had wired Tomkins: 'move troops into Mfumbiro district.' H. Hesketh Bell submitted a lengthy and forcefully written analysis of the situation on 7 June:[4] he recommended deferment of action until the Belgian government had been notified. Bell considered the size of the Kivu expedition insufficient. H. J. Read in the Colonial Office recorded on 9 June: 'Sir H. Bell has doubts as to the wisdom of the proposed action . . . we discussed the matter fully at the Foreign Office yesterday, with Mr. Tilley and Col. Close, and the Foreign Office are now going to warn the Belgian government that we propose to move into the Mfumbiro district at the end of a certain period. This will give the Belgians time to warn their local officials and if there is any collision, they will be responsible. Meanwhile we should send the enclosed telegram which has been settled in consultation with Sir H. Bell.'[5]

When it was learned that the telegram to defer action had probably not reached the expedition, Crewe wired on 3 July: 'If troops are still in Mfumbiro district, they should remain there, otherwise, in accordance with my telegram of 9 June, troops should remain at Mbarara.'[6] Langley noted: 'The present position is that the Colonial Office having failed to stop the troops before they crossed into the Mfumbiro district finally sent instruction there.'[7] Tilley concluded: 'I cannot say that I think our position very brilliant.'[8]

---

[3] Coote to Boyle, 28 June 1909, incl. 4 in no. 101, C.O. to F.O., 25 August 1909, F.O. 403/411.

[4] In C.O. 536/29.

[5] Read's minute on Bell's memorandum, 9 June 1909, C.O. 536/29; cf. the F.O. minutes: 'The Governor of Uganda says, in effect, that the force in Uganda is so small at present that it would be dangerous. . . . Of course there might be no collision, but in view of our weakness he thinks the risk of trying it too great.' (Tilley, 10 June). 'Sir Hesketh Bell appears to be quite right. It would be foolish to occupy and then to be obliged to withdraw before a superior Belgian force.' (Langley, 10 June). 'It would be very undesirable to run the risk of an armed conflict with a superior Belgian force.' (Charles Hardinge, no date), F.O. 367/127.

[6] Crewe to Tomkins, incl. in no. 54, C.O. to F.O., 9 July 1909.

[7] Langley's minute on 27697, F.O. 367/128.

[8] Tilley's minute on 39097, F.O. 367/129.

Coote had written on 28 June that he could reoccupy the evacuated country without provoking an attack by the Belgians. Crewe wired on 13 July: 'Posts should be reoccupied as soon as possible.'[9] By this time, however, the Kivu force was back in Mbarara. The group set out again on 22 July; Coote hoped to reach the posts now occupied by the Belgians by 1 August. The Belgians, however, had strengthened their force. When Coote arrived in Kigezi, the middle of eastern Mfumbiro, he learned that five Belgians and 200 men were camped at Muhavura, about six miles off. The bellicose Commandant Fredrick Olsen instructed Coote to leave the territory;[1] Tomkins reported on 9 August that if Coote advanced on Rubona there would be a fight.[2] The Belgians had effectively blocked the way to Kivu. Coote established headquarters in Kigezi. There were no more significant troops movements, but 'two armed forces of native troops within four miles of each other, with no limiting line of territory, but both claiming the rights of administration over the natives in their vicinity, is a situation fraught with possibilities of trouble'.[3]

The confusion over the instructions to the Kivu expedition was typical of the disjointed Anglo-German efforts to implement the agreement of May 1909. Baron Griendl, the Belgian Minister in Germany, gathered that the agreement had been steamrolled through the German Foreign Office by the German Colonial Office. In Britain there was little coordination between the War Office, Foreign Office, and Colonial Office. Departmental confusion in the two governments was complemented by inter-governmental chaos. The basic problem was the loosely worded secret supplementary agreement, which stated simply that Britain and Germany would keep each other informed

---

[9] Crewe to Acting Governor Boyle, tel., 13 July 1909, incl. no. 2 in no. 66, C.O. to F.O., 13 July 1909, F.O. 403/411.

[1] The Belgian government ordered Olsen to avoid a conflict on 9 July; he acknowledged the receipt of his instructions in a telegram which reached Brussels on 28 July. On the 15th July the commandant was instructed by the Belgian Colonial Ministry not to form new posts unless the British did, and to abide by the provisional arrangements concluded by the British and Belgian officers. This latest threat, the Belgian Colonial Ministry reported, was probably caused by the British reoccupation of the district. Crewe to Tomkins, 10 August 1909, incl. in no. 95, C.O. to F.O., 16 August 1909, F.O. 403/411.

[2] Tomkins to Crewe, tel., 9 August 1909, incl. 1 in no. 127, C.O. to F.O., 6 October 1909, F.O. 403/411.

[3] Boyle to Crewe, secret, 30 August 1909, incl. 1 in no. 127, C.O. to F.O., 6 October 1909, F.O. 403/411.

about their negotiations with Belgium, and that they would not come to an agreement with the Belgians until both could do so at the same time. It was understood that the British could occupy the territory agreed upon as 'Mfumbiro', but it was not clear when the occupation would occur, nor how the Belgians, who were already administering the western part of the region, would be informed.

Grey received a Belgian protest against an 'act of aggression' on 7 July.[4] The Belgians protested energetically and indignant-ly;[5] they had not even been notified of the British intention to occupy the region.[6] Davignon, the Belgian Foreign Minister, informed Arthur Hardinge, the British Minister in Belgium, on 6 July, that Belgian territory had been violated and that the Belgian troops were advancing on the British expedition; force would be used if the British would not respect the frontier.[7] Davignon assumed there had been a mistake, and talked about the 'exciting effects of the African sun'. The British were prob-ably used to such 'frontier incidents'; to a country like Belgium without the same experience, 'the violation of Belgian territory, which the King had to swear on ascending the throne to defend

[4] See Grey's minute of 7 July 1909 (25578), F.O. 367/128; also Hardinge to Grey, no. 46 (no. 87 Africa), 6 July 1909, F.O. 403/411; and 'Memorandum of Conversation between Granville and Davignon', incl. 1 in no. 46, and the aide-mémoire communicated by the Belgian government, incl. 2 in no. 46.

[5] The Belgian protests, which fully express the position taken by the Belgians at the 1910 conference, may be found in F.O. 403/411. See no. 74, Grey to Hard-inge, 21 July (no. 83 Africa): incl. 1, Davignon to de Lalaing, 19 July 1909; incl. 2, Note communicated by de Lalaing to Grey. This last document reviews the history of the region as well as the legal foundations of the British claim to Mfumbiro, and attempts to prove that the Mfumbiro region was unquestionably Belgian in accordance with the 30th meridian division of the 1894 agreement. It is an impressive statement.

[6] There were two problems involved in the notification of the Belgian govern-ment of the Anglo-German agreement. First, the agreement had to be accepted by both governments. This had been done by the end of May (see Goschen to Grey, no. 34 Africa, 31 May 1909, F.O. 367/127). Second, there remained the problem of when and how the notification should occur. The Germans suggested 15 September to allow time to notify their east African authorities. This placed the British government in an embarrassing position: 'in view of the protest of the Belgian government . . . His Majesty's Government must account for the presence of British troops in the Mfumbiro territory, and will be obliged, therefore, to mention that they have entered into an agreement with Germany on the subject, without the delay.' (Grey to De Salis, no. 52—no. 14 Africa tel.—9 July 1909, F.O. 403/411.) A copy of the first agreement was finally presented to Davignon on 13 July (see Hardinge to Grey, no. 83—no. 91 Africa—26 July 1909, F.O. 403/411). This was long after the Belgians had learned of the Kivu expedition. The supplementary agreement remained secret.

[7] Hardinge to Grey, no. 46 (no. 78 Africa), 6 July 1909, F.O. 403/411.

in its integrity', was indeed serious.[8] The Belgians might have been able to understand such action, Davignon explained, if the Belgian government had refused to negotiate a peaceful settlement.[9]

Hardinge pointed out that Davignon's memorandum of 11 June on the subject amounted to a flat refusal to negotiate and that they must bear the responsibility for any violence.[1]

The incident occurred at a fortunate time for Britain, an inopportune moment for Belgium: after the disappearance of the old Congo State and before the British recognition of Belgium as its successor. This enabled Britain to escape the 'inconvenient provision'[2] in the Anglo-Congolese agreement of 9 May 1906,[3] by which all frontier controversies between Britain and the Congo State would be submitted to arbitration. From the Belgian point of view it was inconvenient for still another reason. As Davignon explained to Hardinge, the 'Belgian public would associate it with Mr. Morel's renewed loud, and impatient demands for vigorous British action in the Congo'.[4]

The Belgians regarded their legal position as unassailable; the boundary was clearly defined and the district under Belgian administration. The British action was, in effect, a forcible and deliberate usurpation of a Belgian territory.[5] Grey and Hardinge answered these arguments at length. Regardless when the British had occupied Mfumbiro, the Belgians were not free to do what they pleased up to the line they claimed; Mfumbiro had been acknowledged both by the Congo State[6] and Germany as a British possession.[7]

While the two governments hurled legal arguments at each other, progress was being made toward a settlement. There can be no doubt that the agreement of May 1909 and the British

---

[8] Hardinge to Grey, no. 50 (no. 83 Africa confid.), 8 July 1909, F.O. 403/411.

[9] 'Memorandum of Conversation between Granville and Davignon', 6 July 1909.

[1] Hardinge to Grey, no. 48 (no. 4 Africa tel.), 7 July 1909, F.O. 403/411; also Hardinge to Grey, 8 July.

[2] Hardinge to Grey, no. 83 (no. 91 Africa), 26 July 1909, F.O. 403/411.

[3] See Hertslet, III, p. 586.

[4] Hardinge to Grey, no. 60 (no. 86 Africa), 10 July 1909, F.O. 403/411.

[5] Grey to Hardinge, no. 74 (no. 38 Africa), 21 July 1909, F.O. 403/411.

[6] By recognizing in the 1894 agreement the British sphere as established by the Anglo-German agreement of 1890.

[7] Grey to Hardinge, no. 74, 21 July 1909, with inclosures; also Grey to De Salis, no. 122 (no. 110 Africa confid.), 27 September 1909, F.O. 403/411.

occupation of Mfumbiro accelerated the diplomacy necessary for a European agreement about Ruanda-Urundi. For if the Belgians were to solve their Mfumbiro problem with Britain, they also had to come to an agreement with Germany about the disputed Kivu region.

German-Congolese relations in Ruanda-Urundi had continued to deteriorate. In November 1908 the Belgian Commandant Derche, with two other Belgians and sixty askaris, had attempted to establish a military station on Lake Bulera, to the southeast of the volcanic mountains. The Germans had illegally occupied the volcanic region, Derche explained; the region obviously belonged to the Congo.[8] The Governor of German East Africa as well as the local German officials howled in protest. The result was the Derche-Kandt agreement[9] of 19 February 1909, by which neither side was to occupy Lake Bulera; the summit ridge was to be regarded as the provisional frontier. A distinction was made between this 'contested territory' and the 'territory affected by the Bethe-Hecq agreement', but, in effect the Derche-Kandt agreement of 1909 was a corollary to the Bethe-Hecq agreement of 1899. The Belgian government, however, refused to recognize the 1909 arrangement.

The Anglo-German agreement of 1909 was evidence of the impatience of the German Colonial Office with this endless controversy with the Belgians. Dernburg, who was responsible more than anyone else for the German side of the treaty, had not foreseen, however, all the consequences of the secret agreement. The Germans were astounded to learn of the British Kivu expedition. Lindequist observed that it was 'remarkable and obvious' that the British were dead set on using the May 1909 agreement to bring an end to the quarrel with the Belgians. Germany should use the British initiative to settle the

---

[8] Dernburg observed that even by the Declaration of Neutrality most of Lake Bulera was still in German territory. The Belgian maps, however, showed the lake to lie in undisputed Congo territory. The difficulty was that there still existed no agreement about the median of Lake Kivu; if a diagonal line were drawn from the Belgian median, almost all of the lake would be beyond the 'contested territory'. The German line still left the tip of the north of the lake as undisputed Belgian territory; but the Germans claimed sovereignty up to the volcanic ridge. See Renkin to M.A.E., 21 January 1909, M.A.E. 1/38/5. Also Dernburg to A.A. 19 December 1908, A.A. 3/2. The most important documents, including the exchanges between the local officials, are in M.A.E. 1/38/5.
[9] A copy may be found in M.A.E. 1/38/5.

dispute without delay. Even after the May 1909 agreement, there still lurked the fear in the German Colonial Office that Britain might come to a separate peace with Belgium at Germany's expense.[1]

The German Foreign Office was unenthusiastic about the Anglo-German agreement. It was largely the product of the German Colonial Office, with which the Foreign Office had merely cooperated and to which it had given its consent. Wallwitz, the Minister in Belgium was especially regretful about the agreement. After the Belgians had complained to him of the German role in the Kivu expedition, he wrote to the German Foreign Office, that all the good will between Germany and Belgium which had been built up over a period of years had been destroyed overnight. The repercussions would be felt in German-Belgian relations.[2]

The Kivu mission had also had local effects. Dernburg learned in September 1909 that the Governor of German East Africa was alarmed at the excitement in Ruanda-Urundi over the British expedition and the possible consequences of an Anglo-Belgian armed clash.[3] Lindequist, who usually tended to magnify things out of proportion, had already foreseen the possibility of a rebellion in Ruanda, but for a different reason. Ruanda was 'dismembered' between Germany and Belgium: if a settlement were not reached soon there would be a revolu-

---

[1] Lindequist to A.A., 27 July 1909, A.A. 3/3.

[2] Van der Elst hinted to Hardinge that he thought the German attitude more conciliatory than the British; Germany was at least willing to negotiate and to discuss the Belgian claim, while Britain apparently thought only of overt 'acts of aggression'. Hardinge observed: 'I dare say the Germans have tried to put the blame of the brutal *fait accompli* on us, but I do not believe that they will consent to relax their grip on a single square foot of the Kivu-Ruzizi district.' Hardinge to Grey, no. 126 (no. 110 Africa confid.), 1 October 1909, F.O. 403/411.

See also Flotow to A.A., 28 May 1910, A.A. 3/6: '. . . technical officials . . . who naturally did not take political aspects into consideration, conducted the negotiations [of May 1909]. No one here [Brussels] found the German claims unjustified, and Belgium would have been ready at any time, if these questions had been broached, to consider them in a spirit of friendship. The whole tendency of the Belgian government, the King included, is to work as closely as possible with Germany. This is why the surprise of our May agreement with England was so painful and distressing.'

[3] Dernburg to A.A., 8 September 1909, A.A. 3/3. The report from Dar es Salaam disclosed that the Belgian troops in the volcanic region included 20 whites and 900–1,100 Africans; the British force was reputed to consist similarly of over 20 whites but only 200–300 Africans. These numbers were grossly overestimated; to protect the 'indigenous population' from this invasion from the north, a company of 70 men had been despatched from the Usumbura garrison to the northwest of the colony. Dernburg to A.A., 27 August 1909, A.A. 3/3.

tion, which would be worse than the one in southwest Africa, would spread to all of German East Africa, and could only be smothered at tremendous human and economic expense.[4] If Belgian claims in Ruanda-Urundi were realized it would mean only a small, insignificant addition to the already gigantic Congo; but for the German colony it would have the direst consequences.[5]

Lindequist's alarmism was extreme, but nevertheless typical of the rising wave of indignation directed against the Belgians in the German Colonial Office. In this atmosphere of frustration, the Germans had no trouble convincing themselves that Leopold was guilty of fraud.

The exasperating aspect of the Kivu controversy from the German point of view was that if the German government had stuck to the original boundary of November 1884 there would have been no dispute. They had not. The Germans had accepted without objection the boundary described by the Declaration of Neutrality of 1885, which divided Ruanda-Urundi. All the legal facets of the early treaties were exhaustively discussed by the German Colonial Office; they themselves admitted that their case was weak. By accepting the Declaration of Neutrality they had at least implicitly renounced their claims to the boundaries indicated on the maps attached to the Congolese-German treaty of 1884 and the Congolese-French treaty of 1885. Yet they had not done so explicitly; and the Declaration of Neutrality was based on 'previously concluded treaties'. Was it possible to show that there were discrepancies in the earlier maps, that the Germans had agreed to a copy of the map attached to the Congolese-French treaty of 1885 which did not correspond to the original? If so the German case would be much stronger; for if it could be proved that the maps of the 'previously concluded treaties' contained contradictions, or even fraud, then presumably the boundary issue would have to be settled on the basis of the first treaty of November 1884.

The German Foreign Office in 1885 had retained only a copy of the map attached to the Congolese-French treaty. Dernburg's efforts to locate an original in Brussels and London

---

[4] Lindequist to A.A., 15 August 1909, A.A. 3/3.
[5] Dernburg to A.A., geheim, 11 January 1910, A.A. 3/4; also Lindequist's memorandum of 21 October 1909, A.A. 3/3.

proved fruitless. Finally in January 1910 the German Embassy in Paris discovered in their archives an 1885 map by E. Desbuissons, who was the archivist and cartographer of the French Foreign Ministry in 1885. Dernburg judged that the map had 'an undoubtedly official character'. The boundary running from the north end of Lake Tanganyika coincided exactly with the one on the map of the Congolese-German treaty of 1884 (the curve to the west). The map was an original; it would be highly surprising, Dernburg thought, if it was not the real map of the Congolese-French agreement.[6]

The point of the German discovery of the Desbuissons map was that it raised suspicions that the map commonly accepted as the one attached to the Congolese-French treaty might be bogus. If the Desbuissons map and the map of the Congolese-French treaty were identical, there were only two possibilities: either Desbuissons had made a mistake, or the originals in Brussels and Paris did not correspond, which meant either an accident or falsification. Dernburg ruled out the possibility that Desbuissons had erred; he had the reputation of being an exacting academician. The possibility could not be excluded, Dernburg concluded, that in 1885 the Congolese authorities submitted a fraudulent map to the German government.[7]

It was possible, of course. But the Desbuissons map did not prove there had been forgery; it only aroused suspicions. Dernburg requested the German Foreign Office to try to persuade the French government to let the German officials in Paris see the original map. Secrecy would be necessary so as not to put the Belgians on guard.[8]

The discovery of the Desbuissons map occurred on the eve of the Kivu-Mfumbiro Conference of 1910. The Germans were already long exasperated with the unyielding Belgian policy toward Ruanda-Urundi. The agitation of the Colonial Office over Kivu was reaching a climax. The Desbuissons map contributed its share.

As in the crisis of 1894, the more the Germans considered the problem, the more indignant they became; as in 1894 this led to a German demand for complete satisfaction. The Anglo-German agreement of May 1909 accomplished its purpose. The Belgian government could not withstand the combined

[6] Ibid.   [7] Ibid.   [8] Ibid.

assault of Britain and Germany; the Belgians agreed to negotiate.[9] 'An Anglo-German combination about their affairs is to them as alarming a monster as an Anglo-Russian one to the Persians.'[1] When the German delegation arrived in Brussels, however, they were not prepared to negotiate, but to demand Belgian capitulation.

[9] 'The Belgians are very indignant, but they miss the point of our agreement with Germany. By that agreement we have made good our title to Mfumbiro as against Germany and any claim that Germany had to the territory has reverted to us. It is for the Belgians to show that they have a better claim than Germany can show.' Langley's minute on 27697, F.O. 367/128.
[1] See note G, p. 274.

VIII. THE GERMAN, BELGIAN, BRITISH KIVU-MFUMBIRO CONFERENCE OF 1910

... I could not conceal from myself the more I listened to the arguments that both our cases against Belgium were bad, but that the German case was a good deal worse than ours. (Sir Arthur Hardinge, British Minister in Belgium, 1910)[1]

LESS than two months before the representatives of the three powers were to gather in Brussels to discuss Ruanda-Urundi, Leopold II on his deathbed admonished his ministers that the Germans and British should never be allowed to grab the Kivu-Mfumbiro region, even if force was necessary to prevent them.[2] His death on 17 December 1909 foreshadowed the events of the conference, and enabled the Belgian government to conclude a settlement that Leopold himself would no doubt have considered humiliating.

The Kivu-Mfumbiro Conference[3] convened at the Belgian Foreign Ministry in February 1910. The negotiations fell into three chronological and topical divisions. The first, 7 to 26 February, may be described as a period of presentation, which was occupied with discussion about the claims of the three powers. The second, 11 to 17 March, was a period of deadlock, which was concerned with practical discussion about how the disputed territory could be divided. The third, 18 April to 14 May, was a period of compromise, in which the final settlement was reached.

The first weeks of the conference were filled with long speeches from the senior delegates: Ebermaier, van den Heuvel, and Hardinge.[4] The Kivu-Ruzizi problem was discussed first.

[1] Hardinge to Grey, no. 17 Africa confid., 11 February 1909, F.O. 367/174. Cf. Van Zuylen, *L'Echiquier Congolais*, pp. 405–10.
[2] Comte Louis de Lichtervelde, *Leopold of the Belgians* (English translation; New York, 1929), p. 217; Col. Sir Charles Close, 'A 50 Years Retrospect', *Empire Survey Review*, II, July 1933, p. 136.
[3] The official title was 'Conference respecting Frontiers between Uganda, German East Africa and the Belgian Congo'.
[4] The German delegates were: Ebermaier, head of the Africa Department of the C.O., subsequently Governor of the Cameroons; Danckelmann; and Baron von Lersner; Belgian: van den Heuvel, formerly Minister of Justice; van Malde-

It soon became clear that the German and Belgian delegates differed on a fundamental point: what was the real, legal frontier? Ebermaier had begun the conference with an 'historico-political exposé', which gave, as van den Heuvel admitted afterward, an impartial and fair account of the history of the controversy from 1884. The gist of Ebermaier's argument was that the Declaration of Neutrality of 1885 interpreted, but did not alter, the provisions of the earlier treaties.[5]

Van den Heuvel disagreed. The Belgians, he said, were willing to substitute a new frontier for the old, but there could be no doubt that the true legal boundary was established by the Declaration of Neutrality, which rectified the old maps by common agreement.[6]

The German and Belgian delegates developed their arguments from these two points of view. Ebermaier contended that Bismarck must have regarded the Declaration of Neutrality as an interpretation, rather than an alteration of the earlier treaties; otherwise he would have surrendered German rights. Such a surrender would have to be explicitly expressed, not merely presumed. Furthermore, van den Heuvel was defending an astronomical boundary line; this might work on paper but not in practice. It started from the 'northern extremity of Lake Tanganyika'; but there were two northern extremities, which varied depending on rainfall. Which was meant? The reason why Germany had waited until 1895 to object to this 'mathematical' boundary, Ebermaier explained, was because before then the contested territory had not been occupied by either power. Besides, the Germans could not consider the Declaration of Neutrality as a binding agreement because it was based on 'insufficient and defective materials'.[7]

ghem, President of the Court of Cassation; and van der Elst, Director-General of the Ministry of Foreign Affairs; the British: Hardinge, C. F. Close, subsequently President of the International Geographical Union; and J. A. C. Tilley, subsequently British Minister in Brazil. Captain Behrens attended for the first half of the conference. The secretaries of the conference were de Bassompierre, subsequently Belgian Minister in Poland, and Pierre Orts.

⁵ Ebermaier to Dernburg, 19 and 21 February 1910, A.A. 3/4; 'Commission Internationale pour l'examen de certaines litiges de frontières en Afrique Orientale', 8 and 9 February 1910, M.A.E. 1/38/4.

⁶ Ibid.

⁷ Hardinge commented on the discussions: 'The clearly proved inconsistency and constantly shifting character of the German claims was very damaging, nor was Herr Ebermaier's explanation amongst other defences of them that these claims had increased in extent *pari passu* with the increase in geographical know-

Van den Heuvel replied to the German arguments in a manner which struck Hardinge as 'remarkable for moderation, its good humoured and conciliatory spirit'. There could be no question of the surrendering of German rights in 1885, van den Heuvel pointed out, because in 1885 Germany was not a neighbour of the Congo State. One of the purposes of the Declaration of Neutrality was 'to substitute for rough and inconsistent boundaries a clear definition of frontiers', which all the powers would be invited to recognize. The astronomical line superseded the earlier boundaries. The point was whether the German government had clearly accepted the Declaration of Neutrality. This was what van den Heuvel attempted to prove. He reviewed the exchange of notes in 1884–5; Hatzfeldt's acceptance[8] was 'explicit and precise'. When the Germans in 1895 pointed out a 'trifling inaccuracy' on a map which reproduced the boundary of the Declaration of Neutrality the frontier was corrected to correspond to the astronomical line; this showed that in 1895 the German government still regarded the mathematical boundary as binding. This was true also in Africa. In July 1896 Captain Ramsay had crossed the astronomical line to give a German flag to the African chief Kakali. In reply to the complaint by the Congo government, Alvensleben declared Ramsay had made a mistake and had withdrawn the flag. It was not until the turn of the century that Germany claimed the frontier of November 1884. Although the Belgians were now prepared to substitute a natural frontier for the astronomical, the Germans would have to concede that the latter must be the basis for all discussion.[9]

By 17 February Hardinge thought that the abstract, legal aspects of the problem had been sufficiently thrashed out. The next step, he proposed, should be for the German and Belgian delegates to mark out their claims on the blank maps prepared by the Belgians. Ebermaier agreed, but first wished to ascertain

ledge and discovery to my mind at all a convincing one. Our own claims although they rested on the intentions of three separate treaties, those of 1884, 1890 and 1894, with respect to certain visible definite and tangible geographical features, at least complemented, but did not contradict one another.' Hardinge to Grey, no. 31 Africa confid., 27 February 1910, F.O. 367/174.

[8] 25 August 1885.

[9] Hardinge to Grey, no. 17 Africa confid., 11 February 1909, F.O. 367/174; Ebermaier to Dernburg, 19 February; 'Commission Internationale', 11 February 1910, M.A.E. 1/38/4.

whether the boundaries on the original map attached to the Congolese-French treaty in Paris agreed with the original in Brussels. Ebermaier was convinced, of course, that the original in Paris would be identical with the Desbuissons map. He and Danckelmann suggested that the map in Paris should be examined. The Belgians, to the surprise of the Germans, readily assented. Von Lersner and Bassompierre, representing Germany and Belgium respectively, were to go to Paris, request the French Foreign Ministry to let them see the map, and report to the conference.[1]

A map was found in the Paris Foreign Ministry archives. Although the Germans doubted that it was the original, the differences between it and the map attached to the Congolese-French treaty in the possession of the Belgians did not affect Ruanda-Urundi. The German case based on the Desbuissons map therefore collapsed—at least as far as the Belgians and British were concerned.[2]

Hardinge had been careful 'to stake nothing on this German conjecture or speculation and had displayed little interest in this particular aspect of the German case, which [the British delegates] . . . always regarded as rather doubtful. . . .'[3] Even had the map been proved identical with the Congolese-German map of 1884, it was still questionable whether this would annul the Declaration of Neutrality. Hardinge regretted, however, that the Germans were not able to prove their supposition.

---

[1] Ebermaier to Dernburg, 19 and 21 February; also Hardinge to Grey, no. 24 Africa confid., 17 February 1910, F.O. 367/174. 'The Germans asked, Baron Danckelmann rather irritably and hotly, as though there had been double-dealing on the part of the late King, how it was that the maps communicated by him to the French and German governments were not identical. . . . M. van den Heuvel then returned to his old theory that it was precisely because the map communicated to France differed slightly as a statement of his claim from that communicated in the previous year to Germany that the King had in the text of his subsequent Declaration of Neutrality given a new description of his claims to Prince Bismarck, which the latter had accepted, and which must therefore be held to supersede the frontier of the earlier map annexed to the German treaty, and which he had shown in his earlier statement dealing with Count Alvensleben's negotiations had been so unquestionably regarded until about 1908.' Cf. 'Commission Internationale', 15, 17, and 22 February 1910, M.A.E. 1/38/4.

[2] The German hunch about the Desbuissons map was never proved. There were two variations in the Belgians maps, neither of which greatly affected Ruanda-Urundi. Copies of the photographs taken at the conference of 1910 which appeared in the *Deutsches Kolonialblatt* in 1916 ('Der Kiwusee-Grenzstreit') may be found, with additional comments, in M.A.E. 1/1/16.

[3] Hardinge to Grey, no. 29 Africa confid., 25 February 1910, F.O. 367/174.

For two reasons. First, there could be no doubt that it would have strengthened the German case, which would have made it easier for the British to support them, as was agreed in May 1909. Second, the Desbuissons map indicated a boundary which would have given Britain the whole of the Mfumbiro district.[4]

The Mfumbiro negotiations proceeded parallel with the Kivu-Ruzizi transactions. Since the British and Germans had reached a provisional agreement about the territory included in the Mfumbiro region[5] in the May 1909 agreement, it was now up to Hardinge to argue the British claims against the Belgian.[6] The basic stands taken by the two sides were simple. Britain based her claim to Mfumbiro on the Anglo-German treaty of 1890; Belgium claimed all territory west of the true 30th meridian, the established boundary between the Congo and Uganda by the Anglo-Congolese agreement of 1894.

Hardinge explained the British delay in occupying Mfumbiro; only after the turn of the century, after the pacification of Uganda and the capture of Mwanga and Kagerega, was it possible for Britain to organize the western province of Uganda. Germany and Britain had not agreed about the territory to be considered as Mfumbiro; when it was discovered that Mfumbiro lay west of the true geographical meridian, Congolese claims became involved also. The Belgians, however, treated the British claims as baseless and refused even to discuss them. When the Congo government repeatedly told the British to go to Berlin to settle disputes south of the first parallel south latitude, explained Hardinge, the British adopted the suggestion; in Berlin the British and Germans agreed that in accordance

---

[4] Ibid.

[5] But never any agreement about 'Mfumbiro' itself. The German note to the Belgian government explaining the 1909 agreement 'purposely abstained from going more closely into the Mfumbiro question' because the May 1909 negotiations had exchanged territory ('Austauchverhandlungen') rather than established a definition ('Auslegungsverhandlungen'). (Note by Baron Schoen, 27 October 1909, incl. in Goschen to Grey, 5 November 1909, no. 70 Africa confid., F.O. 367/129). De Salis noted whether it was called an 'Austausch' or an 'Auslegung' the result was the same. (De Salis's memorandum incl. in Goschen to Grey, 5 November 1909.) Langley noted: 'The German government is pretty stiff in tone. . . . If the Belgians are suffering from the delusion that we are discussing with the Germans the whole question of the Congo this communication will not relieve their minds.' (40911, F.O. 367/129.) Grey: 'The last paragraph of the German memorandum is very friendly to us. The Belgians will not like this at all and will probably endeavour to disturb this harmony by a very conciliatory attitude to Germany.' (40911, F.O. 367/129.)

[6] See Hardinge to Grey, no. 27 Africa confid., 21 February 1910, F.O. 367/174.

with the old maps and intentions versus mere descriptions of astronomical lines, the Germans were justified in claiming Mfumbiro, and therefore in transferring it to Britain in accordance with the treaty of 1890. The British might, however, hinted Hardinge, be willing to modify their claims.[7]

Van der Elst, Director-General of the Belgian Foreign Ministry, replied by emphasizing how the British had changed the character of Mfumbiro: first it was an isolated mountain, then a chain of mountains, then an entire district. The Anglo-German agreement of 1890, the basis of the British position, could not dispose of territory west of the true 30th meridian; therefore it was clear that Mfumbiro belonged to the Congo and the British should have received compensation from Germany somewhere else. Furthermore Britain had negotiated with Germany behind the back of the Belgian government and subsequently had violated Congolese territory which had never been questioned by Britain and which was being effectively administered by Belgium. The only just solution of the problem, said Elst, was for Britain to recognize that she had acted 'mistakenly and hastily' and should restore Mfumbiro to Belgium.[8]

Just as it had been hard for Britain to reach a settlement with Germany about Mfumbiro, so it was similarly difficult for her to agree with Belgium. The discussions in February led to no agreement.

Hardinge described the Mfumbiro-Kivu discussions as rounds in a 'diplomatic tournament'; there was much 'inconclusive skirmishing'; few practical victories. By the end of February the British delegates, especially, were weary of academic lectures about 'true conventional juridic' frontiers; nothing new was being said; at best old positions were being

---

[7] Hardinge summarized the German contribution to the Mfumbiro discussion: 'Herr Ebermaier followed with a very lengthy juristic statement, the only interesting feature of which was the distinction which he sought to establish between the legal rights ("Rechte") and the actual or past claims ("Ansprüche") of Germany on the eastern Congo frontier. His point was that whereas Germany would by herself have been satisfied with a frontier which would have given her the Ruzizi, Lake Kivu, and the line of the volcanoes south of Mfumbiro, she had a right under the treaties of 1884 and 1885 to further territory to the north, and could not refuse, when we called upon her, to claim that territory on our behalf under the treaty of 1890 to do so as against the Congo State, although she might have been, by herself, content to waive or compromise her rights.' Hardinge to Grey, 25 February; cf. 'Commission Internationale', 19 and 22 February 1910, M.A.E. 1/38/4.
[8] Ibid.

stated in new ways.[9] The first period closed on 26 February; the delegates were to confer with their governments about possible practical solutions.[1]

The British delegates thought the German case weak. The agreement of May 1909 was based on the assumption that both British and German claims against the Congo were, roughly, equally valid. Now it appeared that if there were to be a practical settlement it would have to be at the expense of British Mfumbiro claims; if eastern Mfumbiro were not abandoned to the Congo, Belgium would never agree to the Ruzizi-Kivu boundary. Grey was willing to grant the Germans this 'favour' of relinquishing part of the British Mfumbiro demands. Germany could compensate Britain's loss in Mfumbiro by substituting the natural Kagera boundary for the one of 1° south latitude.

The British and German delegates, in accordance with the May 1909 agreement to work together, met after the close of the last meeting of the first period. The British group had a proposal, which Grey had authorized. The German case, they explained, was far from strong—it would never win in arbitration—but obviously the Germans could not be expected to yield any part of Ruanda-Urundi. The Ruzizi-Kivu boundary was mandatory. The difficulty was that the Germans had little to offer Belgium in return; except, perhaps, part of the north shore of Kivu and, in the middle of the lake, the large island, which the Germans were reluctant to give away because of the German missionaries there. The Belgians, however, attached great importance to the north shore of Lake Kivu and the western part of the parallelogram claimed by Britain as Mfumbiro. A Belgian road was under construction from Lake Kivu to Rutshuru. The British proposal was to give Belgium this western part of Mfumbiro, which had never been under British administration anyway; Britain would retain the more valuable half of Mfumbiro and could stipulate for a road across western Mfumbiro to Lake Kivu. The British could make some further concessions in the north to facilitate the arrangement. Germany, on her side, would restore to Belgium a small section

[9] Hardinge to Grey, no. 24 Africa, 17 February 1910, F.O. 367/174; Hardinge to Grey, no. 27 Africa confid., 21 February 1910, F.O. 367/147.
[1] Hardinge to Grey, no. 31 Africa confid., 27 February 1910, F.O. 367/174; 'Commission Internationale', 26 February 1910, M.A.E. 1/38/4.

to the north of Lake Kivu, with the boundary running north-east to Mount Karisimbi; and give Britain the Kagera boundary.

The German delegates thought the proposal would be un-acceptable to the German government. They were especially reluctant to consider the Kagera boundary; the area between 1° south latitude and the Kagera was reputed to be rich in forests. They would, however, discuss the proposed compromise with their government.[2]

The second phase of the conference began in mid-March. On their return from London and Berlin, the British and German delegates met on 11 March. The German group had been right: the British proposal had been rejected at Berlin. Until the dis-crepancies on the various maps were cleared up satisfactorily, explained Ebermaier, the only course for the German govern-ment was to take its stand on the 1884 map. The 'great curve' legally gave Germany territory to the west of Lake Kivu; but Germany in a 'spirit of conciliation' was ready to waive her rights and be content with the line of the Ruzizi and a line drawn across Lake Kivu, giving Germany the large island and the east shore as far north as Limboge, but leaving Belgium the west shore. This was their maximum concession. In short, the Germans refused to give up anything.

The conference reassembled on 14 March. After preliminary skirmishing about who should show his hand first, the Belgians presented a map indicating the concessions they were prepared to make. Toward the Germans they were conciliatory: the Belgians were willing to yield the Ruzizi-Kivu frontier and a line drawn across Lake Kivu giving Belgium the island Idjwi and part of the north shore. Toward the British the Belgians were adamant: they refused to abandon any part of Mfumbiro. They were, however, prepared to make concessions to the British farther north.

Ebermaier then presented the German demands, which included the island Idjwi and the Bugoye district on the north shore. Hardinge explained that the British government would insist on western Mfumbiro and access to Lake Kivu.

The negotiations reached deadlock at this point. The further meetings of the second period were abortive, filled with more 'inconclusive skirmishing'.

[2] Ibid.

Ebermaier attempted to prove an ethnographic connection between the inhabitants of Idjwi and Ruanda; moreover, he argued, Germany could not be expected to abandon the island because of the mission established there by German missionaries—one of whom had tutored the German Emperor! This drew the rejoinder from van den Heuvel that it was an established fact that there was no ethnographical connection between the Africans on Idjwi and in Ruanda, and that the presence of missionaries could not prejudice territorial rights. Ebermaier contended that the Germans had, in fact, conceded a great deal; the Belgians retained an important military road from Bobandana to Rutshuru; the Germans would be left with a mere 'native cow path' from Goma. The Belgians replied that a division based on these grounds was entirely insufficient.[3]

The British Mfumbiro proposal was also unsatisfactory to the Belgians. Belgium would be left the less valuable western region composed chiefly of lava—while Britain would retain the rich eastern valleys. There could be no agreement on these proposals. The second period of negotiations closed with this note of stalemate.[4] Hardinge wondered whether the whole question would have to be submitted to arbitration.[5]

Whether or not the negotiations miscarried depended on the Germans with their absolutely uncompromising position. Ebermaier hinted to Hardinge before his return to Berlin over the Easter adjournment that Germany might accept compensation for yielding Idjwi and might even grant Belgium some territory on the north shore. But if Germany gave Bugoye to Belgium, Ebermaier explained, Britain must give back some of the Mpororo region ceded to her by Germany in 1909. An equivalent to the Bugoye or Goma district was that part of Mpororo ruled by the chief Kateraya. Germany might also consider the Kagera boundary. The British delegation was divided: Close and Behrens—who had both attended the 1909 conference—thought Ebermaier's proposal feasible; Hardinge and Tilley did not.[6]

Grey regarded the point as small, but important. There was

[3] 'Commission Internationale', 16 March 1910, M.A.E. 1/38/4.
[4] Hardinge to Grey, no. 46 Africa, confid., 17 March 1910, F.O. 367/174; 'Commission Internationale', 14 and 16 March 1910, M.A.E. 1/38/4.
[5] See note H, p. 275.
[6] Hardinge to Grey, 17 March.

'little practical disadvantage in cutting off a small corner of
Mpororo', but the 1909 agreement did not mean that if
Germany chose to give up part of the slopes of Mfumbiro that
Britain should restore part of Mpororo. This would enable the
German government to say that all its demands had been satis-
fied without German sacrifices; Grey could see no reason why
Britain should pay the price of a satisfactory settlement because
of a weak German claim against Belgium. In Grey's opinion
the Germans should simply yield the north shore of the lake.[7]
Crewe agreed.[8]

The anti-Belgian team of May 1909 had broken down. Grey
bluntly stated to the Germans that they had failed to prove their
case against Belgium, and that he hoped the German government would authorize their delegates to make concessions
which would bring about a settlement. He hoped that the
Germans would not be 'unreasonable'.[9]

For the Belgians the German obstinacy made things extremely difficult. Davignon told Hardinge at the end of March
(between the second and third periods) that the Belgians would
be able to meet the British Mfumbiro requirements, but that
the Germans must let go of Idjwi: the Belgian Parliament
would never ratify 'an agreement too obviously one-sided and
unfair'. 'Ours is', said Davignon, 'a small country, but this
makes it all the more important for us if we are to justify the
confidence of Parliament to show that we are jealous and
tenacious of our independence, our dignity, and our rights.'[1]

The Germans were out to get all they could, but they did not
intend to wreck the negotiations. The trouble was that Dernburg and Lindequist thought the German case much better
than Ebermaier had been able to prove to the British and
Belgian delegates at the conference. Since the British would not
support the Germans in their effort to punish the Belgians by
taking all the disputed territory, the alternative was to give up
hope of reaching a settlement, or yield on several minor points.
Lindequist instructed the German delegates before their return

---

[7] F.O. to C.O., 29 March 1910, F.O. 367/174.
[8] C.O. to F.O., 8 April 1910, F.O. 367/175.
[9] Grey to Goschen, no. 34 Africa, 11 April 1910, F.O. 367/175.
[1] The final settlement, however, got through the Belgian Parliament with no
difficulty whatever. See Chambre des Représentants, *Annales parlementaires*, 23
December 1910, p. 405, 9 March 1911, p. 878, and 4 May 1911, p. 1212. Cf.
Hardinge to Grey, no. 64 Africa confid., 13 April 1910, F.O. 367/175.

to the third period of negotiations. The German group was authorized to renounce to Belgium some of the disputed region in the north, but they were to do all in their power to win back Kateraya's part of Mpororo[2] from the British. The island of Idjwi had similar priority. But, said Lindequist, the negotiations should not founder because of an island: the German delegates were empowered to divide, if necessary, the island between Germany and Belgium.[3]

The conference resumed its work on 18 April. Hardinge announced that the British government would accept the Belgian Mfumbiro proposal.[4] Van den Heuvel welcomed this as an important contribution toward the general settlement.[5]

The British were trying at the same time to solve their Mfumbiro-Mpororo problem with the Germans. The question was whether the British should compensate Germany by restoring a section of Mpororo to Germany because Germany had not acquired all the disputed region north of Lake Kivu; 185 square kilometres was to be given to Belgium. The Germans said that the 1909 agreement was contingent on Germany's receiving all the disputed territory; the British argued that Germany had yielded the Mpororo area without qualifications. The agreement itself was vague.[6]

The British delegates pointed out to the Germans that, in accordance with Grey's instructions, Britain could not, in principle, admit the German interpretation of the 1909 agreement. The British might, however, agree to boundary modifications that would be to the advantage of both sides: Kateraya's portion of Mpororo (about 400 square kilometres) would be

[2] See below, p. 195, note 4.

[3] 'Anweisung für die deutschen Delegierten für die Verhandlungen in Brüssel', 8 April 1910, A.A. 3/5.
    Hardinge wrote on 18 April: 'Baron Danckelmann stated in the course of conversation that a suggestion which I made to the German delegates at an earlier stage of our negotiations that Idjwi should be divided between Germany and Belgium, just as Saghalien was divided at the Peace of Portsmouth between Russia and Japan, might in the last resort be accepted by his government.' Hardinge to Grey, no. 67 Africa confid., 18 April 1910, F.O. 367/175.

[4] See note I, p. 275.

[5] Hardinge to Grey, 18 April; 'Commission Internationale', 18 April 1910, M.A.E. 1/38/4.

[6] This became an issue because the Governor of German East Africa, von Rechenberg, had 'protested violently' when Ebermaier and Danckelmann ceded the district of Mpororo to the British in 1909. 'They now want to recover what they ought not to have given up.' See the minutes of 21 April 1910 and Tilley's private letters in F.O. 367/174.

restored to Germany for some German compensation on the Kagera. The British would lose about forty square miles in the exchange. Hardinge recommended the barter to Grey; even though the British sacrifice was greater than the German it provided a reasonable way out of deadlock.[7] Grey notified the Germans that they should regard the sacrifices as proof that the British were doing 'all they can to bring about a satisfactory settlement of the whole question'.[8] It was not clear, however, whether the territory which the Germans wished to exchange—Ndorwa[9]—was or was not part of Ruanda; after German assurances that Britain would in any case receive 'an exactly equal area in the Kagera valley if Ndorwa was found to be a part of Ruanda', an agreement was quickly reached.[1]

The crisis of the conference was the German-Belgian stalemate. Ebermaier offered on 22 April to partition Idjwi, but the Belgians flatly rejected the proposal. Ebermaier was beginning to fear a rupture of negotiations. On 22 April he had written to Dernburg that the German cession of Goma and Idjwi was the only way to save the conference.[2] On 22 April, the date of the Idjwi partition offer, Ebermaier stated that this proposal represented the utmost limit of their possible concessions; the Belgians would have two days to consider it—if they did not accept, the Germans would leave for Berlin, thus breaking off negotiations. This was not merely bluff. Ebermaier's instructions authorized him to go no farther than partition—which the Belgians might or might not eventually be bullied into accepting; if no settlement were reached this would jeopardize the Anglo-German agreement.

The German Colonial Office finally concurred. On 27 April Ebermaier announced that he was empowered to surrender to Belgium the landing place at Goma and to draw the frontier half-way between Goma and Kisenyi so that it would run about one and one-half kilometres east of the Belgian road from Goma to Rutshuru. Idjwi was to be Belgian on certain commercial

[7] Hardinge to Grey, no. 69 Africa, 20 April 1910, F.O. 367/175.

[8] Hardinge to Grey, no. 71 Africa confid., 27 April 1910; F.O. to C.O., 2 May 1910, F.O. 367/175.

[9] Ndorwa is a district in eastern Kigezi; see H. B. Thomas and Robert Scott, *Uganda* (London, 1935), p. 459.

[1] See Ebermaier to Dernburg, 23 April 1910; Ebermaier to Dernburg, 30 April 1910, A.A. 3/5.

[2] Ebermaier to Dernburg, 22 April 1910, A.A. 3/5.

conditions and assurance of security for the German mission-aries.[3] The crisis had passed.

The only remaining problem was the British road to Lake Kivu. Crewe had insisted on the retention of the passageway in the agreement because it would 'even at the worst, be useful to obtain such a concession with a view towards bartering it for something else at a future date'.[4] On Grey's recommendation, however, Hardinge was authorized to abandon the right to construct a road; but British subjects were to have unrestricted access to Lake Kivu.[5] The Colonial Office made this concession only on the understanding that no further points would be raised.[6] The Belgians made no objections.[7]

Separate protocols between Germany and Belgium, Germany and Britain, and Britain and Belgium were signed on 14 May 1910. Boundary commissions were appointed; after the frontiers were demarcated, the protocols were signed by the boundary commissioners,[8] formally ending the Kivu-Mfumbiro controversy.

[3] See Hardinge to Grey, no. 75 Africa confid., 27 April 1910, F.O. 367/175. This document also discusses how the islands in the lake were divided between Belgium and Germany. Cf. 'Commission Internationale', 27 and 29 April 1910, M.A.E. 1/38/4.

[4] C.O. to F.O., 9 May 1910, F.O. 367/175.

[5] Hardinge was instrumental in the British abandonment of the Kivu project. 'I entertain considerable doubt, after studying the geography of Kivu . . . as to the value of a port or warehouse . . . nor do I believe that in practice it will prove at all a useful acquisition for the purposes of trade between Uganda and the Tanganyika region, the western shore of Kivu being even more rugged and destitute of landing facilities than the eastern, whilst the navigation of the Ruzizi between Kivu and Tanganyika is interrupted by the existence of rapids. . . . I imagine that the Cape to Cairo railway whenever it reaches the eastern portion of the Congo State is more likely to follow the course of the Upper Congo via Ponthierville to Stanleyville than close enough to Lake Kivu to affect in any sensible degree the commercial development of that region.' Hardinge to Grey, no. 77 Africa confid., 29 April 1910, F.O. 367/175.

[6] C.O. to F.O., 9 May.

[7] 'Commission Internationale', 6 May 1910, M.A.E. 1/38/4.

[8] A copy of the agreement signed at Brussels on 14 May 1910 along with the convention between Belgium and Germany confirming the agreement (signed at Brussels 11 August 1910) may be found in *British and Foreign State Papers*, CIII, pp. 372–5. The 'Exposé des Motifs' of 16 December 1910, M.A.E. 1/38/4, reviews the work of the conference. For references concerning the ratification of the agreement and the demarcation of the boundaries, see the version of this chapter to appear in *Bulletin de l'Academie Royale des Sciences d'Outre-Mer.*

IX. THE STRUGGLE FOR
RUANDA-URUNDI

GEOGRAPHICAL ignorance lay at the bottom of the Kivu-Mfumbiro controversy. Boundaries were drawn through Ruanda-Urundi in 1884–5, and in 1890, with total lack of knowledge of local country. Even the Cape to Cairo route in 1890 and 1894 was projected through a group of volcanic mountains.

In contrast to the Cape to Cairo route, which was an imperial dream on a grand scale, the carving of Ruanda-Urundi was a practical, and, after the turn of the century, an almost day-by-day affair. The documentation is voluminous. The 1910 conference itself lasted over three months. But the problems of Ruanda-Urundi and the Cape to Cairo route must be seen in the perspective of European diplomacy; it is easy to exaggerate their importance. The negotiations, unlike those of Fashoda and Morocco, were conducted at the leisure of the powers involved, without public pressure—or even interest. The Kivu-Mfumbiro controversy scarcely brought the great powers to the brink of war. Ruanda-Urundi was an African problem, which, like most other African problems, was subordinated to graver issues of war and peace in Europe. But its history throws considerable light on the way Africa was partitioned.

The policies which culminated in 1910 were determined differently in each country. In Britain the 1890 African partition was the work of Salisbury himself, who guided the settlement through the Cabinet and Parliament. In 1894 Percy Anderson was responsible for the inclusion of Article III, of which Kimberley and Rosebery approved. The War Office —Colonel Close and Captain Behrens in particular—showed as great an interest in Mfumbiro as the Foreign Office. Later policy was determined by inter-departmental committees composed of representatives from the War Office, Foreign Office, and Colonial Office. The only time the Colonial Office had a noticeable impact on policy, however, was in 1909, when Sir H. Bell's advice was followed. Usually the Colonial Office assented to the ideas of the Foreign Office and War Office. As Walter

Langley in the Foreign Office expressed it: 'The Colonial Office do not help at all, which is scarcely fair treatment, since Mfumbiro is really their concern.'[1]

In Germany the policy-making procedure was simpler, determined almost solely by the Colonial Office. Even in 1894 the colonial experts were instrumental in shaping German African policy; only in 1890 was it determined by the Foreign Secretary and the Chancellor. In the later years Dernburg and Lindequist were almost entirely responsible for German policy toward the Kivu controversy; the Foreign Office acquiesced in whatever they decided.

In Belgium there was an even simpler process. Although the Colonial Ministry prepared the reports and the Foreign Ministry conducted the negotiations, the basic policy was determined solely and consistently by one man: Leopold II. His death was the only reason why a settlement was possible at all. Then the Belgian government quickly came to terms; Close remarked that when the conference convened in February 1910 the ladies at court were still wearing black in mourning for the King.[2]

The arguments presented in 1910 were basically the same as those used when the region was opened up in the 1890s. In the long run the German case proved the most forceful—natural and ethnic frontiers, so far as possible, should not be violated. The dispute was settled in favour of the Germans. It seemed to be the triumph of an enlightened principle over the artificial boundaries of the original partitions. The imperial powers began with arbitrary boundaries, but they finished with natural frontiers and minute on-the-spot delimitation. Yet whether a settlement along ethnic rather than astronomical lines could have been possible without Leopold's death is highly questionable. The division of Ruanda-Urundi was such a flagrant violation of natural frontiers that only Leopold could perpetuate what the Belgians themselves called an absurd dispute.[3] Leopold, however, should not receive all the blame. The German position was undoubtedly the weakest legally; the Belgians at the 1910 conference felt with justification that what Belgium

[1] Memorandum of 16 August 1909, F.O. 367/128.
[2] Close, 'A 50 Years Retrospect', p. 136.
[3] See 'La conférence de la frontière orientale du Congo belge', *Mouvemen Géographique*, XVII, February 1910, pp. 106–7.

received was disproportionate to the validity of her position. The Germans considered Leopold's condition of negotiation—a strip of territory running to Lake Victoria—unreasonable; but in the end took practically everything and left the Belgians nothing. The Germans and British claimed to uphold natural frontiers, but if they appear as champions on the side of Africans, it is at least in part because it was to their advantage to press the Congo State for natural boundaries. They had common complaints against Leopold; this was why they found it easy to work together in 1909. There was agreement between Britain and Germany that Ruanda-Urundi should not be divided; but none of the three powers hesitated to divide the smaller ethnic groups. One is struck by the way in which small pieces of Mfumbiro were bartered for portions of Mpororo, how compensations were determined by 'exactly equal areas'. When the three civilized European powers quibbled over '50 square miles of rock and lava' in the middle of Africa the dispute began to border on the ludicrous.

Who should have what was determined by diplomacy rather than legality. In 1894 the Germans justified their objections to the corridor because of what they considered a violation of their treaty rights; what really concerned them were the commercial and political implications of the Cape to Cairo route, which were removed by diplomacy. At all the later conferences there was much debate—which the British called academic—about the true legal positions. Colonel Close commented after the 1910 conference that these debates 'served no very useful purpose—except, perhaps, that the delay enabled the delegates to become well acquainted with each other . . .'[4] The issues became emotionally charged, and no agreement was ever reached over a point such as whether the line drawn by the Declaration of Neutrality was the true legal frontier. Settlements were made by drawing lines on maps, by giving one piece of territory in return for another. The British and Germans never agreed on what 'Mfumbiro' was; they came to terms in 1909 by simply agreeing that the British could have certain designated land.

Discussions about the validity of old maps and the origins of the disputes comprised the 'inconclusive skirmishing' of the

[4] Close's memorandum of 25 May 1910, F.O. 367/174.

conferences. As Colonel Close expressed it, each side was intent on not being 'scored off' by the other. The real facts of many of the episodes—such as the way the successes of the Kivu expedition were botched—never, of course, came out at the conferences. Indeed, 'all the arrangements of real value' at the 1910 conference were settled outside the formal meetings, with the British usually mediating between the Belgians and Germans. They were practical gatherings; the delegates talked of how to divide the country rather than the historical significance of the disputes. Seldom indeed did they question their right to partition the region in the first place.[5]

The Germans were naturally indignant about the variations on the Belgian maps. Yet by 1910 the point of which was the correct map or boundary made little difference. Even had the Germans proved their case about the Desbuissons map, it is still debatable whether this would have invalidated the Declaration of Neutrality. The main point is that in 1910 the Germans could not have been any more demanding, nor the Belgians any more conciliatory. Dernburg regarded the Anglo-German 1909 agreement as an understanding that the two governments would join to punish Belgium for her monarch's misbehaviour in central Africa[6], and his uncompromising attitude nearly ruptured the negotiations of 1910.

One of the most remarkable aspects of the negotiations was the tendency to read a purpose into the actions of statesmen in the 1884–94 period which must have been at least in part unintentional. The Germans and Belgians formed elaborate explanations of why Leopold drafted the Declaration of Neutrality and why Bismarck accepted it. In fact, Leopold probably altered the previous boundaries merely for simplification and because the boundary of the Declaration of Neutrality lopped off a little more territory for the Congo; Bismarck and the German Foreign Office indifferently accepted it. The Germans read into Article III of the 1894 agreement a deliberate plot to encircle their east African territory; the British themselves later came to regard Article III as a grand attempt which failed. It was, in fact, a colossal blunder. Perhaps the

---

[5] See Leonard Woolf, *Empire and Commerce in Africa* (London, 1920), p. 291.
[6] See 'Instruktionen für die deutschen Delegierten zur Besprechung in Brüssel am 8 February 1910', geheim, A.A. 3/4.

most striking aspect of the whole controversy, however, was the
German failure to question the British claim to Mfumbiro. The
British themselves never questioned their right: Mfumbiro,
whatever its origin, was explicitly guaranteed to them through
the treaty of 1890. There is no evidence that the British ever
examined or even attempted to locate the original documents
which might have given a hint as to what 'Mfumbiro' was. The
negotiations of 1890 were not even studied; consequently the
myth grew that Mfumbiro was included in the treaty in return
for ceding Kilimanjaro to the Germans, and it was assumed that
approximately the same amount of territory was meant to be
included.[7]

Of the imperialists who were involved in the Ruanda-
Urundi entanglement, only Arthur Hardinge can be compared
to Salisbury for grasp of issues and cogency of argument. The
Belgians, in particular van den Heuvel, were more consistent
in defence of their claims than either the British or the Germans.
Ebermaier was unrivalled in bombast and haughty nationalism,
except, perhaps, by Lindequist. Anderson's competence was
surpassed only by his own ability to blunder.[8] Colonel Close
was by no means a self-denying imperialist, but diligently tried
to find sensible solutions. Hardinge was the most reasonable of
all, and more than once exposed the folly of wrangling over
such matters as who should own the highest volcano in Mfumbiro. The Kivu-Mfumbiro controversy produced talent and
statesmanship as well as incompetence. The fortitude of Coote
and the manoeuvres of the Kivu expedition were perhaps the
most remarkable episode in the whole controversy, despite the
bungling of the British Colonial Office. But the whole affair
had rotten roots. If the German suspicion about Leopold and
the map of the Congolese-French agreement of 1885 was never
proven, there can be no doubt about 'Mfumbiro'. Stanley's
claim to 'Mfumbiro' was a monumental fraud.

Salisbury remarked during the 1890 negotiations: 'To some
minds just at present, both in Germany and in England, the
interior of Africa in the line of the great lakes occupied the

---

[7] See E. Hertslet's memorandum 'Mfumbiro as a *quid pro quo* for Kilimanjaro',
17 April 1906, F.O. 367/10.

[8] As I have been reminded by Agatha Ramm, in some respects this is a superficial
judgement of Anderson. But I contend that it is an accurate evaluation of his role
in the negotiations of 1890 and 1894.

position and offered the attractions of the El Dorado of the 16th century. I did not think such anticipations were grounded upon fact, and these feelings would probably melt away as practical experience increased. . . .'[9] Salisbury was wrong; this was not the way imperialism worked. Regardless of the economic value of a region, competition for scraps of territory waxed rather than waned; Ruanda-Urundi became the object of much imperial bickering.

The 1910 conference brought to a close the imperial competition of a quarter of a century. It was a conclusive settlement, which lasted until the reverses of the First World War. The agreement was dependent on the treaties of 1884, 1885, 1890, and 1894—all of which were based on imperfect geographical knowledge. The Congolese-German boundary commission survey of 1904 provided the information necessary to make a precise final settlement. The Anglo-German Mfumbiro conference of 1908 showed that the British and Germans might be able to work together against the Congo State, while the Anglo-German May 1909 agreement and the British Kivu expedition effectively forced the Belgians to meet the Anglo-German terms. In 1910 Ruanda-Urundi became completely—but not finally—German.

[9] Salisbury to Malet, no. 186A, 21 May 1890, F.O. 84/2030.

PART TWO

RUANDA-URUNDI AND COLONIAL RULE

X. THE EXPLORATION OF
RUANDA-URUNDI

I have always thought that long, straight routes through Africa
ceased to be of anything more than very ordinary value when once
the main features of the continent had been determined; and that
to turn a somewhat hard and uncertain profession to its best account,
the latter day explorer had best select a circumscribed district and
work it thoroughly . . . (Major A. St. Hill Gibbons, 1901)[1]

THE heroic odysseys during the nineteenth century of the great
European explorers in search of the source of the Nile led them
to the region of the great lakes of Tanganyika and Victoria.
The first descriptions of Ruanda and Urundi are recorded in
the stories of their travels.

Burton and Speke were the first to visit what they called 'ill-
famed Urundi' as they explored Lake Tanganyika; they hoped
that they might discover the beginning of the Nile at the
northern end of the lake. On 14 April 1858 they reached
Wafanya, the southern limit of Urundi, 'the only port in that
inhospitable land still open to travellers'.[2] Burton described the
people of Urundi there as noisy, insolent, addicted to drunken-
ness, and when drunk, quarrelsome and violent. The Rundi,
'many who stand upwards of six feet high . . . are evidently
natives of a high cold country; they are probably the "white
peoples resembling the Abyssinians", and dwelling near the
lake, of whom European geographers have heard from in
Zanzibar'.[3] Urundi, according to Burton's information from
the Arabs, was a 'monarchical' country, governed locally by
chiefs who at regular intervals sent tributes to the mwami,
the sovereign of the country.

Burton and Speke did not stay long in Urundi. After two
miserable days at Wafanya, they left for Uvira, on the northwest of the lake, where they hoped to solve the riddle of the
Nile. There they learned that the Ruzizi river—the natural

[1] Major A. St. Hill Gibbons, 'Explorations in Marotseland and Neighbouring
Regions', *Geographical Journal*, XVII, February 1901, p. 107.
[2] Richard F. Burton, *The Lake Regions of Central Africa* (2 vols.; London, 1860),
II, p. 106.
[3] Ibid., p. 145.

western frontier of Ruanda-Urundi—flowed into and not out of the lake. Burton wrote that he felt sick at heart. Lake Tanganyika was not the source of the Nile.[4]

The attempt to prove that Lake Victoria was the Nile source led Speke in November 1861 through Karagwe, where he viewed in the distance the lofty peaks of Mfumbiro.[5] The redoubtable Stanley provided more detailed information about Ruanda and Urundi. Stanley and Livingstone skirted the 'wooded heights of Urundi'[6] to the north end of Lake Tanganyika, where, by visiting the mouth of the Ruzizi, they verified the report given to Burton and Speke. 'The question, "was the Ruizizi an effluent or an influent?" was answered forever.' Stanley learned from the chief Ruhinga that the Ruzizi 'rose near a lake called Kivo [Kivu]';[7] north of Urundi was Ruanda, which was said to be a 'large country'. In *How I Found Livingstone* Stanley recorded the first detailed information about the Rundi districts north of Lake Tanganyika.

During his march through Karagwe in 1876, Stanley learned from the Arab Hamed Ibrahim that 'the Ruanda are a great people, but they are covetous, malignant, treacherous, and utterly untrustworthy'. 'They have never yet allowed an Arab to trade in their country, which proves them to be a bad lot.'[8] Thirteen years later Stanley again passed through Karagwe, again described the fierce, warlike people of Ruanda. '. . . it is almost a proverb with the Arab that it is easier to get into Ruanda than to get out of it . . . Mohammed, the brother of Tippu Tib, has tried to penetrate Ruanda with 600 guns, and failed'.[9] Stanley added to the accumulating ethnographical and geographical knowledge of the region, as did, in a greater way, Franz Stuhlmann, who accompanied Emin Pasha on the Emin expedition of 1890–2. Emin and Stuhlmann skirted the north-eastern edge of Ruanda, and passed to the north of the Mfumbiro range. Stuhlmann collected information that confirmed rumours that Ruanda was rich in ivory; he also discussed the

[4] Ibid., p. 145.
[5] *Journal of the Discovery of the Source of the Nile* (London, 1863), p. 213.
[6] H. M. Stanley, *How I Found Livingstone in Central Africa* (London, no date), p. 422.
[7] Ibid., pp. 416–18.
[8] *Through the Dark Continent* (2 vols.; London, 1878), I, p. 455.
[9] *In Darkest Africa* (2 vols.; London, 1890), II, p. 332.

ancient pastoral invasion of the Tutsi, the tribal structures, and the dialects of the inter-lacustrine region.[1]

Neither Stanley nor Stuhlmann entered Ruanda-Urundi itself.[2] Arabs had apparently visited part of Ruanda-Urundi as early as 1850; Tippu Tib stated in 1888 that 'Ruanda . . . belongs to me . . . there are my people supplied with munitions of war'.[3] But this was an empty boast. Ruanda-Urundi had remained off the Arab trade route,[4] just as it had also remained unvisited by the early European explorers. Through a combination of geographical features of mountains in the west and north and swampy rivers in the east, which discouraged the exit of the inhabitants and entry of travellers—as well as a reputation for hostility of the inhabitants—Ruanda-Urundi had remained isolated; the region was not opened up until comparatively late in the history of European discovery of Africa, and its exploration followed, rather than preceded, the political scramble.

The era of the great explorations of Africa ended around 1890. A few scientific expeditions, such as the Duke of Mecklenburg's in 1907, continued to traverse Africa; but these expeditions were exceptional. Explorations after the Anglo-German partition of 1890 became inseparable from colonial administration. Important problems of geography were still unsolved; after 1890 it was usually colonial officials working within the boundaries of their sphere of influence who attempted to provide answers. This change in the pattern of African exploration was not merely a result of the partition. The great explorers had indicated the locations of mountain ranges, deserts, and lakes; they had seldom given definitive information about specific geographical features. The explorations of Oskar Baumann and Count von Götzen were the transition between exploration of Africa on a grand scale to the exploration of Ruanda-Urundi in local detail.

'An admirable example of the thoroughly trained scientific

[1] Franz Stuhlmann, *Mit Emin Pascha ins Herz von Afrika* (Berlin, 1894), chapters XI and XII.

[2] On 9 and 10 March 1876, however, Stanley had actually reached Kisaka, in eastern Ruanda, but on meeting the hostile inhabitants he turned back toward Karagwe. *Historique et Chronologie du Ruanda*, pp. 12–13.

[3] This quotation is from a letter from Tippu Tib to Mahomed Masood and Seif Bin Ahned, incl. in Euan Smith to Salisbury, 2 January 1889, which was extracted by Sir John Gray and shown to me by Alison Smith.

[4] Cf. Louis de Lacger, 'Premiers contacts avec les blancs le règne de Rwabugiri', *Grands Lacs*, 1938–9, pp. 60–61.

explorer',[5] Oskar Baumann, an Austrian leading the Masai expedition of the German anti-slavery committee, left Charlie Stokes's station at Bukoni on Lake Victoria and crossed the Kagera into Urundi in September 1892. He received a friendly welcome from the Hutu, who regarded him as a liberator from Tutsi domination. After marching four days through northern Urundi, Baumann crossed the Akanjaru—the river dividing Ruanda and Urundi—into Ruanda on 11 September. He found the villages in Ruanda cleaner than in Urundi, the agricultural products more diverse. Declining an invitation to visit the mwami of Ruanda, Baumann crossed the Akanjaru back into Urundi. The Hutu were as hospitable as before. The Tutsi, however, attacked Baumann's expedition; they were easily repulsed. On 19 September he arrived at what he regarded as the 'origin of the Kagera [sic],[6] the mighty head stream of the Victoria Nyanza, which Englishmen call the Alexandra Nile, because it is the source river of the Nile; we stood at the *source of the Nile*'. Baumann confirmed rumours that to the south of the 'Mfumbiro' mountains was Lake Kivu, from which flowed the Ruzizi river.[7]

The discovery of Lake Kivu on 16 June 1894 by Götzen was of major historical and geographical importance; as was his visit to the volcanic region north of Ruanda. In mid-May 1894 Götzen and his party had crossed the Kagera into Ruanda. On his entrance to Ruanda he had seen in the distance a red glow, which indicated that some of the volcanoes must be active. On 11 June 1894 he ascended Tshanina-Gongo; it took Götzen two hours to walk around the edge of the crater. His group then travelled south to Lake Kivu, which he described as 50 miles long and 18–25 miles wide, studded with picturesque islands; the shores, he said, resembled an Italian lake. Götzen was received cordially by Rwabugiri, the mwami of Ruanda, and despite a later attack by Tutsi warriors of Bisangwa in the Bugoye district, regarded his welcome to Ruanda as peaceful.[8] 'If a country such as Ruanda . . . should come under German

---

[5] 'Dr. Baumann between Victoria Nyanza and Tanganyika', *Geographical Journal*, I, March 1893, pp. 228–30; see also IV, September 1894, pp. 246–50.

[6] Baumann actually traced the course of the Ruvuvu.

[7] Oskar Baumann, *Durch Massailand zur Nilquelle* (Berlin, 1894), p. 152; see especially chapter IV.

[8] *Historique et Chronologie du Ruanda*, p. 13.

sovereignty, we should rejoice in the thought that when the inhabitants met the first representatives of the white race they also met considerate and peaceable people.'[9]

The Baumann and Götzen expeditions marked the beginning of a series of explorations by German officers: Langheld, von Trotha, von Bethe, and Ramsay.[1] Of these Ramsay's was the most important. Ramsay's party in January 1897 ascended the Ruzizi, the valley of which he described as a wide, treeless plain; the region abounded in elephants. Ramsay disagreed with Baumann about the source of the Nile. Ramsay traced the courses of the Ruvuvu, considered by Baumann to be the head-stream of the Kagera, and the Akanjaru; he considered the latter more important. Ramsay also described how the mwami of Ruanda, Mibambwe IV Rutarindwa, had been murdered in 1896 because of his 'unpopularity and greed', and how his brother Yuhi V Musinga had triumphed in the struggle for accession. 'Musinga, with whom I concluded blood-friendship, placed himself under German protection, and received a German flag and letter of protection [*Schutzbrief*] . . . that I achieved this in a peaceful way seems to me to be the most important political result of the expedition.'[2]

The results of the expeditions by the German officers were significant; but they were overshadowed by the work of one man, who might well be called the pioneer of Ruanda-Urundi: Dr. Richard Kandt.[3] Kandt's scholarly work over a period of years did much to fill in the gaps of knowledge concerning the Ruanda-Urundi region. At the end of January 1898 Kandt set out on one of his most important expeditions, the purpose of which was to solve the problem of the source of the Kagera. From Tabora Kandt travelled to the junction of the Kagera and the Ruvuvu, which he reached in mid-May 1898. There, by measuring the volumes of the two streams, he ascertained that the Ruvuvu was decidedly less important than the Kagera, that Baumann's solution to the Nile problem was wrong.

---

[9] G. A. Graf von Götzen, *Durch Afrika von Ost nach West* (Berlin, 1895), p. 155; see especially chapter VI.

[1] The details of these expeditions are summarized and discussed in August Vetter, *Die Ergebnisse der neueren Untersuchungen über die Geographie von Ruanda* (Darmstadt, 1906).

[2] Hauptmann Ramsay, 'Uha, Urundi und Ruanda', *Mitteilungen aus den deutschen Schutzgebieten*, X, pp. 177–81; cf. *Historique et Chronologie du Ruanda*, p. 13.

[3] See below, p. 146, note 3.

Kandt followed the Kagera upstream, where he reached the confluence of the Akanjaru and the Nyawarongo; there he ascertained that the Nyawarongo, and not the Akanjaru—as Ramsay had assumed—was the main source of the Kagera. After ascending it for six days he reached the mouth of the Mukungwa, its largest tributary. Kandt marched on to the volcanic region; from there he travelled to the north end of Lake Tanganyika. At the end of December 1898 he ascended the Ruzizi valley, which he plotted cartographically for the first time. From the west bank of Kivu he marched northwards to the north of Mfumbiro under considerable hardship through regions stricken with famine. He returned across the volcanic range to the east shore of Lake Kivu and the Ruzizi. His circumambulation from the north of Lake Tanganyika around Lake Kivu and the volcanic region allowed him to produce the first detailed map of the region. Kandt facilitated the work of the Congolese-German boundary commission of 1902–4 by placing the results of his researches at their disposal. Dr. Kandt settled on the southern bank of Lake Kivu, at his zoological station 'Bergfrieden'; from here he made more excursions. From 19 October to 3 November 1899 he explored the east bank of Lake Kivu and the large island in the middle of the lake, Idjwi. At the end of July 1900 Kandt began a more thorough exploration of the Akanjaru and the upper-Kagera; he verified again that the Nyawarongo, not the Akanjaru, was the true, if theoretical, source of the Kagera Nile.[4]

Until 1892 most of the information about Ruanda-Urundi had come from the great explorers who had painted the lines of the African continent with a broad brush. Local explorations—sometimes as difficult and tedious, but seldom attracting as much attention as the sensational transcontinental adventures—were needed to fill in detail. In Ruanda-Urundi this was done within a decade, and was due mostly to the efforts of German explorers and officers, who provided the answer to one of the great geographical puzzles of east and central Africa: the ultimate source of the Nile. The beginning of the twentieth century saw the passing of Ruanda-Urundi as unexplored territory.

---

[4] Kandt's explorations and early impressions of Ruanda are recounted in detail in his *Caput Nili* (2 vols.; Berlin, 1919 edition).

XI. THE TUTSI, THE HUTU,
AND THE TWA

Ruanda is certainly the most interesting country in the German
East African Protectorate—in fact, in all central Africa—chiefly on
account of its ethnographical and geographical position. (The Duke
of Mecklenburg, 1910)[1]

FROM the German researches before the First World War
emerged a clear picture of the peoples of Ruanda-Urundi.[2]
Rundi and Ruanda societies were composed of three ethnic
groups: the Twa (pygmoids), the Hutu Bantus (or negroids),
and the Tutsi, assumed by the Germans to be of Hamitic
origin.[3] The Twa, pygmoids related to the forest negroes of the
Congo, were thought to be the oldest inhabitants, and to have
been in Ruanda-Urundi since time immemorial. They were
found mostly in the western Mfumbiro region and swampy
country in the north, where they were mainly hunters; in other
parts of Ruanda-Urundi there were a few Twa who were metal
workers and potters, dancers and buffoons. Both the Hutu and
the Tutsi scorned the Twa, and regarded them as outcasts;
a few Twa mingled with some of the Hutu. Jan Czekanowski,
the ethnographer of the Mecklenburg expedition, estimated
that there were 3,000 Twa in Ruanda in 1907;[4] Hans Meyer,
the German authority on Urundi, recorded 4,000 in Urundi
around 1913.[5] These figures corresponded more or less with
those estimated by the German authorities. The Twa were an
insignificant but in some places bothersome minority—less than
one per cent of the population.

[1] *In the Heart of Africa* (English translation; London, 1910), p. 44.
[2] I have drawn this account mostly from the German documents in Ruanda-
Urundi, especially the annual reports, which describe in detail the ethnic groups
and political organization; my purpose is to recreate the impression of the country
and its peoples that a German might have had if he had visited Ruanda-Urundi
before the First World War. I do not pretend to be an anthropologist; but I have
tried to correct some of the erroneous German notions by following the anthropo-
logical works cited in the bibliography.
[3] Cf. Audrey I. Richards, ed., *East African Chiefs* (London, 1960), chapter I.
[4] Jan Czekanowski, *Forschungen im Nil-Kongo Zwischengebiet* (5 vols.; Leipzig,
1917), I., p. 134.
[5] Hans Meyer, *Die Barundi* (Leipzig, 1916), pp. 158–62.

The Hutu came to Ruanda-Urundi later than the Twa, but little was known of their origin. They were an agricultural people, thought to form about 85 per cent. of the population. The other group was the pastoral Tutsi, who were assumed to have invaded Ruanda-Urundi around or before the fifteenth century. The penetration of the Tutsi into the region was a slow, apparently peaceful process. They first subjugated the indigenous inhabitants in eastern Ruanda, then gradually extended their dominion toward the west. The Tutsi absorbed the Bantu language of the Hutu; throughout Ruanda-Urundi the three ethnic groups spoke basically the same language with local modifications. The extent of Tutsi domination over the Hutu varied from region to region. The Tutsi-Hutu relation in the semi-independent heavily populated districts of northern Ruanda, where few Tutsi penetrated, for instance, differed from the total subjugation of the Hutu under Tutsi chiefs in central Ruanda. The proportion of Hutu to Tutsi also varied from Ruanda to Urundi. Czekanowski estimated the Tutsi population of Ruanda at 10 per cent.; Meyer calculated that they comprised much less of the Rundi population—about 3 per cent.

During the early years of the German administration there was a tendency to overestimate the total population. The population of the two countries was unevenly distributed; the inhabited regions were hills, which were often separated by uninhabited valleys filled with swamps. Mosquitoes, steep slopes, and high temperatures in the valleys accounted for the density of population on the hills; the Germans frequented the more heavily populated region; their ideas were often distorted concerning the population of the other parts of the country. One observer guessed that a total of four million people lived in Ruanda-Urundi in 1906–7. Hans Meyer estimated a total of five million as late as 1913–14; in 1916 he estimated more realistically the population of Urandi at one and a half million. Ruanda alone was assumed by some as late as 1914 to have a population of three million. Czekanowski, who was trained as an ethnographer, however, gave the population of one and a half million for Ruanda in 1907. Apart from the German administrators, Czekanowski was the only investigator who provided an explanation of his method of calculation. He estimated the density of population on the basis of the number of huts seen in certain districts. From the area of the district and the number of huts he calculated the number of inhabitants.[6] Obviously this method could not lead to precise results, but Czekanowski's estimates corresponded favourably with the calculations made by the local authorities over a period of years.

Ruanda-Urundi was assumed to be the most densely populated region in Africa. The Residents for this reason, in part, tried to make informed guesses about population numbers. In each of the annual reports for Ruanda and Urundi there were detailed population statistics of the white, 'coloured' (including everyone who was not white or African), and African populations. In 1911 the Urundi administration began to take definite measures toward a census by asking the chiefs to report the number of huts in their districts, by which the Germans calculated the total population in a method similar to the one used by Czekanowski in Ruanda. The Urundi Resident in 1914 estimated the population of Urundi at one and a half million. In Ruanda the census methods were more advanced. Under Dr. Kandt's supervision, counts by the askaris (African soldiers) and the police force were taken locally in various administrative districts. These surveys indicated that the population of Ruanda was around two million. Thus, the total population of Ruanda-Urundi before the First World War, according to the German documents, was around three and a half million.

There were no accurate ways to determine the rate of population growth. The impression of the German officers was that the birth-rate surpassed the death-rate. This was obvious, they thought, from the number of babies; one seldom saw a woman who did not have a baby strapped to her back.

The great density of population created the problem, of course, of food supply. Although the Hutu hoe-farmers cultivated their crops intensively, and almost every cultivable spot

---

[6] These figures are compiled from Czekanowski and Meyer, and from various articles that appeared in colonial journals; most of these sources are discussed in detail in the United Nations study, *The Population of Ruanda-Urundi* (New York, 1953). This is a good study, but uses only published sources; it does injustice to the official German calculations. The U.N. report implies that the German officials grossly overestimated the population of Ruanda-Urundi; in fact the unpublished documents show that the Germans with their rough census methods arrived at the same conclusions as the U.N. experts.

was used, famines were not uncommon, in part because of the irregularity of rainfall.[7]

The Hutu were agriculturalists; the Tutsi were breeders of long-horned cattle. Socially and economically the Tutsi dominated the Hutu. Cattle were wealth, the key to political and social standing; and the cattle were owned almost exclusively by the Tutsi. The Hutu desire to own cattle was the fundamental reason for their subjugation. The Hutu wanted cattle; the Tutsi wanted servants and labour for their crops. The Tutsi despised agriculture. To acquire cattle the Hutu obligated themselves to perform services for the Tutsi. In Ruanda this took the form of a cattle agreement called the *ubuhake*, which enabled the Hutu to obtain cattle, provided they were loyal to the Tutsi who granted them the cattle. The cattle agreement involved subjugation on the part of the Hutu to the extent that in some places, in return for the use of cattle, the Hutu relinquished their pastures and arable land, and were bound to provide crops as well as personal and military services for the Tutsi. In this way the Tutsi wielded almost total political and economic power over the Hutu. On the other hand, the personal allegiance between the Tutsi and Hutu ensured protection for the latter. The Tutsi exploited the Hutu, but also provided security.

Over a period of centuries the Tutsi had gradually usurped the ownership of the land from the Hutu. All land, theoretically, became the property of the mwami, the absolute and semi-divine sovereign, whose symbol of authority was the *kalinga* (in Urundi the *karyenda*), or sacred drum from which were hung the genitals of the enemies of Ruanda killed by the mwami. To the mwami all subjects were obliged to pay tributes. The collection of these tributes was the responsibility of a complicated administrative hierarchy. Administratively below the mwami was a council of ministers, *batware b'intebe*, below them the chiefs who governed the provinces, and beneath them the sub-chiefs. The mwami was required to consult the *biru*, or council of guardians of traditions, for important decisions. Supreme judicial authority was vested in the mwami, who

[7] The long rainy season usually occurred, roughly, during October, November and December; a short dry season during January and February; a short rainy season during March, April and May; and the long dry season during June, July and August.

delegated authority to courts composed of great chiefs, who in turn delegated authority to more local courts. In a similar way, the mwami distributed land and cattle among his subjects, who in return administered regions, paid the tributes, and provided military services. The great chiefs, in short, held responsibilities and obligations to the mwami for land, cattle, and military service; this system of obligations and tributes descended from the mwami to the most common farmer. Obligations were not usually to the same person; one might be bound to one chief for cattle, to another for land, and yet another for military service.

This intricate society more or less characterized both Ruanda and Urundi. Descent in both societies was agnatic. Both Ruanda and Urundi were ruled by absolute sovereigns who were considered divine. In both countries the bami (plural of mwami) distributed their land and cattle among their feudatories, who in return rendered administrative and military services. But there were differences as well as similarities. The system of obligations in Urundi was less strict than in Ruanda; the cattle holding provision for Urundi, for instance (called the *ubugabira* instead of the *ubuhake*) was similar but less binding than in Ruanda. Land ownership in Urundi was not as splintered as in Ruanda. The most important difference between the two societies, perhaps, was the absence in Ruanda of the *ganwa*, or princes of the royal blood. As a mwami acceded to power in Urundi, he received one of the four dynastic names: Ntare, Mwezi (Kissabo's other title), Mutaga, Mwambutsa.[8] Their descendants were named Batare, Bezi, Batanga, and Bambutsa, respectively. They were *ganwa*, princes, until the accession of an mwami who received the same name as their eponymous ancestor; then they became *bafasoni*, a less important, honorary title. The position of these members of the royal family were similar to the ruling Tutsi in Ruanda; but they had less prestige than their counterparts in Ruanda. Each of the *ganwa* or great chiefs (*ganwa* were 'great chiefs'; but not all great chiefs were *ganwa*) had his own army, and could not be controlled as easily by the mwami as in Ruanda. The result was a far less centralized government in Urundi than in Ruanda.

[8] In Ruanda the dynastic names were Cyirima, Kigeri, Mibambwe, Yuhi (Musinga's other title), and Mutara, which also followed in sequence.

Ruanda at the beginning of the twentieth century became known to the German explorers as a highly centralized state in which the power of the great chiefs was strictly limited. Urundi, in contrast, was a conglomerate of territories whose rulers were semi-independent and whose allegiance to the mwami was more in theory than in practice. There was a tradition of rivalry and war between the two domains.

The physical characteristics of the peoples of Ruanda-Urundi were as striking as the country which they inhabited. The Tutsi were tall, handsome, slender, and well-proportioned, sometimes over seven feet. The Twa, in contrast, were grotesque little creatures whom the Germans referred to as dwarfs. Between the two stood the stocky aboriginal Bantu, the Hutu.[9] The country inhabited by this unlikely trio was sometimes referred to as the high plateau of the central African rift valley, which formed the watershed between the Congo and the Nile; but the terrain gave the impression of sugar-loaf mountainous country rather than a plateau, with the height averaging around 6,000 feet. The mountains were in many places denuded of forest, which aggravated the problem of erosion. Götzen observed that a remarkable feature of Ruanda was the total absence of wood; grass was used for fuel. The average yearly temperature was about 70° F., 'like a warm day in Germany', as one German officer described it. Ruanda was divided from Urundi by the Akanjaru river. The western frontier of Ruanda-Urundi was marked by Lake Kivu and the Ruzizi river. In the northwest were the Mfumbiro mountains; in the northeast and south natural frontiers were less pronounced, but were formed to some extent by the Lumpungu and the Malagarasi rivers. As the German explorers crossed these frontiers into Ruanda-Urundi they were impressed, almost without exception, with the great beauty of the country. 'Ruanda is a gigantic high plateau with neither tree nor bush; only banana trees . . . in the villages. It is incredibly populated, in general very fertile, and very cultivated; there is almost no difference between it and Urundi, the most beautiful land in our colony.'[1] 'If all were not so stark' Lt. von Parish wrote in 1902,

---

[9] Anthropologists have shown, however, that the physical characteristics distinguishing the three groups are not sharply defined.
[1] Ramsay, 'Uha, Urundi and Ruanda', p. 181.

'it would be almost an ideal beauty'.[2] These were the countries and peoples which became part of German East Africa.

[2] 'Bericht des Leutnant von Parish über den vom 16.12.02 bis 14.1.03 von Kishenyi nach Ishangi durch Ruanda ausgeführten Marsch'. USU. I I/D/28.

One of the most picturesque and sensitive descriptions of Ruanda-Urundi during the early German period is given by Lt. von Parish. Parish was appointed in 1901 as commander of Ischangi, a German post on Lake Kivu; his health suffered and he was ordered home. He died almost immediately on his return to Germany. See 'Zwei Reisen durch Ruanda, 1902–3; Aus Tagebüchern, Briefen und hinterlassenen Papieren des Oberleutnants F. R. von Parish, zusammengestellt von Oskar Freiherr Parish von Senftenberg', *Globus*, 1904, LXXXVI, pp. 5–13 and 73–79.

XII. THE GERMAN PACIFICATION OF URUNDI AND ESTABLISHMENT OF AUTHORITY IN RUANDA, 1896–1906

The organized native population included in the sultanates [of Ruanda and Urundi] presents such virgin and malleable material, that with patience, consciousness of purpose, and insight, the goals of the German protectorate, in my opinion, can be realized without difficulty. (Haber, Acting Governor of German East Africa, 1906)[1]

THE German East Africa government extended its authority to the borders of Uganda and the Congo during the 1890s. In 1896 the 'Militärstation Usumbura' was founded.[2] From Usumbura the German officers established relations with one-eyed Kissabo, the mwami of Urundi, and Musinga, the mwami of Ruanda.

Unlike the sovereigns of Ruanda, the potentates of Urundi during the nineteenth century were unable to control their chiefs and to achieve sovereignty over their country.[3] Unlike Ruanda, Urundi was not a centralized state. The reign of Mwesi IV—Kissabo—(1860–1908) was an internecine struggle against refractory chiefs. Kissabo pretended to wield absolute power, in accordance with the traditions of the Rundi; he was in fact a potentate of limited power. He regarded the German intrusion as a threat to his already precarious position. Captain von Bethe's first contacts with Kissabo in 1899 were friendly; Kissabo promised Bethe submission to German authority and assured him of his eagerness to cooperate. Kissabo was in fact deceptive; he really hoped to defeat his enemies and establish his own absolute sovereignty without German interference. But Kissabo saw more defeats than victories in the Rundi wars at the turn of the century; his authority diminished rather than increased. The Germans at Usumbura did not intervene.[4]

[1] Haber to A.A., Kolonialabteilung, 18 June 1906, RU. I I/D/28.

[2] Cf. *Historique et Chronologie du Ruanda*, p. 14.

[3] See Hans Meyer's discussion of pre-colonial Urundi in *Die Barundi*, pp. 151–65, and especially J. Vansina's 'Notes sur l'histoire du Burundi', *Aequatoria*, XXIV, (1961). The Germans referred to Ruanda and Urundi as 'sultanates' and their rulers as 'sultans'.

[4] See Pierre Ryckmans, *Une page d'histoire coloniale* (Brussels, 1953), p. 5. Some of the early documents which Ryckmans used in Ruanda-Urundi are not in the Usumbura archive.

Captain von Beringe described events in Urundi in a long political report in July 1902. Kissabo, Beringe was convinced, was an enemy of Europeans; although most of the population of Urundi was not anti-German,[5] most of the Tutsi chiefs in Urundi were enemies of Kissabo. Urundi, in short, was in 'chaos'. Beringe requested permission for an 'Urundi expedition' of three months. He did not want to depose Kissabo, but to gain once and for all his submission to German rule. Then there would be a basis on which to build in Urundi an authority as strong and effective as the one in Ruanda.[6] Götzen, now Governor of German East Africa, was sceptical; he was mainly concerned with Musinga in Ruanda. To Götzen the most important function of German rule in Urundi was not to detract from the good German relations in Ruanda, and therefore German actions in Urundi should be peaceful rather than punitive.[7] Beringe replied that the situation in Urundi continued to deteriorate. The Mugera mission was in danger; Kissabo was a threat to German authority. The only way to restore order in Urundi would be by a punitive expedition; this would require reinforcements from Tabora. Beringe was trying to convince his government that there was only one course to follow: war against Kissabo.[8]

Beringe's renewed request for a punitive expedition against Kissabo arrived in Dar es Salaam while Götzen was on home leave. Stuermann, the official who replied to Beringe's latest report, was as unenthusiastic as Götzen about Beringe's bellicose plans; German relations with Kissabo must remain 'peaceful and diplomatic'. Stuermann ordered Beringe not to take any action unless it was approved by Götzen.[9]

Two difficulties confronted Beringe. First, he had to convince his superiors in Dar es Salaam that a punitive expedition against Kissabo was a wise policy; this he had failed to do. Second, if there was to be a punitive expedition, Beringe needed reinforce-

[5] Dr. England, 'Bericht über die Urundi Expedition von 24 März bis 25 Juni 1902', USU. I I/D/28.
[6] Beringe to Gouvernement, 15 July 1902, USU. I I/D/28.
[7] Götzen to Usumbura, 13 September 1902, USU. I I/D/28.
[8] Beringe to Gouvernement, 12 December 1902; also 'Klagen gegen den Sultan Mwezi Kissabo in Urundi', 30 July 1901; and Beringe to Gouvernement, 15 December 1902, USU. I I/D/28.
[9] Stuermann to Usumbura, 11 February 1903, and to A.A., Berlin, 18 March 1903, USU. I I/D/28.

ments. On 12 December 1902 he had requested from Götzen a detachment of fifty men from Tabora; Götzen had refused. Beringe was resourceful; he requested support from Bismarck-burg (i.e. Kasanga), the German post on the south end of Lake Tanganyika. He also tried Bukoba, the German post on Lake Victoria; Bukoba, however notified Dar es Salaam.[1] Stuer-mann's response was a telegram to Bukoba forbidding them to take any part in the Urundi expedition.[2]

Beringe was not to be stopped. He bombarded the government in Dar es Salaam with reports of increasing anarchy and terrorism in Urundi.[3] In his report of 14 April 1903 Beringe described the recent events in Urundi in a way designed to clear himself from any suspicion that he might be disobeying orders, and to create the impression that immediate intervention in Urundi was necessary. The chiefs whom Kissabo was fighting, Beringe explained, were the ones who had recognized German authority. This was an intolerable situation which Beringe was determined to correct with or without the aid of the central government and the neighbouring military stations.[4]

The policy of the central government remained unchanged. In a memorandum of 7 June 1903 Götzen instructed Beringe that the situation in Urundi did not justify a military expedition, and to get busy with road construction.[5] In the meantime, however, Beringe had written that a detachment from Bismarckburg had arrived in Usumbura to participate in the Urundi expedition.[6]

---

[1] Bukoba to Gouvernement, 2 February 1903, USU. I I/D/28; also Bismarck-burg to Gouvernement, 16 April 1903, USU. I I/D/28.

[2] Stuermann to German Consulate, Entebbe, 11 March 1903, USU. I I/D/28.

[3] Beringe's reports sometimes contradicted the reports arriving in Dar es Salaam from his own subordinates. See Lt. Pfeiffer's report of 5 January 1903; Beringe to Gouvernement, 23 January 1903; 10 March 1903; and 14 April 1903; USU. I I/D/28.

[4] Beringe to Gouvernement, 14 April 1903.

[5] Götzen to Usumbura, 7 June 1903, USU. I I/D/28.

[6] Beringe mobilized all military support in the Urundi area, which gives some idea of German strength at this time. The expedition consisted of:

Abteilung Usumbura I: *Hauptmann* von Beringe, *Stabsarzt* Dr. Schörnich, *Unter-offizier* Gebel, 35 askaris of the IX Company, 60 *Hülfsmannschaften*, one maxim gun and 3.7 *Schnelladekanone*.

Abteilung Usumbura II: *Feldwebel* Münzer, 20 askaris of the IX Company, and 67 *Hülfsmannschaften*.

Abteilung Bismarckburg: *Oberleutnant* Fr. von Ledebur, *Stabsarzt* Dr. Exner, *Unteroffizier* Federonski, 35 askaris of the VI Company and 82 *Hülfsmannschaften*.

Abteilung Ischangi; Leutnant Pfeiffer, 25 askaris of the IX Company, 25 *Hülfs-mannschaften*, and 60 Ruanda Tutsi.

Beringe vigorously prosecuted his campaign against Kissabo, converging on him with four columns. He notified the central government on 23 June 1903 that the expedition had been a 'great success'. Kissabo had submitted to German authority on 6 June, having lost 200 men. Only three of the German force were killed, two injured.[7]

Kissabo recognized the 'Militärstation Usumbura' and German sovereignty (*Oberhoheit*); he also agreed to leave the Mugera mission in peace, and not to molest caravans passing through Urundi. Four hundred and twenty-four head of cattle were to be given by Kissabo to the German authorities as a penalty for his malfeasances since 1899. He was to recognize, in addition, the independence of the chiefs Kilima and Machoncho, who had allied themselves with Beringe against Kissabo. In return, the Germans would recognize Kissabo as the mwami of Urundi, and would support his efforts to consolidate his country.[8]

Beringe had flouted his superiors. Götzen was furious. The military station at Usumbura, Götzen said in a letter of reprimand, had not been seriously threatened by Kissabo; Beringe had exaggerated beyond reason the gravity of the situation in Urundi. While it was true that the Mugera mission had been in danger, three askaris would have been enough to protect it. The recognition of independence of any chiefs in Urundi was in direct contradiction to Götzen's specific orders; the unity of the country had been destroyed. Beringe had taken upon himself a grandiose project which could endanger German relations with the two most powerful African domains in the whole colony. Decisions about such gravely important matters were for the Governor of German East Africa himself, and his orders had been intentionally disregarded.[9]

Beringe had achieved his goal: the submission of Kissabo. Events after the conclusion of his treaty seemed to prove Beringe

---

[7] Beringe to Gouvernement, tel., 26 June 1903; also his telegram of 29 July 1903 and his exhaustive report of 24 July 1903. Beringe's report listed 8 killed and 7 wounded in the German force.

[8] Beringe's report of 24 July.

[9] Götzen to Usumbura, 23 September 1903, USU. I I/D/28. News of Beringe's expedition had appeared in the *Tägliche Rundschau* on 16 July 1903; Götzen received a letter from the Colonial Section of the Foreign Office in Berlin shortly afterwards demanding a report explaining why the expedition had been authorized. See A.A., Kolonialabteilung, to Götzen, 23 July 1903, with clipping, USU. I I/D/28.

right and Götzen wrong. Beringe reported in October 1903 that the situation in Urundi continued to improve;[1] Götzen's fears that the punitive expedition might adversely affect German relations in Ruanda had not been realized. Two views had clashed: Beringe's, that the country must be pacified before it could be efficiently administered; Götzen's, that the political situation in Urundi would settle without German interference and that the immediate goals of the military station at Usumbura should be the occupation of the disputed territory and the construction of roads. The former thought that Urundi would be governed best by recognition of the most important chiefs; the latter, that German authority would be most easily established by recognition of the traditional sovereign of all Urundi, and through cooperation with him. Beringe had triumphed because he commanded the Usumbura military station. But Beringe had disobeyed his superiors; he was replaced by von Grawert.[2]

Götzen tried to repair the damage. In April 1904 he ordered Usumbura to regard all chiefs as subordinate to Kissabo, on the condition that Kissabo would continue to recognize German sovereignty.[3] The chiefs to whom Beringe had granted independence consequently renewed hostilities against both Kissabo and the Germans. Grawert might have thought it debatable whether Götzen's policy of complete centralization under Kissabo was more satisfactory than Beringe's policy of limited centralization under Kissabo with independence of some Rundi chiefs; but Grawert was in a difficult situation, complicated by the contradictions between the instructions of the central government and the local actions of Beringe.

[1] Beringe to Gouvernement, 8 October 1903, USU. II I/D/28.

[2] A memorandum of 3 June 1904 stated that Beringe was returning to Germany and would not return to the colony. Beringe had interviews with Götzen in Dar es Salaam, but the details were not recorded.

The advent of Grawert, incidentally, marked the beginning of typewriters in Ruanda-Urundi.

[3] Grawert, in accordance with Götzen's instructions, recognized Kissabo as sovereign of Urundi; the formal ceremony between Kissabo and Grawert by which Germany recognized Kissabo as absolute ruler of Urundi did not take place, however, until 8 October 1905. Grawert 'explained in the name of the Governor that Kissabo was the recognized Sultan of Urundi, adding that as long as he met our wishes we would regard his political enemies in Urundi as our enemies'. See Grawert's 'Bericht über die Bezirksreise im Sultanat Urundi in der Zeit vom 25 August bis 25 October 1905'; also Götzen to Usumbura, 13 April 1904; 23 December 1903 and 4 June 1904, USU. II I/D/28.

Götzen, incensed at Beringe's disobedience, expected Usumbura to follow the instructions of the central government to the letter; this limited Grawert's initiative. Grawert in his reports at first concentrated on problems concerning the disputed Kivu territory, the administration of the military posts, and the construction of roads. He avoided as much as possible the hot issue of Rundi politics.[4]

The problems were too great to ignore. The chief Machoncho —to whom Beringe had granted independence—attempted to murder Grawert with a spear in early May 1905; he feared that Grawert would try to hang him because he had systematically attempted to overthrow Kissabo and had even plotted to attack Usumbura. Grawert shot in self-defence. Machoncho died a few days later.[5]

During the autumn of 1904 Grawert had travelled through Urundi; he made it a point to ask Hutu whom he met what their relation was to Kissabo. 'Everywhere there was a real awareness that he was their real sultan . . . everywhere it came to light that they feared subjection to the greatly increasing power of the smaller chiefs (Kilima, for example).' Since Beringe had granted Kilima independence, Grawert thought it best not to intervene in the small war between Kilima and Kissabo; he would, however, prevent other chiefs from attacking Kissabo. Grawert regarded his moderate support of Kissabo as a return to the policy of Götzen. 'I was delighted to explain to the missionaries throughout Urundi that the support of Urundi under the Mwesi Kissabo was not a new but a restoration of a previously recognized general policy that is completely practicable, a policy which will be, as far as I am concerned, carried out without deviations. . . . Father van der Burgt, one of the people most intimate with Urundi, said to me in private conversation that he thought our present policy was the only correct one, and that the Dutch in the east Indies, trying to attain the same goals, had had good experiences with the same system.'[6] This statement is one of the earliest expressions of German 'indirect rule' in Ruanda-Urundi. 'The ideal is: unqualified recognition of the authority of the sultans from us,

[4] See Usumbura to Gouvernement, 2 April 1904; 12 May 1904, USU. II I/D/28.
[5] Grawert to Gouvernement, 17 May 1905, USU. II I/D/28.
[6] Grawert to Gouvernement, geheim, 5 December 1904, USU. II I/D/28.

whether through taxes or other means, in a way that will seem
to them as little a burden as possible; this will link their
interests with ours. This ideal will probably be realized more
easily and earlier in Ruanda, which is more tightly organized,
than in Urundi, where we must first re-establish the old
authority of the sultan, which has been generally weakened by
wars with Europeans and other circumstances.'[7]

Whatever policy the German East Africa government may
have had at this time, it was not easy to apply to Urundi,
which continued to be tempestuous. Beringe's punitive expedition had weakened Kissabo's control over the Rundi chiefs;
the problem facing Grawert was how to bring refractory chiefs
under Kissabo's authority. Kissabo had never been an absolute
despot; Grawert's plan would not only restore what strength
Kissabo had before Beringe's expedition, but would also give
Kissabo a control over his country which he himself had never
before been able to achieve. To determine who supported
Kissabo and who opposed him was one of the purposes of
Grawert's expedition of August–October 1905. Grawert was
surprised to learn that the powerful chief Luhindikira in southern Urundi acknowledged Kissabo's authority. He also discovered
that the chief Tschoja in northern Urundi regarded himself
as Kissabo's subject. Grawert concluded that 'through the
recognition of Kissabo as overlord we are on the right path'.[8]

The conspirators against Kissabo were sometimes his close
relatives, who hoped to overthrow him and to rule themselves.
Apart from them the principal offenders were Lussokossa in
the northeast, Lusengo in Bugufi, and Kilima—the real cause
of trouble in Urundi—who led major conspiracies against
Kissabo. After formally recognizing Kissabo as the ruler of
Urundi at Mubekeje in October 1905, Grawert tried unsuccessfully to take Kilima by surprise through a quick march
to northwestern Urundi, Kilima's stronghold. Kilima eluded
his pursuers, but the German show of force demonstrated to his
subjects that he was now contending not only against the
recognized ruler of Urundi, but also against a determined and
invincible European power. On Grawert's return to Usumbura,
two rebel chiefs, Tunguse and Kibamba, formerly adherents to
Kilima, approached him to say that they had deserted Kilima

---

[7] Grawert's report of 21 November 1905, USU. II I/D/28.   [8] Ibid.

to recognize Kissabo as their ruler. Then in April 1906 a patrol of Grawert first destroyed Kilima's village and appropriated ninety-six head of his cattle; Kilima was seized by a group of Ruanda after a skirmish in which five Ruanda and eight of Kilima's men were killed. Kilima himself had been wounded over his left eye and brought to Usumbura.[9]

The capture of Kilima marked the consolidation of Urundi under Kissabo. The 'divide and rule' policy of Beringe had been abandoned; the Germans ruled Urundi through the traditional sovereign of the country. Ostensibly the Germans had centralized Urundi. 'It is certain that in the greater part of Urundi Mwesi [Kissabo] is recognized as overlord, even though the recognition is often only nominal and the degree of his influence might vary.'[1] Urundi was now to be administered with the same success which the Germans had had in Ruanda.

The consolidation of Ruanda occurred over a period of centuries; under the invincible Kigeri IV Rwabugiri (1853–95) Ruanda acquired the frontiers which the Germans found in 1894. Kigeri IV died in 1895; his son Mibambwe IV Rutarindwa succeeded him, but in the struggle to retain his throne Mibambwe IV was killed. Yuhi V Musinga (1896–1931), another son of Kigeri IV, became mwami in 1896.[2]

As in Urundi, the Germans did not intervene in Ruanda politics at the turn of the century. In part this was because there was no need; Götzen's expedition had produced friendly relations, which were perpetuated by Ramsay's treaty of protection with Musinga. But it was also at least in part because they had no choice. By 1902 the permanent German force in Ruanda consisted of Lt. von Parish and 21 askaris at Ischangi and *Unteroffizier* Ehrhardt and 4 askaris at Kisenyi.[3] The aim of

---

[9] Grawert's 'Bericht über die Bezirksreise vom 17 Januar bis 31 März des Jahres 1906', 25 April 1906, USU. II I/D/28. Kilima was subsequently deported to Neu-Langenburg.

[1] Not until 1908, however, was stormy northeastern Urundi brought under control by the Germans. Lusengo, who along with Mbanzabugabo and Busokoza had bought rifles in Karagwe to wage war against Kissabo, finally submitted to the authority of the mwami. Busokoza and Mbanzabugabo escaped, but Grawert appropriated their cattle; this marked the end to their opposition. See Grawert to Gouvernement, 7 December 1907, RU. II I/D/33.

[2] Cf. Kandt, *Caput Nili*, II, p. 768.

[3] Beringe, 'Bericht über die politische Lage im Bezirk Usumbura', 15 July 1902, USU. II I/D/28.

German occupation in the Kivu region was simply the prevention of Belgian occupation. It clearly would be disastrous if the Germans could not stay on good terms with the Ruanda. German policy from the outset was to try to establish the friendliest of possible relations with Musinga. Götzen instructed Usumbura in 1902 to work with Musinga 'in an absolutely peaceful way'; Usumbura was to regard Musinga as the ruler of Ruanda and was not to intervene in any way there without Musinga's permission and cooperation.[4]

The Germans were happy to discover that Ruanda presented few of the difficulties with which they were faced in Urundi. Unlike chaotic Urundi, Ruanda was stable; unlike Kissabo, Musinga genuinely wanted to cooperate. The German officers found Musinga intelligent and shrewd. Dr. Kandt later wrote that Musinga knew he could not in the long run defeat the Germans, who had modern weapons, in a prolonged war; he could on the other hand manipulate the Germans to his own advantage.[5] From the German point of view nothing could be better; pacification of a hostile Ruanda would be a costly if not impossible venture. Mutually advantageous relations were the result: the Germans used Musinga to establish their authority in the northwest of the colony; Musinga used the Germans to strengthen his own position in Ruanda.

German-Ruanda relations continued without difficulty. Musinga sent emissaries, the chiefs Lugambarara and Sengura, accompanied by sixty Ruanda, to Usumbura in a gesture of friendship in July 1902.[6] Beringe reciprocated by a visit to Musinga in October–November 1902.[7]

Lt. Parish travelled through Ruanda in December 1902–January 1903; he reported that not only were German relations good with the Tutsi rulers, but also with the Hutu. Ruanda was at peace; the only trouble came from the persecuted Twa. At the end of his report he waxed poetic: 'May the beautiful country of Ruanda, with her rich resources, and her marvellous, healthy climate, soon be opened to colonization; and may she be developed economically into the pearl of our protectorate;

---

[4] Götzen to Usumbura, 13 September 1902, USU. II I/D/28.
[5] See Kandt's 'Bericht über die Verwaltung in Ruanda', 15–16 August 1906, RU. I I/D/33.
[6] Beringe to Gouvernement, 26 July 1902, USU. II I/D/28.
[7] Beringe to Gouvernement, 28 March 1903, USU. II I/D/28.

this she deserves by virtue of her countless, intelligent population as well as her richness in crops and cattle.'[8]

Fair Ruanda, the pearl of German East Africa! 'Deepest
peace' reigned in Ruanda.[9]

Despite the glowing reports, there were two serious problems
facing the German officers who attempted to administer
Ruanda. The first was how to provide adequate protection for
missionaries; this involved the fundamental problem of main-
tainance of order and respect for German authority. The second
was how Ruanda and Urundi were to be opened to trade, while
at the same time protected from unscrupulous merchants. Both
problems plagued the Germans to the end of their administration.

Beringe had justified his punitive expedition against Kissabo
by professing, among other reasons, the need to protect the
Mugera mission from Tutsi attacks. The missionaries in
Ruanda faced similar difficulties. By 1904 the White Fathers
had established five missions in Ruanda. Musinga accepted the
presence of missionaries as a part of his acceptance of German
authority; his attitude toward the missionaries, as Grawert
described it, was 'thoroughly correct'. The difficulty was that
some of Musinga's chiefs did not share his views. Grawert
investigated the relations between the missionaries and the
Ruanda as he travelled through Ruanda in late 1904. In
November he visited Father Barthelemy of the Nyundo
mission, who had recently been attacked by Tutsi; this was only
one incident in many during the previous months. Grawert sent
a patrol to capture if possible the chiefs guilty of offences against
the missionaries and to burn their villages; Tibakunsee,
Luwamagabo, and Lukarra were the main offenders. After a
holiday at the Zaza mission to celebrate the birthday of the
Kaiser, Grawert despatched another patrol to try to capture
one of the leaders of the trouble, Billabonneje, while Grawert
himself burnt the villages of the culprits and destroyed their
banana groves. Musinga cooperated with Grawert and made
every effort to punish his guilty subjects. But the hostilities

[8] Parish, 'Bericht von Leutnant von Parish über den vom 16.12.02 bis 14.1.03
vom Kishenyi nach Ishangi durch Ruanda ausgeführten Marsch', 26 March 1903.
[9] Grawert, 'Bericht über die Expedition nach Ruanda und die dort vorge-
fundenen Verhältniss sowie den Rückmarsch durch Urundi', geheim, 5 December
1904, USU. II I/D/28.

directed against the Europeans seemed likely to get out of hand despite the combined efforts of Musinga and Grawert.[1]

The causes of the unrest were more complicated than simply the Tutsi dislike of missionaries; more important sources of trouble were connected with the problem of opening the region to commerce.

Economic exploitation of what the Germans regarded as the virgin, rich countries of Ruanda and Urundi was a main goal of their administration in east Africa. This they wanted to do on their terms, however; the Germans did not want their virgin raped by an unworthy suitor. Grawert was disturbed to learn from Father Pouget of the Zaza mission in Kisaka in November 1904 that Europeans recently had forcefully stolen cattle from Africans. Investigation showed that it was not exactly theft, but a form of business. An Austrian and a South African Boer were the cause of the trouble. The way Shindelar, the Austrian, and Praetorius, the Boer,[2] conducted business was to wander from hill to hill looking for cattle; as soon as they found a herd they would select the best cows and force the Africans to accept cheap cloth in payment. When the Africans saw that they were being robbed, they objected, but were daunted by the violence of Shindelar and Praetorius. A chief called Kaschugi was not only tied but also whipped by Shindelar. Sometimes Shindelar and Praetorius held women as hostages to force the Africans to 'sell' their cattle.[3]

Cattle theft was a serious crime. 'People sell their cows very seldom, very unwillingly, and at a high price; a bull would usually be exchanged for cloth worth at least 20 rupees;[4] average market prices for beef cattle is 25 rupees, and this is taken as the lowest rather than the highest price.' Schindelar and Praetorius obviously could not be allowed to continue their 'concealed robberies'.[5]

Schindelar and Praetorius were a flagrant example of the

[1] Ibid.

[2] The German documents give their nationalities as Greek and Goan respectively; but it is more probable that they were Austrian and Boer, as is mentioned in *Historique et Chronologie du Ruanda*, p. 15.   [3] Ibid.

[4] Rupees were the currency of German East Africa; 100 hellers equalled one rupee. One rupee was worth approximately one and one-third German marks, or 1/4d. sterling; 15 rupees equalled one pound sterling.

[5] Praetorius and Schindelar were subsequently arrested and imprisoned. Praetorius was a British subject; he complained to the British Consul in Zanzibar that he had been imprisoned for over a year and that his 300 head of cattle were

small invasion of Ruanda by petty merchants, most of whom were Indians and Goans, who came from Uganda and the region around Lake Victoria. Their impact on Ruanda-Urundi should not be underestimated, Grawert warned. 'The influx of these merchants will be a continued threat to the peace of the country as long as we are not in a position to protect immediately the natives from the attacks of these people.' The missionaries urged Grawert to declare Ruanda and Urundi out of bounds for coloured merchants and other undesirable characters. Grawert, however, regarded the development of trade in Ruanda-Urundi as highly important. 'To forbid trade, even temporarily, seems to me to go too far; it would not be in the interest of the colony.' He conceded, however, that the situation was so serious that the Governor would have to take immediate action of some sort.[6]

Grawert had enough problems for the moment anyway. As he travelled through Ruanda in 1904 he discovered that rumours had spread that he had been murdered. Was this an indication that the Ruanda were looking for an excuse to overthrow German rule? For if it were true that the German leader had been killed, then it should not be difficult to destroy the rest of the German force. Grawert regarded these rumours as part of the agitation directed toward the missionaries and coloured merchants. The missionaries placed the entire blame on the merchants and the trouble stirred up by them, combined with Tutsi hatred of any foreign intervention. Grawert did not think that the missionaries themselves were entirely innocent; in their zeal to proselytize they had been too forward in their relations with the Tutsi. The unrest in 1904 had its origins in the scandalous dealings of the traders, the resentment of the Ruanda toward the missionaries, and even the reluctance of the Ruanda to accept the presence of German officers them-selves—but it also had a more fundamental and serious cause.

sold by order of the judge, although his case had never been before the court. See the British Consul General to the Acting Imperial German Governor, 21 August 1906, 17 September 1906, 14 December 1907; for Praetorius's and Schindelar's further offences in Ruanda, see Grawert to Gouvernement, 8 January 1905, 15 March 1905, USU. II I/D/28.

[6] Grawert's report of 5 December. By March 1905 the coloured traders had extended their activity to Urundi; Grawert requested a decree to ban the traders from Ruanda and Urundi; 'Musinga's relation to the whole affair can only be described as praiseworthy.' Grawert to Gouvernement, 15 March 1905.

Musinga, though recognized as the absolute sovereign of Ruanda, was more limited in power than the Germans had at first suspected. To be sure, Kissabo was a petty chief in comparison to the mighty ruler of Ruanda. But within the court of Musinga, two powerful factions contended against one another for the favour of Musinga, and, in case of his death, for control of the choice of his successor. One faction was the Wega, led by the chief Kaware; the other was the Banjiginja, guided by Kansogera, the mother of Musinga. Ostensibly Musinga's rule was a monolithic and absolute despotism; in reality he survived only because he shrewdly manipulated these contending forces. Musinga had recognized the advent of the Germans as a chance to consolidate his own power; if the Germans would persecute his enemies, he would grant the Germans nominal sovereignty over Ruanda while he retained the real power over his people. There were in any case many other benefits to be gained through friendship with the Germans. From the German point of view, recognition of Musinga as mwami was the only way to avoid a war with the most powerful African state in German East Africa; there was everything to be said in favour of 'indirect rule'. But it was not until 1904 that the Germans learned that beneath the veneer of absolutism was political turmoil that could lead to civil war. Recent agitation against the missionaries and traders was at bottom directed against the rule of Musinga himself.[7]

From the beginning German policy had consistently supported Musinga. If this policy was to remain successful, it was essential that aliens in Ruanda cooperate with the German authorities. This the missionaries knew; they were responsible only in small part for the unrest in Ruanda. Activities of the petty coloured merchants, however, could lead eventually to an explosive situation.

The ordinance of the German East Africa government of 10 March 1905[8] decreed that special permission in the form of a licence must be obtained before expeditions could travel to Ruanda-Urundi and before trade could be conducted there. The ordinance was not designed to retard the economic development of Ruanda and Urundi, but to protect the Africans

---

[7] Grawert to Gouvernement, 5 December.
[8] *Amtlicher Anzeiger für Deutsch Ostafrika,* 10 March 1905, VI, no. 7.

from the unscrupulous methods of the coloured merchants. It was a temporary measure, to last only until 'specified markets can be built, where trading can take place. . . . This system seems to me to be the only one that will make supervision possible.'[9] The difficulty in 1904–6 was that the German force was not adequate to ensure fair trade between the Africans and the merchants.

Yet Ruanda and Urundi had a large military force compared to other parts of the colony. By 1905 the Germans had established posts at Tschiwitoke, Ischangi, and Kisenyi; all were under the command of the military station at Usumbura. The main purpose of this military force was to occupy the disputed Kivu territory; German activity in Ruanda-Urundi was more a military occupation than a colonial administration.

In 1906 this was to change. The protectorate force would continue to defend German territory against the Congolese troops; but civil authority was to be established. By 1906 the military had achieved a great deal in Ruanda-Urundi. The sovereignty of Kissabo over Urundi had been restored; Beringe's 'divide and rule' policy had been corrected to Götzen's original policy of 'indirect rule'. In Ruanda, friendship with Musinga was effective and auspicious. It was time to move ahead politically and economically with the 'pearl of German East Africa'. In 1906 military occupation of Ruanda-Urundi was to end and colonial administration was to begin.

[9] Grawert to Gouvernement, 5 December 1904.

XIII. THE URUNDI RESIDENCY, 1906-14

The mwami himself has nothing to say except in his own village. . . .
In short, his political influence is non-existent; he exists because
tradition says that he must; but he is not the ruler of the country.
(Von Stegman, Resident of Urundi, 1911)[1]

By the time that German rule had established itself firmly in
the northwest of the colony around the turn of the century, the
central government at Dar es Salaam had experimented, not
always successfully, for over a decade with ways to rule an
African colony. One result was a division of German East
Africa into administrative and military districts (*Bezirke*),
which corresponded roughly with natural geographical features
and tribal boundaries. As a district was pacified it passed from
military to civil administration. Ruanda and Urundi were part
of the 'Ujiji district' until the founding of the military station
at Usumbura in 1896; they then became the 'Usumbura
district' until 1906. The districts of German East Africa were
administered by district officers (*Bezirksamtmänner*), how in
many cases—as in Ruanda-Urundi—were officers in the
protectorate force (*Schutztruppe*). The counterpart of the protectorate force was the police force (*Polizeitruppe*) of the civil
administration. The military and civil hierarchies overlapped,
and in some instances duplicated each other's functions. Although officers in the protectorate force became civil administrators (in part because of the great shortage of civilian staff)
they sometimes remained under the jurisdiction of the protectorate force, which was in turn subordinate to the civil
authority of the Governor of German East Africa. The key to
the basic administrative policy of this complicated civil-
military bureaucracy was the hut tax, which varied from region
to region depending on local circumstances. The purpose of
the hut tax, according to Götzen, was not to raise large revenues for the government, but to educate Africans to continuous
and responsible labour. The collection of the hut tax was one

[1] Urundi Jahresbericht 1910/11, I/A/8.

of the main responsibilities of the district officer; he was assisted by *akidas*, minor coloured officials, and *jumbes*, 'headmen' appointed by the district officer in each of the tribes. The abuses of the *akidas* and *jumbes* was one of the causes of the bloody Maji-Maji uprising in 1905, and was also one reason why the German administration decided not to try to establish the same system in Ruanda-Urundi.

The basic reason why Ruanda-Urundi was to be administered in a fundamentally different way from the rest of the colony, however, was the constant fear that too much interference with traditional Tutsi authority might incite an uprising that would be disastrous for German rule. The Tutsi could not be bullied and intimidated with the same success the Germans had had with Africans in other parts of the colony. And the German administration was flexible enough to recognize that different circumstances demanded different policies. 'I am as convinced as ever', wrote the Acting Governor in June 1906, 'that it would be mistaken to try now to break up the great and well established sultanates for the purpose of imposing German government in the form of district administration dependent on single negroes or the smallest communities. The present tightly organized political structure of the sultanates offers a favourable opportunity to administer and develop culturally the natives through their traditional rulers with the least expense concerning paid administrators and least recourse to European force.'[2] Haber, the Acting Governor, did not think that civil administrators could replace the officers of the protectorate force at that time, because of the shortage of civilian staff; but the protectorate force had several responsible and experienced officers who could serve for the present as civil 'Residents' of Ruanda and Urundi. As in other parts of German East Africa, the relations between the civil and military authority would be a problem. 'The introduction of the German system at the courts of the sultans might appear a duality, with on the one hand, a company commander with several European officers and non-commissioned officers and strong, well-drilled African troops; and, on the other hand, a Resident and a secretary and a clerk, and a few police. . . .' Cooperation

---

[2] Haber to A.A., Kolonialabteilung, 18 June 1906, RU. I I/D/28.

between the civil and military personnel would be absolutely essential because of the importance of the experiment.[3]

As Grawert became the Resident in 1906 (while at the same time retaining military command of the IX Company at Usumbura), he continued successfully to maintain good relations with Kissabo;[4] by 1908 Kissabo, with Grawert's help, had brought the remaining refractory chiefs under his control. This marked the most successful point in German Urundi policy; if Urundi were still not so centralized and efficiently administered as Ruanda, at least there was more stability than ever before, as well as indications that the situation would continue to improve.

1906–8 saw the triumph of German indirect rule in Urundi; but a period of indecision and recurrent failure followed. The establishment of the Residency in Urundi had the misfortune of coinciding with a period of transition in the German East Africa government. Von Rechenberg became the new governor; Grawert returned to Germany for home leave in 1908; he was succeeded by a bewildering number of Residents in Urundi.

Even if the new German authorities had been determined to continue the policy of indirect rule, they would have found the ideas of Götzen and Grawert impossible to implement. For Götzen and Grawert had not anticipated the collapse of the entire Rundi political system in 1908. German control over Urundi that had taken years to achieve was destroyed by the death of the sixty-three year old Kissabo. The German Resident reported as late as 1911: 'The Residency in the far south, east and northeast of the district does not have the slightest influence.'[5] Although the Resident had made earnest attempts to cooperate with Mutaga, Kissabo's successor, Mutaga and his mentors had responded with 'lies, empty promises and opposition'.[6]

Kissabo's death was followed not by revolution—as one of the new Residents, Göring, had feared—but by what the Germans

---

[3] Ibid.

[4] 'Grawert filled his difficult post with diplomatic adroitness and great circumspection, and he had a masterly way of bringing the natives—who at first were somewhat refractory—under the control of the German government.' Mecklenburg, *In the Heart of Africa*, p. 45. Cf. J. von der Burgt, *Gott Will Es!*, 1901, XIII, pp. 161–7.

[5] Urundi Jahresbericht 1910/11, I/A/8.   [6] Ibid.

regarded as chaos, not a new phenomenon in Urundi. The young mwami Mutaga IV (1908–15) had no influence at all; the Rundi government, as far as there was one, was dominated by his numerous older relatives, of whom the most important and oldest was Ntarrugera (Seruschanya). Mutaga, about fifteen years old, was recognized by most of the Rundi chiefs as the nominal ruler of Urundi, but only in central Urundi could it be said that the mwami actually controlled his subjects.[7] In northeastern Urundi, the chiefs Lussokossa, Bansabugabo, and Lusengo had renewed their old struggle for independence. Other chiefs who had been loyal to the old mwami saw the weakness of Mutaga as a chance to strengthen their independence at his expense. Kiraranganya and Senyawatara in eastern Urundi continued to pay tribute to Mutaga by sending him gifts, but in fact 'completely do as they please'. In southern Urundi the situation was worst; Mutaga and his group did not even know the names of the chiefs who opposed him. Von Stegman, the Resident in 1911, pointed out that it was erroneous to believe that the mwami was an omnipotent ruler: 'It is also an error to assume that this "mwami" has the power to rule and does rule, and that each follows his orders without question. This is simply not the case—the mwami is only in tradition the predestined possessor of a sacred title; he received this through circumstances of birth, by having a mother from a certain family, and further because of certain mystical indications, and finally because of practical considerations of his clan. These practical considerations are decided in every case in favour of a prospective sultan who is a minor, and who therefore will be the instrument of his clan. . . .'[8]

[7] See Urundi Jahresbericht 1909/10, I/A/8.
[8] Urundi Jahresbericht 1909/10, I/A/8. Jacques J. Macquet describes the selection of the mwami in Ruanda: 'Royal succession was not completely fixed by custom. The heir was chosen by the king from among his sons. He was generally one of the youngest because the strength of Ruanda was magically connected with the king's strength. The name of the chosen one was kept secret. Even the future mwami did not know it. It was revealed only after the king's death by the three most important *biru* whom the mwami had entrusted with his decision. The other sons and their mothers generally did not agree willingly to the choice and there was often a period of unrest, even of civil war, before the new mwami became an effective ruler.' *The Premise of Inequality in Ruanda* (London, 1961), p. 125. As Professor Vansina emphasizes, Maquet's description does not apply to Urundi; in Urundi there were no *biru* in the Ruanda sense. In a letter to me of 8 November 1962.

The Tutsi rulers were trapped by their own tradition; the chosen mwami was incapable of ruling Urundi. Mutaga was the eldest son of Kissabo's favourite wife, Ndirikumutima, of the Banjakarama clan. Ntarrugera had been appointed by Kissabo as Mutaga's regent (*Reichsverweser*). Ntarrugera became the dominating personality in Urundi, 'the greatest and richest man in Urundi, whose . . . views are listened to at Mutaga's court because he is feared.' Ntarrugera could control the young mwami and central Urundi, but Ntarrugera himself was as incapable as Mutaga of ruling all of Urundi; this only could be done by a strong mwami. Most of Urundi fell to the powerful chiefs.[9]

Rechenberg, Götzen's successor as governor, tried to adapt indirect rule to the new circumstances. Would it not be best to 'conserve or create' domains (*Sultanaten*) that were 'practical and natural'? In this way the Götzen ideal could be realized; the only difference would be several domains instead of one. The Germans would profit in addition from the old maxim of 'divide and rule'; they would have the best of both worlds.

The Resident was instructed by Rechenberg that Urundi should be divided into three categories. First, the independent chiefs: Busokoza, Mbanzabugabo, and the son of Kilima, with several others in the east and south. These chiefs would no longer be required to recognize the mwami as overlord, but must, of course, continue to recognize German authority. Second, the chiefs who had in the past recognized Kissabo, and who would continue to recognize Mutaga in the future. Third, chiefs who in the past were more or less independent, such as those in the Ruzizi valley, who might with the guidance of the Resident be brought under Mutaga; but these cases would have to be considered on their own merits.[1]

Rechenberg misunderstood the Rundi political system. As Pierre Ryckmans has pointed out, new domains did not have to be created; they were already there, varying from year to year in accordance with the strength of the chiefs. The Rundi chiefs resembled satellites, their separatist tendencies held in check by the power of the mwami. There were also other divi-

---

[9] Urundi Jahresbericht 1911/12, I/A/8.
[1] Ryckmans discusses Rechenberg's policy at length in *Une page d'histoire coloniale*, pp. 16–24.

sions in Rundi society, the most important of which were the factions of the royal family and the old tension between Tutsi and Hutu. Beringe had undermined this delicate system by his defeat of Kissabo; the sovereignty of the mwami had been restored only by great effort. The death of Kissabo, however, weakened the Rundi political structure to a point where even the Germans were unable to restore the mwami's control over Urundi. Rechenberg wanted to preserve the existing authority of the young mwami and his family in central Urundi and at the same time to make peace with the separatist chiefs. Perhaps this was the only way that the Germans could effectively administer Urundi. But Rechenberg did not see that the authority of the mwami was more easily weakened than strengthened, and that separatism throughout Urundi would gain momentum if the great chiefs were allowed to entrench themselves in positions of independence. Rundi government splintered to the end of the German era.

From 1908 to 1912 events seemed uncontrollable to the German officials. In part this was because of the rapid succession of Residents: Fonck, Göring, von Stegman, von Bock, and von Langenn-Steinkeller, few of whom were given the chance to become thoroughly acquainted with Urundi. The annual reports during this time reveal that their understanding of the Resident's responsibility in Urundi often differed from the governor's instructions. Rechenberg wanted to support as far as possible the mwami, giving independence only to a limited number of chiefs. The Residents, however, had little sympathy for the royal family; they tried to 'divide and rule', 'to play one chief off against the other'. Far from theoretical questions of indirect rule, the Residents were concerned with mundane questions such as settling boundary and cattle quarrels between the Rundi chiefs.

In the northeast of Urundi the Resident had to intervene in the small wars of Lusengo, Lussokossa, Tschoja, Muhini, Wirirakusura, Sengobana, and Senyawarungu. After Kissabo's death the feud between the royal family and the family of Kilima (who was now represented by his son, Kasliwami) was resumed. In June, July, and August 1909 the Resident delimited definitely the boundary between the two and announced that he would not tolerate further aggressions on the part of

Mutaga's people. Nonetheless in February 1910 a chief of Mutaga called Karagi invaded Kasliwami's territory and burnt a number of huts, injuring three people. Lt. Wintgens was despatched to punish Karagi.[2]

Kilima was allowed to return from exile in 1910. He was no longer regarded by the German authorities as a danger to the mwami, and therefore as a danger to German rule, but as a salutary counterweight to the disruptive influences of Mutaga. 'Kilima has grown older, but still makes a vigorous impression; he seems to have acquired in exile a whole series of new experiences, and also the intention of making use of them now in his own territory.' Kilima's return had had a noticeable effect on Mutaga's clan: 'they fear him very much. And that is good!'[3]

All this was a complete change in attitude on the part of the German officers. Until 1908 Grawert had regarded the activities of Kilima, Lusengo, Lussokossa, and Bansabugabo as undermining German rule itself. The separatist efforts of these chiefs were now welcomed as a means to secure a stability which Mutaga was incapable of providing. This was true also of the increasing independence of Wirirakusura and Muhini near Lake Tschohoha; Tschoja, near Lake Rugwero; Senyawarungu, near the Muyaga mission; Kiraganja, to the south, and Ndugu, in the hinterland from Lake Tanganyika. All of these chiefs now dealt directly with the German officers, and more or less cooperated with the German efforts to increase crop productivity, conserve forests, and construct roads. In the Tanganyika valley the semi-independent chiefs (who still gave token submission to the mwami) by 1912 also had direct relations with the Resident, and helped him in the German attempts to combat sleeping sickness. By 1912 the Germans were able to maintain an uneasy peace between the chiefs in the north and northeast; central Urundi remained under the control of Mutaga. Only in southern Urundi was German authority non-existent.[4]

The disregard of German authority in southern Urundi was an extreme example of a common problem. German rule

[2] Urundi Jahresbericht 1909/10, I/A/8.
[3] Urundi Jahresbericht 1910/11, I/A/8.
[4] Urundi Jahresbericht 1911/12, I/A/8.

diminished in direct proportion to the distance from Usumbura. The Germans could never hope to rule Urundi successfully as long as the Residency remained at Usumbura; only by moving inland could the Germans impose on the Rundi a respect for order and permanent stability. Von Langenn-Steinkeller, one of the later Residents who understood Urundi better than most of his colleagues, recognized that from an inland station the Resident would at least be able to keep the Rundi chiefs under constant supervision.

There was another reason why the Germans regarded the transfer of the Residency inland as necessary. In contrast to the cool, healthy, densely populated highlands of the interior of Urundi, the Tanganyika coastal plain was hot, unpleasant, sparsely populated, and ravaged with tropical diseases. Every year the German authorities and Africans alike suffered from malaria, dysentery, and worms. Despite preventive measures, six Europeans during 1910–11 had become infected with sleeping sickness. Moving the Residency from Usumbura to Kitega would free at least part of the German staff from the anxieties of poor health and the strenuous prophylactic efforts necessary in a tropical region infested with disease. As had been expressed in the German reports for several years, the stimulus given German morale by moving from Usumbura would itself invigorate German administration.

The raising of the German flag over Kitega on 15 August 1912 and the advent of the conscientious and energetic Dr. Heinrich Schnee as Governor of German East Africa marked the beginning of the final period of German rule in Urundi.

The new Residency at Kitega was 'very favourably situated in a central location, about four hours south of the Mugera mission, on a well watered high plateau which commands a good view; it is close to Ntarrugera's territory. . . . Mutaga and Ntarrugera, as well as all of the chiefs who have visited the Resident here or whom he has met during his district travels, vivaciously express their delight over the founding of the Residency at Kitega'. The location itself belonged to Mutaga, who immediately declared it as 'Crownland' (*Kronland*) of the German East Africa government. In July 1913 the IX Company, a detachment of whom had stayed at Kitega during the

early months of the Residency there, returned to the Usumbura
garrison. The civil administration at Kitega was left with three
Europeans.[5]

Schimmer, the last German Resident during peace time, and
Langenn, his predecessor, were the first German officers fully
to understand the complexities of Urundi. They saw that as in
Ruanda the royal family was divided into factions competing
for the favour and control of the mwami. The dominant influence on Mutaga was his mother, Ndirikumutima, a Muniakar-
ama; she was an intelligent and shrewd woman. Ndirikumutima's arch-rival was Ntarrugera, the regent of Mutaga.
Ntarrugera regarded himself as a pure *ganwa*, or 'prince of the
royal blood'. Mutaga during his formative years was caught
between these two influences. This division in the royal family
between Mutaga's mother and his regent enabled the separatist
Rundi chiefs to withdraw beyond the influence of the mwami;
this was greatly facilitated by the Germans, who after the death
of Kissabo, recognized their independence. What appeared to
the Germans in 1908 as 'chaos' was in reality a struggle for
domination between Ndirikumutima and Ntarrugera. Both
wanted to preserve the territorial integrity of Urundi in face
of the seceding chiefs; but neither could succeed while contending against the other. The powerful Kissabo himself had only
with the utmost difficulty succeeded in gaining nominal submission from Rundi chiefs.[6]

The German officers in 1908 had not understood these forces
in Rundi politics. They had seen only a weak mwami incapable
of ruling his country. The only alternative to chaos, they
thought, was the recognition of the most important chiefs. This
policy had not been entirely unsuccessful. By 1912 the German
authorities were able to maintain order and had prevented
war between the chiefs. But things were far from the way the
Germans might have preferred them. If there was general
peace, there were also continual border quarrels and cattle
disputes between the chiefs. The Germans were forced to act
as arbitrators in an unceasing wrangling and bickering over
things that a strong mwami would have settled for them.
Was there a hope that Mutaga might develop into an mwami
capable of alleviating the German administrative burdens in

[5] Urundi Jahresbericht, 1911/12.   [6] Ibid.

Urundi? In 1911 the local German authorities still regarded the situation in Urundi as basically hopeless although Mutaga and the authority of the mwami had not yet suffered decisive defeat.[7] In May 1914, however, Schimmer wrote that Mutaga had grown into manhood; he was much less shy, often dressed in European clothes, and had begun to learn to read and write Swahili. Schimmer occasionally took Mutaga with him on district trips; in this way the mwami was gaining a first hand knowledge of his country. The influence of Mutaga's mother seemed to be diminishing; Ntarrugera confined himself more and more to his own territory, although he was said still to have great influence over Mutaga. The mwami was assuming more responsibility. Yet his own territory in central Urundi continued to splinter. Despite Mutaga's increasing personal authority, Rundi government by 1913 was so fragmented that it was impossible to begin again to centralize it. In the north, east, and south the great chiefs were almost independent of Mutaga; Schimmer in 1913 thought that the best policy would be to complete the break, 'to divide these territories generally and with as little friction as possible from Mutaga'. In holding this view, Schimmer was acting in accordance with the instructions of Governor Schnee.[8]

Schnee was following basically the same policy as Rechenberg. In June 1913 Schnee instructed the Resident of Urundi to continue to support the authority of Mutaga only 'in the territories where he really possesses authority'.[9] Schnee was optimistic about German administration in Urundi; he thought things would improve with time and patience. Yet by the end of 1915 the situation in Urundi was perhaps worse than at anytime during the German era.

There were three reasons for this sudden deterioration. The first was the continued rivalry between Ndirikumutima and Ntarrugera, complicated by the increasing independence of Mutaga. The second was the outbreak of the First World War. The third was the unexpected death of Mutaga at the end of 1915.

The annual report of 1913 stated that Ntarrugera still exerted considerable influence on Mutaga. But this rapidly

[7] Ibid.   [8] Urundi Jahresbericht 1913/14, I/A/8.
[9] Schnee to Residentur Urundi, 15 June 1913, UR. IV I/D/8.

changed. Ndirikumutima allied with the chiefs in the northeast against Ntarrugera; Mutaga himself soon looked for the opportunity to rid himself of his regent. In October 1914 Ntarrugera and his brother Rugema arrived at Kitega to demand that the Resident recognize their independence. Mutaga, they said, was nothing but an instrument of his mother's views. Ntarrugera was granted independence by the Acting Resident, Wolf, in June 1915 on grounds that Mutaga and his mother were provoking the chiefs in the northeast against him. At this time Ntarrugera was at war with Bansabugabo; Mutaga saw this as a chance to ally himself with the chiefs in the northeast against Ntarrugera—this was a new combination in Rundi politics.

In the midst of these troubles war had broken out between the great powers; to add to Germany's difficulties in Urundi, the Resident Schimmer was killed in the Luvungi engagement in 1915.[1] Langenn, who returned after Schimmer's death to become the last Urundi Resident, ignored Ntarrugera's independence, and, in fact, called upon him to serve again as regent after the death of Mutaga. The events leading to Mutaga's death had been preluded by the death of his twelve-year-old brother in September 1913 and another brother, Bangura, in October 1915. Mutaga claimed that they had been poisoned; no member of the royal family could die a natural death. This theory is not entirely implausible, as Ntarrugera during the later years refused to visit the court of Mutaga for fear of poison. It is more probable, however, that at least one of Mutaga's brothers and he himself, according to the German documents, were victims of malaria. Mutaga died on 30 November 1915.[2] This was a crowning blow to the almost unbelievably poor luck which the Germans had had in administering Urundi. In late 1915 the German situation in Urundi was critical; they had only a token force against overwhelming enemy numbers; the collapse of the authority of the mwami increased their difficulty. German rule in

---

[1] See below, pp. 211-2.

[2] Langenn's telegram is in UR. IV I/D/34. Cf. the information given to Professor Vansina: 'Nduwumwe (the later regent) told me that Mutaga had quarrelled over a woman with Bangura and each had wounded the other. Both later died from the wounds. Poison according to him was to be ruled out.' In a letter to me of 8 November 1962.

Urundi ended shortly after the proclamation of Mutaga's son Mwambutsa IV as mwami on 16 December 1915.[3]

Through the years of administration in Urundi, the German officers gained complete cooperation from neither Kissabo nor Mutaga, neither the members of the royal family nor the great chiefs, neither the rulers of Urundi nor the populace. 'The well-known passive resistance of the Rundi comes to light as soon as the hand of the government is not held directly over the chiefs; if he is far away . . . then he does not bother about the administration. . . . Administration is not a pleasant thing for the Rundi.'[4] The Germans had failed to maintain consistently good relations with the rulers of Urundi; they were also passively resented by the bulk of the population. It is not surprising that the German administration was attacked publicly for its shortcomings.

An article appeared in the missionary journal *Afrika-Bote* in July 1913[5] entitled 'Die Gottvergessenheit in Urundi', written by a White Father, P. J. Gassldinger. This article is of especial interest because it was a sharp indictment of German colonialism in Urundi. Solf, the German Colonial Secretary, ordered an investigation to see whether the charges were justified.[6] The local authorities consequently prepared a point by point defence for the German Colonial Office. The controversy illuminates the main problems that the Germans faced in Urundi, and the accomplishments and failures of the administration.

The charges against the Urundi administration fell into three parts. The first was a specific accusation that the Residency at Kitega was being built by 'starved and exhausted' unpaid workers—'even Sunday is not a day of rest'. This charge applied to all public works in Urundi. The second charge was that the policies followed by the Residents were retarding the economic development of the region. The third accusation was the most damning—that the Germans had failed in their

[3] Some of the documents for the last years of the German period are in UR. IV I/D/34. Many of the ones which Ryckmans used, however, are now missing from the Usumbura archive; so see Ryckmans's *Une page d'histoire coloniale* for further detail.

[4] Urundi Jahresbericht 1913/14.

[5] X, pp. 305–10.

[6] Solf to Gouverneur, 16 July 1913, UR. IV I/D/33.

civilizing mission, that they were ruling an oppressed people filled with 'sullen anger and hatred' for the administration.

Langenn and Schimmer began their reply[7] to the first charge by explaining the general difficulties the administration had had with the Rundi while the Residency was at Usumbura. The Rundi feared diseases along the coast; therefore they stayed inland, where it was hard for the Resident to make contact with them. For this reason it had been impossible to levy taxes, except to a limited extent along the coast of Lake Tanganyika. Even when the Resident moved to Kitega it was still impossible to collect taxes because of the 'shyness' of the Rundi and the long period of time required for them to adjust to European administration. 'If taxes are to be collected', Schimmer wrote, 'then the people must be advanced enough not to run away; for collections do not come readily from fugitives.' But the German officers had made a start: 'when the Residency began its work at its new location of Kitega, it tried to establish a closer feeling with the people.' In accordance with the customs of the country, the Resident received support from the mwami and the great chiefs, who said that groups of their people would be glad to help the Germans build their new Residency. It was difficult for many Rundi to pay taxes; but by helping to construct the Residency they would fulfil their tax obligations.[8] Gifts were also given to the chiefs, and sometimes one or two cows to the workers themselves. In this way the Rundi 'become accustomed to Europeans and are trained to work'. The allegation of 'starved and exhausted' labourers, Langenn and Schimmer said, was nonsense; a group of about fifty Africans under one chief would come for approximately a month; these fifty did not stay for the entire month, however, but were replaced after a week by others, who brought fresh provisions with them. This system had great advantages. It brought the Resident into contact with more and more people, who were given the opportunity to see Kitega, Europeans, and the administration. Schimmer noticed that when he made trips around the country fewer people ran away; some even approached 'to say something friendly'; usually they were

[7] Langenn's 'Bericht an das Reich-Kolonialamt', 25 September 1913, and Schimmer's letter to the central government, 29 September 1913, UR. IV I/D/34. Schimmer's letter is more detailed.
[8] See note J, p. 275.

those who had worked at Kitega. And there were many other things of positive value learned at Kitega; for instance, that if sick one could receive medical treatment, although admittedly, Schimmer said, only in serious cases because the administration had no doctor.[9] As for the charge that the Africans were forced to work on Sunday, what difference did it make, since the Rundi were neither Christians nor Mohammedans? The administration had, however, stopped work on Sundays since there was no rush to finish construction. Another justification of compulsory labour at Kitega was that the Africans were learning to use latrines, 'which must seem ridiculous to a Rundi', but which had important hygienic results in fighting diseases. If the missionaries were asked whether their Africans used latrines, 'they would blush and say that their people were not so far along.' All in all, Langenn and Schimmer concluded, the experience of the Africans on the German public works led them to trust the administration and convinced them of its justice and propriety.[1]

The second accusation was that the administration in Urundi was retarding the economic development of the region. Urundi was 'sealed off' from the rest of the colony; Europeans were not allowed to settle there. Gassldinger charged that 'money is unknown' in Urundi and that the Resident even refused to permit the Rundi to leave the country to work on projects such as railway construction. In reply to these charges, Langenn and Schimmer began by admitting that there had been some confusion over the ordinances restricting immigration of the coloured merchants into Urundi, but after the establishment of the Residency at Kitega the government had clearly announced in 1913 that the region was now open to trade.[2] A market at Kitega had been constructed so that the administration could supervise the transactions between the traders and the Rundi. Money was well-known at Kitega and would always be accepted by Africans, although sometimes not eagerly. 'The Resident diligently encourages circulation of money and explains its worth in relation to the exchanged goods.' That money was not better known in Urundi, Schimmer stated, was

[9] See note K, p. 276.
[1] Langenn's report of 25 September 1913 and Schimmer's letter of 29 September 1913.
[2] See below, chapter XV.

the fault of the missionaries, who preferred barter exchanges because they profited from the Africans more that way. What money there was seemed to be possessed mostly by the chiefs; but money would gain more general circulation with the growth of trade. The difficulty was to attract commerce to Urundi; contrary to Gassldinger's criticisms, the administration did encourage trade and wished that European traders in particular would come to Urundi. Only in southern Urundi was immigration still prohibited; that region would remain closed until a police post could be established there.[3] The rest of Urundi, however, was completely open to trade; but none had come. The *Internationale Handelsgesellschaft* had said in August 1911 that they were going to establish a firm in Kitega, but the only representative so far was an Arab who lived in a straw hut. 'This is the way it has been with other Europeans: words, letters, but no actions, even though the Resident wants to smooth the way for them.' There would be greater difficulties for planters who might want to come to Urundi, because of the shortage of land. 'For where the Hutu do not have their own crops, all the rest of the good land is used by the great cattle herds as pasture.' Even the missionaries, who mostly required only small plots of land, had found it extremely difficult to find appropriate places. Trade, however, was a different question, Langenn explained: 'to attract white traders to Urundi has been a zealous striving of the Resident.' As to the charge that Africans were not permitted to leave Urundi to earn money on plantations and railway construction, Schimmer stated, this was 'untrue'. On the contrary, 'the Resident would be delighted if people freely left'. But the Resident did not intend to permit Urundi to be used as a source of labour supply for the rest of the colony. If Africans were deported *en masse* from Urundi they would quickly succumb to tropical diseases unknown in the highlands of Urundi; their eventual return would contaminate Urundi itself. Langenn and Schimmer concluded that Urundi had a hopeful economic future, but that it was dependent on responsible European traders. European trade in Urundi, despite encouragement from the Residents, had failed so far to materialize.[4]

[3] The Niakassu police post was established in southern Urundi on 12 December 1913.
[4] Same as footnote 1, p. 141.

The last charge against the German administration in Urundi was that it had failed in its mission of guiding a backward people toward 'civilization and culture'. Langenn and Schimmer replied that this was untrue, and that most of the missionaries themselves readily acknowledged the splendid job accomplished by the Resident. As far as 'civilization' was concerned, Schimmer said, Father Gassldinger had several wrong ideas. The Rundi were not an especially pleasant and 'gemütlich' people who could be easily guided to civilization, although they were highly industrious compared to other negroes. One of the main problems was that 'the negro lies, the Hutu to a high extent; the Tutsi is a master of lies'. 'There is a Rundi proverb: he lies like a Tutsi.' The administration had to contend with 'insubordination and impertinences' on the part of a large number of the population, who in the north and south were almost entirely 'uncivilized'. This was no 'native paradise' which could be easily civilized, but the administration had taken some important steps in that direction. For instance, a great problem was that the Rundi tended to use their weapons freely; there were many instances of injuries and even murder in which the Germans had to administer justice. To curtail the indiscriminate use of weapons the Resident had forbidden the Africans to carry spears, bows and arrows while in Kitega or Usumbura or other German posts, or when with a caravan going through the country. This had had results: 'the Rundi has learned that one can go without weapons.' Deaths by fights with spears had diminished, 'especially in Usumbura and Kitega, where fights between drunk men are now for the most part unbloody'.[5] As for the allegation that none of the German officers could speak Rundi, this was more or less true, but with the appearance of the *Deutsch-Kinyaruanda Sprachführer* it would be easier to learn the language. The French White Fathers had had for some time a *Französisch-Kirundi Grammatik* which had helped them, but in any case the White Fathers seemed to have a special talent for languages. It would be surprising and even pitiful, moreover, if the White Fathers, who had been in Urundi since 1896, could not speak Rundi. A Protestant missionary who had mastered two other Bantu languages had told Schimmer that Rundi was an especially difficult language. 'The

[5] Ibid.

German officials have only been in Urundi a short time; because of the shortage of staff and because there is much other work to be done, there is little time left to learn Rundi.'[6]

The really important charge, however, was that the Germans were ruling an oppressed people. And this, Schimmer said, depended upon one's point of view. If by this charge was meant that 'the oppressed, the Tutsi, highly dislike our administration and regard it as something to which they must adjust themselves, this I readily admit. I do not know anyone, however, who believes that the negro loves us'. There was no use trying to deceive oneself that the Africans in Urundi were especially fond of German administration; but were they anywhere else? German rule in Urundi had been peaceful. Considering the ups and downs of Rundi politics, the Germans had achieved a great deal. By 1914 the Resident could say that many Rundi now recognized the advantages of 'law and trade'.[7]

But if Gassldinger's article was nothing more than sensational journalism, it nevertheless raised questions to which the German administration in Urundi could not always give entirely satisfactory answers. Gassldinger was not the first to make the charge that German administration in Urundi had been a failure. As Governor Schnee stated in 1913: 'The history of Urundi since the German occupation is unfortunately not pleasant, and stands in contrast to the . . . peaceful and pleasant state of things in Ruanda.'[8]

---

[6] Ibid.

[7] Ibid. See also the Jahresbericht for 1913/14. Schimmer thought that Gassldinger's article was libellous, and that Langenn and Bock, the Residents against whom the article was directed, should legally prosecute him. Gassldinger, however, died of sun-stroke at the Save mission on 14 October 1913 while on his way to a meeting of White Fathers in Ruanda. See 'Dem Andenken des Missionspreisters Joseph Gassldinger', *Afrika-Bote*, XX, pp. 102–4.

[8] 'Die nordwestlichen Gebiete Deutsch-Ostafrikas—Aus dem Reisebericht des Gouverneurs Dr. Schnee', *Kolonialblatt*, XXI, September 1913, p. 752.

XIV. THE RUANDA RESIDENCY, 1907–14

> The fundamental principle is the same with all Residents. It is desired to strengthen and enrich the sultan and persons in authority, and to increase thereby their interest in the continuance of German rule, so that the desire for revolt shall die away, as the consequences of a rebellion would be a dwindling of their revenues. At the same time, by steadily controlling and directing the sultan and using his powers, civilizing influences would be introduced. Thus by degrees, and almost imperceptibly to the people and to the sultan himself, he eventually would be nothing less than the executive instrument of the Resident. (The Duke of Mecklenburg, 1910)[1]

THE mwami of Ruanda during the German era came closer to absolute rule than his counterparts in Urundi. The same patterns of social and political organization existed in both countries. But Ruanda was more organized than Urundi. In Urundi the goal was civil administration, but the Germans achieved only military occupation. The history of Ruanda, in contrast, was the history of a more successful attempt to introduce principles of European law and commerce.

During 1906 and through part of 1907 Grawert served as Resident for both Ruanda and Urundi. During this time his main concern in centralizing Ruanda was with the refractory chiefs in the north—Ruanda's equivalent to Urundi's separatism. Southern Mfumbiro had never been integrated into Ruanda, just as southern, southeastern and northeastern Urundi had not been part of Urundi before Kissabo. Musinga's authority over northern Ruanda was only nominal; in some cases the chiefs were completely independent from his control. The powerful Muhumusa (the wife of the mwami Rwabugiri, who fled to northern Ruanda after Rwabugiri's death and Musinga's accession) in particular refused to recognize the authority of Musinga, although the region under her sway was still considered as part of Ruanda. In general, however, northern Ruanda was not characterized by powerful chiefs, but by petty rulers who exercised power only within limited regions.

---

[1] *In the Heart of Africa*, p. 46.

In February 1907 Grawert suggested that the German administration should bring the refractory chiefs under the control of Musinga; this would facilitate administration and would be consistent with the policy of centralization in Ruanda. But, said Grawert, the pacification of northern Ruanda should be delayed until the establishment of a separate Ruanda Residency in Ruanda itself; the extension of Musinga's rule in the north would have to be backed by German force.[2]

The five-year interval between the founding of the Residency at Kigali in 1907 and the one at Kitega in 1912 was one reason why the Ruanda Residency was more successful. Another reason for the comparative success of the Ruanda Residency was that it did not suffer from so great a turnover in personnel. The selection of the first Resident offered no problem. Was there anyone more qualified as a prospective Resident than the explorer, poet, and scientist of Ruanda, Dr. Richard Kandt?[3]

Kandt arrived in Kigali to assume his responsibilities as Resident in August 1907. A year earlier he had submitted to the central government two long memoranda about Ruanda government.[4]

Kandt described the political and social organization in the same way as have some anthropologists—in the language of feudalism. The absolute monarch, the king, was the semi-divine mwami. The Tutsi were the aristocrats, the Hutu the commoners. The feudal system of obligations worked through land, military service, and cattle.[5]

Regardless of the accuracy of describing an African society in terms of European feudalism, there could be no doubt, as

[2] Grawert to Gouvernement, 17 February 1907, RU. II I/D/33.
[3] Born 17 December 1867 in Posen; studied medicine in Leipzig, Würzburg, Heidelberg, and Munich. Practised as a medical doctor in Munich, where he became interested in African exploration. Studied African languages and geography in Berlin, and subsequently assumed an important role in the exploration of the northwestern part of German East Africa during the late 1890s. Represented the German East Africa government as Resident of Ruanda from 1907 to 1913, when he returned to Germany for home leave. On the outbreak of the First World War he volunteered as a medical doctor and died as a result of gas poisoning on 29 April 1918. See 'Dr. Richard Kandts Heimkehr aus Africa', *Afrika-Bote*, IX, 1903, pp. 2–4; and his obituary by Franz Stuhlmann in the *Kolonialzeitung*, XXXV, May 1918, pp. 74–75.
[4] Entitled 'Denkschrift über die Aufgaben der Verwaltung in Ruanda', dated 13–14 August 1906 and 15–16 August 1906, RU. I I/D/33; see also 'Politische Organisation der Eingeborenen in Ruanda', by Gudovius, undated, in RU. IV I/D/33; and the Ruanda Jahresbericht 1911/12, I/A/8.
[5] Ibid.

Gudovius, a later Resident of Ruanda, expressed it, that this was an 'uncommonly complicated' society. From the beginning the Germans had no intention of changing it, although they regretted that it was not more conducive to European administration. There were several reasons for this decision. The bulk of the population seemed content with the system; any attempt to alter the authority of the chiefs over their regions or to group them into convenient administrative districts would cause 'discontent and bitterness'. In addition, Musinga would regard land reform or any tampering with the system of obligations as a threat to his own authority. It was expedient for the Germans to remain on good terms with Musinga; it was quite impracticable to try to reshape or reform Ruanda society, especially since there was no obvious remedy. The decision not to interfere basically with the social and political institutions of Ruanda was consistent with the policy of support for Musinga.[6]

For years Musinga had urged the German authorities—including the Duke of Mecklenburg when he passed through Ruanda—to banish Muhumusa, his rival in northern Ruanda. Muhumusa was the mother of Bilegea, the half-brother of Musinga and pretender to the title of mwami. She was Musinga's deadly enemy and could arouse much trouble in northern Ruanda with her magical powers. In mid-1909 Gudovius captured Muhumusa and brought her to Kigali. This was a mistake, for as they approached Kigali rumours spread among the Hutu that Muhumusa and Bilegea with the help of the Germans would abolish the rule of Musinga. Gudovius's arrival in Kigali with Muhumusa coincided with the arrival of the troops from Usumbura sent to protect Ruanda from the 'invasion' of the British Kivu expedition. This gave further impetus to the rumour, which gained such strength that the Hutu in eastern Ruanda were ready to overthrow their Tutsi chiefs. Muhumusa was quickly deported to Bukoba and the agitation subsequently died; but for a short time the German action had the opposite from the desired effect. Through the unfortunate combination of circumstances the rule of the mwami had threatened to crumble rather than crystallize. Eventually, however, Musinga was grateful that

6 Ibid.

his enemy had been removed. The Germans had taken a definite step towards the pacification of northern Ruanda.[7]

Apart from the Hutu unrest encouraged by Muhumusa, the
main cause of trouble in northern Ruanda were the pygmoid
Twa. In other parts of Ruanda and Urundi, scattered Twa
lived peacefully as potters. 'Next to the ruling, cattle-rearing
Tutsi and the agricultural Hutu, they form to a certain extent
the remaining lowest caste, an ancient people despised, feared,
hated by the other natives, and excluded from the community
of eating; they are nevertheless tolerated and occasionally
mingle with the lowest Hutu.' In northern Ruanda, however,
there were less peaceful 'forest or swamp Twa', who lived south
of the volcanoes in primeval forests and east of the volcanoes in
the great swamps, especially in the Mruschaschi swamp. These
hostile Twa refused to acknowledge Musinga as their overlord;
through their frequent robberies and raids they had become 'the
plague of the country'. Their number was small—there were
only about 100 'warrior' Twa—but they had been strengthened
by outlaw Hutu, who had fled to the north as fugitives from
the mwami and the Germans. 'Neither the intelligent and
normally energetic Tutsi nor the Hutu, with their masses, dare
to drive the dwarfs out of their lurking places and to punish
them.' One source of strength was their inaccessible territory;
they could easily retreat into the forest or swamps. Another
was the superstitious fear by the Tutsi and the Hutu of the Twa:
'one-half dozen dwarfs emerging from the swamp are enough to
rout hundreds and thousands of Hutu.' Formerly the 'forest
dwarfs' had been content with the occasional abduction of
children and theft of food. The Africans in their immediate
area had appeased them by placing provisions at their disposal;
like the elves of German folklore, they vanished with their booty
into the forest. Recently, however, the Twa had become more
aggressive with blatant robberies. With all his numberless
subjects the mwami was powerless against a 'handful of dwarfs'.
Musinga complained to the Resident. The German officials
had, in fact, tried unsuccessfully for years to establish relations
with the Twa leaders; the Twa always withdrew into their
forests or swamps. Finally the Twa chief Bassebja was appre-

[7] Gudovius's report of 3 December 1909, RU. III I/D/33; also Ruanda Jahresbericht 1909/10, I/A/8.

hended and sentenced to death in 1911.[8] This made such an impression on the swamp Twa of his tribe that they agreed finally to submit to Musinga and live peacefully. Over a year later Gudovius succeeded at last in September 1912, by travelling through the inhospitable mountainous region southeast of the Rugesi swamp, in negotiating with Bungrure, the son of the notorious Twa chief, Grue. In a few days the chief himself with his family and people appeared. They promised to refrain from perpetrating further offences against the inhabitants of the surrounding areas, including those in British territory. In return, the Germans pardoned them for their past outrages. At the same time Wintgens, commander of the Ruhengeri post, established contact with the Twa south of Karisimbi and drew them out of their inaccessible habitat. These Twa also promised to refrain from attacking their neighbours and in return were offered protection of their forest villages by the Germans. Gudovius hoped that the Twa would eventually become assimilated with the Hutu; but at the same time he regretted that 'Africa would then again be poorer for the loss of one of her most interesting ancient and primitive races'.[9]

The disturbances in the north resulted in the death of several German personnel and a missionary. The victims for the most part were askaris. The fatalities were few, however, and were restricted almost entirely to the northern border region, 'where the power of the chiefs fails or at least is weakly founded'. Although unfortunate, Kandt said in discussing the murder of Father Loupias in 1910,[1] these occurrences were only 'of purely personal meaning'. The peace of the country was not threatened —at least until 1911. Isolated acts of violence such as murder or robbery were not a problem of security, but of administration and justice.

As in the rest of German East Africa the officers in charge of Ruanda-Urundi had jurisdiction over all the inhabitants of their region. Any death sentence or imprisonment over six months, or fines of over 200 rupees, however, were subject to

---

[8] See below, p. 127.
[9] Accounts of the Twa are found in many of the reports of the expeditions through Ruanda in RU. I/D/33; an undated memorandum by Gudovius in RU. IV I/D/33, from which the above quotations are taken, draws together and summarizes much of this information.
[1] See below, p. 178.

confirmation by the governor. No person sentenced to flogging could receive more than twenty-five lashes at one time, and not more than two floggings could be given for one offence, with an interval of two weeks between each flogging.[2] Women, Indians, and Arabs could not be flogged, and children under sixteen could only be caned. No one could be enchained for more than fourteen days. Appeals against the decision of the district officers could be made to the governor within a month of the sentence.[3]

The judicial and administrative systems of Ruanda and Urundi were elaborate and carefully considered. The statutory code defined the relationship between the Resident, the mwami, his subjects, and immigrants; the control of land alienation and natural resources; and the organization and duties of the police force. Ordinances complied with the basic statutory code of German East Africa, but could be modified by the Residents; local statutory deviations or innovations were subject to approval by the governor, or, depending on the ordinance, other officials or departments of the central government.

The Resident recognized the mwami as the paramount African ruler. As a symbol of this recognition the Imperial German Government presented the mwami with a document and authorized only to him a flag, 'an insignia of honour similar to those used in the Dutch Indies'. The Resident guaranteed protection to the mwami from his enemies, both domestic and foreign. The mwami and his chiefs, to whom he delegated responsibility, retained jurisdiction over all his people, who were subject to customary law. The Resident reserved the right,

---

[2] See note L, p. 277.

[3] According to the penal code, crimes were divided into five categories: (1) crimes against the State and public order (such as treason and arson); (2) crimes against the person or morality (such as slavery, kidnapping, and rape); (3) crimes against property (such as theft); (4) miscellaneous crimes; (5) misdemeanours. The criminal statistics given in the Urundi Jahresbericht 1909/10 are a good illustration of how the German judicial system worked. In the first class, crimes against the State, 2 were imprisoned between 6 and 12 months; 9 were imprisoned under 6 months; 3 were fined; total: 14. In the second class, personal offences, one was sentenced to death; 3 imprisoned for one year or more, 17 to 6 months to a year, 9 for less than 6 months; one was fined; 3 were flogged; total: 34. In the third class, mostly theft, one was sentenced to over one year, 4 from 6 months to a year, 49 for less than 6 months; one was fined; 6 were flogged; total: 61. In the fourth class, 'misdemeanours', 3 were imprisoned for less than 6 months; one was fined; 7 were flogged; total: 11. In addition there were other punishments meted out to those sentenced above; 5 paid additional fines; 81 received additional floggings.

however, to intervene in individual cases; he could advise the African judge, and could suspend sentences 'when the type of punishment contradicts to a high extent European concepts of culture and justice, or when there is a clear inconsistency in the law'. The Resident also reserved jurisdiction over immigrants, Africans in the employment of immigrants, and Africans guilty of an offence against immigrants. The mwami was allowed to punish those guilty of witchcraft, provided there was sufficient evidence. To curtail feuds the mwami was bound to see that each murderer was brought before a court; in a case where this was not possible, as in the escape of the culprit, his family would be held responsible. The mwami was also required to provide protection of individuals and families, such as Christians, who might be subject to persecution or 'social boycott'; in return 'the Resident offers the same protection to heathen Ruanda'. 'Attempts to estrange a Ruanda from his faith through force or threats, or to prevent religious instruction or religious customs, shall be handled judicially.'[4] The question of religion was also connected with the problem of land alienation.

Since there were no settlers, and few government posts,[5] most land alienation involved missionaries. The mwami was recognized by the government as owner of all property, all ground and minerals,[6] all crops, all animals;[7] in short, the mwami was the possessor of all objects. He could present his property as gifts, give it as a fief, lease it, sell it. The only exception to this rule were the primeval bamboo forests in the region of the volcanoes, which were declared 'Crownland' of the German East Africa government. All other land was the property of the mwami or his subjects. The mwami acknowledged the right of Christian missionaries to build settlements. The mwami could not be forced, however, to sell a particular site on which he did not want a settlement. To avoid difficulties, missionaries were to propose three possible places; each was to be at least fifteen

[4] The administrative and judicial system is outlined in detail in an unsigned, undated memorandum in RU. IV I/D/33.

[5] See note M, p. 277.

[6] See note N, p. 277.

[7] The mwami was granted the right to hunt freely, as well as to retain ivory in his and his subjects' possession. He was obliged to try to curtail the Twa's hunting elephants, and, if possible, to forbid entirely the killing of cow-elephants and young animals. The mwami himself was allowed to kill up to 12 elephants a year. Hunting and weapon licences were issued by the local authorities; in Ruanda and Urundi this was only a small source of revenue.

kilometres apart. The mwami was not obliged to yield any more than a limited, reasonable amount of land in the immediate area of the mission which would be used for crops. These transactions between the mwami and the government and the missionaries were carefully controlled by the Resident and recorded in the form of contracts.[8]

To enforce regulations the Resident organized an African police force. Chiefs on each hill, usually those holding the land fief (or their representative), were appointed to 'positions of honour'; each was given a brass badge in the shape of a half-moon which they wore on their breasts. This was their symbol of authority. These 'police' helped control the smuggling of arms, which was prohibited in the same ordinance of 1905 which barred coloured merchants from entering the country. The privilege to sell alcohol was allowed only to those with written permission from the local German authority; this licence cost from twelve to sixty rupees per year. Only mild alcoholic beverages such as beer made from grain, honey, or bananas were allowed; strong intoxicants, opium, hashish, or other opiates were forbidden. The police chiefs were to assist in the enforcement of these ordinances. Their main duty, however, was to maintain good relations between the Africans and the non-indigenous populations, especially merchants who might be passing through with caravans. The police chiefs were required to find suitable camp sites for them and assist with provisions. In case of attack by Africans on the caravans, or of merchants on Africans, the police chiefs were to arrest the culprits and to bring them to the nearest government or military post. The police chiefs were empowered to settle minor disputes between the inhabitants of their hill independent of the German authorities.[9]

Complementing the 'police chiefs' were the 'government chiefs'. This was a system begun by the Resident in 1911; it was a regional authority, an intermediary between the local police chiefs and the German officials. With the consent of Musinga, the great chief Ruamaga was appointed as 'government chief' for the Mutara district. Ruamaga was a fortunate choice, an example of the type of African the Germans liked to draw into government service. He had been entrusted with governmental

[8] Same as footnote 4, p. 151.   [9] Ibid.

duties before and had proven his competence and willingness to assist; he was respected throughout the country for his sagacity and great wealth. He had the additional virtue, from the German point of view, of holding the land fief for the entire Mutara district. In other regions the cattle, military, and land fiefs were entangled and fragmented to the extent that on a single hill one would not meet the original holder of any of the three fiefs, but 'mostly only representatives of their representatives'.[1] By the outbreak of the First World War the Resident, while leaving intact the complicated fief system, had managed to divide Ruanda into seven administrative districts: Kigali, northeast Induga; south Buganza; west Kisaka; east Kisaka; Bugessera; north Buganza. These districts did not cover the whole of Ruanda. Although elaborate in theory and more advanced than Urundi, the administrative structure of Ruanda was still rudimentary.

The most prominent features of the administration in Ruanda were not the day by day judicial problems, but the punitive expeditions, which were in contrast to those in Urundi. The purpose of military expeditions in Urundi was usually merely to punish chiefs who refused to submit to German rule, or to settle quarrels between the chiefs. The power of the mwami vacillated, as did the policy of the administration. There was never any serious threat to German rule. In contrast, the goal of the punitive expeditions in Ruanda was always to strengthen the authority of the mwami; expeditions were less frequent, but usually more serious. German administration in Ruanda was more efficient and organized than in Urundi, but also more vulnerable to revolution. The most important punitive expedition in Ruanda during the German period aimed at suppression of a revolutionary movement in northern Ruanda. The Ndungutze movement which culminated in 1912 aimed to overthrow both Musinga and German rule.

Musinga's rival for the title of mwami was the pretender Bilegea,[2] the son of Muhumusa and Musinga's half-brother. Muhumusa managed to escape from Bukoba into British territory in 1909; she was helped by a Tutsi called Ndungutze. Muhumusa and her followers in collaboration with the Twa

[1] Ruanda Jahresbericht 1911/12, I/A/8.
[2] Cf. Kandt, *Caput Nili*, II, pp. 8–9.

chief Bassebja had managed to intimidate and rule for a short time the inhabitants of British Ndorwa; Muhumusa, however, was arrested by the British and deported to Kampala.[3] Ndungutze and Bassebja eluded the clutches of the British authorities and began to plot revolution in Ruanda. Ndungutze was the grandson of Rwabugiri (Kigeri IV, mwami, 1853–95), and the son of Mibambwe IV (mwami, 1895–6), Rwabugiri's successor who had been killed shortly after his accession. Ndungutze was also the half-brother of Bilegea (another son of Rwabugiri) through Muhumusa.[4] Sometimes Ndungutze claimed the title of mwami for Bilegea; at other times he claimed it for himself. In any case he enjoyed enormous popularity, especially in northern Ruanda. Ndungutze also gained support throughout Ruanda from those who believed that Mibambwe IV had chosen Bilegea and not Musinga to succeed him, and from those who were opposed to Musinga for other reasons. Ndungutze directed his agitation against the clans who were responsible for Musinga's successful struggle to become mwami: the Wega and the Bazobe. Allied with these two groups were the Baletwa, the chiefs who were especially influential in questions of land. Opposed to Musinga were the Baha, the family of his mother, and the Wanyiginya, who were the family of Rwaburgiri. In addition, Ndungutze acquired mass support from the Hutu, to whom he promised freedom from working the land for the Tutsi. By 1912 Ndungutze and his supporters were boldly making raids from Rukiga in northern Ruanda, burning villages and farms of those who opposed him. He had gained the open or passive support of many important chiefs.[5]

Musinga, deeply alarmed at the force of the Ndungutze movement, begged the Resident to take stringent measures against those who were fomenting revolution. The intelligent

---

[3] See the very interesting file on Muhumusa in the archives of the Entebbe Secretariat. She lived to extreme old age—until June 1945, when she died in Kampala, still a political prisoner.

[4] Cf. M. J. Bessell, 'Nyabingi', *Uganda Journal*, VI, 1938–9, pp. 73–86, which is a good first hand account of the revolutionary movement in southwestern Uganda and northern Ruanda called Nyabingi, of which the Ndungutze movement was a part, and which is important as a manifestation of anti-white sentiment and the Hutu-Tutsi cleavage in Ruanda. Other accounts are: J. E. T. Philipps, 'The Nabingi, an anti-European Secret Society in Africa, in British Ruanda, Ndorwa and the Congo', *Congo*, I, 1928, pp. 310–21; P. T. W. Baxter, 'The Kiga', in *East African Chiefs*; M. M. Edel, *The Chiga of Western Uganda* (New York, 1957).

[5] Gudovius to Gouvernement, 3 February 1912, RU. III I/D/33.

and capable Gudovius, who acted as Resident when Kandt returned to Germany for home leave in 1911, at first did not take Ndungutze or his followers seriously—until he learned that rumours were rapidly spreading that the Germans were harmless, that from their guns 'only water would come'. These rumours were remarkably similar to the ones which preluded the holocaust of the Maji-Maji uprising of 1905. They were rooted in superstition and resentment at the advent of the white man. The rumour ran that the Europeans would be impotent against the magic protection and the power of the great chiefs. Gudovius also saw that the Ndungutze movement could incite a revolution of Hutu against Tutsi.[6]

Ndungutze had allied himself not only with the Twa chief Bassebja, but also with the murderer of Father Loupias, Lukarra, and with those guilty of a murder of two askaris on the island Nunanira in Lake Bulera. The Rukiga district in northern Ruanda had become a haven for outlaws. The inhabitants of this region were the Kiga, many of whom were using Ndungutze merely as a means to increase their independence. In many instances, Gudovius reported, the movement was 'an expression of hostility towards askaris and Europeans' as well as an indication of the antagonism of Hutu towards Tutsi. In any case it was a movement which would spread rapidly unless curtailed. The specific region in which this unrest was especially apparent was between the great Twa swamp (Mruschaschi), Lakes Bulera and Luhondo, the road between Kigali and Ruhengeri, and the Tschohoa-Basse. Musinga's authority was 'seriously endangered' only five hours north of Kigali. Unless the Germans intervened 'the districts of Rukiga and Mulera will be lost'; Ruveruka, Boyoka, Kabuje, Ruhondo, Kibare and Bumboge were also endangered. Passive and sometimes open resistance was noticeable throughout the country.[7]

Gudovius moved quickly. On 5 February 1912 he despatched *Polizeiwachmeister* Pursche and fifteen askaris to form emergency posts immediately south of the troubled region; this measure effectively stopped the rebel raids, although plundering con-

[6] Gudovius to Gouvernement, 31 March 1912, RU. III I/D/33.
[7] There are several reports about the Ndungutze movement in RU. IV I/D/33; they are summarized in 'Bericht über die Expedition der Polizeiabteilung Kigali und einer Abteilung der 11. Feldkompagnie gegen den Gegensultan Ndungutze und den Zwergenhäuptling Bassebja vom 8.4 bis 20.5 1912'.

tinued in the Rukiga district itself. By the end of March the chiefs of the Bushiro-Buhoma district had declared themselves in alliance with Ndungutze. As in other instances, Gudovius observed that this was more an attempt to strengthen their own independence than a closely knit conspiracy. Gudovius carefully planned a surprise attack. The purpose of the expedition was 'punishment of the insubordinate districts and their peoples and chiefs by causing the greatest possible damage until complete submission; otherwise, destruction of crops and settlements, and occupation of the theatre of operations by chiefs appointed by the Resident who are faithful to Musinga'. To ensure a decisive victory Gudovius requisitioned a detachment of the XI Company of about sixty men led by Lt. von Linde. Gudovius himself commanded the police detachment of Ruanda of about thirty men. The plan was for Linde to occupy the tempestuous region between Lakes Luhondo and Kabuje while Gudovius attacked the village of Ndungutze. Surprise was essential; otherwise Ndungutze and his followers would flee into British territory. Gudovius was well aided by two young Tutsi spies, who provided information about Ndungutze's region, village, and movements.[8]

Gudovius's contingent left Kigali on 8 April. Two night marches across mountainous terrain and swamps brought them to Ndungutze's village immediately before dawn on the 10th. All was still; no one suspected their approach. One of the spies reported that Ndungutze was there. No one stirred. Pursche took command of the encircling troops; Gudovius entered the village. He was immediately descended upon by a throng of warriors armed with spears. Gudovius and his escort fired continuously, killing about fifty. Most of the villagers attempted to break out of the circle of surrounding soldiers; most were slaughtered. Ndungutze himself was killed during the fighting.[9] Gudovius burned the village; nothing was left but ashes. 'With this the last resistance was broken.' Gudovius's men had suffered only slight casualties. It had been a brilliant military manoeuvre —if slaughter can be considered laudable.

In the meantime Lt. Linde and his men had completed their

[8] Ibid.
[9] Cf. Bessell, 'Nyabingi', p. 82; Bessell states that Ndungutze was arrested in 1913 in Uganda at Mbarara.

assignment of burning villages and killing those who resisted their advance. The chief Lukarra was executed after 'summary proceedings' on 18 April for the murder of Father Loupias; the Twa chief Bassebja was shot on 15 May. During this time the German 'Demonstrationszug' had ravaged the countryside; toward the end of the expedition, Gudovius reported, less violence was needed because the people were thoroughly intimidated and 'obedient'. The Africans in northern Ruanda had learned that it was best to submit to German authority. German justice, despite its elaborate judicial scaffolding and its scrupulous fairness in individual cases, sometimes was heavy-handed. But the mission had accomplished its purpose; the sparks of a revolution had been quenched. Martial law was lifted on 20 May. 'Complete peace has been restored to the country where Ndungutze and Bassebja and their followers rebelled against Musinga.'[1]

Despite the brutality of German rule, northern Ruanda in general and Rukiga in particular remained pacified for only a short while. Agitation after 1912 was never so serious as the Ndungutze disturbance, but askaris continued to be murdered and caravans robbed. The German authorities never found an entirely adequate solution for the stormy and rebellious north-ern part of Ruanda.[2]

The result of the Ndungutze expedition, however, was a strengthening of authority of the mwami and the German administration. 'The sultan himself knows full well that he has only the government to thank for the total subjugation of his fearful rival, and has expressed his thanks to the Residency through a special delegation and the presentation of a great elephant tusk.' Gudovius reported after the conclusion of the expedition that the administration could continue to count on 'complete loyalty of Musinga' and could be assured that he would try to fulfil every wish of the Resident.[3]

Yet even with the full cooperation of Musinga, German rule neither encompassed all of the population of Ruanda, nor pro-

---

[1] See the report cited in footnote 7, p. 155. The pretender Bilegea was known to have visited Ndungutze, but had left the country; he was said to be living in Urundi. Gudovius reported that he would now not dare to make a bid for power in Ruanda.

[2] See especially Wintgens to Gouverneur, 27 April 1914, RU. IV I/D/33.

[3] Gudovius's report of 1 June 1912.

duced all the desired results. As in Urundi—although to a lesser extent in Ruanda—the Germans discovered that the power of the mwami was much weaker in practice than in theory. Captain Wintgens—who had commanded the Ruhengeri post, and become the last German Resident after Kandt returned to Germany for home leave in 1913—said in the annual report for 1913 that although Musinga's subjects continued to pay him the traditional tributes, his actual authority over them was 'little indeed'. 'As soon as anything new, especially anything unpleasant, is required, he [Musinga] is as good as helpless; only after long entreaties and threats on our part toward the disobedient will the request sometimes be carried out.' Kandt had written in 1910 that the 'somewhat playful character' of Musinga was an impediment to the further development of Ruanda; he hoped that the visit of Governor Schnee would shape in the minds of Musinga and his subjects 'a concept of the "Kais. Gouvernement" which until now has been abstract and anonymous. . . .' Wintgens saw a more fundamental reason why German administration in Urundi and Ruanda was difficult, a reason beyond the failure of the people to grasp the meaning of German government and beyond the obvious lack of authority of the mwami. Wintgens reached the same conclusion that Schimmer had reached in Urundi. The trouble was the character of the Tutsi and the Hutu. 'Indolence and indifference' were the great enemies of German rule. 'Open refusal to obey is not in the Tutsi character; he makes promises in the usual way; the result for us is the same . . . no practical results.'[4]

'Indolence and indifference' of the Tutsi and Hutu did not present the same type of problems as did the weakness of authority of the mwami. An interesting example is found during the tax collection of 1914. The Resident was collecting taxes in the districts of Kisaka, Kigali, Kisenyi, Shangugu, and Bugessera. Shortage of personnel restricted activity to these regions. Musinga and a few great chiefs had, however, 'on grounds of the great willingness of the population to pay us the tax' attempted to collect taxes in some of the regions untapped by the German authorities. One attempt had been successful; the second ended in 'complete failure'. The chiefs who tried to

[4] Ruanda Jahresbericht 1913/14, I/A/8.

collect the tax for Musinga in the Ruhengeri region met with 'absolute resistance of the population, who explained to them that they wanted to pay the money-tax to the government, but not to Musinga'. Musinga's tax delegation finally went to the Catholic mission at Rwaza and asked that they use their influence to make the Kiga pay the tax; the delegation lied, saying that the taxes would be turned over to the Resident. The missionaries wrote to Wintgens; Wintgens replied that he had naturally forbidden this 'private tax collection'. Musinga was now in a compromised position, where his subjects refused to obey his command. Had his delegation used force, and had there been bloodshed, the Resident would have been forced to intervene and 'would have had to suffer again for the faults' of the mwami. Fortunately nothing had come of the incident.[5]

The one rupee per head tax in 1914 was the first general tax collection in Ruanda.[6] The decision to levy this tax was made after careful consideration by Wintgens, in collaboration with the Resident of Urundi, who was to try the same experiment in Urundi. There were two main reasons why tax collection had not been attempted before 1914. The first was the shortage of coins, of which only a few were in circulation in Ruanda. The second was the lack of an industry or livelihood through which the bulk of the population could make earnings to pay taxes. Wintgens challenged both these assumptions. In the first place, public auctions of cattle had shown that there was a surprising amount of coin in Ruanda. But the main reason behind the decision to levy taxes was 'not because so few coins are available . . . but just the opposite: because there are no required taxes, there are few coins'; taxes would draw more coins into the country and stimulate the economy. The Ruanda would eventually exchange their products not for cloth and beads, as was

[5] Wintgens to Gouverneur, 24 July 1914, RU. IV I/D/33.

[6] Hut taxes had been collected in Kisenyi, Ischangi, Bugaramma, and Kigali since 1910. Previously a small tax had been collected only from immigrants; the revenues were very small, less than 1,800 rupees per year. Cf. *Historique et Chronologie du Ruanda*, p. 22.

In Urundi, hut, house, head, and business taxes were collected only in Usumbura from immigrants. In 1913–14 business taxes brought in 8,825 rupees as opposed to 3,469 rupees the previous year; house, hut and head taxes, 10,765 rupees as opposed to 5,560 the previous year. The Resident planned a general tax collection similar to the one in Ruanda for 1915; head tax in inner-Urundi would be one rupee; in the neighbourhood of Usumbura, 3 rupees. Those who helped the Germans in the fight against sleeping-sickness were exempted from taxes. See Urundi Jahresbericht 1913/14, I/A/8.

now customary, but for money; the interest aroused by taxes in money would facilitate the organization of potential industries of Ruanda into productive enterprises. In the past it was thought that tax collection would be impossible because there was no great number of German officials; but because of the close relations with Musinga and his chiefs the taxes could be collected through them under supervision of the German authorities. Musinga himself opposed taxes because he feared the Hutu would regard the payment of taxes to the government as a chance to say to the Tutsi that their services had been rendered, that by paying taxes to the Germans they were no longer indentured to the Tutsi.

Musinga's fears in fact were realized. Wintgens reported in July 1914 that the tax collection had been a great success, and that the collected taxes would amount to at least 150,000 rupees. 'One can even speak of a joy of payment . . . even old people, children and sick people come either to pay or to request exemption.' This was remarkable, since inability to pay the one rupee tax would lead to two weeks labour on public works, mostly on road construction or improvement. But Wintgens did not deceive himself that the Ruanda 'delight in the payment of taxes in and for themselves'. The reason the Hutu were glad to pay was because they thought the Germans would then 'protect them against the despotism and injustice of the Tutsi'.[7]

The tax collection of 1914 showed that the Germans were not unpopular in Ruanda. It demonstrated that the Ruanda, unlike the Rundi, were aware of the meaning of government, the 'double-dominion'; if asked, an average Ruanda would say 'Musinga rules over me, and the Resident rules over me'.[8] The tax collection of 1914 also showed that shortly before the outbreak of the First World War there were reasons to believe that the economic future of the region was hopeful.

[7] Wintgens's elaborate explanation of taxes in Ruanda is in Wintgens to Gouverneur, 1 February 1914 and 24 July 1914, RU. IV I/D/33.
[8] See the annual reports for Ruanda and, K. Roehl, 'Ruanda—Erinnerungen', *Koloniale Rundschau*, XXI, 1925, pp. 289–98.

XV. RAILWAYS, TRADE, AND
CIVILIZATION

. . . to submit barbarism to civilization . . . (Cecil Rhodes, 1899)[1]
We must turn Ruanda and Urundi into *coffee lands* . . . (Richard
Kandt, Resident of Ruanda, 1913)[2]

PART of the imperialist vision was that central Africa would
be opened to trade and civilization. This was to be done through
a permanent means of communication—railways. Railways
would bring trade; trade would bring civilization. The Cape to
Cairo route was a commercial and civilizing enterprise as well
as a political symbol of empire. The idea of a German empire
stretching across the African continent had been shattered by
the Anglo-German agreement of 1890. But the notion of German trade flowing across Africa still continued.

These grand imperial ideas were tested by Ruanda-Urundi.
It was Ruanda-Urundi that their proponents struggled for and
with; it was there that both schemes met defeat. For Ruanda-
Urundi was the missing link in the Cape to Cairo route. It was
also the most western region of German East Africa, the only
part of the colony that abutted on the Congo. If German trade
was to flow through central Africa, and if Ruanda-Urundi
itself was to be developed economically, then the German East
Africa railway would have to be extended to what at one time
had been considered as darkest Africa.

The history of the missing Cape to Cairo link from 1894 to the
First World War is the story of Cecil Rhodes's negotiations with
Leopold II and the Kaiser in the attempt to connect the
British spheres in the north and south of Africa. His Trans-
Continental Telegraph had reached the southern shore of Lake
Tanganyika by 1899.

Rhodes arrived in Brussels in February 1899 to discuss his
project with Leopold. Leopold received Rhodes at a luncheon,
attended mainly by persons who had distinguished themselves

---

[1] As reported in Lascelles to Salisbury, no. 24 Africa very confid., 15 March
1899, F.O. 10/215.
[2] Kandt's memorandum of 8 September 1913, RU. IV I/D/33.

in the service of the Congo State, such as Colonel Wahis, the recent Governor-General, and Colonel Thys, the organizer of the Congo railway.[3]

Rhodes told Leopold 'that he would shortly ask Her Majesty's Government to remind His Majesty of the Vth Article of the Anglo-Congolese convention of 1894,[4] and obtain leave for him to push the works of his telegraph line across the Congo State'. Leopold replied that he had already started to build a telegraph line along Lake Tanganyika and that this would provide the connecting link with the north.

Mr. Rhodes strongly objected to thus breaking his line by handing over the working of an important section of it to a foreign administration. He explained, moreover, that the line which the Congo State government was laying was a very inferior affair, quite unsuited to the large business which he hoped to attract to his through line from Cairo to the Cape. That he knew exactly the nature and the value of the material to be employed, as most of it had been sent from Europe by the Nyasa route; that if wooden poles were employed they would be destroyed by white ants in a few months; and that if the wires were stretched from tree to tree, where that might be feasible, the result would be frequent breakages and interruptions.[5]

Leopold insisted that he was quite capable of constructing a telegraph; Rhodes said that he would stand by the right conceded to Britain by Article V.

Finally the King appears to have said that his treatment of Great Britain in regard to Article V would depend on how far she kept her engagements towards the Congo State under the lease granted by Article II. . . . The King said that he could not suppose that Great Britain would fail in her word toward him in the Bahr el Gazal; but on her conduct to him there, would depend his conduct towards the telegraph connection.[6]

Since Leopold would be 'extremely hard to deal with', Rhodes thought the wisest course would be to try to come to terms with the Kaiser so that the telegraph could be run through German East Africa.

---

[3] Plunkett to Salisbury, no. 19 Africa, 4 February 1899, F.O. 10/720.
[4] See above, chapter IV.
[5] Plunkett to Salisbury, no. 20 Africa confid., 4 February 1899, F.O. 10/720.
[6] Ibid.

The next month Rhodes went to Berlin to negotiate with the German government about the Cape to Cairo route.[7] Rhodes and the Kaiser were congenial, stimulating one another by their august imperial ideas. Rhodes planned to convince the Kaiser that the future of the German empire abroad lay in the Middle East; Germany with a grand Middle-Eastern empire could easily afford to allow Britain the completion of her Cape to Cairo route.

Sir Frank Lascelles, the British Ambassador in Germany, called on Rhodes on 12 March to congratulate him on 'the favourable impression he had created on the Emperor'. Rhodes replied 'that he had noticed that as soon as he mentioned the word "Mesopotamia" he had won his case, and that then he had referred to the glories of Nineveh and Babylon'.[8] The Kaiser had said that 'Germany had begun her colonial enterprise very late, and was, therefore, at the disadvantage of finding all the desirable places already occupied'. 'To this Mr. Rhodes had replied that there was still one quarter in which much remained to be done, and in which, in former ages, mighty empires had flourished. He referred to Asia Minor and Mesopotamia.' 'The Emperor at once became enthusiastic, and Mr. Rhodes took the opportunity of pointing out that the prosperity of the great empires which had flourished in those parts was due to irrigation rather than to war.' Rhodes said to Lascelles that 'he hoped he had done no harm in favouring the Emperor's ideas'.[9]

The Kaiser agreed in principle on 11 March that Rhodes could build the telegraph, to be followed by a railway, through German East Africa. The details remained to be cleared up. Rhodes seemed anxious lest the Kaiser might feel obliged to provide him with a large escort when he reached German East Africa; this he wished to avoid for economic reasons.

[7] Lascelles to Salisbury, no. 24 Africa very confid., 15 March 1899, F.O. 10/215. Rhodes had already reached an agreement with the Egyptian authorities to build the telegraph through their territory; the rate per word through Egypt and the Sudan was to be two and one-half pence.

Rhodes's visits to Berlin and Brussels are touched on in Sir Lewis Michell, *The Life and Times of the Right Honourable Cecil John Rhodes* (London, 1912), pp. 337–8; on Rhodes's visit to Berlin, see Vindex, *Cecil Rhodes* (London, 1900), pp. 633–4; for further references, see Langer, *The Diplomacy of Imperialism*, p. 622.

[8] Lascelles to Salisbury, 15 March.

[9] Ibid.

The Telegraph Company was, in fact, himself. He had no share-holders, for although his associates were fond of philanthropy and five per cent., they did not care so much about the former without the latter. He had already spent 100,000 pounds upon this enter-prise, and it would be a serious consideration for him to be saddled with the expense of a large escort, for which he did not see the necessity. He was convinced that His Majesty, with his large ideas, would sympathize with him . . . he did not wish to spend more than was necessary for personal protection.[1]

The railway, Rhodes said, would be up to the southern frontier of German East Africa within five years. The Kaiser replied that he would be ready for him by that time.[2]

The agreement between the German government and the Trans-African Telegraph Company, which was concluded in collaboration and with the approval of the British government, authorized the company to continue their telegraph line through German East Africa at their own expense. The railway negotiations were left open.[3]

The Kaiser regretted that 'Mr. Rhodes was not his Minister, as with such a man his Majesty could have done great things'.[4] Some elements of German opinion feared that Rhodes with British capital was 'a gigantic spider silently and unobtrusively spinning its web around Germany's African possessions';[5] but the Kaiser and his advisers were convinced that Rhodes's visit to Berlin would produce 'the most satisfactory results'.[6] The Cape to Cairo route was to complement the German East Africa system of telegraphs and railways; it was to be mutually advantageous to both Germany and Britain.

The telegraph reached Ujiji, but not Ruanda-Urundi. Rhodes died shortly after his interviews with the Kaiser and Leopold; with him was interred the dream of the Cape to Cairo route, which was not exhumed—so far as Ruanda-Urundi was concerned—until the First World War. In the meantime the German East Africa government continued to expand its own railways.

[1] Lascelles to Salisbury, no. 25 Africa very confid., 16 March 1899, F.O. 10/215
[2] Ibid.
[3] Lascelles to Salisbury, no. 28 Africa, 22 March 1899, F.O. 10/215.
[4] Lascelles to Salisbury, 15 March.
[5] See the interesting analysis of the German press attitudes towards Rhodes's negotiations in Stephen to Salisbury, no. 9, 21 March 1899, F.O. 10/215.
[6] Lascelles to Salisbury, 16 March.

Plans for the 'Urundi-Ruanda railway' did not materialize until late in the history of the colony. Although the possibility of a railway had been discussed earlier by the local authorities, the immediate impetus to the scheme was given by Governor Schnee; the purpose of his visit to Ruanda and Urundi in 1913 was in part to gather information about the proposed railway. But Schnee envisaged an extension of the central railway from Tabora only 'to where the Ruvuvu empties into the Kagera'. A railway through Urundi and Ruanda themselves would be impracticable because of the great cost involved in construction over mountainous territory.[7]

Schnee's proposal received sharp criticism from the Europeans in Ruanda-Urundi. What was the point, they asked, in building a railway to Ruanda-Urundi that would hardly touch it, that would end in a poor, sparsely inhabited, swampy region to the east? The controversy was taken up in the German colonial press.[8]

One opponent of the government proposal suggested that the railway from Kilimanjaro should be extended to Lake Victoria, and from there to Ruanda. But this suggestion was not considered seriously. The main lines of the controversy were drawn by Schnee and Father van der Burgt, one of the respected and acknowledged authorities on Urundi.

Schnee argued that the railway from Tabora to the Ruvuvu-Kagera confluence would be approximately 450 kilometres long, that it would entail great expense; the cost of a railway into mountainous Ruanda-Urundi itself would be astronomical. The purpose of the termination at the Ruvuvu-Kagera confluence was that from there shipping on the Nyawarongo, Akanjaru, and Ruvuvu could be developed; they were said to be navigable for 500 to 600 kilometres. This would 'connect' Ruanda and Urundi to the rest of the colony, and would be the most economical method of opening the region to trade.[9]

[7] The governmental proposals are outlined in a lengthy memorandum of 20 July 1911, in RU. III I/D/33.
[8] The railway is discussed at length in two articles: M. Moisel, 'Die Urundi-Ruandabahn', *Kolonialzeitung*, XXX, June 1913, pp. 418–20; and Emil Zimmermann, 'Zur Linienführung der Kagerabahn', *Kolonialzeitung*, XXXI, January 1914, pp. 38–39. These two articles cover all the important points made in the unpublished documents in the Usumbura archive. There is also an important discussion in the last pages of chapter XI of Hans Meyer, *Die Barundi*.
[9] See the Moisel article. The Urundi administration established a new post in the region, at the south end of Lake Tschohoha, in 1913. This location was chosen

Van der Burgt replied persuasively to these arguments. Although he should be content, perhaps, that the railway would terminate in the neighbourhood of his mission, Friedberg in Ussambiro, he thought that 'in the best interest of the colony' the line should run farther to the west. As Emil Zimmermann expressed it, the railway hardly 'scratched' Ruanda-Urundi, for which the railway was being built. Van der Burgt pointed to the absurdity of a railway ending in a swamp. He advocated a railway that would go 'through the heart of Urundi and Ruanda to Lake Kivu'. 'In this way these magnificent highlands with their hundreds of thousands of workers would be actually opened. . . . It is correct that the Tabora-Kivu railway is 200 kilometres longer than the Tabora-Kagera railway, and therefore costs more; but it should be considered also that the Rundi and the Ruanda within their country could work by the hundreds of thousands on the railway and in this way could pay their taxes; this is now impossible, for apart from their cattle, they do not possess anything other than their healthy poverty.'[1]

The debate about the 'Urundi-Ruanda railway' was interrupted by the cataclysm of the First World War.[2] The Urundi-Ruanda railway, like the Cape to Cairo railway, was never built. Ruanda-Urundi was never 'connected' to east Africa.[3]

because of the friendliness of the Africans in the region and because water connection with the terminus of the railway would be possible.

[1] Ibid.; also Pater J. M. M. van der Burgt, 'Die Urundi-Eisenbahn', *Deutsch-Ostafrikanische Zeitung*, 1913, numbers 82, 83, 84.

[2] Construction of the railway from Tabora, however, had already begun; work continued until 1915. Additional documents on the Urundi-Ruanda railway may be found in a file marked 'Ruandabahn, XII J/2' in the Ministry of Railways and Harbours, Dar es Salaam. These documents have been examined by M. F. Hill in preparation for his *Permanent Way*, vol. II, 'The Story of the Tanganyika Railways' (Nairobi, 1959), which contains some interesting comments about the development of railways during the German era and about German administration in general.

[3] Although Ruanda-Urundi was never connected by railway to the rest of the colony, communication by the First World War was frequent and regular. The telegraph extended only to Tabora, but the railway went all the way to Kigoma. The steamer 'Hedwig von Wissmann' connected Usumbura to Kigoma; it called at Usumbura 12 times a year; by the First World War Usumbura was the main door through which trade passed in and out of Ruanda-Urundi (cf. J. van der Burgt, 'Vom Norden des Tanganyika-Sees', *Gott Will Es!*, XIII, June 1901, pp. 161–7; van der Burgt foresaw many of these developments). From Usumbura the main roads led to Kisenyi, Kitega, and Kigali, and from Kisenyi to Kitega. Caravans passed over these roads on their way to and from Bukoba. Mail was delivered in Kigali once a month after the arrival of the 'Hedwig von Wissmann' in Usumbura. A telegram could arrive within ten days at Kitega after its arrival at Tabora overland by way of Uschirombo.

The railway was to have opened Ruanda-Urundi to trade. Some trade had been developing in Ruanda-Urundi independently from the plans for the railway; and two aspects of this trade and the implications of opening up Ruanda-Urundi had been argued vigorously for many years by the local authorities, the officials in the central government, the German Colonial Secretary, and the colonial circles in Germany. The first was the idea that the labour supply of Ruanda-Urundi could be exported and used in other parts of the colony, especially on the plantations in the east. There was unanimous agreement between the local officials and the central government that this would be impracticable and unwise; the Rundi and the Ruanda, accustomed to healthy highlands, would never acclimatize to the diseases and tropical climate of the rest of German East Africa. As Hans Meyer expressed it, it would be 'wholesale massacre' to deport labour *en masse* from Ruanda-Urundi. Whether this theory was correct was never proven, because without the railway mass deportation from Ruanda-Urundi was economically impracticable; the question remained speculative.

The second problem of trade in Ruanda-Urundi, however, was practical; opinions about it divided sharply, and the heated debate raged all the way from the local Residents to the German Colonial Secretary. This was the problem of the coloured merchants, referred to in the German despatches as the 'Inder Frage' or Indian question.

The 'Indian question' (by 'Indians' was meant everyone except Europeans and Africans) was controlled through the Governor's ordinance of 10 March 1905. '. . . until further notice entrance to the sultanates of Ruanda and Urundi is permitted only from the military station of Usumbura, and only with written permission from the district officer, or his representative, who is authorized to grant permission . . .' The phrase 'until further notice', as the Central-Afrikanische Seen-Gesellschaft pointed out to the Colonial Office in March 1908, seemed to imply that this was a temporary provision.[4] Two parts of an ordinance of 7 March 1906 were also relevant to Ruanda-Urundi.

[4] Central-Afrikanische Seen-Gesellschaft to K. A., 6 March 1908, RU. II I/D/33.

no. 2. Sojourns of non-indigenous natives in the restricted territories are only permitted to those who receive personal authorization
from the administrative authority of the district where the restricted
territory is located.

no. 10. Natives . . . are forbidden during sojourns in restricted
territories to possess firearms. . . . Natives who do not belong to an
African negro tribe can be forbidden in individual cases or in
general to make sojourns in the restricted territory by the local
administrative authorities.[5]

Did the ordinance of 1906 supersede the one of 1905? This
was the question asked by the Central-Afrikanische Seen-
Gesellschaft, who said that they were greatly interested in the
possibility of salt mines in Ruanda-Urundi. The Colonial Office
replied that there was 'no doubt' that the ordinance of 1906
cancelled the one of 1905; the ordinance of 1906 was intended
to keep out 'natives'.[6] But in fact, the new ordinance was far
from clear. Grawert interpreted it in September 1906 to mean
that 'every coloured leader of a caravan is permitted entry to
the sultanates as long as he does not have weapons. How is this
to be controlled?' Grawert envisaged the 'greatest danger';
'all of the Indian and European firms in Bukoba, not to mention
Mwanza, Tabora, and Ujiji, will immediately send hundreds of
people into the country'.[7]

The precise meaning of the two ordinances remained indefinite until 1910, when the 'Inder Frage' became a public controversy. In July an article by Emil Zimmermann[8] appeared in
the *Deutsche Tageszeitung* entitled 'Ruanda'.[9] Indians, he
reported, were 'unfortunately' overrunning Ruanda. Ruanda
was 'the most valuable part of our whole east African possession'; why were the German officials allowing it to be spoiled?
Before the German discovery of Ruanda, there were no Indians
there at all; to decide how to open the region was not easy, but
the government had acted wisely in adopting Grawert's

---

[5] *Amtlicher Anzeiger für Deutsch-Ostafrika*, VII, no. 8, 1906.
[6] K. A. to Central-Afrikanische Seen-Gesellschaft, 24 March 1908, RU. II
I/D/33.
[7] Grawert to Gouvernement, 25 September 1906, RU. II I/D/33.
[8] Zimmermann was a well-known colonial writer, disliked by the officials in
German East Africa. Langenn reported that Zimmermann's articles about
Urundi 'abounded in errors'; the Governor commented that the only remarkable
feature about Zimmermann's travels in east Africa was his inordinate consumption
of liquor.
[9] 28 July 1910, clipping in RU. III I/D/33.

suggestion to make it a restricted territory. Now, however, Indians were pouring into the country; if this continued Ruanda might as well 'be handed over to the Indians, Levantines and Greeks'. Who was responsible for this unwise policy? Rechenberg had told Zimmermann that it was up to the Resident of Ruanda, Dr. Kandt, to control immigration. 'Kandt is unfortunately a free-trader.'[1]

Lindequist, the German Colonial Secretary, requested an explanation.[2] Kandt defended himself by discussing the problems of development of European commerce in Ruanda.

When he came to Ruanda in September 1907 to establish the Residency at Kigali, Kandt said, he recognized that Ruanda could not be opened immediately to trade. On the other hand, 'I had nothing against the immigration of Indians, whose activity, I have learned, is generally useful for the economy. Of course my greatest sympathies were with my compatriots, however.' The only German merchant whom Kandt knew who might be persuaded to come to Ruanda was Herr Schiele in Bukoba. 'I told him that for several months the country would remain closed to coloured merchants, but that a *duka* [shop] would be necessary and that he could establish one in the vicinity of the Residency.' If coloured merchants came later, then Schiele would have the advantage of several months' previous activity over them; if Schiele himself could not come then he could send an industrious representative. Kandt volunteered to supervise the activity of the shop; 'yes, even more'. 'I knew that because of his previous bankruptcy he had no credit, so I advanced 1,000 rupees to him out of my private funds, so that he would have a certain credit with the firms on the coast for the purchase of cloth. . . .' After a long wait of four months a caravan finally arrived at Kigali with a representative of Schiele; this representative, however, presented to Kandt a further bill for 1,500 rupees. Before Kandt could raise objections, a second caravan arrived, which put him in debt even further. 'I had then to open in a manner of speaking a *duka* myself; in other words, I had to sell the stuff for months to get rid of it and to pay my debts.' Kandt lost several hundred rupees; '. . . even today, three years later, there is still a pile of matches in my shop that I cannot get rid of'. Kandt's relations

---

[1] Ibid.   [2] See Lindequist to Gouverneur, 18 August 1910, RU. III I/D/33.

with Schiele, needless to say, were ruptured. Kandt had not planned to open shop at Kigali; but shops were needed. Since no Europeans seemed to be interested, he had written to the German post at Bukoba and had asked them to send some Indian merchants. This was how the first large number of Indians had come to Kigali. That they had multiplied, Kandt wrote, was not surprising; even the European firms regarded Indians and Arabs as indispensable for their businesses and sent them to Ruanda.[3]

Lindequist debated the merits of Indian traders in a long letter to the Governor of German East Africa in October 1911. Lindequist was willing to admit three things: first, that it was undeniable that without a money economy it would be impossible to levy taxes; second, that circulation of money was not possible without trade; third, that from the point of view of big businesses Indian traders might be useful. But, said Lindequist, 'successful small trade leads to big trade; and big trade retains connections and associations'. This was especially true of 'oriental trade'. Opportunities given to Indians in east Africa would make the east African economy more and more dependent on them; this was a 'national danger'. There were other hidden dangers. Most of the Indians in the north of German East Africa were British subjects. Trade controlled by a foreign power 'could become a powerful weapon in the hands of an enemy'. Germany had felt occasionally 'the pressure of England' in east Africa; if Britain were to gain more control of trade in the German colony it would give the British a chance 'to interfere in the affairs of the administration, if not to cause great disturbances'. The history of German colonialism on the west coast of Africa had shown that the colonies could be developed independently of Indians; east Africa should follow the example given there of providing schools for Africans so that they could learn to defend themselves against the 'un-reliability of the Indian merchants'. Dr. Kandt's attempts to defend free-trade were 'little worthy of imitation'. The 'virgin territories of Ruanda and Urundi' could be developed without the Indians, said Lindequist; the ordinance of 1905 which prohibited their entry was to be strictly enforced.[4]

---

[3] Kandt's undated memorandum in RU. III I/D/33.
[4] Lindequist to Gouverneur, 28 October 1911, RU. III I/D/33.

Lindequist thought the Indian problem so serious that he considered transferring the control of Ruanda-Urundi immigration to the Colonial Office in Berlin rather than leaving it to the discretion of local officials. Lindequist withdrew his proposal in view of the Governor's strenuous objections, but his instructions left no doubt about the policy of the government toward Indians. The Governor, and especially the local authorities, did not share all of Lindequist's views,[5] but they were obliged to enforce his orders. The ordinance of 1905, of course, gave some margin for local interpretation; in individual cases the Resident could permit an Indian to settle in Ruanda or Urundi. But Lindequist's interpretation of this ordinance indicated that few Indians would qualify. Finally in 1913 (after Lindequist's resignation as Colonial Secretary) the Governor received permission to enact a more liberal policy. In an instruction of June 1913 the Governor declared that Ruanda and Urundi were to be considered as open to trade. 'I do not intend that the formerly restricted territories of Ruanda and Urundi should be open for every sort of immigration; for then there would be a flood of inappropriate elements who would disturb the peace.' Labour recruiters and cattle buyers were to be forbidden, as formerly. But merchants, coloured as well as European, were to be allowed entrance unless there was an obvious reason why they might be undesirable.[6]

Lindequist probably exaggerated the danger of Ruanda-Urundi being 'overrun' by Indians, just as he was too optimistic about the economic future of the country. The effectiveness of his restricted immigration policy is difficult to judge, but in any case there was not a great abundance of Indians in Ruanda-Urundi by 1914. In the Usumbura district there were seventeen

[5] The Acting Governor, Mether, in January 1912 replied to Lindequist's comments by drawing a distinction between the 'Indians' and the 'Swahili merchants'. 'In all of the colonial newspapers one reads about the atrocities of the Indian vampires, who exploit the poor blacks and swindle them out of their hard earned money. I was a native judge for years, and I must say that in most cases the Indian swindle far less than the Swahili merchants. They both want to make a profit; that is why they are merchants; but my impression of the Indians I have met here and there is that they have a certain feeling of truth and faith in trade. The Swahili merchants lack this almost entirely, and these people are the ones who played a fateful role in the southern districts before the rebellion of 1905.' Mether thought the Indian merchants resembled 'the Polish Jews', who could under proper supervision benefit the economy. Mether to K. A., 6 January 1912, RU. III I/D/33.
[6] 'Reinconcept', 15 June 1913, UR. IV I/D/34.

non-European firms; in the Kitega district, also seventeen non-European firms. In all of Ruanda there were only twenty-eight non-European firms. Many of these 'firms' were in fact a single Arab or Indian. The few European enterprises were usually represented by Arabs or Indians. The Max Klein firm in Usumbura was directed by a German; the other two European firms in Usumbura, the Central-Afrikanische Seen-Gesellschaft and the Deutsch-Ostafrikanische Gesellschaft, were directed by an Arab and a Goan respectively. The only European firm in Kitega was the Internationale Handelsgesellschaft, represented by an Arab. In Ruanda, only the Internationale Handelsgesellschaft, Max Klein, the Deutsch-Ostafrikanische Missions-Handelsgesellschaft and the Societa Italiana had branches. It would be difficult to maintain that Ruanda-Urundi on the outbreak of the First World War was a thriving commerical centre.[7]

What had become of the El Dorado of central Africa? There were several reasons why Ruanda-Urundi failed to attract commercial enterprises. One obvious reason was the policy of restricted immigration, which kept out Indians, and therefore, to some extent, trade. But this itself does not explain why Ruanda-Urundi failed to develop economically; for while Indians were discouraged, the administration made several efforts to encourage European firms. Few had come. The vision of Ruanda-Urundi as a centre of great wealth had dimmed. Natural resources of the region were still mostly unknown; what exploration had been done had not produced favourable results. There was the possibility, perhaps, of salt and iron deposits; but there were neither diamonds nor gold. Apart from the Ruzizi valley, Ruanda-Urundi was poor in big game. German-Congolese relations had improved after the conclusion of the treaty of 1910, but imports of valuable commodities such as ivory and rubber from the Congo remained insignificant. Fishing was of importance only locally around Lake Tanganyika. But if there were no diamonds, gold, or ivory, there

---

[7] See the annual reports for Ruanda and Urundi of 1913/14. Many of these firms bought native products, especially skins, with coins, more often with cheap cloth, still more often with beads about the size of a pea; the favourite colours of the beads were deep blue and light yellow. After beads and cloth, brass and copper goods were the main imports. The Residents thought that the traders made excessive profits.

remained the products of the soil, the domestic animals, and the labour supply of one of the most densely populated parts of Africa. These were the resources that the Residents tried to organize.

Ruanda-Urundi's agricultural products were diverse, including beans, peas, red sorghum, tobacco, eleusine, cassava, millet, bananas, peanuts, and maise.[8] Of these, beans and peas were grown in great quantities and were the staple diet. In some places, especially in parts of Urundi, bananas were consumed as a principal means of nourishment; in other places, especially in parts of Ruanda, bananas were used only for the preparation of beer. Honey was valued by the Ruanda and the Rundi, and gathered throughout the country, although inefficiently; many of the bees were often killed and the wax wasted, despite the attempts of the Residents to introduce German beehives. Domestic animals were abundant, but mostly uneconomical. In some parts of the country sheep and goats were not eaten by the inhabitants; mutton was especially despised as an item of diet. For this reason sheep and goats played an unimportant role in the economy, and were used mostly as an object for barter. Traders often received and gave more for the skins of the animals than for the animal itself.

Since social standing was conceived in terms of cattle, the Germans had difficulty in persuading the Tutsi, who owned almost all livestock, that cattle had an economic as well as a social and political value. The Tutsi preferred to breed imposing looking tough and scrawny cattle with long lyre-shaped horns. Cattle were Ruanda-Urundi's most abundant and valuable product; but 'they have neither high slaughter nor high milk value'. Milk cows were sold reluctantly by the Tutsi; what milk there was often was bitter because of poor pastures. The pastures themselves were overstocked. Perhaps the cattle in Ruanda-Urundi could be used to economic advantage, Gudovius reported in 1911, but there was no prospect of this until modern transport was available.[9]

Modern transport—the railway—was to be the key to economic success in Ruanda-Urundi. The railway was to bring trade,

---

[8] See 'Die Wirtschaftliche Bedeutung von Ruanda', *Nachrichten aus der Ost-afrikanischen Mission*, XXIII, 1909, pp. 63–66, 76–78.

[9] The annual reports for Ruanda and Urundi of 1911/12 have the best discussions of agriculture and domestic animals.

trade was to bring money, money was to bring taxes. The rail-way was both a hope and an excuse; a hope, that the economy would flourish as soon as the railway was built; an excuse, that there was no money economy because there was no railway. Just as Wintgens challenged similar notions about taxes, so Kandt challenged the assumption that Ruanda-Urundi would become a new Jerusalem of prosperity and progress once the railway was built.

A railway would doubtless reduce the cost of exports from Ruanda-Urundi, but what was there to export? Beans and peas? Scrawny cattle? Where would they be shipped? Dar es Salaam? Would the freight cost justify transport of such common or inferior products? And there were other problems. The railway itself would not guarantee that the Tutsi would be willing to sell cattle, or that the economy could be reorganized to ensure delivery of beans and peas at the railway terminus. Crops in Ruanda-Urundi were grown almost exclusively by the Hutu, who, like other east African Bantu, used primitive agricultural methods. The Hutu were industrious; their crops were grown intensively and all cultivable land was used. But the result was a subsistence economy; Ruanda-Urundi produced enough food to feed its population, and little more—as the Germans had discovered at their markets in Usumbura, Kitega, and Kigali. A railway over a long period of time might stimulate crop production, but it was hard to see how it would produce immediate results, or how the amount of beans and peas available for export would justify the cost of transportation, not to mention the cost of railway construction. The railway would be invaluable, however, for the exportation of a product of world-wide significance.[1]

'We must turn Ruanda and Urundi into *coffee-lands*', Dr. Kandt wrote in 1913. In accordance with their instructions, the Residents had for years experimented with crops of commercial value, such as cotton, tobacco, and rice. None had grown so successfully as coffee. Coffee had the further advantage of growing in regions considered uncultivable by the Hutu; especially appropriate were the groves after groves of bananas. For other crops, such as peanuts or cotton, the Germans would have

---

[1] Kandt's long memorandum of 8 September 1913, in RU. IV I/D/33; see also Wintgens to Gouvernement, 1 February 1914, RU. IV I/D/33.

to compete with the Hutu for suitable ground, almost all of which was already in use. The banana groves were practically unused, and were peculiarly suited for coffee. The soil was moist, and the banana trees would protect the coffee trees from the wind and sun. 'Should we be frightened because of the high costs?' 'Brazil was also originally not a coffee country, Ceylon not a tea country, and the Malay states not a rubber country. This last example shows how with favourable conditions a completely new productive character can be stamped rapidly on a country.' With concentration of energy and effort, one million coffee trees could be planted in 1914, and increased by one million a year; by 1920 there would be six million coffee trees in Ruanda-Urundi, and a modest estimate would be that two pounds of coffee per tree could be harvested. Ruanda-Urundi would become the coffee farm of Germany. Ruanda and Urundi alone could meet Germany's coffee needs, and there would be enough left for the world market. The economy of German East Africa would be diversified, and the enormous labour potential of Ruanda-Urundi at last organized and used.[2] Coffee was the German vision of the economic future of Ruanda-Urundi. Like other visions, it was shattered by the First World War.

By 1914 the dream of railways and commerce in Ruanda-Urundi had not been realized. The railways had not been built; there was little trade. What civilization there was had been brought less by the traders than by the missionaries.

[2] Ibid.

XVI. THE MISSIONARIES

The only civilization and culture we will reach here will be entire
. . . through education. (Father Gassldinger, 1912)[1]

THE first missionaries arrived in Ruanda-Urundi before the
German explorers. As early as 1879 an expedition of Cardinal
Lavigerie's White Fathers ventured along the eastern shore of
Lake Tanganyika into Urundi. Two years later a group of
White Fathers were massacred in Rumonge.[2] As late as August
1896 Father van der Burgt and Father van der Biesen were
forced to flee for their lives from the attacks of a chief called
Musabiko.[3] In the same year the first permanent Catholic
mission was built at Muyaga. Mugera was founded around
1900, Save, Zaza, and Nyundo in Ruanda shortly afterwards.
Within the next five years Buhonga and Kanyinya were established in Urundi, Rwaza, Mibirizi, and Kabgayi in Ruanda. By
1904 Ruanda alone had acquired five Catholic missions. When
Pastor Johanssen of the Protestant Bielefeld Mission first
travelled through Ruanda-Urundi in 1906 he repeatedly heard
from Africans that 'this country belongs to the French [i.e. the
White Fathers]'.[4]

Grawert described the Catholic missionaries in 1904 as
reflecting to a high extent the characteristics of their superior,
Bishop Hirth, the Apostolic Vicar of Southern Nyanza (from
which Ruanda and Urundi were separated in 1912 to become
the Kivu Province under Bishop Hirth at Kabgayi). 'His ideas
and his biases are absolutely typical of his priests. Bishop Hirth
is in my opinion an intelligent man, not completely open, and
not anything other than a person friendly to Germans; if he
had his way, however, the government would go to hell and he
would establish an African church-state.' Grawert reported
that the missionaries had been instructed by Hirth to avoid

---

[1] This is an extract from a letter signed in the name of Father Gassldinger; see
below, p. 187, note 3.
[2] Mgr. Gorgu recounts the early missionary activities in Urundi in *En zigzags
à travers l'Urundi* (Namur, 1926), pp. 10–13.
[3] *Kolonialzeitung*, X, April 1897, p. 155.
[4] *Ruanda—Kleine Anfänge, Grosse Aufgaben* (Bethel bei Bielefeld, 1915 edition),
p. 32.

anything that could lead to interference with the affairs of the government; they should use restraint in their relations with the 'worldly authorities'. Grawert judged that this attitude of studied indifference to the administration was not entirely appropriate from those who were quick to criticize the German officials, yet thought that the government had an obligation to protect them. Grawert informed Bishop Hirth that he wanted the full and unreserved cooperation of the missionaries, who in some instances might be able to provide the administration with information which might avert situations which could imperil them all, and be of the 'greatest danger' to the whole country.[5]

Grawert thought that Bishop Hirth had been well chosen by his Catholic superiors; the priests in Ruanda-Urundi were on the whole a competent group. The only problem child for Hirth, Grawert reported, was Father Zuembiehl, who was a deeply biased and immature Jesuit. 'For him the main principle is to have two irons in the fire and never to forget that the Belgians may become masters of the presently disputed territory, and therefore to pay them frequent visits.' The imperious Father Brard of the Save mission; the peasant-like cloddish Father Barthelemy of Nyundo, 'who directs his whole faith towards heaven'; the reverent Father Classe of Rwaza, who 'is always praying'; the narrow-minded but incredibly well-educated Father Pouget of Zaza—these were Grawert's descriptions of the Europeans with whom the German officers found themselves in deepest Africa.[6] Antagonism as well as good will characterized the relations between the German authorities and the missionaries.

The German administration protected the missionaries from hostile Rundi and Ruanda. Beringe's reasons for his campaign against Kissabo in 1903 had been, in part, to protect the Mugera mission. Attacks on missionaries were regarded by the German authorities as attacks on the administration itself; those guilty of offences against the missionaries were punished in the same way. The most important instance during the German period in Ruanda-Urundi of crime, punishment, and missionaries, was the murder of Father Loupias in 1910.

[5] Grawert to Gouvernement, geheim, 5 December 1904, USU. II I/D/28.
[6] Ibid.

Father Loupias was a respected and dedicated missionary at the Rwaza mission in northern Ruanda who was murdered in April 1910 when he tried to intervene in a cattle dispute concerning a rebel border chief called Lukarra. Loupias, attempting to persuade Lukarra to return some stolen cattle, had seized him by the arm when he saw that Lukarra would try to escape, and Lukarra's followers had killed the priest with their spears.[7]

Dr. Kandt wanted to punish Lukarra as an individual criminal. Loupias's murder, however, occurred shortly after the disturbances in northern Ruanda caused by the British Kivu expedition and during the unrest of the Ndungutze movement. Lukarra attacked Ruhengeri,[8] the military post newly established to pacify the region, thus entangling civil, military, and missionary affairs. A punitive expedition was despatched from Ruhengeri, but the results were abortive. Lukarra and his followers had escaped into the Congo.

Months later, an askari attached to the Ruhengeri post for the purpose of maintaining order and, if possible, apprehending Lukarra, met a group of African women gathering wood in the volcanic region. He seized a pretty girl, raped her, and returned her to her mother only after receiving a bribe. 'With this heroic act he was still not content; he then appropriated some small grazing cattle in the neighbourhood.'[9] When the bridegroom of the raped girl discovered what had happened, he quickly gathered his friends and relatives and ambushed the askari. The askari fired, tearing off the ear of an African. The Africans then rushed on the askari and killed him with their sickles.

'As understandably human as was the attitude of the natives,

[7] The administrative reports concerning Loupias's death are missing from the Usumbura archive, but it is discussed in detail in 'Ermordung eines Missionars in Ruanda', *Kolonialzeitung*, XXXV, April 1910, pp. 295–6; and Egon Fr. Kirschstein, 'Zur Ermordung des Paters Loupais in Ruanda', ibid., May 1910, p. 307. Cf. *Historique et Chronologie du Ruanda*, pp. 140–2. Professor Vansina tells me that the murder of Loupais seems to have been motivated by the erroneous notion of the Hutu that Loupais was an agent of Musinga. In a letter to me of 8 November 1962.

[8] The Ruhengeri post was typical of the German military posts in Ruanda-Urundi; it had been established in March 1909, then abandoned, then reoccupied for a specific purpose. Even Kisenyi was not occupied permanently until July 1907. The military posts usually consisted of a small detachment of askaris—20 askaris was considered the minimum number for an effective force—under the command of a European who might be either an *Unteroffizier* or an *Offizier*. Military posts were under the command of the protectorate force, although their services could be requisitioned by the civil authorities.

[9] Kandt to Gouvernement, 25 January 1911, RU. III I/D/33.

punishment of the lyncher could not be avoided on many grounds.' The Africans involved should have lodged a complaint with either the mission in the neighbourhood or the Ruhengeri post; to allow them to go unpunished would lower the prestige of the Germans in the eyes of the Africans, and would lead to more disturbances in the already restless region of northern Ruanda. Lt. Wintgens, *Polizeiwachmeister* Pursche, and 'a handful of askaris' (10 police askaris and 800 'Hülfskrieger') were assigned to punish the culprits. Wintgens's orders were typical of those given to German punitive expeditions in Ruanda. 'Men who do not submit immediately shall be killed, women and children taken as captives.' The result: around 65 Africans killed, 60 women and children captured, 230 head of cattle confiscated.[1] This 'local' punitive expedition still did not lead to the capture of Lukarra.

Lukarra eluded his German enemies for almost two years. He was finally apprehended and executed 'in the interest of the restoration of public peace and security' during the Ndungutze bloodbath of April–May 1912.[2] Lukarra while chained had tried to escape; he was shot, but still alive enough to be tried by 'summary proceedings' for the murder of Father Loupias. His execution—only one of the enormous number of killings—made a 'great impression' on the local Africans.[3] The missionary had been avenged, but at a terrible cost.

Protection was the main way in which the administration assisted the missionaries. This was their bond of friendship; they united as Europeans against Africans. The main source of antagonism, on the other hand, was what the German authorities referred to as missionary interference in administrative affairs. Grawert in 1904 had observed 'inconsistencies' in the attitude of the missionaries towards the German authorities; he thought that in some of the missionaries' dealings with the Africans they might be advised to consult more closely with the administration, if for no other reason than to learn about various governmental policies. Grawert was surprised, for example, that Bishop Hirth had discussed with Musinga the possibility

---

[1] Wintgens, 'Bericht über die militärische Tätigkeit der Postenbesatzung von Mruhengeri bei den polizeilichen Massnahmen in Sache der Ermordung des Askari Rissassi der 11. Feldkompagnie am 31.12.1910", RU. III I/D/33.
[2] Gudovius to Gouvernement, 20 May 1912, RU. III I/D/33; see above, pp. 155-7.
[3] Ibid.

of more Catholic missions in Ruanda without consulting the
Resident.[4] The reluctance of the missionaries to confide in
those outside the Church was their own concern; it did not
bother the German authorities except when governmental
affairs were involved, and especially when established German
policies were violated.

This issue of the missionaries' 'policy of interference' came
to a head in 1911. 'One might have hoped', Dr. Kandt wrote,
'that these events [concerning the death of Loupias] might have
made the missionaries more cautious; but these hopes have
disappeared with the passing of time.' The Resident of Ruanda
had complained for years to the central government about the
attitude and activities of the missionaries, Kandt explained; but
neither the entreaties of the government nor practical experience could lead the missionaries to common sense. Father
Schumacher of the Kabgayi mission was now repeating all of
the unfortunate errors of Father Loupias. In recent months
Schumacher had tried to meddle in an 'entirely internal dispute
of the natives'; the case in which Schumacher was interested
had appeared twice before the legitimate African judge. By
interference, Schumacher had provoked a 'crass incident'
which had led to 'unbearable circumstances'.[5]

On 1 January 1911 Musinga had learned that there had been
some difficulty between a missionary, Father Schumacher, and
some of his subjects. Five years previously Musinga's chief
Ruhigirakulinda had punished a subject for not participating
in a military expedition against the Twa by taking four cows
away from him. This man had taken his punishment peacefully
for five years; he was not a Christian, and did not go to the
mission for catechization. In December 1910 his chief punished
him again for disobedience by taking three more of his cows.
About this time the man began to attend services at the mission;
Kandt observed that he presumably did this because of his
dispute with his chief, in the hope that the missionaries would
intervene on his behalf. Schumacher, however, decided that the
man had been punished by his chief because he wanted to

[4] Musinga informed Grawert about Hirth's supplications; Musinga explained
to Hirth that 'there were already five missions in Ruanda, and that was enough';
he wanted no more 'Faranza' (Frenchmen) in the country. Grawert to Gouvernement, 5 December 1904.
[5] Kandt to Gouvernement, 3 January 1911, RU. III I/D/33.

become a Christian. 'If, as often', Kandt wrote, 'a Christian wins a legal proceeding, good—because he has won by the strength of his rights.' 'But if he loses, then the reason immediately invoked is that it is because he is a Christian.' Kandt thought this was impossible to explain to the missionaries.[6]

'What have things come to', Musinga asked Kandt, 'if missionaries all over the country can intimidate and threaten to banish the chiefs who punish someone who is disobedient?' Kandt answered Musinga: 'That is foolishness. You know as well as I that a missionary cannot banish one of your chiefs. And if one demands it of you, all you need to do is refuse.' With this Musinga seemed much relieved, but the affair for the Resident was not finished.[7]

For years, Kandt said, the Resident had preached to the missionaries that 'the Residency by instruction and in agreement with the *Kais. Gouvernement* has striven in view of the obstinate character of the Hutu to support and to strengthen the precarious authority of the chiefs, great chiefs and the sultan'. 'Nothing helps. Because of the allegedly insurmountable resistance to conversion of the Tutsi, the missions remain a principal opponent of governmental policy.' By trying to force the chief to return the cattle, Schumacher was violating German policy; he not only demanded the return of the cattle recently taken for punishment, but also those that had been confiscated five years ago. '. . . in my opinion this is nothing other than an attempt at power made by an ambitious man who seeks to rule, who is too vain to say to the natives who turn to him that his power is not so great.'[8]

The crux of the issue between the administration and the missionaries was whether or not to support the Tutsi as the rulers of the country. Even in Urundi, where independence had been granted to some of the great chiefs, the German administration had consistently supported the Tutsi domination. Tutsi justice was sometimes unjust; 'the decisions of European justice are also not always just'.[9] The missionaries, however, had a different view toward Tutsi rule and justice, which resulted

[6] Ibid.   [7] Ibid.
[8] Ibid. See also Schumacher to Kandt, 1 January 1911; Kandt to the Kabgayi mission, undated; memorandum of 11 February 1911; and Kandt to Schumacher, 17 January 1911; RU. III I/D/33. Schumacher received censure from the German East Africa government.   [9] Kandt to the Kabgayi mission, undated.

from the attitude of the Tutsi toward Christianity. 'The Catholics in their characteristic mixture of orthodoxy and rationalism', Kandt said, found the Tutsi spiritually impossible; 'they ignore the Tutsi as inconvertible and turn to the Hutu, above all to the children'.[1] The German authorities turned to the Tutsi for efficient government, the missionaries to the Hutu for the spread of Christianity. The missionaries regarded the Tutsi as religious imbeciles, impossible to convert; the German authorities regarded the Hutu as 'savage and disposed to opposition and disobedience'.[2] The missionaries thought that the Tutsi were unjust to the Hutu and tried to protect them from Tutsi despotism; the German authorities thought that 'the best way to destroy authority would be to support complaints of the Hutu against the Tutsi'. 'That there are injustices is clear; but where are there not? And those who are most unjust are the missionaries in their uncritical support of their [Hutu Christian] people.'[3] The missionaries' partiality for the Hutu interfered with the German scheme of administration, and was a main source of antagonism.

Beneath the clash of views over practical issues were cultural and national differences. Langenn reported in 1911 that 'as always it is much to be regretted that those attached to the mission stations are for the most part from foreign countries; A French element is strongly preponderant'. Even the 'German' members of the Catholic missions were mostly Alsatians; the common language was French, and it was used almost exclusively. 'It is clear that this preponderant French element and French mentality provides a base for neither the German language, nor . . . German national ambitions.'[4] It was not surprising that the German authorities found the German Protestant missionaries more compatible. The Protestant Bielefeld Mission arrived in Ruanda in 1907;[5] the Neukirchner Missionsgesellschaft in Urundi in 1911.[6]

[1] Kandt to Gouvernement, 3 January 1911, RU. III I/D/33.
[2] Ibid.   [3] Ibid.
[4] Von Stegman, who signed the Urundi annual report for 1910/11 copied the identical words from the report of 1909/10. He apparently was either so unimaginative that he had nothing new to say, or was greatly impressed by the observation. Langenn rephrased the same thought in the report of 1911/12. Cf. Kandt, *Caput Nili*, I, p. 225.
[5] See *Nachrichten aus der Ostafrikanischen Mission*, XXI, 1911, pp. 178–96.
[6] Cf. Franz Gleiss, *Führer durch die evangelischen Missionen in Deutsch-Ostafrika* (Wuga, Usambara, 1914).

Doctrinal differences between Catholicism and Protestantism were reflected in the work of the missionaries. In 1910 Dr. Kandt reported that the Catholic missionaries in Ruanda included 24 priests, 5 brothers, and 6 sisters; in total, 35 persons. The Protestant mission had 4 pastors and 3 deacons, along with 4 women and 4 children; total, 15 persons. The Catholics in 1910 claimed around 5,000 Christians and 2,000 catechumens; the Protestants had baptized no one. By 1911 the Catholic Christians and catechumens had grown to around 8,000; the Protestants had baptized 17.[7] 'The Protestants place the main emphasis on preaching.' Both missionary movements were 'very content' with the results of their work;[8] as far as Dr. Kandt was concerned, this was 'the main point'.[9]

The missionaries freely admitted, however, that they faced great difficulties with the 'reserved and mistrustful character'[1] of the Rundi and the Ruanda, who 'decline any foreign religion, including Islam'. Langenn in 1912 judged that the real success in conversion was 'very slight'; 'the absolute requirement of monogamy which comes along with the Christian religion seems especially impossible for the chiefs'.[2] Yet Langenn also admitted that 'the missionaries before the baptism demand a long strict period of observation'.[3] Perhaps the success of the missionaries was greater than Langenn thought.

By 1914 missionary work was one of the more thriving European activities in Ruanda-Urundi. In Urundi the White Fathers had established missions at Mugera, Buhoro, Muyaga, Rugari, Kanyinya, and Buhonga; the Protestants had missions at Iwanga, Kogawami, Iruwura, and Muyewe. There were 19 Catholic and 6 Protestant missionaries.[4] In Ruanda the White Fathers had missions at Kabgayi, Save, Nyundo, Rwaza, Mibirizi, Zaza, Rulindo, Murunda, and Nyaruhengeri, with 17 other stations directed by converted Africans; there were 44 European Catholic missionaries. The Protestants had 6

[7] See the Ruanda annual reports of 1909/10 and 1910/11; cf. 'Eine ersehnte Stunde', *Nachrichten aus der Ostafrikanischen Mission*, XXVI, 1912, pp. 3–8.
[8] Ruanda Jahresbericht 1909/10.
[9] Ruanda Jahresbericht 1913/14; cf. 'Das Urteil eines deutschen Offiziers [von Parish] über die Mission in Ruanda', *Afrika-Bote*, 1904, pp. 280–2, and 'Egon Fr. Kirschstein und die Kath. Mission in Ruanda', ibid., 1909–10, p. 239.
[1] Urundi Jahresbericht 1909/10.   [2] Urundi Jahresbericht 1911/12.
[3] Ibid.   [4] Urundi Jahresbericht 1913/14.

missions, in Rubengera, Kirinda, Remera, Dsinga, Shangugu, and Idjwi (Kitembe). There were 11 European Protestant missionaries.[5] The total of 80 missionaries was a substantial part of the white population of Ruanda-Urundi; as Dr. Kandt pointed out, one missionary blessed with many children could, by leaving or coming, greatly influence the white population statistics for one year. With their superior numbers the cultural influence of the missionaries on the mass of the population probably surpassed that of the German officers. And the way in which this influence was exerted was perhaps more through education than through religious services.

Grawert wrote to Bishop Hirth in December 1906 that he hoped the 'impact of knowledge' would reach the Tutsi in particular, because they tended to remain aloof from Europeans and European culture. 'I freely admit that I believe that at first, attempts at religious instruction and attempts at conversion must be dropped; but I also think that by wisely using his influence the teacher who gains is the one who knows how to enthral his students; in this way a school prepares the way for Christianity without religious instruction. Even the Tutsi, who probably still will not be moved to adopt Christianity for a long time, will be subjected to Christian influence, which they will receive unnoticeably and inescapably through the school.'[6] Grawert was trying to suggest to Bishop Hirth that the missionaries would defeat their own religious purpose as well as the purpose of education as a goal in itself if they tried to use it simply as a tool to proselytize. He was also expressing the fear of the administration that the missionaries would educate the Hutu but not the Tutsi.

Each mission had a school or schools of some sort. In 1911 Langenn reported that there were 70 mission schools with 1,440 pupils in Urundi;[7] in the same year Gudovius reported 35 schools and 2,001 pupils in Ruanda. Instruction was mostly in the indigenous language, although some of the Catholic missionaries taught in Swahili. Kandt commented in 1913,

[5] Ruanda Jahresbericht 1912/13; the statistics for Ruanda 1913/14 are not complete. In 1913 Kandt reported that the Catholics had 8,522 Christians and 5,932 catechumens in Ruanda; the Protestants had made 45 baptisms. Similar statistics for Urundi are not available.

[6] Grawert to Hirth, 31 December 1906, RU. II I/D/35.

[7] Urundi Jahresbericht 1911/12.

perhaps reflecting his own bias: 'I have the impression that more is learned in the Protestant schools.'[8] By 1913 the Catholic Kabgayi mission had begun an 'advanced class' (*Seminar*), which Wintgens thought 'has a special value because the German language is taught'. The pupils at the highest level could already converse slowly in German and could sometimes write dictations without errors.[9] The pupils of the Catholics were predominantly catechumens; religion was associated with education. 'Apart from the catechumens, going to school is not especially exciting. The natives, when they do not intend to become Christians, approach with a certain mistrust; for in spite of the existing good will, the missionaries cannot free themselves from the habit of injecting religious material in the instruction.'[1] Just as most of the converts to Christianity were Hutu, so the Hutu were the recipients of the missionary education. The Tutsi remained aloof. Only Pastor Johanssen, the head of the Protestant missions in Ruanda, seemed to make any progress with the Tutsi.

Pastor Johanssen and his Protestant colleagues tried especially to educate the mwami and the great chiefs. 'With moving zeal Pastor Johanssen undertakes the difficult work of informing the sultan and the great chiefs about Protestantism. He is astonished over the growing comprehension.'[2] By 1911 Musinga could speak fluent Swahili; he could also read, but to write was difficult because his hand was not limber enough; so he had ordered a typewriter through the Resident.[3] Mutaga in Urundi made similar progress with Swahili.[4] Swahili itself did not spread rapidly through Ruanda-Urundi during the German period, although Gudovius commented in 1912 that the people had a good talent for languages and those who had the opportunity to learn Swahili 'learn it easily and well'.[5] Schimmer in 1914 spoke of the 'thirst for knowledge of the Rundi'.[6]

As in other parts of German East Africa, the administration itself began schools. A government school was established in Usumbura in 1909. The first year the school had twenty-five

[8] Ruanda Jahresbericht 1912/13.   [9] Ruanda Jahresbericht 1913/14.
[1] Ruanda Jahresbericht 1911/12.
[2] Ruanda Jahresbericht 1912/13; see also Johanssen's book, *Ruanda*.
[3] Ruanda Jahresbericht 1911/12.   [4] Urundi Jahresbericht 1913/14.
[5] Ruanda Jahresbericht 1911/12.   [6] Urundi Jahresbericht 1913/14.

pupils, about three-fourths of whom were Rundi children, the rest children of askaris and traders. Two of the pupils were sons of neighbouring chiefs. The school was taught by a coloured teacher sent from Dar es Salaam. By 1911 the school at Usumbura had grown to thirty-six pupils, by 1913 to two classes with forty-five and sixty-three pupils each; askaris received instruction in addition. With the transfer of the Residency to Kitega a school was built there also; in 1913 it had thirty-five pupils. In Kitega the administration made a special effort to attract Tutsi children.[7] The failure of the missionaries to provide education for the Tutsi created a problem for the Germans. 'It lies in the immediate interest of the Resident to instruct the Tutsi, for we must deal directly with them in administration as the rulers of the country.'[8] Education of Tutsi became the special purpose of the Ruanda government school established in Kigali in 1910. As in Urundi, the school was taught by a teacher sent by the central government. But the first year the results were not great and the school was attended mostly by the children of askaris and traders. In 1912 the administration built a new 'large, attractive school with four classrooms'. But to the end of the German era the school in Ruanda suffered from incompetent teachers,[9] and the administration's experiments in education in Kigali perhaps resembled less the energetic efforts of the missionaries than the feeble attempts to educate made by the representatives of Islam.

A small, miserable Koran school in Usumbura somehow struggled on year after year to teach the children of a few askaris and traders. This was the only noticeable Islamic activity in Urundi. Islam in Ruanda was also never a problem to the administration, but Dr. Kandt liked to speculate about its implications for the future of the country, because the rumours of 'Islamization' affected the German restrictive immigration policy. Kandt said that he doubted whether Islam in Ruanda-Urundi would ever make much progress. The mwami and the Tutsi were especially antipathetic toward it. Kandt thought that the Rundi and the Ruanda were so

[7] Urundi Jahresberichte, 1909 through 1914.
[8] Ruanda Jahresbericht, 1913/14.
[9] Ruanda Jahresberichte, 1909 through 1914.

spiritually content that Islam could not offer them much. The few Mohammedans among the population had usually acquired Islam as children, and as they became older they usually were careful to conceal it from their compatriots and sometimes abandoned it altogether. Kandt was particularly concerned with the myth propagated by the missionaries, and accepted by many German officials, that if given a chance—opening the country to trade, or even by a large influx of Mohammedan askaris—Islam would sweep the country. Kandt had decided to test this theory. At Kigali there were thirty Mohammedan police askaris, who together had fifty-five 'boys' (African servants). From the latter Kandt excluded three, who came from places such as Tabora and along the coast where Islam was endemic. Of the rest one from the Congo was excluded along with one Ruanda. This left fifty Ruanda 'boys'. They had been in the service of the askaris for years; none were Mohammedans. From this Kandt concluded that either the askaris were poor proselytizers, or that Islam, especially in unfavourable circumstances, was not the force it was often said to be.[1] In any case the Ruanda and the Rundi were at least as impervious to Islam as they were to Christianity.

Fear of Islam was one of the few forces which united in spirit the Catholics, Protestants, and German officers in Ruanda-Urundi. The relations between the three groups were gracious but seldom cordial—'correct but stiff', Schimmer commented in 1914.[2] The Protestants and the Catholics were as remote from each other as they were from the German officers. Together they tried to bring European civilization to Ruanda-Urundi. And there is no doubt that the missionaries succeeded where the German officials failed. For regardless of their religious success, they taught reading and writing. One of the missionaries wrote to Langenn in 1912: 'If I no longer had any schoolboys around me I would simply give up.' The only civilization which the missionaries would succeed in bringing to Ruanda, he said, would be through education.[3]

[1] Ruanda Jahresbericht, 1910/11; cf. Roehl, 'Die Ausbreitung des Islams im südwestlichen Ruanda', *Nachrichten aus der Ostafrikanischen Mission*, XXV, 1911, pp. 132–4.
[2] Urundi Jahresbericht, 1913/14; cf. Johanssen, pp. 32–34.
[3] These sentences come from a letter from the Buhonga mission in reply to Langenn's inquiry of what the missionaries thought of the German administration. The letter, dated 4 September 1912, is typical of the replies, filled with praise for

This was a modest view, which reflected the character of many of the missionaries; they were men of good will with dedicated ambitions. Among their most notable achievements were Father van der Burgt's French-Rundi dictionary and Pastor Johanssen's translation of parts of the Bible into the indigenous language, which stand as monuments in the cultural history of the country.

The German officers sometimes regretted that the missionaries were not instruments of German nationalism. The missionary movements in Ruanda-Urundi were, in fact, less nationalistic and secular than international and religious. Some of the missionaries in Ruanda-Urundi experienced Belgian as well as German administration. The former was perhaps as nationalistic as the latter, and both as secular as the missionaries were religious.

the administration; ironically it is signed in the name of Father Gassldinger as the superior of the Buhonga mission. UR. IV I/D/34.

XVII. BELGIAN AND BRITISH RUANDA

The Belgian soldier in these parts is a professional looter, and is capable, whether on his account or by order of his superiors, of sucking as much out of an acre as professionals born and bred to the work. (Captain de Courcey Ireland, Kivu Expedition, 1909)[1]

GERMANY at the Kivu-Mfumbiro Conference of 1910 had been reluctant to yield to Belgium the large island in the middle of Lake Kivu, Idjwi. One of the main reasons had been the presence of the German Protestant Bielefeld mission on the island. To avoid rupturing the negotiations Germany had finally agreed that Idjwi should be Belgian, if Belgium would guarantee the security of the missionaries and grant Germany certain privileges on the island. The details of the 'privileges' were settled in a protocol of 30 October 1911: the Germans were to be allowed to gather wood and chalk on Idjwi. The Belgians later regretted their generosity, and described the agreement as a 'heavy servitude'; they claimed that the Germans would deforest the island, and requested a modification of the agreement.[2] The Germans refused. Relations between the local officials were a minor source of friction between the two countries until the First World War.

The missionaries provided more delicate problems. The following incident between them and the local Belgian officials gives a glimpse of colonial administration in part of Belgian Ruanda—for Musinga claimed Idjwi as part of his domain.

The Protestant missionary Wiemers, who lived with his parents on the German island Wau on Lake Kivu, discovered in April 1913 that some African girls, about seven or eight years old, had been molested by the Belgian commandant Derche on some of the small islands in the lake. Derche's sexual perversions were sufficiently grotesque to motivate Wiemers to climb into his small boat and go to the Belgian post on Idjwi to complain indignantly. Jussiamt, the Belgian

---

[1] 'Diary of the Kivu Mission . . .', F.O. 403/411.
[2] See Roehl, 'Politische Fragen auf der Insel Idschwi', *Nachrichten aus der Ost-afrikanischen Mission*, XXIX, 1910, pp. 234–7; Beyens to Zimmermann, 23 October 1913, RU. IV I/D/33.

officer in command of the post, professed ignorance of Derche's activities and urged Wiemers to drop the matter. Wiemers replied that the Africans in the neighbourhood were aroused because of the incidents, and that some sort of justice was necessary. Wiemers departed in anger at the indifference of Jussiamt. He also objected to Jussiamt's imprisonment of an African chief called Mugenzi 'because he refused to provide provisions for the soldiers'. Later in the month Wiemers claimed that Jussiamt offered him 'in the name of the commandant 500 or 1,000 francs . . . and on top of that a good milk cow' to forget the Derche escapades; Jussiamt subsequently denied under oath that he made the proposal.[3]

Wiemers reported the incidents to Pastor Johanssen. He also submitted a report to the Resident of Ruanda, which claimed to give an accurate account of 'Belgian maladministration'. According to Wiemers, the inhabitants of the small island of Kinyawaranga, who could not number over fifty, were required by the Belgian post on Idjwi to deliver fifty fish every other day to the post. Wiemers said that this was an impossible demand that the people simply could not fulfil, especially during the unfavourable dry season. Yet if they did not meet the demands they were subjected to 'chicaneries' by the Belgians. One of the chiefs, Wikuba, was required to deliver one hundred loads of food to the Belgian post every third day; Wiemers said that this might be possible only during the harvest season, that even then it would be a great burden on the people. There were many instances of cattle appropriation; Wiemers said that cattle were scarce on the islands of Kivu, that they were valued even more than in Ruanda. In August 1913 Belgian askaris appeared one evening on Wau and took away three cows and two steers. 'Such harshness and beatings given by the black soldiers one would have to see to believe.' According to Belgian law, Africans were to be remunerated for all labour and supplies; women and children were not permitted to work for Europeans. Yet in August 1913, Wiemers reported, 'thousands of men, women, including some who were heavily pregnant, boys and girls were forced to work many days without pay from six in the morning to seven in the evening with

[3] Wiemers's 'Bericht über Ereignisse auf Idschwi im Zeitraum vom 16 bis 28 April 1913', RU. IV I/D/33.

only very short rest breaks'. According to Belgian law, Belgian authorities were forbidden to burn huts without some justification; yet huts had been burnt indiscriminately on the heavily populated island of Kijiji. Wiemers himself had been mistaken for a Belgian once when he wanted to buy a fish; the fisherman had shouted at him: 'Your brother in Nakarenga burnt our huts and destroyed our bananas, and I will not sell any fish to you robbers.' The missionaries feared for their lives because of the unrest which the Belgians were creating. 'The fact is that the black soldiers wander through the country and rob and destroy to their personal gain.'[4] The missionary accounts of these atrocities on Lake Kivu led to an inquiry by the Colonial Ministry, which sent Commissar Henry, Major Molitor, and Judge Voisin to investigate.

The elder Wiemers wrote to the Resident of Ruanda on 12 October 1913 that he was anxious about his son's safety. Voisin had appeared on the island along with sixteen armed askaris; after an hour's inquiry about Derche, Voisin had obliged the younger Wiemers to accompany him to Belgian territory, where the parents of Wiemers thought he was now being detained.[5] Pastor Johanssen wrote later in the month that he was afraid that Wiemers would be deported to Stanleyville; Wiemers had incriminating evidence against the Belgian administration which they wished to conceal. Was there nothing the German government could do? The meaning of the incident was greater than the safety of one individual; it involved also the security of the whole mission on Idjwi and the welfare of the Africans. 'It is not as if we were requesting protection simply for ourselves. We have come here to serve the natives. Missionary Wiemers took the complaints of the natives loyally and directly to the Belgian authorities in the hope that there would be a way in which to redress them. . . . Not as a political agent for German interests did he go to the Belgians, but out of sympathy for the natives.'[6]

At this point Dr. Kandt, though suffering from malaria, began inquiries about the relations between the missionaries and the Belgians, and about the alleged Belgian atrocities on

---

[4] Wiemers's report of 16 September 1913, RU. IV I/D/33.
[5] Wiemers to the Kigali Residency, 12 October 1913, RU. IV I/D/33.
[6] Johanssen to Busse, 26 October 1913, RU. IV I/D/33.

Lake Kivu. Kandt himself had no especial love for the Belgians; he had collided more than once with Derche over frontier questions. When Kandt himself had learned of Derche's sexual perversion he naturally had found it abhorrent, and had hoped that the German government would not in the future have to deal in military and diplomatic ceremonies with a man who had placed himself in such a compromising position. Kandt was uncertain whether all the missionaries' allegations against Derche were true; but in any case he had advised the missionaries to remain silent. Against his wishes an article had appeared in their missionary journal attacking the Belgian administration.[7]

Kandt regarded Wiemers as an unreliable source. In the past Kandt had been obliged to reprimand him for his behaviour in Ruanda, and finally to forbid him entrance to the country. During his encounter with Jussiamt on Idjwi, Wiemers had been reminded by him that his own morality was not beyond reproach; Kandt concurred in Jussiamt's opinion. Without more information from other sources it would be difficult to tell whether Wiemers's description of Belgian activities on Lake Kivu was accurate or not. But after the missionaries had spread the rumour that the Belgian authorities would take vengeance on Wiemers for the attacks made on the Belgian administration, Kandt held himself responsible to do what was within his power for his compatriot. Kandt had visited the Belgian judicial authority in Goma, who assured him that the incident would be handled in good faith, that there was no reason to fear that the Belgian government would persecute Wiemers for the attacks of the Protestant missionaries. The Belgian authorities who had been sent to investigate the incident were men of integrity; Kandt was sure that they would handle the matter with justice.[8]

These were sordid affairs. Derche personally was guilty of perversion, just as the Belgians as a group were guilty of corruption. Although the accuracy of the German missionaries' descriptions of Belgian activities on Lake Kivu was open to question, there could be no doubt that the local Belgian officials had abused their authority by intimidating the Africans and by requiring services from them for which they were not justly

[7] Kandt to Gouvernement, 8 December 1913, RU. IV I/D/33.   [8] Ibid.

compensated. Administration in Belgian Ruanda was, in short, a scandal. The flight from Idjwi of the chief Wera with two hundred and fifty of his people in January 1914 demonstrated the unpopularity of Belgian rule. Kandt regarded Belgian tyranny on Lake Kivu merely as an abuse of authority by local officials; when this had been called to the attention of the Colonial Ministry they had promptly ordered an investigation. Kandt thought that Voisin would restore the Africans' confidence in European justice. Derche had left on home leave before the arrival of the committee of inquiry; he would hardly be expected to return. The missionaries would remain subject to the 'arbitrary treatment and chicanery of the Belgian functionaries'; but this was a failing of integrity and competence of local Belgian colonial officers rather than of the intentions of responsible Belgian colonial statesmen.[9]

Kandt's judgement of Belgian colonialism was balanced, moderate, and probably accurate. As late as 1913 the intentions of the high Belgian colonial administrators were not always fulfilled by the local authorities. The notes made during the Kivu expedition by the British officers who came in contact with the other part of 'Belgian Ruanda'—the part north and west of the volcanoes at one time claimed by Musinga—confirm Kandt's views. Ireland recorded: 'The Belgians take 12 fr. per head, poll-tax and hut-tax inclusive annually. This amount is said, I believe untruly, to be remitted by the inhabitants bringing in free food for the askaris, and being credited with the amount of food brought in. In any case, only headmen are paid, and these gentry never pass on payment to the peasants who supply the food. Much discontent is rife on this score alone.'[1]

Apart from sheer exploitation, colonial rule in 'Belgian Ruanda' consisted of little more than procurement of food and porters. Payment, when made, was by cloth and beads.[2] There was no elaborate system of administration and justice, in part because the British pushed out the Belgians before Belgian

---

[9] Ibid.   [1] 'Diary of the Kivu Mission'.

[2] T. V. Fox, 5 July 1911, 'Report on Territory lying west of the 30th meridian between the Mfumbiro volcanoes and Kahinga channel proclaimed British on the 10 May 1911'. This document summarizes Belgian activity at the time of British occupation and discusses the principles on which British Ruanda was later administered. E.S. 1875.

activity was any more than a nominal occupation. Mfumbiro[3] became 'British Ruanda' as Coote's Kivu force occupied the region in 1909.

Just as the Germans around the turn of the century had been reluctant to intervene in Ruanda-Urundi, so the British, ten years later, thought it 'not desirable to interfere with the native regime until we are more firmly established in this new country [Mfumbiro]'.[4] The 'Kigezi district'[5] could not be added formally to the Uganda Protectorate until the international boundaries were finally demarcated in 1911.[6] Meanwhile Mfumbiro was considered under military occupation, and the despatches were signed by the head of the 'Kivu Mission'. Coote's replacement, T. V. Fox, was also uncertain as to 'the purpose for which the post is still maintained here. . . .'[7] But as Fox became more acquainted with the region, he, like his predecessors, waxed enthusiastic about the future of Mfumbiro.

Fox in July 1911 described the new district as 'high, healthy, and difficult for travelling . . .'; the Kigezi district fell into two distinct parts, 'Ruanda' and 'Rukiga',[8] which were known to the German administration in Kigali as simply part of the Rukiga district of northern Ruanda. The British Rukiga district (north of British Ruanda) was 'essentially a country of small independent clans owning no paramount chief and owing to the bickering that goes on amongst these clans there is very little intercourse among them. . . .'[9] The Bantu inhabitants of the area, whose 'characteristic feature is the hair dressed in string all round the head', were 'more uncouth and uncivilized'

---

[3] 'The name Mfumbiro which has become established by long use as the name by which the line of volcanoes is known among Europeans and has been loosely used of late for Ruanda and even for the whole of the former disputed area south of the 1° south of latitude is that of a stretch of country in the immediate neighbourhood of Kigezi Post and is not otherwise used by natives.' Fox's report of 5 July.

[4] 'Memorandum by Acting Chief Secretary', 2 October 1911, in Kigezi Monthly Reports, 1911, E.S. 1450A.

[5] The Kigezi district included more than the Mfumbiro region. Fox suggested that the district should be called Mfumbiro instead of Kigezi, but his proposal was not accepted.

[6] Acting Chief Secretary to the Government, 12 August 1911, Administration of Kigezi, E.S. 1857.

[7] Fox to Chief Secretary, Entebbe, 3 December 1910, Kigezi Monthly Reports, E.S. 1450.

[8] Fox's report of 5 July 1911.

[9] E. H. Reid to Chief Secretary, 5 March 1912, Kigezi Monthly Reports, E.S. 1450B.

than the Africans of 'British Ruanda'.[1] British Ruanda was under the sway of Nyindo, the half-brother of Musinga. 'Some of the [British] Ruanda chiefs have fairly large tracts of country with sub-chiefs under them and have considerable influence. Most of them, including all who have been in touch with Kigezi, are well-disposed and having been subject to European control in the past may be expected to conform to methods of regular administration.'[2]

During the Belgian occupation of Mfumbiro, Nyindo had fled from the Belgians as a refugee to northern Kigezi; he had been unable to control his chiefs, or to see Musinga. Upon the British arrival, Nyindo was granted permission to visit Musinga for two months. 'Nyindo certainly abused this privilege by remaining absent for some eight months, and the absence of the hereditary chief at this early stage of the development of the district caused serious inconvenience'; but Nyindo was recognized by the British authorities as the paramount African chief, on the condition that he would cooperate with their attempts to administer the region.[3]

At the Kivu-Mfumbiro Conference of 1910, the German delegates had placed great emphasis on the necessity to preserve the territorial integrity of Ruanda.[4] Gudovius wrote to the political officer at Kigezi in February 1912 that the German government would be grateful if the British administration would permit Nyindo to pay visits to Musinga, and to let him continue to pay the traditional tributes to Musinga of honey, beer, skins, and cattle.[5] The British agreed, on the condition that this privilege would not interfere with Nyindo's obligations to the British government.[6] Musinga in this way was less unwilling to see part of his domain pass under British control. Nyindo, on his part, 'professed unadulterated admiration and loyalty towards the Government of His Britannic Majesty'. But Nyindo's true feelings lay, if not with the Germans, with his

---

[1] Fox's report of 5 July.

[2] Ibid.

[3] E. H. Reid to Chief Secretary, 7 March 1912, Kigezi, E.S. 2489.

[4] As was illustrated by the German insistence on acquisition of the region under the sway of Kateraya, when they learned that Kateraya was Musinga's subject. The delegates at the 1910 Conference do not appear to have known about Nyindo.

[5] Gudovius to Political Officer, Kigezi, 24 February 1912, attached to Reid's letter of 7 March.

[6] Reid's letter of 7 March.

brother Musinga; on the outbreak of the First World War Nyindo revolted against British authority.[7]

Kigezi was established as a district in the Western Province of Uganda in 1911. Civil administration followed the military occupation on the Kivu expedition; as in German East Africa, military officers assumed civil responsibility because of shortage of civilian staff.[8] The main problem which faced T. Grant, the Western Provincial Commissioner, as he tried to organize Kigezi administratively, was whether to establish courts and collect taxes through indigenous 'chiefs', or whether to import African 'agents' from other parts of Uganda who had had administrative experience—this was a problem similar to the one the German officers had dealt with in Ruanda-Urundi. Grant recommended that Nyindo receive recognition as the paramount chief in British Ruanda; this decision was taken not only because Nyindo was the most influential chief in the region, but also because the British authorities feared that 'he might join his brother in German territory with a large following from the Kigezi district. . . .' In the Rukiga district, however, there was no chief of importance, and Sebalija, 'a superior type of Muganda . . . Mr. Coote's right hand man on the Kivu mission', was appointed as 'agent'.[9]

Grant was sceptical about bringing Baganda 'agents' into Kigezi, and thought they should be employed only when absolutely necessary. 'They should be carefully supervised with a view to the avoidance of any cause for complaints against them by the natives. Baganda in their position are inclined to be overbearing and unsympathetic with the natives. They are in no sense to be regarded as chiefs, but as advisers to the native

[7] 'When in company with Mr. Sullivan, I [S. Browning, Provincial Commissioner, Western Province] thought he rather overacted the part of allegiance and devotion; which soon proved to be the case, for in August of the same year [1914], Nyindo metaphorically threw himself into the arms of some Germans, who, disguised as White Father missionaries, visited him at sundown. Nyindo and Katuleggi have both been persistently disloyal from then until now and have assisted the Germans in every possible way against ourselves and the Belgians.' 'Western Province', Annual Report, 1915/16, E.S. 33/14C. Nyindo surrendered to the British authorities in May 1916 and was subsequently deported. See the Annual Report for 1916/17, Western Province, E.S. 314D. Cf. below, p. 213.
[8] The most prominent officer in the early years of the Kigezi administration was Captain E. H. Reid, of the 4th Kings African Rifles.
[9] C. E. Sullivan, 'Scheme for the Organization of Rukiga', 12 March 1912, 'Native Courts in Kabale', E.S. 3851.

chiefs, and their services will only be retained until it is considered that they can be dispensed with.'[1]

The idea behind the 'agent' system was to educate and supervise the indigenous chiefs, who, as soon as they were competent, were to replace the Baganda agents. The agents were to be appointed at fixed salaries; the local chiefs were to receive a 'sum equivalent to the difference between these salaries and the five percent rebate on taxes collected. . . .'[2]

In March 1914, however, C. E. Sullivan, Assistant District Commissioner in charge of Kigezi, proposed that the five percent rebate should be paid to the Baganda agents, leaving nothing for the local chiefs. This suggestion involved an important point of administration. W. E. F. Jackson, Assistant Chief Secretary at Entebbe, decided that the Baganda agents should be paid fixed salaries only, because they might abuse their authority if their income was dependent on the amount of taxes collected. The local chiefs, on the other hand, should receive 'small sums by way of percentage'. 'They may not be of much assistance, at present, in the collection of taxes, but I think that even very small payments would help in emphasizing the principle that they are expected to assist the Baganda in this work and would serve, by degrees, to give them some interest in the collection of taxes.'[3]

British tax systems were more advanced than the German. When the British occupied Mfumbiro, they assumed it would be only a matter of time before money from Kigezi would flow into the coffers of the Uganda Protectorate; the British, unlike the Germans, did not stop to debate whether tax collection was possible without a money economy. Grant said simply that the poll-tax of three rupees was 'not to be unduly pressed', and that 'until the natives pay poll tax it may be possible to arrange for them to perform a certain amount of labour, unpaid. . . . They ought to maintain and improve roads and make paths which may be necessary to facilitate touring.'[4]

---

[1] Grant to Chief Secretary, Entebbe, 11 October 1912, with attached memorandum, 'Administration of Kigezi', E.S. 1857, II.
[2] W. E. F. Jackson to Chief Secretary, 1 October 1915, 'Administration of Kigezi', E.S. 1857, III.
[3] Ibid. Jackson's decision was ratified by the Governor; see W. E. F. Jackson to Provincial Commissioner, Western Province, 9 October 1915, 'Administration of Kigezi', E.S. 1857, III.
[4] Grant's memorandum of 11 October.

Tax collections began in 1913–14,[5] and continued through the war.[6]

Apart from tax collection and appointment of chiefs, the most important British accomplishment in Kigezi before the First World War was the establishment of 'native courts for the hearing of petty cases'. The purpose of the courts was to 'guarantee the elementary security of life and property, and the free and guided development of the communal existence of the natives. . . .'[7] Courts were to be considered as 'an executive organization of the tribes',[8] consisting of those appointed by the Governor; jurisdiction extended over (1) 'civil cases in which the amount or subject matter in dispute does not exceed in value 200 rupees'; and (2) 'criminal cases, except cases punishable with death or transportation for life, provided that no punishment of either kind not exceeding three months or a fine not exceeding 150 rupees shall be imposed'. Appeals from the native courts were heard by the district court at Kabale.[9] One county court and five 'sub-divisional' courts were established.[1] The judicial system in Kigezi was still in the stages of preliminary organization when war broke out between the great powers.

At the outbreak of the First World War, which brought local administration to a 'standstill',[2] the Kigezi district had been under British administration for less than five years, under civil administration for less than two. The British administration in Kigezi, like the German in Ruanda-Urundi, was concerned with problems of health, agriculture, education,[3] and communications.[4] In both Kigezi and Ruanda-Urundi the main sources of revenue were taxes, court fines, and beer and game licences.

[5] G. D. Smith to Chief Secretary, Entebbe, 28 June 1913, 'Administration of Kigezi', 28 June 1913, E.S. 1857, III.
[6] In 1916–17, for example, 19,524 rupees were received through poll-tax out of a total revenue of 57,740 rupees for the Kigezi district.
[7] Sullivan, 'Scheme for the Organization of Rukiga'.
[8] Memorandum by W. E. F. Jackson, 26 March 1914, in 'Native Courts in Kabale', E.S. 3851.
[9] Headquarters of the Kigezi district was transferred from Kumba to Kabale in early 1914. See 'Administration of Kigezi', E.S. 1857 III; cf. Thomas and Scott, p. 462.
[1] 'The Courts Ordinance, 1911 . . . Kabale Native Courts', E.S. 3851.
[2] See J. E. T. Philipps to Western Provincial Commissioner, 14 August 1920, 'Kigezi, Land', E.S. 6448.
[3] The Church Missionary Society and the White Fathers each had one mission in Kigezi; each had a school.
[4] See the monthly and annual reports from Kigezi, 1910–20.

Both the Germans and the British attempted to introduce indirect rule. The main difference between the administration of Kigezi and Ruanda-Urundi—so far as comparison is possible—was the 'agent' system in British Rukiga. On paper, British justice and tax collection were more elaborate than the German. Belgian colonial administration in Ruanda, in contrast to both British and German, seems little more than a military occupation; but the Belgian Colonial Ministry before the First World War had begun to reform local administration —Belgian officials began to pay Africans for labour and provisions, and to administer justice—and there is no reason to believe that Belgian colonialism would not eventually have compared favourably with British and German.

The Commissioner of the Western Province of Uganda commented on the general state of affairs in Kigezi in the annual report of 1917/18:

The poll tax collection is better than I anticipated and the improvement reported in the work of the native courts is an encouraging sign. Many are addicted to excessive beer-drinking at certain seasons and when under that influence are (like other people) very quarrelsome; and sticking spears into one another on these occasions is no uncommon occurrence. Their domestic habits are sadly in need of reform, for their huts and compounds are dilapidated and filthy. However one must bear in mind that these people are only just emerging from the condition of savages and be on one's guard against the too frequent mistake of expecting too much of them.[5]

The same conclusion might be drawn about British administration in Kigezi. Considering the very few years before the First World War in which Britain had administered her lost province of 'Mfumbiro', not much could be expected.

'British and Belgian Ruanda' were hardly significant. Britain and Belgium happened by chance to receive small fragments of Ruanda. Ruanda-Urundi was administered almost entirely by Germany. If judgement of pre-First World War colonialism in Ruanda-Urundi is to be given, then it is the German administration which must be judged.

[5] E.S. 3314/E.

XVIII. GERMAN RULE AND RUANDA-URUNDI

FAILURE characterized German colonialism in Ruanda-Urundi more than success. The German administration succeeded in planning for the economic future of the country; it failed entirely in economic development. In part this was because German colonial administration was lopped off in 1914. If the 'Urundi-Ruanda railway' had been built, the history of Ruanda and Urundi might have taken a different course; Ruanda-Urundi would have been 'connected' to east Africa. But the failure of the imperial dream to open central Africa to trade and civilization had deeper causes than simply the failure to build a railway. As Kandt and Wintgens recognized, the railway itself would not bring prosperity, nor would it mean necessarily that Ruanda and Urundi would become profitable to the administration.

The Germans failed in their goal of economic development; they succeeded only partially in the maintenance of order and recognition of German sovereignty. In both Ruanda and Urundi, the Germans attempted 'indirect rule'. This was a purely German invention, and was not copied from foreign imperial systems and grafted on to Ruanda-Urundi. Whenever it was compared to the indirect rule of other imperial powers, the analogy in the minds of the Germans was the Dutch Residencies in the east Indies rather than the various British systems.

In Ruanda 'indirect rule' was successful because there was an organized African domain with an mwami strong enough to impose his authority on his subjects. If the Germans were shrewd enough to see that recognition of Musinga as overlord of Ruanda and cooperation with him was the only safe way to maintain peace, Musinga was shrewd enough to see that he could manipulate the Germans to his own advantage. But even with German assistance, northern Ruanda remained rebellious. In Urundi the Germans were much less fortunate. Instability was endemic, but the immediate trouble began with Beringe' egoism. He sacrificed his government's policy to gratify his lust for conquest. His defeat of Kissabo weakened the foundation of Rundi government. Grawert succeeded in restoring Kissabo as overlord of Urundi and in defeating Kissabo's enemies; but the whole system of Rundi government collapsed on Kissabo's death in 1908 and the German officers reacted with bitterness and frustration. This explains to some extent their inconsistent policies. They granted independence to great chiefs and at the same time tried to curtail separatism. The Germans regarded Rundi politics as chaotic, and tried to impose order; but as soon as they seemed to succeed the structure would fall again, as in 1915 with the death of Mutaga. This was colossally poor luck.

In both Ruanda and Urundi the Germans discovered that the power of the mwami was less in practice than in theory, more a myth than a reality. Even in Ruanda the mwami was powerless to control his subjects in direct proportion to their distance away from him and the unpopularity of his command. By the end of the German era the Residents understood the complexities of Rundi and Ruanda politics; they saw that behind the façade of monolithic absolutism individuals and groups competed for power, and that the mwami sought to use the conflicting forces exerted by individuals and groups to his own advantage. In Ruanda Musinga was successful; in Urundi after Kissabo's death, Mutaga was as unsuccessful as the Germans in controlling Rundi politics.

The Urundi Residency was plagued by changes in personnel; no fewer than six Residents served between 1908 and 1914. All were officers in the protectorate force. For the most part they regarded their Urundi assignment as simply another command, a stepping stone to take them farther in their career as soldiers; they lacked dedication to Urundi itself. Military rather than civil mentality prevailed, although the Resident was a civil authority. The Residents almost without exception failed to understand completely the idea of the Residency, even when presented in a modified form by Rechenberg. In theory the Resident was to recognize the paramount African rulers, and cooperate with them; the German officers and the African rulers were to administer Urundi together. In practice the Resident found little cooperation, and his principal task was keeping peace among the Rundi chiefs, rather than working with them toward a common goal. The German officers admitted frankly that the 'common goal' was an increase of authority of the Resident and economic exploitation of Urundi;

perhaps to some extent this was why they found the Rundi less than eager to cooperate. The later Residents tried 'to play one chief off against the other' instead of strengthening the authority of the great chiefs over their subjects. This was one reason why separatism flourished. But if the later Residents failed to comply with the letter of their instructions, there was never in the later years a case of flagrant violation of trust such as Beringe had perpetrated. The later Residents were a competent group. Of them, the mild-mannered, diligent Langenn and the gruff, realistic Schimmer stand out as the most effective Residents after Grawert. Schimmer admitted bluntly that the Rundi were not especially fond of the Germans—but that nowhere else did Africans show an especial love for German tutelage either—that the best thing to do would be to recognize that there would never be congenial relations between the two races—but that there could be economic development which would be mutually advantageous. Surely Schimmer's views stand as a classic and realistic expression of the attitudes of many German colonialists toward Africans. Some, like Dr. Kandt, took a more optimistic view.

Dr. Kandt towers over all others as the greatest German colonial administrator in Ruanda-Urundi. He dedicated his life to Ruanda. Kandt was eccentric, a poet, medical doctor, and scientist as well as an administrator. He was not, in contrast to most other German administrators in Ruanda-Urundi, a soldier. Kandt never hesitated to state his unpopular views about 'Indians' and trade; his commonsensical ideas contrasted strikingly with the fantastic theories of Lindequist. Kandt was a pedant; but he also had a sardonic humour and capacity for original thought. Wintgens, who resembled Schimmer in his abruptness and energy, was the only person who can be compared to him for ingenuity and foresight—although Gudovius was probably as intelligent as either.

In Ruanda, Kandt and Wintgens succeeded where the Urundi Residents failed. The average inhabitant of Ruanda was aware of the 'double dominion', the rule of the German government as well as of the mwami. This was not true in Urundi, in large part because of the weakness of the mwami. In both Ruanda and Urundi, however, the Residents could say by 1914 that the Africans recognized the advantages of European law and commerce, at least around the German posts. Coins circulated; the Ruanda tax collection of 1914 was a success, although the success was due to the Hutu notion that by paying taxes to the Germans they would be protected from the injustice and tyranny of the Tutsi.

In theory the judicial system was elaborate, in large part because it had to conform to the judicial system of the whole colony. In practice it was a crude type of retribution. Petty offences among Africans were left for customary law. If an African offended a European, however, or committed a crime great enough to violate a European sense of propriety, he would be punished by the German authorities, usually by flogging. The Germans considered flogging the most effective punishment, and the Residents raised indignant protests in 1914 when the Governor instructed them that a Tutsi should never be flogged except in exceptional circumstances. Justice was an instrument to ensure white man's supremacy; but in fairness it must be said that European justice in both Ruanda and Urundi was not inhumane in comparison to justice in other parts of Africa, nor does there appear to have been flagrant abuse of the judicial system.

But the principal means of maintaining German authority was the punitive expedition. These were often brutal. When a chief refused to submit to German rule, or, especially in Ruanda, to the authority of the mwami, a German officer would set out to destroy systematically the villages and agriculture of the 'rebel', and would appropriate his cattle. In the most serious cases, such as during the Ndungutze expedition of 1911, the main offenders were hanged. In many cases, however, they were simply deported, as Muhumusa was sent to Bukoba and Kilima to Neu-Langenburg. In Urundi the punitive expeditions were usually less serious than in Ruanda. For in Urundi the chiefs were so divided among themselves that they seldom posed a threat to German rule. Villages were burned and the refractory chiefs eventually made to obey whatever policy the German officers in Urundi might have been following at the time. Cattle were confiscated, which meant ruin for many people. But the Urundi punitive expeditions were seldom as violent as the ones in Ruanda. In part this was because the cleavages in Ruanda society differed from those in

Urundi. In Urundi the splits were between members of the royal family and the great chiefs; there was less emphasis on the Hutu-Tutsi difference. This meant that in Urundi there were tendencies toward anarchy, but less toward revolution. In Ruanda the Hutu were generally subjected to greater servitude and tyranny by the Tutsi. Absolutism was greater in Ruanda than in Urundi, but there still existed individuals and factions who vied for power. And in Ruanda those who opposed the mwami were more dangerous than those who competed against the mwami in Urundi. For in Ruanda the rebel chiefs could incite the latent hostility of the Hutu against the Tutsi, which did not exist to the same extent in Urundi. This was a powerful and potentially revolutionary force. The antipathy of the Hutu toward the Tutsi explains more than any other reason why Ndungutze succeeded in gaining mass support, and why both Musinga and Gudovius thought that the movement could overthrow both the mwami and German rule. Had it been successful, the revolution encouraged by Ndungutze would have resulted in independence for the Hutu and a breakdown of the highly organized Tutsi system of government. This explains why Gudovius used such appalling brutality to crush the Ndungutze movement. The Ndungutze expedition was the worst example of German brutality, but it would be euphemistic to call the other punitive expeditions a form of justice. There is perhaps something more tragic than comic about a German officer in darkest Africa who interrupted his task of burning banana groves to celebrate the birthday of the Kaiser. The Germans who administered Ruanda-Urundi did not question their right to mete out justice and to rule the two countries, just as the diplomats in Berlin, Brussels, and London did not question their right to partition Africa.

The most astounding aspect of German rule in Ruanda-Urundi was that so much was accomplished by so few people. In 1914 the white population of Ruanda-Urundi was about 190. Of these about 130 were missionaries. Of the remaining 60, a few were traders; most, about 40, were soldiers stationed at Usumbura and Kisenyi. In 1914 there were only *six* civil authorities in Urundi, *five* in Ruanda. Eleven administrators in a region nearly twice the size of Belgium. Are not the successes of German colonialism in Ruanda-Urundi more surprising than the failures?

PART THREE

RUANDA-URUNDI, THE FIRST WORLD WAR, AND THE PEACE SETTLEMENT

XIX. THE GERMAN-BELGIAN WAR IN EAST AFRICA

The valour and the strength of our army! (Octave Louwers, Belgian Foreign Ministry, 1921)[1]

It is not too much to say that without the British contribution, gladly given, in such vital matters, the Belgian invasion could hardly have succeeded. (British Official Account)[2]

THE outbreak of the First World War was accompanied by a resurgence of German colonial ambitions in central Africa. As the ardent German colonial enthusiast Hermann Oncken expressed it, 'we are fighting for an Empire in central Africa'.[3] A German *Mittelafrika*—the central African empire which had its roots in the activities of Peters and Emin—was finally to be realized through the First World War. Africa was to be 'repartitioned', mostly at the expense of the Belgian Congo. German East Africa would be linked to the Cameroons and South West Africa; the industries of imperial Germany would exploit the raw material of tropical Africa and find there a market for their products; *Mittelafrika* would dominate strategically the trade and military routes of the Atlantic and Indian oceans and would end forever the British threat of a Cape to Cairo route. *Mittelafrika*, in short, was to be a German empire in Africa worthy of the German empire in Europe.

These dreams of imperial grandeur were short lived. Only in German East Africa was Germany able to conduct an extended military campaign which lasted until the armistice. Even in east Africa, German forces were not sufficiently strong to wage

---

[1] *La campagne africaine de la Belgique* (Brussels, 1921), p. 15.
[2] *Military Operations in East Africa* (2 vols.; London, 1941) I, p. 460, note 2. This is the British official history of the east African campaign, based on a draft of Major H. FitzM. Stacke, and compiled by Lt. Col. Charles Hordern; the second volume has not yet been published.
[3] The doctrine of *Mittelafrika* played a prominent part in the writings of Karstedt, Leutwein, Delbrück, Oncken, Rohrbach, Kolbe, von Rechenberg, Trietsch, and Solf. Extracts from their works appear in Emil Zimmermann's anthology, *Das deutsche Kaiserreich Mittelafrika als Grundlage einer neuen deutschen Weltpolitik* (Berlin, 1917; English translation, *The German Empire of Central Africa*, with introduction by Edwyn Bevan, London, 1918). See also Octave Louwers, *Le Congo Belge et le pangermanisme colonial* (Paris, 1918); and 'Principes généraux de la politique coloniale belge', A. G. R., van den Heuvel papers, 30.

anything but defensive war. Von Lettow-Vorbeck, the talented German commander, knew from the outbreak of hostilities that military operations in east Africa would be subsidiary to the major campaigns in Europe; 'I knew that the fate of the colonies, as of all other German possessions, would only be decided on the battlefields of Europe'.[4] Von Lettow's task was to prevent his enemy in east Africa from sending troops to Europe; if he could with a small force inflict injuries on the British, and attract to east Africa large numbers of his enemy which would otherwise join Allied forces in Europe, then perhaps the east African campaign might influence the outcome of the war.[5] Von Lettow's strategy was to threaten his enemy's most sensitive point: the Uganda railway. 'From these considerations it followed that it was necessary, not to split up our small available forces in local defence, but, on the contrary, to keep them together, to grip the enemy by the throat and force him to employ his forces for self-defence.'[6] This meant concentration of the bulk of German troops in the northeast corner of the colony; it is in this light that the campaign in Ruanda-Urundi must be seen.

Just as east Africa was a subsidiary theatre in the world war, so Ruanda-Urundi was a subsidiary theatre in east Africa. The Ruanda-Urundi region nevertheless played an important part in the struggle for military supremacy. The only part of German East Africa contiguous to the Congo was Ruanda-Urundi, the logical base for attacks against the Congo, and, conversely, a major Belgian military objective.

The pre-world war diplomatic and military entanglement in Ruanda-Urundi had been coloured by national pride and imperial ambition; the Kivu-Mfumbiro Conference of 1910 had defined formally the boundaries of Ruanda-Urundi, but had not soothed the indignation of the Belgians, nor fulfilled the ambitions of the chauvinists of the German Colonial Office. The Kivu-Mfumbiro controversy had involved a comparatively heavy concentration of military forces in the Ruanda-Urundi region, which were still intact at the outbreak of the war. It was not surprising that one of the first actions of the east African campaign occurred in Ruanda-Urundi.

[4] General von Lettow-Vorbeck, *My Reminiscences of East Africa* (London, no date) p. 3.   [5] Ibid., p. 3.   [6] Ibid., p. 4.

On 18 September 1914 the German motor boat on Lake Kivu armed with a 37 mm. gun and a machine gun captured the larger of the two Belgian whalers; this established German control of Lake Kivu. On the night of 23 September the energetic Resident of Ruanda, Captain Wintgens, along with a force of about 50 men and a machine gun embarked in canoes from Ishara to conquer Idjwi. The Belgians at dawn sighted some of Wintgens's boats that had lost their way, but most of the force had already landed on Idjwi behind the Belgian post. After a creditable resistance the Belgians were forced to surrender; the Germans captured the post along with the Belgian steel boat.[7] Germany was now the master of Idjwi and Lake Kivu as well as all of Ruanda-Urundi. This was the closest Germany came to the realization of her *Mittelafrika* ambitions during the First World War.

The German capture of Idjwi raised the question whether the neutrality of the Congo had been violated. The Governor of German East Africa, Dr. Schnee, had himself hoped that hostilities would not spread to Africa.[8] According to the Berlin Act of 1885 any power with territory within the conventional basin of the Congo had the option to proclaim itself neutral;[9] in fact, neither Germany nor Britain invoked neutrality.[1] The Belgian Congo, on the other hand, was 'perpetually neutral', according to the Declaration of Neutrality of 1885. Neutrality was declared by the Belgian authorities at the beginning of the war.[2] A telegram sent by the Belgian government to the Congo authorities on 6 August 1914 stated: 'German army invaded Belgian territory 4 August. Belgium does not want to carry the

---

[7] *Military Operations*, I, p. 50; cf. the Belgian official account, *Les campagnes coloniale belges* (3 vols.; Ministère de la Défense Nationale; Brussels, 1925–32), I, pp. 162–6; and a manuscript at the Bundesarchiv, Koblenz, by Ludwig Boell, 'Der Feldzug in Ostafrika, 1914–18', which is condensed into *Die Operationen in Ostafrika* (Hamburg, 1951), pp. 61–62. The Belgian official account and the Boell manuscript describe the military engagements in Ruanda-Urundi in such detail that further research is practically superfluous. I have therefore tried to concentrate on events which have been inadequately treated or not touched on—especially those which eventually led to Belgium's acquisition of Ruanda-Urundi.
[8] Heinrich Schnee, *Deutsch-Ostafrika im Weltkriege* (Leipzig, 1919), p. 28.
[9] Berlin Act, Article X; the conventional basin of the Congo extended far beyond the political boundaries of the Belgian Congo.
[1] Germany submitted through the United States government a proposal for neutralizing the African territories on 22 August 1914, but by this time both sides were already involved in an African war.
[2] See *Les campagnes coloniale belges*, I, pp. 17–23.

war to Africa. Maintain strictly defensive attitude on frontiers of the Congo and the German colonies accordingly.'[3]

Regardless of the 'perpetual neutrality' of the Congo, 'the British and German protectorates in east Africa never were neutral territory, either juridically or by implication'.[4] In retrospect it is hard to see how the Congo itself could have remained neutral, if for no reason other than the temptation offered to the Belgians to join the victorious British forces; for once South African support arrived in east Africa the odds were overwhelmingly against the Germans.

At the beginning of the war, however, Belgium had good reason to fear German aggression. The Kivu controversy, not to mention the utterances of the *Mittelafrika* advocates, had shown that the German colonial jingoes were sceptical about Belgium's capacity to rule a colony many times her own size, and that few German imperialists would hesitate to seize what they could of the Congo in the event of a new scramble for and partition of Africa. The First World War posed the question whether there was to be a *Mittelafrika* or a scramble for the German colonies instead. This was a momentous alternative; the Belgians had every reason to feel intimidated by their powerful Teutonic neighbours.

Yet the German force in east Africa was not strong. Outbreak of war caught the Germans—as well as the British and Belgians —unprepared. Schnee was a pacificist,[5] and actually thwarted von Lettow's plans for the defence of the German colony. At the beginning of hostilities there were only 14 military units in German East Africa, composed of 260 Germans and 2,472 Africans, spread over an area nearly twice the size of Germany itself. The force was designed for nothing other than internal security. In comparison with the rest of the colony, Ruanda and Urundi were under heavy military occupation, with the IX

---

[3] The events in Ruanda-Urundi concerning neutrality illustrate the difficulties of isolated local officials in ignorance of the policy of their governments. On 26 September 1914 Lt. Lang at Kisenyi sent a representative to parley with the Belgians. The Belgian Lt. Terlinden said that he had received no news of the outbreak of hostilities, but also that he could not guarantee the eventual neutrality of the Congo. 'After this evasive answer, Captain Wintgens did not believe that the Belgians would respect the Congo Act.' Boell MS, pp. 479–80.

[4] *Military Operations*, I, p. 529.

[5] 'Dr. Schnee . . . a nice little man, weak, no character and rather typical of all second-rate civil servants; he admitted to me that von Lettow was too strong for him.' Colonel R. Meinertzhagen, *Army Diary, 1899–1926* (London, 1960), p. 105.

Company at Usumbura and the XI at Kisenyi. In accordance with von Lettow's strategy of concentration of troops, however, the two companies had been withdrawn from Ruanda-Urundi shortly after the outbreak of war; this left at considerable risk the region practically denuded of protection. The Belgians nevertheless grossly overestimated German troops in Ruanda-Urundi at 2,000 men. The actual number of German troops in Ruanda-Urundi in October 1914 was:

	European	askari
Kisenyi	5	47
Tschiwitoke	1	25
Usumbura	18	80
	24	152

'. . . As soon as the Belgians discover that we have very weak forces in Ruanda and Urundi, they will cross the Ruzizi, and we shall not be able to prevent them.'[6]

The Germans in Ruanda-Urundi nevertheless gave the impression of a large and well-disciplined force. On 4 October 1914 Wintgens defeated a Belgian attempt to take Kisenyi; on 20 and 30 November and again on 2 December 1914 Wintgens inflicted heavy injuries on Belgian troops. The close of 1914 saw Germany gain a fragment of Congo territory—Idjwi. Both sides were still acting defensively; neither was able to attempt a major offensive.

More skirmishing occurred throughout 1915. The German problem was to defend Ruanda-Urundi with as few men as possible against Belgian invasion. The Germans had several advantages. The precipitous terrain along the Ruzizi prevented the Germans from inflicting significant injuries on the Belgians, but it also deterred for the time being a Belgian invasion south of Kivu. The most important early action fought in Urundi was the abortive German attempt to take Luvungi, in the Ruzizi valley, where Commandant Henry was concentrating Belgian troops. Captain Zimmer, the German commander at the Usumbura garrison, detailed Schimmer to storm Luvungi with 16 Europeans and 111 askaris with 2 machine guns.

[6] In *Military Operations*, I, p. 49; Zimmer to Col. von Lettow-Vorbeck, 21 October 1914.

Schimmer divided his force into two groups, which advanced on Luvungi on 12 January 1915. The Germans managed to take the Belgians by surprise, but Schimmer was killed almost immediately; 'Der Hauptmann ist tot', cried *Vizefeldwebel* Reupke. Lt. Falkhausen took command and tried to continue the attack, but was forced to withdraw when his right flank was surrounded. The German attack was repulsed, but Belgian losses were substantial and the Germans regarded Luvungi as a victory. Urundi had lost her most colourful Resident, however, and the Urundi troops were consequently demoralized.[7]

The small Urundi detachment under Resident Langenn, now Major, who replaced Schimmer, could fend for itself in the minor engagements along the Ruzizi, as could Captain Zimmer and his force at Usumbura. This freed the remaining German troops in Urundi for wherever else they were needed.[8] Three detachments from Urundi in December 1915 had been transferred to the central railway; two detachments from Urundi had joined Wintgens in Ruanda. Of the Ruanda posts, Kisenyi was the most strategic. Situated on the north shore of Lake Kivu, it controlled the entrance to Ruanda. Against Kisenyi the Belgians directed their major attacks. In February 1915 several small battles were fought around Kisenyi and along the Congolese-German frontier. On 28 May Lt. Lang defended Kisenyi against a Belgian force said to be over 700 men with 2 machine guns. Again on 5 July and 3 August Belgian troops were repulsed by the Germans at Kisenyi; the XXVI Company arrived from Mwanza to relieve the beleaguered post in August 1915. Wintgens was now capable of minor raids; on 31 August he defeated a Belgian group, killing 10 Belgian askaris; on 2 September he stormed a Belgian stronghold held by 100 askaris with 3 guns and 1 machine gun. During September and October military action increased; hardly a day passed without at least a minor engagement. On 3 October about 250 askaris were repulsed from Kisenyi. On 26 November the Ruanda force with reinforcements from Bukoba inflicted heavy losses on the Belgian enemy, which possessed machine guns, 2·75 mm. howitzers and over 1,000 askaris. The German force

[7] See the Boell MS, pp. 595–607; cf. *Les Campagnes coloniales belges*, II, pp. 171–2
[8] See Boell's interesting comments in chapter VII of *Die Operationen in Ostafrika* on the conflicting views of the civil and military authorities toward strategy in th Ruzizi valley.

in December 1915 numbered 350 rifles, 4 machine guns and 2 guns. On 12 January 1916 Wintgens surprised a Belgian column north of Kisenyi, killing 11 Belgian askaris; on 27 January Captain Klinghardt repulsed another Belgian attack on Kisenyi itself.[9]

The Germans benefited from their good relations with the Ruanda. Musinga at the beginning of hostilities had persuaded his half-brother Nyindo, in Kigezi, to revolt. The Tutsi burnt the camp of the British Assistant District Commissioner in Kigezi and routed British authority.[1]

At the outbreak of war the British had regarded as a remote possibility any serious German invasion through the wilds of southern Uganda, and considered that the greatest danger to British possessions lay east of Lake Victoria. The Uganda government sent all four available companies of regular troops to assist the British East Africa Protectorate. Ankole, the district bordering Kigezi, remained firmly under British control. The revolt in Kigezi was the only British set-back in Uganda. Apart from this minor incident the Anglo-German frontier remained quiet.[2] The main activity occurred along the German-Belgian frontier.

Belgian troops vastly outnumbered their German opponents in Ruanda-Urundi. At the end of September 1915 Belgian forces, mostly Africans under the command of Europeans, between Lakes Tanganyika and Edward consisted of the following strength:[3]

Rutshuru	135
Bobandana	190
Idjwi	50
Nya Lukemba	325
Uvira	375
	1,075

Belgian estimates of the German troops in Ruanda-Urundi included the IX Company at Usumbura and the XI at Kisenyi; in fact, these companies had been withdrawn shortly after the

[9] Von Lettow has a succinct review of these actions in *Reminiscences*, chapter IX; cf. Boell, *Die Operationen*, chapter VII.
[1] See the lengthy report entitled 'The Kigezi Operations' in the archive of the Entebbe Secretariat.
[2] *Military Operations*, I, pp. 24–26.   [3] *Les campagnes coloniales belges*, I, p. 160.

outbreak of war, leaving less than 200 German troops there. The German force north of Lake Tanganyika was incapable of launching a major offensive against the Congo; but the Belgian headquarters at Rutshuru, overestimating the German strength in Ruanda-Urundi, had adopted a policy of defence until a concerted invasion could be planned with the British forces. The Belgian authorities feared that Uvira and Belgian transport and communications might be exposed to German attack unless Belgian and British offensives were coordinated.

The Anglo-German combination against the Congo had ceased after the Kivu-Mfumbiro Conference of 1910. In 1914 the alliance was reversed; the antagonism over Mfumbiro was forgotten; German East Africa had become a common menace to the Belgian Congo and the British possessions alike. The bond of Anglo-Belgian cooperation was forged by the outbreak of war.[4]

The Kabati Conference of October 1914 was the first meeting of representatives of British and Belgian forces in east and central Africa. Commandant Henry, who had assumed command of the eastern provinces of the Congo, found himself in 'cordial agreement'[5] with Captain E. S. Grogan, Assistant Intelligence Officer in Uganda. Since immediate action was considered impossible, Belgian policy was to remain defensive until Britain needed Belgian assistance. When the British were ready for a major invasion of German East Africa, Belgian troops would either strike at the same time or would support British forces.

The first cooperation resulting from the Henry-Grogan accord occurred a few months later. In January 1915 the British Commander in Uganda requested Belgian assistance to restore order in the Kigezi district. A Belgian force of 500 men with 2 guns quickly pacified the region.

Meanwhile the principle of Anglo-Belgian cooperation had been approved by the British and Belgian governments. Brigadier-General Malleson reached Rutshuru on 14 February 1915 on a mission assigned by the British War Office to 'endeavour to arrange the fullest possible cooperation' between the British and Belgian forces.[6] Malleson had envisaged a

---

[4] *Military Operations*, I, p. 29; cf. Meinertzhagen, *Army Diary*, pp. 109–10.
[5] Ibid.   [6] Ibid., p. 199; cf. *Les campagnes coloniales belges*, II, pp. 196–9.

British advance from Uganda against Ruanda; by a coordinated Belgian attack against Usumbura and advance through Urundi, the northwest part of German East Africa would fall into allied hands. Difficulties of communication between Uganda and the Congo, however, made this plan infeasible until later in the war.[7]

On his arrival in Rutshuru, Malleson found that the Belgians had altered their defensive policy. By 1915 the Belgians had obtained more accurate information about the size of the German Ruanda-Urundi force opposing them; by drawing on reserves and garrisons in the interior of the colony Belgium could bring troops north of Uvira up to 7,000. An invasion of Ruanda was planned for April 1915. The Belgian assaults on Kisenyi throughout 1915 were not intended as defensive border skirmishes, but as prelude to a full-scale Belgian invasion of the northwest part of German East Africa. Belgian troops, however, suffered from shortages of transport and munitions. No major effort was possible by Belgian forces until they received arms; Henry requested British aid. Arms and munitions consequently arrived at the Congolese posts in the spring of 1915 via Nairobi and Kampala. Malleson hoped that the Belgians would eventually be able, in concert with British forces, to strike as far inland as Tabora and the central railway, but no definite plans were made at this time. Malleson learned from Henry on 23 March 1915 that Tombeur[8] in Katanga was to assume command of Belgian forces; Henry regarded himself as divested of authority and Malleson returned to Nairobi. Before leaving Rutshuru, however, Malleson wrote to Tombeur to emphasize his view that Tabora and the central railway should be the Belgian military objective. Tombeur himself, abandoning plans for a Belgian advance from the southwest of German East Africa, by July 1915 was certain that Ruanda could be conquered without assistance of British troops[9]—if the British could provide additional transport facilities.

At a meeting on 6 February 1916 at Lutobo, Sir Frederick Jackson, Governor of Uganda, and Tombeur agreed that

---

[7] Ibid., p. 199; cf. *Les campagnes coloniales belges*, II, pp. 196–9.
[8] Tombeur had served as *Inspecteur d'Etat*, and Acting Vice-Governor of Katanga. He was subsequently commissioned as Colonel, and promoted to Major-General on 23 January 1916. *Campagnes coloniales*, I, p. 85, p. 219.
[9] Ibid., I, pp. 203–11.

Belgium would invade Ruanda-Urundi as soon as 5,000 carriers organized under British officers and an oxtrain of 100 wagons reached the Congo. Britain was also to provide medical services and reassume control of the Kigezi district. The Belgian government was to defray the cost of transport and supplies. Inevitable delays in delivery across the mountainous Mfumbiro region—as well as the defensive strategy of the British—forced the Belgians to postpone their invasion of Ruanda-Urundi until April 1916.[1]

Belgian offensives against German East Africa raised the question of how the occupied territory would be administered and what would eventually become of it. On 17 April 1916 Sir Francis Villiers, the British Minister to the Belgian government (now at Le Havre), notified the Belgian Minister of Foreign Affairs that the British government hoped that 'all occupation by British or Belgian troops should be regarded as provisional and temporary and that the close of hostilities must be awaited before a final settlement is made. . . . In order, however, to prevent confusion, to secure uniform action and to promote the communication of the Allies the British government are prepared to undertake the whole control and administration of occupied territory until the conclusion of the war'.[2]

The Belgians had anticipated conquest of part of German East Africa: in a long letter to General Tombeur of 27 March 1916 the Belgian Colonial Minister, Renkin, had sketched the double purpose of Belgian invasion: exclusive Belgian occupation of the conquered territory, and establishment of a rudimentary administration. This document expressed clearly in 1916 Belgian policy until the Peace Conference.

I. One of the goals of our military effort in Africa is, as you know, to assure possession of German territory for use as a pawn in negotiations. If when the peace negotiations open, changes in possession of African territories are envisaged, the retention of this pawn would be favourable to Belgian interests from every point of view. But it is indispensable that the conquered territories be occupied by us to

---

[1] *Military Operations*, I, chapter XII; cf. *Campagnes coloniales*, II, pp. 119–220, which emphasizes the change in British policy from defence to offence in December 1915; until Britain assumed the offensive, it was obviously impossible for Belgian troops to invade German East Africa.

[2] Villiers's 'Note Verbale' of 17 April 1916. For explanation of unidentified sources in this chapter, see above, p. xvii.

the exclusion of foreign authority. . . . It is impossible for me to set in advance the limits of our occupation to the east. They will depend on circumstances and the means at your disposal. I would call to your attention, however, that it is of the greatest importance that our occupation stretch to the western shore of Lake Victoria at one point at least. . . . It is clear that it will not be necessary to increase our centres of occupation to justify our claim, but that it will be sufficient if we hold in each region either the administrative centre held by the enemy or the most strategic point.

II. There is no question of establishing in the conquered territory a civil administration of the order of the administrative organization of our colony. The country will be under military government, and I should think divided into a small number of large districts coincid-ing with the big territorial divisions of the German administration. At the head of each of these districts you should place an officer of your preference chosen from those who have had overseas colonial service. . . . Your experience in Africa makes it unnecessary for me to insist on the necessity that you endeavour to win the cooperation of the native chiefs. . . . Our occupation should be restricted to the maintenance of the peace of the country and especially the security of our lines of communication. . . . The native population must give up their arms; they should be notified that any seditious movement, any difficulties caused to our occupation, and any attack against our convoys will be rigorously repressed. The commandants of each district must act with great firmness, but they must not tolerate any act of repression by their European subordinates unjustified by circumstances. Discipline among the military units in charge of the occupation and protection of our communications must be strictly maintained and those guilty of marauding and violence should be strictly punished.[3]

Renkin's orders to Tombeur obviously show that as early as March 1916 the Belgians intended to use any territory which might be conquered by them during the war as a pawn in the east African peace settlement. To make their claim effective the Belgians intended to occupy and administer exclusively the German territory taken by Belgian troops. On 21 April 1916 Pierre Orts in the Belgian Foreign Ministry drafted a memoran-dum to inform the British government that the Belgian govern-ment was willing to accept the view that British and Belgian occupation was to be 'provisional and temporary', but that it was necessary to maintain under Belgian authority the territory

[3] Renkin to Tombeur, 27 March 1916.

taken by Belgian troops. Orts gave the reason that otherwise the Belgian lines of communication might be broken.[4]

Villiers replied on 30 April 1916:

A report from General Smuts that the officer commanding the Belgian forces in the northern district will shortly proceed to Kigali . . . and that he has declined a proposal that he should be accompanied by a British political officer. Ruanda . . . is a province of importance with a large population and is under a sultan with whom the Germans have been careful to maintain good relations. It is possible therefore that the natives will keep faithful to German rule and that they will offer some resistance to the Allied troops. It is true that warfare of an open character is not likely because the nature of the tribes is unwarlike; nevertheless the British officers who are on the spot feel convinced that embarrassment may arise if the areas occupied are not placed, so soon as may be possible, under British administration. His Britannic Majesty's Government hold strongly to the principle of adopting wherever practicable an uniform system for the districts of German East Africa which may be occupied. Note has of course been taken of the military reasons . . . for which the Belgian government were unable to accept the suggestion of British control, but in fact it is not anticipated that there would be interference with the control by Belgian officers of their military lines of communication. Instruction would be given to the British political officials entrusted with the administration of occupied districts to facilitate in all possible ways the transit of Belgian forces and would in no manner interfere with the lines of communication or with the conduct of the military operations. It will be no doubt realized, Sir Edward Grey goes on to state, that the reasons which General Smuts puts forward in recommending administration by British political officials are not only of the highest importance but also of a military character, and in the circumstances it is hoped that the Belgian government will consent to issue at once to their military officers instructions in the sense which His Britannic Majesty's Government so earnestly desire.[5]

These problems of Anglo-Belgian administration were still unresolved at the time of the Belgian invasion.

Until the spring of 1916 the Germans successfully defended their western frontier. Ruanda and Urundi fell in April–May 1916 as the German force withdrew before the concentric attack

---

[4] Orts to M. le Ministre des Affaires Etrangères, 21 April 1916.
[5] Villiers to Beyens, 30 April 1916,

of superior Belgian and British troops. German troops in the northwest of the colony were under the command of General Wahle at Tabora, the strategic railway centre in the west of German East Africa; he gradually withdrew his detachments from the frontiers toward Tabora as the British troops advanced from the north along the western shore of Lake Victoria and the Belgian from the west and north through Ruanda-Urundi.

Strengthened by British munitions and transport,[6] the Belgians in February 1916 prepared an offensive against German East Africa; 5,200 troops with 32 guns and 32 machine guns were concentrated north of Lake Kivu, 2,500 with 20 guns and 20 machine guns along the Ruzizi.[7] The German troops opposing them in Ruanda-Urundi were ludicrously inferior. In January 1916 a German document gave the following numbers:

	German	askari	guns	machine guns
Ruanda	111	957	2	10
Urundi	55	450	1	2

By 17 April, however, part of the German force had already been withdrawn, leaving the Wintgens detachment in Ruanda with only 55 Germans, 600 askaris, with 3 guns and 5 machine guns based at Kisenyi; the Urundi detachment had 36 Germans, 250 askaris, with 2 guns, 3 machine guns, based at Kitega.[8] The problem of a Belgian advance was therefore with supply, transport, and terrain rather than the strength of the opposing German force.

Ruanda-Urundi and the western shore of Lake Victoria were the major Belgian military objectives. Ruanda's high, mountainous plateau, denuded of forest, facilitated troop movement; the problem was how to get there. The Mfumbiro region north of Lake Kivu was a natural frontier difficult to cross; south of Lake Kivu, the Ruzizi river presented similar difficulties. South of Lutobo, however, there was easy entrance to northern Ruanda and no strong German fortifications. It was therefore decided that the principal Belgian thrust would be made by the

---

[6] The Belgians and the British disagreed about the cost; the figures agreed to at Lutobo and ratified by the Belgian government were nearly doubled by the actual cost; 'the danger of a breakdown in the arrangements for cooperation was averted by the British government generously consenting to bear the difference'. *Military Operations*, I, p. 402.

[7] Ibid., p. 400.   [8] Boell, *Die Operationen*, p. 260.

Lutobo road, while subsidiary engagements would be opened north and south of Lake Kivu. In early April the Uganda Police Service Battalion assumed control of the Kigezi district, thus freeing 500 Belgian troops, and creating the impression that the major Belgian attack would occur north of Lake Kivu.[9]

South of Lake Kivu Lt.-Col. Olsen—whose bellicose actions against the Kivu expedition a few years earlier had inflamed Anglo-Belgian relations—commanded the southern brigade, which was divided into three units, of which the two smaller groups were to demonstrate while the third, composed of three battalions, would cross the Ruzizi near Shangugu and penetrate Urundi to Nyanza, 60 miles to the east. North of Lake Kivu Colonel Molitor commanded the northern brigade, organized in two groups. The first, 4 battalions, 10 guns, under Major Rouling, was to demonstrate 10 miles north of Lake Kivu at Kibati; Colonel Molitor commanded the second group of 4 battalions, 2 batteries, and the Kigezi detachment. Molitor was to strike from Lutobo at Kigali. As a preliminary to divert the enemy's attention, the southern brigade demonstrated on 12 April on the lower Ruzizi; a week later Major Muller, commanding the northern unit of the southern brigade, crossed the Ruzizi near Shangugu.[1]

On 20 April, Wintgens, leading the German troops in Ruanda, prepared for the defence of Ruanda with only 65 rifles and no reserve. On 25 April Molitor crossed the frontier. Wintgens fell back to Kigali after a minor engagement on 30 April at Kasibu. The German defences in the west were abandoned on 11 May; in the south the German troops fell back towards Nyanza, where the German forces were gathering for a fresh defence.

Belgian movement was hampered by continuous rain. On 5 May Molitor's column reached the western end of Lake Mohasi, where they fought a minor engagement with the Germans, and then pushed on to Kigali without opposition. In Urundi, Muller's column after taking Shangugu reached Bushekere on 7 May; there Muller found that bad roads and floods made the road to Nyanza impossible. After further delays

---

[9] *Military Operations*, I, chapter XXIV.
[1] See 'La marche concentrique sur Kigali-Nyanza', *Campagnes coloniales*, II, pp. 54–55; cf. Boell, *Die Operationen*, chapter XVII.

Muller marched northeast to Nyanza, where on 19 May he received the submission of Musinga.[2]

The Belgian delays caused by weather and poor roads enabled the Germans to withdraw from Ruanda and Urundi without a major battle. Wintgens's Ruanda detachment had retreated before Rouling's column in the north and had passed only a few miles from Muller's column from the west. Langenn, from the Ruzizi, had retreated to Save, where he joined forces with Wintgens; together the two groups crossed the Akanjaru, leaving Ruanda to the Belgians. By 21 May Rouling's troops at Nyanza had established contact with Molitor at Kigali; Belgian troops were in complete control of Ruanda.[3]

The forces of Wintgens and Langenn were now retreating along the Ruvuvu toward Kitega; they were followed by the Belgian columns led by Molitor and Olsen, advancing from Kigali and Nyanza respectively. Molitor's orders were to march toward Lake Victoria, cutting off, if possible, the retreat of the German forces in Karagwe. Having no specific orders, Olsen was free to follow the Germans toward the south. On 1 June he began the 'marche en éventail' toward Kitega and Usumbura. One of Olsen's columns led by Muller fought intensely on 6 June at Kokawani and 12 June at Nyawigi; the Germans resisted vigorously but continued their retreat.[4] Olsen reached Kitega on 17 June; the previous day it had been evacuated by the Germans and taken by a battalion of Rouling. Olsen remained at Kitega to replenish supplies and establish Belgian authority. Olsen's other column had marched on Usumbura on 6 June; they joined Olsen in the vicinity of Kitega on 19 June. On 27 June the young mwami and his regents submitted to the Belgians. This marked the complete Belgian conquest of Ruanda-Urundi. They had achieved their main military objective almost without opposition.[5]

On 12 June Tombeur had received orders from the Belgian government to extend Belgian occupation at least from Usumbura to Lake Victoria. He was to coordinate his actions with British movements, but was to maintain the independence of

[2] *Campagnes coloniales*, II, pp. 234–8.
[3] See 'La marche concentrique sur Kigali', *Campagnes coloniales*, II; *Military Operations*, I, XXVII; *Die Operationen*, XVII.
[4] Ibid.
[5] See 'La marche en éventail', *Campagnes coloniales*, II; *Die Operationen*, XVII.

the Belgian command. Further Belgian objectives were exclusive Belgian occupation of Ujiji and the western section of the central railway. Tombeur agreed with Sir Charles Crewe, the general commanding the British troops in the west, that the Belgian and British forces would converge together on Tabora. Allied advance on Tabora became, in fact, a race between the British and Belgians. Belgian troop movement was facilitated by sufficiency of local supplies; in contrast to the sparsely populated and sterile region through which the British troops were marching, the Belgian troops, composed largely of Africans, were able to live off the country, unretarded by lack of supply columns and depots. Attempts to coordinate the Anglo-Belgian advance on Tabora proved futile because of the vast distances;[6] the result of the Belgian advantages was that on 19 September 1916 the Belgian flag was hoisted over Tabora.[7]

The conquest of Tabora ended a distinct phase of operations. The Belgians had refused to participate further in the east African campaign; they had achieved their objectives and had stated from the outset that Belgian contribution to the war could not be expected after the security of the Congo was assured.[8] Belgian troops, with indispensable British support,[9] had captured not only Ruanda-Urundi but also a considerable part of the west of German East Africa, including Ujiji and the western part of the central railway. Belgian casualties had been few and the rewards many. There was no longer a German threat to the Congo. Yet the Belgian contribution to the east African campaign was not great. The Belgians had caught the Germans on the run, in full retreat. German forces in the west— always a subsidiary theatre of war—had retreated before overwhelming Allied numbers. The Germans had successfully eluded their Belgian pursuers; while leaving the Belgians the western part of their territory, they were still at large. The Belgians succeeded completely in gaining their objective of

[6] *Campagnes coloniales*, II, pp. 490–2.
[7] See *Military Operations*, I, chapter XXVI.
[8] Belgian troops did, however, later participate in the Mahenge campaign.
[9] 'To recapitulate: apart from the British naval contribution on Lake Tanganyika, during the whole period of the Belgian operations material was arriving via Mombasa and Uganda; British supply services were maintained for the Belgian northern brigade, as well as Crewe across Lake Victoria; British signal personnel accompanied the Belgian march to Biharamulo; Uganda carriers served the Belgian northern brigade all the way to Tabora.' *Military Operations*, I, p. 460, note 2.

occupation of German territory; they failed entirely to destroy the German enemy. The German success in eluding the clutches of the Belgians and British, however, was not surprising in view of the problems of supply and communication over the enormous distances which the Allied forces had to cover.[1]

The enemy had escaped, but the Belgians had won a vast and rich territory. The Belgians had, moreover, excluded British influence from the region occupied by Belgian troops.

[1] From Kamwezi to Tabora, for example, the Belgian northern brigade marched over 400 miles. Ibid., note 1.

XX. GERMAN EAST AFRICA AND BELGIAN OCCUPATION

There is no question of establishing in the conquered territory a civil administration of the order of the administrative organization of our colony. (Renkin, Belgian Colonial Minister, 1916)[1]

BELGIUM faced two main problems after her successful invasion of German East Africa. The first was how to administer the occupied territory; the second was how to ensure to Belgium a just reward for her contribution to the east African campaign. The former was simple; the purpose of military occupation was the maintenance of order. The latter was by no means easy, and involved Belgium in long and difficult negotiations with Great Britain.

Villiers had written on 17 April 1916 that the British government viewed occupation of German East Africa as 'provisional and temporary', and that 'to secure uniform action' the British government was ready to administer all occupied territory. The Belgians had replied that they were willing to regard the occupation as provisional, but that all territory conquered by Belgian troops would be administered by Belgian authorities. On 23 May 1916 Villiers wrote to the Belgian Minister of Foreign Affairs that 'in view of the considerations advanced, His Britannic Majesty's Government will not further press the proposal'. The British accepted Renkin's suggestion that a British senior political officer should be attached to Belgian headquarters in Africa to advise on 'administrative methods in the occupied enemy territory'.[2]

Tombeur met Sir Frederick Jackson and General Crewe at Entebbe on 20–21 July 1916 to discuss the future of the occupied territory. There was little agreement, especially about the Lake Victoria region. The British claimed that the administration of the Bukoba district would be greatly facilitated if it were all uniformly under British administration. Tombeur argued, however, that not only had the Belgians reached

---

[1] Renkin to Tombeur, 27 March 1916; for explanation of unidentified sources used in this chapter, see above, p. xvii.　　[2] Villiers to Beyens, 23 May 1916.

Nyamirembe (on Lake Victoria) first, but that the British themselves had urged the Belgians to establish a base there.[3] The
British countered this argument by recalling that the Belgian
invasion would not have been possible without British transport
and supplies, not to mention Smuts's diversion of the main
German forces; this had eliminated opposition to the Belgian
advance. The result of the Entebbe conference was a provisional
arrangement subject to ratification by the two governments.
The understanding was 'dictated solely by present convenience
. . . without prejudice to any post-bellum territorial claims'; it
provided that Ruanda and Urundi, and the Ujiji district
should be administered by Belgium; Mwanza and Mpwapwa
would be administered by Britain. Bukoba and Tabora were to
be 'administered in the name of both governments by British
officials, under the Belgian and British flags, according to
British martial law regulations'.[4] In substance this provisional
arrangement was adopted by the two governments. The main
exception was that no joint-administration in Bukoba and
Tabora was established. Tabora was handed over to the
British in February 1917; the region along the southwest shore
of Lake Victoria remained solely under Belgian occupation.
Belgium also retained complete control over the western end
of the central railway in the Ujiji district.[5]

The Belgians regarded Tabora as much a liability as an asset;
but since it had been captured by Belgian troops, it could be
used to serve Belgian interests. On 6 September 1916 Renkin
prepared a memorandum for the Belgian government; the
British could have Tabora if they would agree that the remaining districts occupied by Belgian troops should be administered
by Belgium until the peace settlement. '. . . occupation by
Belgian troops of the provinces of Ruanda, Urundi, Ujiji, the
district of Karema and the southern part of the province of
Bukoba would assure [Belgium] of a sufficiently great pawn
against Germany.'[6] On 8 September Renkin prepared another
long memorandum explaining why Belgium should relinquish

---

[3] *Campagnes coloniales*, II, p. 410.
[4] *Military Operations*, I, p. 437.
[5] See 'Guide de conversation à l'usage du Ministre de Belgique à Londres',
undated.
[6] Renkin to M. Le Ministre des Affaires Etrangères, 6 September 1916, 'Projet
de note à adresser au Gouvernement Britannique'.

Tabora. Tabora had been a distinctly 'Allied' undertaking; the British would simply never agree to a Belgian administration there. By occupying the last section of the central railway and the southwestern shore of Lake Victoria the Belgians had attained two important objectives far beyond their original plans, which in themselves were of great intrinsic value; Tabora added nothing. In fact, it was a city with a large population in which Belgium had no interest and which would cause great administrative costs. Furthermore, it was the strategic centre of that part of German East Africa; should the Germans return, their main objective would be the reconquest of Tabora, which would involve Belgium in another costly campaign. If, however, the British administered Tabora, they would consequently protect Belgian gains in the northwest. It was time, Renkin said, that the British government knew definitely about Belgium's plans for east Africa.[7]

The Belgians were willing to exchange Tabora for British acknowledgement that Belgian troops would occupy indefinitely the territory captured by them. This was the gist of Renkin's urgent memorandum of 8 September 1916. By early November, however, the British still had not replied, and the Belgians did not have a clear idea of the British attitude. Were the British trying to take advantage of the difficulties of Belgian troops in Tabora? Administration of Tabora was not only costly but also difficult; the Belgians feared unrest among the large non-European population. If Tabora were reduced to anarchy by revolt, then Belgian troops would be forced into an untenable position; either the revolt would have to be repressed with great force, or British troops would have to be called in. In either case Belgium's capture of Tabora would be compromised; the Belgians would be unable to transfer Tabora to Britain in exchange for consolidation of gains elsewhere.[8] Tombeur had been unable to control his troops; reports had reached London and Brussels that Belgian troops were pillaging the villages as

---

[7] In 1934 G. Moulaert published *La campagne du Tanganyika* (Brussels, 1934), which aroused a storm of controversy by attacking the Belgian government's decision to withdraw from Tabora. Louwers argues that the east African campaign was fought for political rather than military goals in 'La conquête du Ruanda-Urundi', *Bulletin de l' Institut Royal Colonial Belge*, VI, 1935, pp. 167–78; 372–8. Other points of view contributed to the same journal in 1935 are those of F. Dellicour, pp. 143–66; M. A. Engels, pp. 359–60; and M. G. Moulaert, pp. 361–71.
[8] 'Guide de Conversation'.

they overran the country.[9] The situation at Tabora and the reports of Belgian pillaging—which could be greatly to Belgium's disadvantage at the peace settlement—caused anxiety in the Belgian government. On 10 October 1916 the Belgians submitted to the British government three long memoranda which frankly discussed Belgian territorial ambitions as well as the administrative problems facing Belgium and Britain in east Africa.

The first memorandum discussed principles of administration adopted by Belgium in the occupied territory. The Belgians wished to form a uniform policy in conjunction with the British authorities concerning the treatment of German subjects, German firms, plantations, and concessions in the occupied areas. There was also a problem of currency. In all of these matters the Belgians declared themselves willing to follow the principles of international law expressed by the conventions of the Hague. The Belgian government approved of the appointment of Captain N. E. F. Corbett as chief political officer with Belgian headquarters in German East Africa for consultation on administrative problems.[1] The Belgians proposed in detail the boundaries delimiting the two spheres of administration and described how General Tombeur was already at work reorganizing public services at Tabora; engineers were being sent from the Congo to repair the western end of the central railway, and it would not be long before Belgian trains would be entering Tabora.[2]

To all these items the British government replied as definite policies were formed. The British government would, as far as practicable, also follow the principles of international law expressed by the conventions of the Hague, with allowance made for any action taken on grounds of public safety. The British agreed that there was a need to discriminate between native populations who were not hostile to the Allied forces and the German white population, in whose case the Belgian and British authorities should take appropriate action depending on the extent they had already given assistance to the

[9] Plundering was not restricted to Belgian troops; Orts pointed out to Villiers in a conversation of 27 October 1916 that the white South African troops were equally guilty. Orts's memorandum of 28 October 1916.

[1] See Villiers to Beyens, immediate, 4 October 1916.

[2] 'Note en 3 partis', 10 October 1916.

German forces or might be likely to do so in the future.[3] As to the liquidation of German businesses, 'it is very doubtful whether it would be possible to justify the liquidation of enemy firms carrying on business in occupied enemy territory. . . .'

Although there is nothing in the fourth convention of the Hague which expressly forbids such action, it seems that it is inconsistent with the general spirit of the convention which aims, so far as possible, at safeguarding private rights and property. The general theory is that the occupying belligerent should allow the life of the occupied territories to go on so far as is consistent with his military requirements, under the same rules as before, and unless it could be maintained that liquidation of small firms was a military necessity it would be found difficult to justify it. . . . The desire of His Majesty's Government to comply with the Hague Conventions may have been to some extent diminished by Germany's disregard of them, still it seems desirable that His Majesty's Government should be particularly careful not to do anything for which they could be attacked in connection with their enemy territory, because German action in territory occupied by Germany forms one of the chief counts of the indictment against the German authorities. Moreover it is obviously undesirable to do anything which might give the Germans an example for liquidating every business in Belgium or northern France.[4]

The British also thought that 'Belgian exploitation of certain sections of the central railway . . . should be confined to those sections in districts subject to Belgian administration'.[5]

Did Belgium have territorial ambitions in east Africa? This was the subject of the second and third Belgian memoranda of 10 October submitted to the British government.[6] Belgium had 'numerous questions to settle with Germany at the peace negotiations, both European and African'. Belgium bluntly acknowledged that she intended to use the territory in east Africa occupied by her troops as a pawn in these negotiations; she intended to profit by her victory in the east African war, whether in Europe or Africa. As far as Africa was concerned,

[3] Villiers to Beyens, 9 November 1916.
[4] Villiers to Beyens, 26 January 1917.   [5] Villiers to Beyens, 17 January 1917.
[6] The third memorandum, in particular, was mostly concerned with Belgium's further participation in the east African campaign; these negotiations are beyond the scope of this study, but will be considered to the extent that they strengthened Anglo-Belgian friendship and influenced the peace settlement concerning Ruanda-Urundi.

'Belgium has conquered one of the most important parts of the German colony'. 'The value of this territory derives from two circumstances: access to Lake Victoria and a part of the German central railway.' It was yet too early to decide whether Belgium would retain this part of German East Africa; if, for instance, Belgium might gain economically and politically by some other concession elsewhere—such as acquiring from Portugal the southern bank of the Congo river, which would give Belgium undivided control of the Congo mouth—then Belgium would consider ceding the territory occupied by her troops in east Africa in return. Quite bluntly put, 'the point of view of Belgium is simple: she intends to derive from her considerable military effort in Africa as great a benefit as possible'. The territory occupied by Belgian troops was obviously of value: for instance, 'Ruanda, fertile, rich in cattle, and favourable for white colonization'. Britain could not help but recognize the justice of the Belgian point of view. The Belgians were furthermore willing on certain conditions to send Congolese troops to the south of German East Africa to contribute toward Allied victory in east Africa.[7]

The Belgian government 'has not hesitated to communicate in utter confidence her concrete views to the British government'.[8] The Belgians had done this in the hope that Britain would acknowledge Belgian claims in east Africa. They were disappointed. The British attitude was reserved, in contrast to the anticipated response that Belgian claims would be respected with the understanding that British claims to the rest of German East Africa would similarly be put forward. The British professed embarrassment at the acquisitive nature of Belgian aims —the British attitude was 'under all reserve'.[9]

. . . His Majesty's Government desire in the first place to express their thanks to the Belgian government for the frankness with which they have communicated their views as to future policy. His Majesty's Government feel it incumbent on them to reply with equal frankness, and to say that some portions of the notes must give rise to embarrassment. It is the understanding between all the Allied powers that enemy territory occupied by any of them is held and administered provisionally until the termination of the war, and the

---

[7] 'Note en 3 partis'.　　　　　[8] Ibid.
[9] Villiers to Beyens, 10 November 1916.

principle is recognized in the Belgian notes. But—if His Majesty's Government rightly understand the language of the notes—it would appear that the Belgian government are disposed to take the view that in the final peace negotiations it is open to them to make separate arrangements with Germany as to the future of the territory in east Africa now occupied by them, exactly as though that territory had passed into their definitive possession. It would not be fair to the Belgian government to leave them under the impression that His Majesty's Government could agree in advance to such a position which has not so far been claimed for themselves, or for any of the Allies as regards German colonies. It follows from what has been laid down as to the provisional nature of all conquests by the Allied powers that His Majesty's Government regard it as premature at the present time to enter into any discussion as to the future; but they are obliged to state that they could not regard with indifference any settlement in east Africa which might prejudicially affect either the safety or the economic development of their possessions in that quarter of the world. The Belgian government no doubt hold a similar view as regards their possessions. But His Majesty's Government have hitherto refrained from discussion on their own behalf or that of others any final territorial rearrangements in Africa. These must be dealt with in the terms of peace when the latter are considered as a whole and cannot be settled now apart from what may have been done or proposed in respect of other theatres of war, or without careful consideration of their bearing on any other arrangements that may be contemplated as between the governments of Great Britain and Belgium and the other Allies.[1]

The British refused to negotiate with the Belgians about the future of east Africa; they refused even to recognize Belgian occupation of east Africa as anything more than 'provisional and temporary'.

Renkin was confident nonetheless. 'The reserve of the British government will change nothing. Belgium will participate in the African peace negotiations because she participated in the war in Africa. . . .'[2] Beneath this veneer of confidence was the fear that had been present from the beginning of the war and that continued until the final African peace settlement—that Belgium might be excluded from the peace negotiations, that Belgium might be robbed of the reward she had justly won.

This uncertainty continued from the end of 1916 to the

[1] Villiers's memorandum of 8 November 1916.
[2] Renkin to M. Le Ministre des Affaires Étrangères, 28 November 1916.

spring of 1919. Little changed in the part of German East Africa under Belgian administration,[3] just as little changed in Belgian and British attitudes about the future of the German colony. Anglo-Belgian friction reached a highpoint over the delays in Belgian evacuation from Tabora, but Orts's mission to London in April 1917 and the subsequent agreement that Belgian troops would continue to cooperate in the campaign repaired and strengthened Anglo-Belgian friendship. Cooperation continued, but so also did the uncertainty of Belgium's position in east Africa.

The end of hostilities in east Africa raised again the question of the future of the German colony. Belgium had successfully met the problem of administration; Belgian troops had maintained order. Belgium had failed, however, to ensure her reward for victory in the east African war. Britain had refused to recognize Belgium's claims in east Africa; the future of the German colony was to be decided by a conference composed of the Allied and Associated powers; Belgium would of course attend, but it was clear that as a small nation she would be dwarfed by the great powers, just as the Twa were dwarfed by the Tutsi. Belgium had occupied parts of German East Africa for almost three years; but the glitter of her victory had dimmed; her statesmen feared that her military effort in Africa had been forgotten even by those who had profited most from it: the British. The British themselves entertained a large number of ideas about the future of German East Africa, including the possibilities of a colony for India, and even for the United States.[4] The only certainty was that German East Africa would not be returned to the Germans. The Belgians waited in suspense.

[3] For a different view see *Historique et Chronologie du Ruanda*, which tends to emphasize the importance of the Belgian administrative policy during the war; the most significant measure was the limitation of the power of the Bami.

[4] See Meinertzhagen, *Army Diary*, pp. 248–50; 'Principes généraux de la politique coloniale belge', A.G.R., van den Heuvel papers, 30; Robert Lansing, *The Peace Negotiations* (London, 1921), chapter XIII; David Lloyd George, *The Truth about the Peace Treaties* (2 vols.; London, 1938), I, pp. 114–31; George Louis Beer, *African Questions at the Paris Peace Conference* (New York, 1923), part VI.

XXI. THE EAST AFRICAN PEACE SETTLEMENT OF 1919

The energy and the will which must be shown in this negotiation must be carried to the extreme limit allowed within our friendly relations with Britain, but not beyond that. (Octave Louwers, Belgian Foreign Ministry, 1919)[1]

. . . to be frank, none of the Belgian reasons for demanding the most healthy and the richest part of the territory [of German East Africa] will stand the test of even the friendliest examination. (*The Times*, 1919)[2]

As the Paris Peace Conference opened in January 1919, the future of the German colonies was still undecided. German East Africa was occupied by Belgian and British troops; yet its fate ostensibly was to be decided by a conference of powers influenced by the liberal principles of President Wilson; 'the League of Nations should become a "residuary trustee" for the inheritance of the Turkish and the German colonial empires, and should administer, primarily for the welfare of their inhabitants, the backward territories once belonging to those empires.'[3]

Belgium, as conqueror of the northern part of the German colony, demanded a share of the spoils; yet Britain, clearly entitled to the rights of conquest, refused to sanction an African peace settlement based merely on military victory. The debate on the African settlement turned on two principles:

The first, held by France and by the British dominions, was to hand over to the final recipients the former German colonies with full sovereignty. The second, presented by President Wilson, would only give them to them to be administered as mandatories of the League

---

[1] Undated memorandum by Louwers, A.G.R., van den Heuvel papers, 30.
[2] 29 May 1919.
[3] Charles Seymour, ed., *The Intimate Papers of Colonel House* (4 vols.; London, 1928), IV, pp. 294–5. As expressed by Wilson, the goal was 'A free, open-minded, and absolutely impartial adjustment of all colonial claims, based upon a strict observance of the principle that in determining all such questions of sovereignty the interests of the populations must have equal weight with the equitable claims of the government whose title is to be determined.' [Wilson's fifth point]. David H. Miller, *The Drafting of the Covenant* (2 vols.; New York, London, 1928), I, p. 101; cf. R. S. Baker, *Woodrow Wilson and World Settlement* (3 vols.; London, 1923), I, chapter XV.

of Nations. Between the two systems under consideration, England has not yet clearly decided.[4]

'Belgium could not, any more than France, adhere to the formula of President Wilson.' By openly opposing Wilson's proposal, however, the Belgians would put themselves in the position of a rapacious conquerer. The problem was to avoid the stigma of imperialism while achieving an imperialistic goal.

One of the great difficulties facing the Belgian delegation at the Peace Conference was that their east African claims were merely a means to achieve a larger and more important end. The Belgians intended to use the territory occupied by their troops in east Africa as a pawn to acquire the southern bank of the Congo river.

The origin of the problem of the southern Congo bank (which the Belgians referred to as the 'left bank') dates back to the beginnings of the Congo State itself. The abortive Anglo-Portuguese treaty of 1884[5] was designed to give Portugal sovereignty over the entire mouth of the Congo, cutting off the Congo State from the sea. 'The plans of Portugal and England were happily frustrated, thanks to the opposition of France and Germany, and the [International] Association [which became the Congo State] obtained its access to the Atlantic Ocean.' The Congo State, however, was left only with a slender band of territory, limited on one side by Portuguese Angola and on the other by the Portuguese enclave of Cabinda. 'This compromise at the time seemed a victory, but not until later did we see its inconveniences.'[6]

The Congo is a capricious river. The sand which forms its bed frequently changes the navigable passages. The ships which ascend the river from the sea, in fact, are obliged to follow a channel in Portuguese waters. . . . We were forced to build our main port at Matadi. It will rapidly become insufficient . . . access to it is difficult, even perilous. No more than three steamers can turn there at the same time. The town rests on steep rock. It is not possible to build there installations adequate for the growing traffic. But we know

---

[4] 'Note', Louwers, undated, A.G.R., van den Heuvel papers, 30.
[5] See especially R. T. Anstey, *Britain and the Congo in the Nineteenth Century* (Oxford, 1962), Chapter VII.
[6] 'Programme des revendications concrètes', A.G.R., van den Heuvel papers, 30. This document contains an excellent discussion of the Congo mouth problem.

that on the left bank of the river there are excellent sites for the creation of a deep water port with all its appendages.[7]

'Even more serious, we are the only ones to use the river, but we cannot regulate its administration, and, in case of hostilities, all of the lower Congo is at the mercy of an unexpected attack of an enemy, who would have merely to bring its vessels broadside in Portuguese waters to hold Boma under their cannons and stop all traffic. . . . It would be even more serious, if, instead of Portugal we had as a neighbour a great power animated by hostile sentiments. It would hold us in complete subjugation. It is therefore necessary to correct the defects of our maritime frontier and to consolidate our position on the Atlantic Ocean.'[8]

Could the conquered territory in east Africa be used as a means to strengthen the Belgian position on the Atlantic? The difficulty, as Octave Louwers, in the Belgian Foreign Ministry, pointed out, was that the Belgian delegation could not bring 'claims on a Portuguese territory' before the conference. The Belgians would have to limit their formal discussion to the problem of east Africa. 'This tactic has no goal other than to transform a precarious claim into a definite claim . . .'; once the Belgians had acquired definitely the east African territory, they could exchange it for the southern bank of the Congo.[9]

To ensure success in their east African transactions, 'it was agreed to present our claim as not implying a preoccupation with conquest, but as a just reparation for damages undergone by three years of colonial war imposed by Germany and as a measure of security for the future of our colony'. 'One word must be underlined. The formula is self-determination.'[1]

Pierre Orts, one of the secretaries of the Kivu-Mfumbiro Conference and in 1919 Belgian Envoy Extraordinary and Minister Plenipotentiary, accordingly presented the Belgian east African claims to the Council of Ten:[2]

---

[7] Ibid.   [8] Ibid.
[9] 'Note' Louwers, undated, A.G.R., van den Heuvel papers, 30.
[1] 'The discussion of the colonial problem, even based on the principles expressed by President Wilson or by the government of Great Britain, cannot embarrass Belgium. . . . As for the part of the German territories overrun by our troops during the course of the war, we know that the [native] populations rejoiced at the departure of their old masters.' 'Resumé du programme des revendications de la Belgique dans le domaine colonial.' A.G.R., van den Heuvel papers, 30.
[2] 'The Council of Ten, which was the Supreme Council of the Peace Conference,

We have never followed a policy of conquest; but in compensation for the damages sustained as a consequence of the African war, Belgium asks only that the territories which she administers provisionally be left to their self-determination.[3]

After the audience before the Council of Ten Orts made two observations: that the Belgian demands had been favourably received; but that Lloyd George, the British Prime Minister, had remarked that it seemed to him inappropriate to hear the remarks of the Belgian delegation. '. . . the question of the Congo was not, in his opinion, under consideration'. Orts found it necessary to remind him that it was not the Congo, but the fate of the German colonies, that the Belgians wished to discuss.[4] Lloyd George's remark was a sombre warning that the Belgian task would not be easy.

On 20 March Orts arrived in Paris for an interview with Lord Milner, the British Colonial Secretary, who had asked informally to see a representative of the Belgian government to discuss some colonial problems. 'We have several questions to settle concerning Africa, mainly the German East Africa one. I think that it would be preferable not to settle these things in the conference, but to reach an agreement between us. I am convinced that the conference would ratify this agreement.' Orts replied that this was also the Belgian feeling, but that it had already been three years since they had broached this proposition to the British, and that they had received no reply. 'I do not know whether there still will be enough time to make up for the lost time.' Milner replied that 'Yes, I think that it will still be possible.'[5]

During this unofficial interview of 20 March, Orts and Milner discussed briefly the main ideas which were to guide their later discussions. Milner refused to acknowledge Belgian claims in

was merely the Supreme War Council under a different name. Sometimes, indeed, when military questions were before it, it met under the old name.' Lord Hankey, *Diplomacy by Conference* (London, 1946), p. 26. For the general organization of the conference, and the development of the Council of Four and the Council of Foreign Ministers, see H. W. V. Temperley, ed., *A History of the Peace Conference of Paris* (6 vols.; London, 1920–4), II, chapter VII.

[3] 'Proces-verbal—Audition de la délégation belge par le Conseil des Dix—', Louwers, undated, A.G.R., van den Heuvel papers, 30; cf. *Foreign Relations of the United States*: 'The Paris Peace Conference, 1919', III, pp. 809–12.

[4] Orts's 'Conclusions à tirer de notre entretien avec Lord Milner le 20 mars 1919', A.G.R., van den Heuvel papers, 30.

[5] Memorandum by Louwers, undated, A.G.R., van den Heuvel papers, 30.

east Africa, and emphasized the importance of British communication between the Cape and Cairo; Orts pointed to the Belgian contribution to the east African campaign and emphasized the importance which the Belgian public put on receiving adequate compensation. Orts claimed for Belgium the territory occupied by her troops in east Africa; Milner asked whether the Belgians would not actually prefer some other arrangement —referring to the problem of the lower Congo. Milner agreed to broach the question with M. le Costa, the head of the Portuguese delegation.[6]

Orts optimistically concluded from his interview with Milner that it would not be difficult to come to an arrangement with the British. This conclusion proved incorrect, because of the disadvantages which Belgium suffered as a small nation among great powers at the conference.

Although Belgium sent three delegates, she was not represented on the Council of Foreign Ministers, nor on the Council of Four (Wilson, Clemenceau, Lloyd George, and Orlando). The Belgians did not even have a way to find out what was happening; it was only through *Le Temps* on 30 April that the Belgian delegation learned that Germany formally renounced her colonies to the five Allied and Associated powers: France, Britain, Italy, the United States, and Japan. Belgium was not mentioned. The Belgian east African claims presented to the Council of Ten had been ignored. On 13 April the Belgian colonial delegate to the conference had proposed that Germany should renounce her colonies to 'the five Allied or Associated powers or other belligerent signatories to the Treaty'; but this proposal had been dropped. The African settlement apparently was to be made without the participation of Belgium.[7]

Finding themselves excluded from the vital discussions on the question of the future of the German colonies, the Belgian delegation had to rely on scraps of second-hand information, which came mostly from de Peretti de la Rocca, Chief of the African section in the French Ministry for Foreign Affairs.

[6] 'Entrevue avec Ld. Milner à l'Hotel Majestic le 20 mars 1919', Orts, A.G.R., van den Heuvel papers, 30.

[7] Cf. O. Louwers, *La campagne africaine de la Belgique* (Brussels, 1921); and Paul Hymans, *Mémoires* (2 vols.; Bruges, ?1957), I, pp. 337–43, 452–61; and van Zuylen, *L'Echiquier Congolais*, chapter XXV. These works are especially illuminating for events at the beginning of the conference.

Peretti assured Louwers that the article in *Le Temps* was correct but misleading; it was true that in a clause in the preliminary draft of the treaty that Germany renounced her colonies to the five Allied and Associated powers, but that the clause probably would be altered to include Belgium.[8]

The question of the phrasing of the clause relating to the German colonies was crucial; if the future of the German colonies was to be decided by the five Allied and Associated powers, then Belgium would be at a distinct disadvantage, if not excluded altogether. She would probably receive no compensation for her contribution to the east African campaign, no territorial aggrandizement; Belgian public opinion 'would be especially indignant on learning that in the colonial matters where Belgian rights were most solidly established the Treaty said "fie" on these rights. . . .'[9] On 2 May Rolin-Jacquemyns, Secretary-General of the Belgian Delegation, was instructed to approach Berthelot, one of the French Ministers Plenipotentiary; at the same time Hymans, the Belgian Foreign Minister, prepared a letter for Clemenceau. Berthelot assured Rolin-Jacquemyns that the clause would be corrected—the decision had been made by the 'Three', where British influence predominated; Hymans's letter led to a promise by Clemenceau that the draft treaty would not prejudice the partition of the German colonies, and a promise by Pichon, the French Minister for Foreign Affairs, that he would intervene on behalf of the Belgians.[1]

The Council of Foreign Ministers reconsidered the question on 3 May. Pichon demanded in the name of France that Belgium be given satisfaction. After some discussion, the phrase was changed to 'the principal Allied and Associated powers'.[2] The Council thought that Belgium in this way could be included.[3]

The Belgian position, however, was much less secure than the alteration of the clause concerning the German colonies might have indicated. A few days later the Belgians received two unpleasant surprises from the newspapers of 8 May. The first was that the Council of Four had decided on 6 May that the

---

[8] Louwer's memorandum of 3 May. For explanation of unidentified sources used in this chapter, see above, p. xvii.   [9] Ibid.   [1] Ibid.
[2] Ibid.; cf. *Foreign Relations*, IV, pp. 659–61.   [3] 'Aide-mémoire', 14 May.

German colonies were to be administered as mandates by the 'Great Powers'.[4] At first the Belgian delegation refused to believe the news; only three days previously the President of the Conference had written to the principal Belgian delegate that the clauses in the preliminary drafts of the treaty concerning the German colonies would not prejudice the decision as to who would administer the territories.[5] The second shock was even more serious: Britain was to receive the mandate for all of German East Africa.[6]

Hymans protested vigorously to Pichon.[7] Belgian rights had been flouted; the decision by the Council of Four ignored Belgian participation in the east African campaign—Belgium had administered the western part of the German colony for three years. The decision to grant Britain the mandate over all of German East Africa could never be accepted by Belgium.[8]

Pichon professed great astonishment at the decision of the Four; he promised to see Clemenceau immediately.[9] Hymans prepared a letter of protest, demanding that Belgium be invested with the mandate over the territory in German East Africa occupied by Belgian troops.[1]

Hymans received a notice by telephone at 9.00 a.m. on 9 May that he could present the Belgian protest to the Council of Four at 10.30 a.m. the same day. He found on his arrival President Wilson, Clemenceau, Orlando, Lord Robert Cecil, Loucheur, Clémentel, and a horde of financial advisers who had come to discuss reparations. They were in groups in different corners, discussing various topics. Lloyd George arrived late. Clemenceau announced to Wilson and Lloyd George that Hymans had come to discuss African questions. Clemenceau himself explained frankly to Hymans that he knew little of the problem and that Hymans should talk to the American President and the British Prime Minister. 'I then had a conversation with M. Wilson, who seemed very surprised to learn that we occupied territories in German East Africa.' Hymans explained briefly the Belgian case to Wilson. He then had a longer con-

---

[4] 'Entretien avec Lord Milner', 12 May 1919.
[5] Ibid.   [6] 'Aide-mémoire', 14 May.
[7] 'Note du M. Hymans du 9 mai 1919'.
[8] 'Hymans to Monsieur le Ministre des Colonies, très confidentielle', 12 May 1919.
[9] 'Note', 9 May.   [1] Hymans, 12 May.

versation with Lloyd George, 'who listened to me sympathetic-
ally; he recalled vaguely that one of us, M. Orts, had expounded
the question before the Council of Ten; but he was ignorant of
our campaign in Africa, the negotiations between the two
governments, the discussions of M. Orts and Lord Milner. He
declared that he was incapable of discussing the question in the
absence of Lord Milner'. Lloyd George immediately gave an
order to Sir Maurice Hankey to request by telegraph that
Milner, who had returned to London, should come to Paris.
Hymans insisted on the necessity of calming Belgian public
opinion; he had to make some explanation to the Belgian press.[2]
Lloyd George authorized Hymans to declare that the British
delegation understood the necessity and urgency for Milner to
come to Paris to re-examine the question. Hymans then read
his letter to the 'Four', in which Belgium claimed the
mandate over the territory in east Africa occupied by Belgian
troops.[3]

Hymans gained the impression from his meeting with Clemenceau, Wilson, and Lloyd George that things might be
arranged to Belgian satisfaction. 'But the incident is evidence
of the carelessness with which most serious matters are treated,
often without discussion, without preliminary study, by men
often incompetent, who have arrogated omnipotence. One cannot imagine a procedure more dangerous, more irrational, more
disdainful of all safeguards of careful examination and reflection,
less respectful of the rights of small nations. "It was done on a
rush", Sir Maurice Hankey said to me, and in fact the question
was decided in five minutes in an impromtu meeting held after
the reception of the German delegates at the Conference of
Versailles.'[4]

---

[2] 'The publication of the statement that it is decided that Great Britain is to
have German East Africa has again greatly perturbed public opinion here
[Brussels]. It had been believed that Belgium would have a voice in deciding the
destinies of the German colonies, and that as a matter of justice she would be
allowed to retain certain advantageous portions of German East Africa which
her troops helped Great Britain to conquer and which she still occupies and
administers. The general impression produced by the news from Paris is that
Belgium has been simply forgotten and that it required M. Hymans's solemn
public protest and personal application to President Wilson to cause Lloyd George
to send for Lord Milner with a view to examining the question afresh. Whatever
may be the true inwardness of the matter the effect produced here is highly
regrettable.' *The Times*, 12 May 1919.

[3] Hymans, 12 May.   [4] 'Note', 9 May.

Milner arrived again in Paris on 11 May[5] to negotiate with Orts. Since Orts's last conversation with Milner earlier in the year, the east African situation had changed; 'the Four have disposed of the totality of German East Africa to the detriment of our rights'.[6] The Belgians were relieved that the British were at least willing to discuss the matter.

Orts told Milner during the first lengthy conversation that he had been shocked to learn from the newspapers that the 'Four' had decided that the German colonies were to be administered by the 'Great Powers'. Milner replied that he too had learned of the decision through the press; he had thought that Belgium's renunciation of German East Africa was probably part of a general agreement between Belgium and Britain. Orts explained that such an agreement had not been concluded. 'Nevertheless, Lord Milner said to me [Orts], you have received such great advantages on financial matters as signatories to the preliminary agreements. I thought that you would renounce German East Africa in exchange for these advantages.'[7] Orts observed that these 'financial advantages' for Belgium were not so significant as Milner seemed to think, that as a just compensation for Belgium's contribution in the east African campaign they were entirely insufficient.

Milner stated that the 'logical frontier' between the Belgian and British possessions in Africa was the great lakes and their tributaries, the Ruzizi and the Semliki. 'You speak of the old frontier, I [Orts] said to him, the one before the war. At present the problem is to find another good frontier more to the east, which will give to Belgium the territories . . . which she has justly acquired by participating in the colonial war.' Milner countered by saying that Belgium had no true 'interests' in east Africa, that it was not her 'natural domain', that it would be by nature a situation which would create difficulties between the

---

[5] 'My dear Colonial Secretary: I earnestly hope that you will not find it necessary a second time to leave Paris without achieving a decision on the important questions entrusted to your charge. There are at least five matters essential to the peace settlement which you alone can pilot to a conclusion—Togoland, Cameroons, German East Africa, Nauru and Somaliland. You will forgive me for saying quite emphatically that there can be no colonial business which more urgently presses for treatment than these affairs.' Lloyd George to Milner, 14 May 1919, in Lord Beaverbrook, *Men and Power* (London, 1956), pp. 330–1.

[6] 'Note en vue d'une entrevue de Monsieur Le Ministre des Affaires Etrangères avec Lord Milner', 10 May 1919.

[7] 'Entretien avec Lord Milner', 12 May 1919.

two countries in the future. 'In short, he clearly indicated that Britain would like us to give up completely our interests in east Africa.'[8]

Orts asked Milner whether he had broached the question of the Congo bank to the Portuguese. Milner replied 'yes'; 'he had found them unyielding'.[9] Milner had not, however, given up hope that Belgium might find 'compensations' outside east Africa. 'Where?', asked Orts frankly. 'On the left bank of the Congo', said Milner. 'It is clear, I [Orts] replied, that if you can procure for us in Angola a territory equivalent to that which we would cede otherwise, we could talk about this; but can you dispose of Angola?' 'No', was Milner's reply.[1]

Orts concluded his conversation with Milner on 12 May by explaining the need to calm Belgian public opinion; this could be done by modifying the clause in the draft treaty concerning German East Africa. Orts proposed that the clause should read: 'Great Britain and Belgium shall themselves determine the future administration of this colony and shall recommend its approval by the League of Nations.' Milner replied that he personally would be in favour of this solution, but that he would have to confer with his government. As they departed Orts told Milner that a settlement advantageous to both sides could easily be found, but if Britain wanted 'to rob Belgium of her rights, this would be a dangerous policy . . . it would produce an irremediable effect on the relations between the two countries.[2]

Hymans prepared for the worst. On 12 May he requested the Belgian Colonial Minister to send the following telegram to the commander of Belgian troops in east Africa:

Peace Treaty given to Germans provides for renunciation by Germany of her former colonies, which are to be administered by the Entente Powers under the League of Nations. Initial decision of Allied Supreme Council gives mandate of the whole of east Africa to Great Britain. Belgium had declared that she cannot accept this decision—that it was due to an error. Question will be re-examined, and I have high hopes that an agreement satisfactory to us will result. In the meantime oppose calmly and with discretion, but also firmly, any attempt to implement this decision on the spot. Take care also to maintain Belgian prestige with the native population,

[8] 'Entretien', 12 May.   [9] Ibid.   [1] Ibid.   [2] Ibid.

and not to let this incident harm the good relations between our compatriots and the English.[3]

Hymans thought this was a 'precaution' which might prevent 'regrettable incidents'. Actually the British were willing to come to terms with the Belgians, as Orts discovered a few days later. On 15 May Milner notified Orts that he would like to see him concerning a matter of considerable importance: in short, 'the Council of Four does not want to drag out this business . . .'; Milner was ready to prepare with Orts an agreement which the British and Belgian delegates would submit to the Council of Four for their approval. Milner repeated the argument used in all previous conversation: the central African rift and the great lakes was the natural frontier between Belgian and British possessions in Africa. Britain, however, was willing to make Belgium two propositions. First, to cede Ruanda to Belgium—on the condition that the Belgians would drop the question of negotiation for the southern bank of the Congo with the Portuguese.[4]

This was a turning point in the Anglo-Belgian negotiations. The British had acknowledged Belgian claims to Ruanda.

The second proposition made by Milner, however, would exclude Belgium from east Africa. The Portuguese would cede to Belgium the left bank of the Congo; the British would give to the Portuguese a larger region in the southeast of German East Africa.[5]

Milner showed Orts a map illustrating the first proposal. Most of Ruanda was indicated as Belgian; the extreme eastern part of Ruanda, however, was lopped off. Milner explained that the Cape to Cairo railway would have to run through the Kagera valley parallel to the left bank of the river. The Cape to Cairo railway, according to Lord Milner, was a 'point of capital importance'.

If the Cape to Cairo railway was important to the British, Urundi was equally important to the Belgians; Urundi provided 'indispensable communication with Lake Tanganyika'. 'If we possessed Ruanda without Urundi, I [Orts] said to him, the communication between Ruanda and the Congo would be

---

[3] Quoted in Hymans, 12 May.
[4] 'Nouvelle entrevue avec Lord Milner', 15 May.   [5] Ibid.

practically impossible . . . with the possession of Urundi, which borders the northeast of Lake Tanganyika, our new domain would be united directly by the lake to all the systems of railways and navigation of the Congo.'[6]

'This argument impressed Lord Milner; he frankly recognized the justice of it, and finally declared that he was ready to cede to us Urundi and Ruanda, the latter delimited in the east as indicated on the map.'[7]

Orts added that Belgium would require 'commercial concessions' at the two points of terminus of the railway: Dar es Salaam and Kigoma. Milner replied that he was unfamiliar with the details, but that in principle he would be willing to grant the Belgians certain concessions which would facilitate commercial transport.[8]

Orts summarized the main point of the discussion. 'If I understand you correctly, the solution which you propose, that is, a Belgian Ruanda and Urundi, would exclude in your mind any British intervention with Portugal for the resolution of the problem of the lower Congo.' ' "Yes" was the reply. "I am ready", continued Lord Milner, "to pay this price to be done with this matter and to free myself from the trouble of a laborious negotiation with Portugal which would involve other claims on the territories of German East Africa." ' Orts observed that one of the essential Belgian goals—the southern bank of the Congo—would not be reached through this solution; Milner replied that it was necessary to choose between Ruanda-Urundi and the left bank of the Congo. 'I [Orts] had the distinct impression that Lord Milner would like to direct us towards Angola.' As they were bringing their conversation to a close Milner asked Orts what he frankly thought of the proposals. 'I replied that there remained the question of the lower Congo. The combination that he offered was unbalanced—it left us no compensation for the considerable territory that we would abandon to England, which, not to mention Ruanda and Urundi, included natural riches (salt mines, coal, etc.), an important section of the central railway, the installations at Kigoma. I then remarked that for two years we had put much work into the region. We had rebuilt the railway, not only to the limit of our zone of occupation, but to Tabora. All of this

<hr>

[6] Ibid.   [7] Ibid.   [8] Ibid.

would have to be taken into account, and must not be lost sight of. Lord Milner asked me tersely whether I would insist on the lower Congo. I replied affirmatively.'[9]

The Belgian government in May 1919 recognized the importance and priority of the Congo-mouth problem. A lengthy memorandum prepared by Louwers and Orts observed that 'for a long time, then, it has seemed to the government that the true interests of our colony are on the Atlantic Ocean'. 'It is there that it is necessary to consolidate our until now precarious position, because the Atlantic Ocean is the natural outlet . . . and because the Atlantic Ocean is assuming a greater and greater importance in international relations.[1]

Admittedly a part of our colony extends toward the Indian Ocean, and it is necessary to make sure that it has easy access to the sea; for this reason it is essential that the agreement with Great Britain contain a clause on this point; but this circumstance does not give to the permanent establishment of Belgium in German East Africa a character of primordial necessity. . . . The Belgian provinces which we could establish, limited as they would be by the proposals of the English, would always be eccentric, cut from our colony by a natural line of the great lakes and the central rift, and sooner or later, on the completion of the Cape to Cairo railway, would pass into the orbit of English influence. The climate and the richness of the soil there would attract Anglo-Saxon elements in mass, and history is there to teach us what a peril to a small colonial state this situation could lead to. With Katanga the new province would give us two centres where we would have to fight against British hegemony; one is enough. Does this mean that we should attempt nothing in German East Africa? No! The part that we occupy presents incontestable advantages, and if we could without much of a struggle with the English preserve it, perhaps we should not hesitate to persuade ourselves that we could solve the problem of the [Congo] left bank, which remains essential, by our own means, that is to say, by abandoning part of our territories. Indeed, we could hope to retain only a part. Access to Lake Victoria and the last section of railway to Kigoma are two important things that we would lose in any case. There remain, nevertheless, Ruanda and Urundi. The advantages which these two provinces would offer us, however, as important as they might be, are of a secondary importance; they would not justify our incurring the risks mentioned above and the anger of England. . . . There is no justification, above all, to pass by

[9] Ibid.   [1] Louwers's and Orts's memorandum of 19 May 1919.

a chance to realize finally our reasonable and normal goal on the Atlantic Ocean. . . . The government therefore should not hesitate in its choice; the second proposal offered by Lord Milner should be accepted.[2]

'It is not, however, without a heavy heart that the authors of this memorandum arrive at this conclusion. The beautiful provinces which we must see escape us are enticing beyond question. After a time—for we have now occupied them for three years—we have become practically accustomed to the idea that we will always have them—our representatives have accomplished a great work of civilization, which has attracted numerous followers to our cause. Politics demand this sacrifice, in order to assure the future. We think also of our dead buried there on ground hallowed by their courage. They will not have died in vain. Their sacrifice will permit the final perfection of the work of the illustrious creator of our Colony.'[3]

The Belgian plan was to exchange their conquered east African territory for the southern bank of the Congo river. Britain would receive the Belgian occupied east African territory; Belgium would gain the Portuguese territory at the mouth of the Congo; Portugal would receive compensation from Britain in the southeast corner of German East Africa for losses to Belgium in the Portuguese Congo Province. The first step for the Belgians in this complicated exchange was to ensure their rights over the territory occupied by Belgian troops in east Africa; Ruanda and Urundi had first to become officially Belgian before the Belgians could barter them for the Congo region.

On 19 May Orts wrote Milner two letters, one private, one official. The private letter explained the necessity for Belgium to exchange her east African territory for the southern bank of the Congo, which would involve British intervention with the Portuguese. There were three conditions attached to the Belgian abandonment of German East Africa: first, that the western boundary of Ruanda-Urundi established by the Kivu-Mfumbiro Conference of 1910 be corrected to the 'true' boundary established by the Declaration of Neutrality of 1885; second, that Britain guarantee 'facilities' to protect Belgian trade flow-

<hr />

[2] Ibid.   [3] Ibid.

ing to the Indian Ocean; third, that Belgium receive a monetary indemnity for the east African territory occupied by Belgian troops to be ceded to Britain.[4]

Orts's official letter of 19 May was designed to bring Ruanda and Urundi under Belgian sovereignty by proposing an agreement with Britain to be submitted officially by both governments to the Council of Four. The official proposal was a step toward realizing the more complicated exchange with Portugal; but if the Portuguese proved intractable the Belgians would at least have gained Ruanda and Urundi, which would be acquired on the same conditions that Britain and France would acquire Togoland and the Cameroons. Belgium aimed at other advantages also. Orts's official letter stated that Belgian troops had made great sacrifices in the east African campaign, that the territories which Britain asked Belgium to abandon were of unquestionable value. Belgian public opinion could not but notice the discrepancy between Belgium's sacrifices and the advantages which Britain would gain as a result of the contribution of Belgian troops in east Africa. Therefore Britain should pay to Belgium a certain sum, to be determined by a committee of experts, which would be used for development in the Belgian Congo, and which would be dedicated to the Belgian military effort in east Africa.[5]

On 24 May Milner discussed the Belgian proposals with Orts. Milner confirmed the arrangement that Belgium would retain Urundi and Ruanda, with the exception of the eastern part of Ruanda necessary for the Cape to Cairo railway. On the question of pecuniary compensation, however, Milner gave a flat refusal. Orts insisted. Milner would have no trouble, Orts said, in defending before the British public an indemnity to Belgium; Britain would retain very great material advantages which were made possible only by Belgium's contribution to the east African campaign. Milner replied that the British Treasury would never agree to a Belgian indemnity. They then discussed the Belgian proposals for commercial facilities in east Africa; these seemed to pose only minor problems.[6]

Conversation turned to Portugal and the lower Congo.

[4] Ibid., and Orts to Milner, 19 May 1919.
[5] Orts to Milner, 19 May.
[6] 'Entrevue avec Lord Milner le 24 mai 1919'.

Milner did not conceal from Orts that he preferred Belgian control of the Congo mouth to a Belgian Ruanda-Urundi; Milner was prepared to offer Portugal territory in the south of German East Africa considerably larger than that which she would abandon in Angola. It would be to Portugal's advantage. But Milner doubted whether the Portuguese would accept. 'They are very distrustful.' Both Orts and Milner preferred the solution of a British Ruanda-Urundi, a Belgian Congo mouth; this solution would be equally advantageous to all parties involved. The British and Belgians were thwarted by what they regarded as an unyielding attitude assumed by the Portuguese.[7]

Milner and Orts ended their conversation of 24 May on the note of indemnity. Milner said he would send the official British reply to the Belgian proposals on 26 May. 'I [Orts] asked him whether it would confirm our agreement. "Yes", he said, "You are going to give us the indemnity then?" "No." "Then we will have no agreement. Think it over. You would have no trouble in granting the indemnity, and then our business would be completed." '[8]

On 26 May Milner wrote two letters to Orts, one private and one official, in response to Orts's letters of 19 May. Milner's official letter confirmed the proposition that Ruanda and Urundi should become Belgian under certain conditions.

Your proposal is that Belgium should retain the districts of Ruanda and Urundi, with the exception of a strip on the east. . . . This strip would be left in British territory. This modification of the boundary was no doubt proposed by you with the view of meeting the requirement, upon which in our conversations I have always told you we were bound to insist, i.e. the retention by us of a sufficiently broad area to the west of Lake Victoria Nyanza, to enable us to maintain communication, and eventually build a railway connecting the British portion of German East Africa with Uganda. I am glad to say that, with a very trifling alteration agreed to by the experts, Colonel Meinertzhagen and Captain Maury, who have examined the matter together, your proposed boundary . . . does meet our necessities in this respect.[9]

Milner next discussed the conditions under which Belgium would receive Ruanda and Urundi.

---

[7] Ibid.   [8] Ibid.   [9]Milner to Orts, 26 May 1919.

You ask that these districts should be handed over to Belgium under the same conditions as apply to the transfer of Togoland and Cameroons to France and Great Britain. It appears to me, however, that the conditions under which these or any ex-German territories are to be transferred to their several mandatories can only be determined by the Supreme Council of the Allies. I am not therefore in a position to say anything about the terms on which Belgium should receive Ruanda and Urundi. But I must own that I do not see the relevance of what is done with respect to Togoland and Cameroons in this connection. The obvious solution would be that Belgium should hold Ruanda and Urundi on the same terms as Great Britain holds the portion of east Africa allotted to her.[1]

Then Milner fully discussed the point of total disagreement: compensation.

I am afraid I do not understand how any question of pecuniary compensation can arise in this matter. In the first place, I cannot altogether accept your assumption that the allocation of territory under a mandate is necessarily of material advantage to the mandatory state. On the contrary, it may, from the material point of view, be a burden rather than a benefit. But, even assuming that mandated territories could be rightly regarded as possessions, and valuable possessions, I do not think that your withdrawal from portions of east Africa at present occupied by you, outside Ruanda and Urundi, would entitle you to compensation. It can hardly be contended that the portions of east Africa, at present held by Great Britain and Belgium respectively, accurately correspond to their respective efforts and sacrifices in the conquest of that country. I do not myself think that our respective efforts should be the only or indeed the principal consideration in determining which part of that country either of us should hold. But even if this were the true criterion, I contend that Belgium in receiving Ruanda and Urundi would be amply rewarded for her share in the east African campaign. It is true that in geographical extent those districts are only a small part of German East Africa, but their economic importance is out of all proportion to their size. They are healthy and fertile highlands, they contain something more than one-third of the population of the whole colony, and, according to my information, more than two-thirds of its chief economic asset—cattle. Therefore they represent a very important share of the former German possessions. It is true that they are only a part of the country at one time over-run by the Belgian forces, but on the other hand, I may remind you that the

[1] Ibid.

Belgian conquest of this portion of the country, however valuable in itself (and I should be the last to belittle the importance of Belgian assistance), was only rendered possible by the fact that the transport and the greater part of the supplies were provided by Great Britain. It was, in fact, an Allied and not a purely Belgian expedition, though I do not wish in the least to deprive Belgium of any military credit which is due to her. From a financial point of view, I am quite sure that the value of Ruanda and Urundi goes much further to indemnify Belgium for any expenses incurred by her in that expedition, than the value of all of the rest of east Africa ever can to indemnify Great Britain for the enormous cost of our east African campaign, not to mention what we spent in assistance to the Belgian forces cooperating with us.[2]

Milner's second letter was private, and discussed the Belgian proposal for territorial exchange with the Portuguese.

I may say at once, that if the arrangement suggested in your private letter could be realized, i.e. if you could obtain the territory giving you control of the southern bank of the Congo mouth, . . . and at the same time you limited your acquisition in German East Africa to the small strip east of Lake Kivu and to the north of Lake Tanganyika . . . I believe this settlement would be better for all parties concerned than the settlement contemplated in your official proposal.
It would be better for Belgium because, whatever the value of Ruanda and Urundi, I believe the importance *for you* of the undivided control of the Congo mouth, so necessary to the development of your vast Congo domain, is greater than any benefit you could derive from an extension of that domain into German East Africa. It would be better for Great Britain; because the separation of Ruanda and Urundi from the rest of German East Africa, and from Uganda, to which they naturally belong, is in itself undesirable and would certainly prove administratively inconvenient. And it is better from the point of view of native interests, because the tribes inhabiting Ruanda and Urundi are related to those of Uganda and German East Africa and are quite distinct from those of the Congo basin.
But while there is thus everything to be said for your suggestion, and while it is one that I think the Supreme Council of the Allies would be more willing to adopt than the other plan, I cannot conceal from you that it may be very difficult of execution.
If we ask the Portuguese to give up the territory which you want

[2] Ibid.

south of the Congo mouth, they will certainly look for territorial compensation. It is not easy to see where such territorial compensation can be found. It may be possible—there are many difficulties but these may not be insuperable—to find it in the southeastern corner of German East Africa, between the Rovuma and the Mbemkuro. But even if the Portuguese accepted the cession of territory to them in this quarter in exchange for what you wish to obtain from them near the Congo mouth, I can see that we should have to encounter considerable opposition to the proposal to hand over any fresh native population to the Portuguese.

While, therefore, I think it is well worth while making the effort to effect the exchanges in question, I do not feel confident of the result. For that reason my suggestion is that we should proceed with your official proposal, and if we can agree on the terms of it, as I believe we can, we should put it before the Supreme Council for their approval. At the same time there should be an understanding between Great Britain and Belgium that, if within a limited time— you suggest a month, but I think that that is rather too short: I would prefer two months—it was found possible to obtain for you from the Portuguese the territory shown in your sketch map, then you should undertake to give up Ruanda and Urundi, except the small strip indicated in your sketch map. Otherwise the division of German East Africa between Belgium and Great Britain put forward in your official proposal, if accepted by the Supreme Council, would stand and would be a final settlement of the question at issue.[3]

Orts, discussing Milner's official and private letters of 26 May, again tried to convince Milner of the justice of the Belgian demand for an indemnity which would compensate Belgium for the difference between the value of territory conquered by Belgian troops and that which would be retained by Belgium. Milner absolutely refused to consider the principle of Belgian indemnity. 'It is clear, I [Orts] said, that the second plan, which in your mind would be substituted automatically for the first, would not be fair unless it included an indemnity.' Without indemnity the second plan was entirely insufficient; Belgian public opinion would never be satisfied by such meagre advantages with which Britain proposed to reward Belgium for her African campaign. Belgium's gain would be reduced to the acquisition of the southern Congo bank—'obviously of con-

[3] Ibid., private.

siderable value to Belgium, but also destitute of any intrinsic value and populated by degenerate negroes'—concessions at Kigoma and Dar es Salaam, and the restitution of 'a small territory east of Lake Kivu which the Germans stole from us in 1910'. 'Lord Milner seemed momentarily shaken by my argument. He asked what the approximate sum of the indemnity would be. Without letting me reply he said suddenly "no, we won't talk about that" '; the British Treasury would never agree.[4]

Without indemnity the plan for territorial exchange with Portugal became completely impracticable to the Belgians; for this reason the negotiations with Portugal died before they had ever really begun. In any case Milner and Orts both envisaged great difficulties and arduous discussions with the Portuguese if the second plan were followed; both regarded it as highly unlikely that the Portuguese would be willing to meet the British and Belgian terms. For these reasons the second plan was abandoned; Ruanda-Urundi was to be ceded to Belgium in accordance with the first and official proposal. 'This was my last interview with Lord Milner; we separated on very cordial terms. . . .'[5]

Ruanda-Urundi became Belgian on 30 May 1919. Belgium yielded on the point of pecuniary compensation; Orts stated in an official letter which accompanied the agreement: 'I am sorry that I was not able to convince you of the justice of the request for pecuniary compensation for Belgium, but, in view of your formal refusal to consider this request, the Belgian delegation will not insist on it.' The Milner-Orts agreement of 30 May 1919 partitioned east Africa; it constituted the official proposal of the British and Belgian governments that part of German East Africa was to be administered by Britain, part—Ruanda-Urundi—by Belgium; it traced in detail the boundary dividing the two spheres. Apart from a few minor problems concerning the Belgian commercial facilities in the part of German East Africa under British administration, the only remaining major problem was the acceptance of the Anglo-Belgian proposal by the Council of Four.[6]

The partition of east Africa between Britain and Belgium was scheduled to come before the Council of Four in the first week

---

[4] 'Entrevue de 28 mai avec Lord Milner.'   [5] Ibid.   [6] See note O, p. 277.

of July 1919. The Belgians had made every effort to speed what they hoped would be a simple procedure of approval of the Milner-Orts agreement. Hymans learned on 28 June, however, that the Council of Four had established a 'special commission'.[7] President Wilson had not thought that Milner's proposals 'provided adequate protection for the native population'.[8]

The Belgians, needless to say, took a dim view of the 'special commission': 'these incidents show the faults and incoherency of procedure followed by the Conference. Two months previously the Council of Four in ten minutes took a sudden and improvised decision on the distribution of certain mandates without taking into consideration the circumstances involved. Now the fundamental problem which was neglected is being studied.'[9]

The Commission on Mandates summoned the Belgian delegation to present their east African claims on 17 July 1919. Henry Simon, the French Colonial Minister, presided in the absence of Lord Milner. Louwers, Baron de Gaiffier, and Comte de Grunne represented Belgium. The Belgians quickly discovered that while the invitation to appear before the commission was 'addressed in the most friendly terms, at bottom it was nothing more than a kind of "capitis diminutio".' 'Once more they have resolved our problems without us, formed objections perhaps without our knowledge, and have, in short, placed us in a humiliating situation.'[1]

During the Mandates Commission's interview with the Belgian delegation, Simon explained to de Gaiffier that the Commission in principle had no objection to Belgium's claims in east Africa,[2] but that the colonial delegate from the United States, G. L. Beer, had observed:

[7] The Commission was composed of Milner; Colonel House, United States; Simon, France; Crespi, Italy; Chinda, Japan. The Commission was to consider (1) the drafting of Mandates; (2) to hear the view of the Aborigines Society in regard to the Belgian claims in German East Africa; (3) to hear the Portuguese claims in regard to German East Africa. *Foreign Relations*, VI, pp. 728–9.

[8] President Wilson said that he believed 'Belgium had reformed her colonial administration, but the difficulty was that the world did not feel that this was the case'. He thought the best plan would be to ask the Special Commission to hear the views of a delegation of the Aborigines Society which had arrived in Paris to protest against handing over parts of German East Africa to Belgium and Portugal. Ibid., VI, p. 728.

[9] 'Note de M. Hymans du 28 June 1919'.

[1] Rapport sur l'Audition de la Délégation belge par la Commission des Mandats', 17 July 1919.   [2] Ibid.

The territory over which there is a question of giving Belgium a mandate had a population of about three million inhabitants out of the seven millions who formed the population of the former German colony of east Africa. This zone is moreover inhabited by tribes whose position, from the ethnical, political and economic points of view, differs from that of the populations of the Belgian Congo, from which they are moreover geographically isolated. This may cause the Belgian administration difficulties which Mr Beer, some weeks before the agreement of 30th May, had thought it his duty to point out to President Wilson.[3]

The Mandates Commission, however, vindicated Belgium's claim to Ruanda-Urundi and sent a favourable report to the Council of Four.

The delay in ratification by the Council of Four was due to the American colonial delegate, G. L. Beer.[4] Beer had persistently opposed Belgian claims in east Africa; his departure for London and his replacement by F. L. Polk, the new American Plenipotentiary, alleviated the Belgian problem. At a dinner with Polk in early August, Bassompierre—who along with Orts had been one of the secretaries at the Kivu-Mfumbiro conference—told Polk that if the Milner-Orts agreement were not ratified in the near future, the Belgian government would be obliged to inform the Belgian public that the 'new difficulty in settling the African affair came from the United States'.[5]

The climax to the struggle for Ruanda-Urundi came on 7 August 1919. At a meeting of the heads of delegations of the five great powers held in Pichon's office at the Quai d'Orsay, German East Africa appeared on the agenda along with some problems concerning eastern Europe. C. Strachey, the British colonial expert, sketched briefly the history of the controversy. Clemenceau asked how much of the German East Africa territory would become a Belgian mandate. Strachey replied one-twentieth of the colony; but that this was the most densely

---

[3] *Documents on British Foreign Policy, 1919–1939*, E. Woodward and Rohan Butler, eds., First Series, I (London, 1947), p. 366. See also 'Résumé de la conversation entre M. Amery, Sous-Secrétaire d'État aux Colonies Britanniques, et Messieurs de Grunne et Louwers après la séance de la sous-commission des Mandats le 17 juillet, 1919'.

[4] I have discussed Beer's role in the African negotiations of 1919 in a separate paper entitled: 'The United States and the African Peace Settlement of 1919: the Pilgrimage of George Louis Beer,' to appear in the *Journal of African History*.

[5] Louwers to Hymans, 6 August 1919.

populated part. Balfour said that 'there were some objections, as Belgian administration, owing to its past achievements, did not inspire universal conviction', but that he supported the views of Milner. Tittoni said that 'in consideration of the great sacrifices made by Belgium during the war, this satisfaction could not be denied her'. Clemenceau agreed. Polk asked to reserve the American vote.[6] The Council then accepted the Milner-Orts agreement. Like the previous consideration of the Conference given to Ruanda-Urundi, it was over in a matter of minutes.[7]

[6] Polk withdrew his reservation on 21 August. *Foreign Relations*, VI, p. 728. The account of the meeting is in *Foreign Relations*, VII, pp. 612–13, and *Documents on British Foreign Policy*, First Series, I, pp. 365–6.

[7] There remained the minor problem of Belgian commercial concessions in the part of German East Africa to be retained by Britain. See 'Convention between Great Britain and Belgium with a view to facilitating Belgian Traffic through the Territories of East Africa', 15 March 1921 (Treaty Series no. 11, 1921), in *British and Foreign State Papers*, CXIV, 1921, pp. 182–6.

The terms of the Mandate were confirmed by the Council of the League of Nations on 20 July 1922. The Belgian Parliament formally accepted the Mandate by the law of 20 October 1924. For the cession in 1923 by Britain to Belgium of the eastern part of Ruanda reserved for the Cape to Cairo route, and the minor boundary adjustments after 1919, see Pierre Jentgen, *Les frontières du Ruanda-Urundi et le régime international de tutelle* (Brussels, 1957).

XXII. GERMANY, BELGIUM, BRITAIN, AND RUANDA-URUNDI

BELGIUM's acquisition of Ruanda-Urundi is surely one of the great ironies in the history of Africa. For her statesmen did not want it. They intended to use Ruanda-Urundi as a pawn to gain the southern bank and mouth of the Congo river, which they considered as indispensable for the security of their colony. This plan failed because of what the Belgians and British regarded as Portuguese intractability and because of British refusal to pay an additional indemnity, a Belgian condition of negotiation. Belgium was left with Ruanda-Urundi.

When President Wilson at the Peace Conference sardonically remarked 'to divide up east Africa' he left no doubt that as far as he was concerned the repartitioners of east Africa resembled two vultures devouring the carcass of a lion. Before and at the Peace Conference there was much loose talk about a colony for India and the acceptance by the United States of responsibilities in Africa. East Africa proved the emptiness of these speculations: the German colony was divided between those who conquered. The British from the beginning of the war tried to secure Belgian assistance, but also tried to bring all conquered territory under their control. Britain professed embarrassment at Belgium's acquisitive aims in east Africa, and persistently refused to recognize claims over territory overrun by Belgian troops. But had the Belgians not obstinately refused the British demand to administer all of German East Africa—for the British said this would be more 'administratively convenient'— can there be any doubt that Belgium would have been excluded from the peace settlement? As late as the Peace Conference itself the British intended to take all of German East Africa. How far the Belgians might have gone in defending their east African claims against Britain is uncertain. Orts recognized frankly that Ruanda and Urundi were not worth 'the anger of England'; but on the other hand Renkin ordered Tombeur to resist 'with discretion but also firmly' any attempt by Britain to grab the Belgian military zone in German East Africa, and Orts admonished Milner that British refusal to recognize

Belgian claims would have 'irremediable effects' on the relations between the two countries. In any case the British would have had a difficult time trying to evacuate Belgian troops.

But even the most greedy British imperialist could hardly refuse his fellow Belgian imperialist a share of the pie. For German East Africa was a very big pie, over four times the size of Great Britain; and the Belgians had their fingers securely around a plum. Britain's gobbling up all of German East Africa would incur the wrath of the other imperial powers, all of whom, especially France, sided with Belgium. Only the United States remained sceptical about Belgian designs in east Africa. But all, including Belgium and with only the exception of Portugal, would have preferred the solution of the southern Congo bank.

The Belgians thought it regrettable that they would not be allowed simply to absorb Ruanda-Urundi into the Congo. Ruanda-Urundi was to become a mandate of the League of Nations. 'This invention is no doubt unfortunate; . . . the ideas of President Wilson had a great influence.' Yet there is no evidence that the Belgian government did not concur with the principle of the mandate, nor that the Belgians did not intend to fulfil their responsibilities. 'Belgium, it goes without saying, will consider it a point of honour to fulfil the mandate which has been conferred upon us with an absolute loyalty and propriety.'[1] The Belgians genuinely believed in their mission of civilization, responsible government, and economic development, just as they believed that they had fairly acquired by conquest one of the richest regions in Africa.

1919, perhaps, saw the apex of happy imperialist expectation. The Teutonic menace had been vanquished, and the repartition of Africa was to open a new era of colonial success and prosperity. Belgium had acquired what she believed to be the El Dorado of central Africa; for Britain there was now no impediment to the Cape to Cairo route. After 1919 the British had all of Tanganyika through which to run a railway, but retained the eastern tip of Ruanda so that the railway could be built through the Kagera valley. The Cape to Cairo route was, above all, a symbol of British domination of Africa. It was never—as Salisbury saw in 1890—an economically feasible

[1] Hymans to Moncheur, 6 May 1920.

project. After 1919 the need for symbol disappeared; Britain obviously was the master of the eastern half of Africa. The Cape to Cairo railway was never built, just as Belgian expectations of great wealth in Ruanda-Urundi were never realized. Britain handed over to Belgium the eastern province of Ruanda reserved for the Cape to Cairo railway in 1923.

The myth of Ruanda-Urundi as the El Dorado of darkest Africa had been exploded by the years of German administration. The Germans discovered that there were no natural resources, only a limited range of agricultural products, and very little profit to be made from scrawny cattle, at least until there was modern transport. The railway for many years was the scapegoat for German economic failure in Ruanda-Urundi. Once Ruanda-Urundi was 'connected' to the rest of the colony, so it was thought, the economy would make a great jump forward and would make Ruanda-Urundi the commercial centre of east Africa. Dr. Kandt saw that this was untrue. He recognized that the great natural resource of the densely populated region was its labour potential; and the problem was to organize this power, not merely to build a railway. Kandt envisaged Ruanda-Urundi as the coffee farm of Germany. Germany lost her prospective coffee farm, but Kandt correctly surmised the economic future of the region.

German colonialism in Ruanda-Urundi never paid. Not until the last years of the German era, in fact, was the administration even able to organize a general tax collection. If the countries were to be profitable, through coffee, perhaps, it would be only through hard work over many years. The German officers by the First World War were disillusioned with the notion of Ruanda-Urundi as a colonial paradise. They began to emphasize the indifference and passive resistance of the Africans more often than the African qualities of industry and alacrity which they had described earlier. Schimmer went so far as to say that the only difference between Ruanda-Urundi and other parts of the colony was that more people lived in Ruanda-Urundi. Yet even the hard-headed Schimmer, with all his contempt for Africans, thought that economic development was possible and would benefit Africans as well as Europeans. As von Lettow-Vorbeck pointed out, until the First World War there was great hope for the future of German colonies. And this was especially true for Ruanda-Urundi. The Germans were disillusioned. But they were by no means pessimistic.

The Germans who ruled Ruanda-Urundi were diverse in personality, just as their motives for being there were different. The most striking difference, perhaps, was the quality of mind and personality of the best of the local authorities and the worst of the high officials. Is there anything more incongruous than the efforts of those in Berlin, Brussels, and London, who tried to carve up Africa by drawing straight lines on maps, and the laborious deliberations of local authorities who tried to discover natural frontiers? Or the fantastic theories of Lindequist about trade and dangers to German nationalism compared to the common sense observations of Dr. Kandt? Coote pointed to the difference between the pipe-dreams of the arm-chair imperialists and practical experiences of local authorities when he tried to discover why the British were so interested in Mfumbiro. Coote 'asked the General or whoever it was I saw at the War Office when I went home in 1911, why they were so set on having this particular piece of Africa, and he said that for one thing Speke had been the first to discover it, and second it would make a nice summer resort, a sort of Simla, for Uganda officials. Having trekked four times over the intervening hills and swamps, I didn't at the time think much of the secondly!'[2] The common sense of people like Dr. Kandt and Sir Arthur Hardinge in the long run usually prevailed. The imperial powers began with arbitrary boundaries, but eventually tried to adjust them to local conditions. Lindequist might dream about the prosperity which the 'Urundi-Ruanda railway' might bring, but Kandt and Wintgens succeeded at last in convincing their superiors that organization of labour and agricultural development was at least as great a problem as transport.

The German occupation of Ruanda-Urundi was, perhaps, not much different from other attempts to impose a European system of government on a primitive people. Only there was probably less bloodshed than usual. If the Germans failed to introduce European commerce, they succeeded generally—

---

[2] Coote, 'Kivu Mission', p. 107.

with only a few notable and violent exceptions—in administering Ruanda-Urundi by peaceful methods. Their rule over the powerful countries was not entirely unwise, nor unsuccessful. And just as colonial administration in Ruanda-Urundi faced the same basic problems of other administrations in Africa, so did the imperial entanglement in Ruanda-Urundi contain all of the classic elements of the partition of Africa: rivalry over unexplored territory; conflicting, arbitrary boundary agreements; and eventually, compromise and adjustment—and repartition in 1919. The imperial powers cut the diamond-shaped territory of Ruanda-Urundi by three main strokes: the western boundaries of 1884–5, which were determined in complete geographical ignorance and were not settled finally until the Kivu-Mfumbiro Conference in 1910; the northern boundary of 1890, in which 'Mfumbiro' was left unspecified, once again in geographical ignorance; the eastern and southern boundaries almost thirty years later, in which Ruanda-Urundi was severed from east Africa and created as a separate African mandate under the tutelage of Belgium. Belgium received Ruanda-Urundi because she happened to be drawn in on the right side of the world war. Ruanda-Urundi was insignificant in the east African campaign, just as east Africa was subsidiary to the battlegrounds of Europe. The British provided indispensable transport, and the Belgians caught the Germans on the run. The Belgian contribution to the east African campaign was not unimportant; but perhaps it also was not the heroic episode which was sometimes portrayed by Belgian statesmen. The battles were small and the rewards great.

The Belgian agitation at the Peace Conference led by Orts and Hymans was a brilliant political manoeuvre, just as the British Kivu expedition and German Ndungutze force were brilliant military manoeuvres. But just as Coote's success on the Kivu expedition was compromised by the bungling of the British Colonial Office, and just as Gudovius's Ndungutze force was marred by savage violence, so the Belgian triumph at the Peace Conference was impaired by national greed and pride. The Belgian statesmen themselves admitted that Ruanda-Urundi would be an eccentric addition to the Congo, that it would be in the best interests of the inhabitants of the region to leave it attached to the rest of the German colony. But

Ruanda-Urundi was Belgium's fair reward for victory, and therefore became Belgian.

What was the imperialist's attraction to Ruanda-Urundi? At bottom it was a deeply romantic vision, expressed by the slogan of the Cape to Cairo route: to open darkest Africa to trade and civilization. And Ruanda-Urundi was a romanticist's delight. For there were the rounded, rolling, brown mountains patched with green and inhabited by the slender, giant Tutsi, the stocky Hutu, and the dwarf-like Twa. The pearl of German East Africa.

BIBLIOGRAPHICAL NOTE

I

THE pre-First World War diplomatic history of Ruanda-Urundi in the first part of this book is based on unpublished documents at the Public Record Office, London; the German Foreign Office archives, Bonn; and the Belgian Foreign Ministry archives, Brussels. For a study spanning many years the British Foreign Office Confidential Prints facilitate research by compressing bulky correspondence into printed volumes. They also contain inter-departmental correspondence which is sometimes difficult to locate in the original manuscripts. The Confidential Prints, however, only supplement and guide: often important minutes and sometimes entire reports were not reproduced; one cannot follow through a Confidential Print the evolution from a draft to a despatch. For periods of crisis and for points of detail there is no substitute for the original documents, the most important of which are in F.O. 84 (Slave Trade); F.O. 10 (Belgium); F.O. 64 (Germany); F.O. 2 (Africa); and F.O. 367 (Africa after 1905). Neither the German Foreign Office nor the Belgian Foreign Ministry had the equivalent of the British Confidential Prints. The German documents are in the Politisches Archiv des Auswärtigen Amtes, Abteilung A, Kongo Kolonie no. 3. The Belgian documents are in the archives of the Ministère des Affaires Etrangères, Af. 1/38/5 and Af. 1/38/4.

It would be pointless to attempt to list even the more significant documents used for the first part of this book, but there are seven memoranda of singular importance from which the outlines of the Kivu-Mfumbiro dispute may be grasped.

H. Hesketh Bell's memorandum of 2 June 1909 (C.O. 536/29) is a forceful but mistaken analysis of the problem of the Kivu expedition as he found it on his arrival in London.

Col. Close's 'Memorandum . . . on the agreement signed in Brussels on May 14, 1910' (25 May 1910, F.O. 367/174) is the best summary of the Mfumbiro dispute.

'Denkschrift über deutsch-ostafrikanisch-kongolesische Streitfragen', undated (1909), A.A. 3/3, is a full review of the controversy.

'Aufzeichnung über dem deutsch-belgischen Grenzstreit' (undated), A.A. 3/5, is not so detailed as the 'Denkschrift', but is less biased.

'Note sur le territoire contesté de la Ruzizi et du Kivu', undated (1908), M.A.E. 1/38/5, is a thorough summary of the diplomatic side of the Kivu dispute, and is especially valuable in clearing up obscure points in the German documents.

'Note resumant l'historique de l'occupation belge dans les territoires contestés de la Ruzizi et du Kivu depuis 1894', 27 January 1910, M.A.E. 1/38/5, exhaustively discusses the events in Ruanda-Urundi.

'Description des territoires contestés de la Ruzizi et du Kivu', 2 February 1910, M.A.E. 1/38/5, is helpful for geographical points.

The Salisbury papers (Christ Church, Oxford) and the Mackinnon papers (School of Oriental and African Studies, London) give some of the details of the Mackinnon agreement and the Anglo-German 1890 negotiations. An insignificant but interesting scrapbook of H. Percy Anderson is in the care of D. H. Simpson, Librarian at the Royal Commonwealth Society, London, who has unsuccessfully tried to trace papers which Anderson may have left. Microfilms of Harry Johnston's papers are also available at the Royal Commonwealth Society, but I have found nothing in them that is not already known about the Cape to Cairo route. The Malet papers (Public Record Office, F.O. 293) throw some light on the 1894 crisis. The papers of Kimberley and Rosebery are not accessible at present.

The German documents concerning the 1890 and 1894 agreements are printed in volume VIII of *Die Grosse Politik der europäischen Kabinette*. Some of the most revealing Belgian documents on the Kivu controversy were printed by the Germans when they opened the Belgian archives during the First World War: 'Der Kiwusee-Grenzstreit mit dem Kongostaat', *Deutsches Kolonialblatt*, XXVII, July 1916, pp. 172–85, is a collection of documents of fundamental importance. Some additional early Belgian documents appear in R. S. Thomson, *La Foundation de l'Etat Indépendant du Congo* (Brussels, 1933), itself a thorough study of the diplomacy which created the Congo State; Thomson's work is complemented by S. E. Crowe, *The Berlin West African Conference, 1884–1885* (London, 1942).

Many of the valuable commentaries on the scramble for

Africa which provide the background to the history of Ruanda-Urundi have been listed in the footnotes of the text, as have the relevant parliamentary debates and parliamentary papers. The works mentioned here are limited to those directly concerned with the rivalry for Ruanda-Urundi.

F. F. Müller throws new light on the background of German colonialism in east Africa and the settlement of 1890 in *Deutschland-Zanzibar-Ostafrika* (East Berlin, 1959). The following studies illuminate various aspects of the 1890 agreement:

H. v. Hagen, *Geschichte und Bedeutung des Helgolandvertrages* (Munich, 1919).

A. v. Hasenclever, 'Zur Geschichte des Helgolandvertrages vom 1 Juli 1890', *Archiv für Politik und Geschichte*, III, 1925.

Günther Jantzen, *Ostafrika in der Deutsch-Englischen Politik, 1884–1890* (Hamburg, 1934).

L. Caprivi, *Die ostafrikanische Frage und der Helgoland-Sansibar-Vertrag* (Bonn, 1934).

D. R. Gillard, 'Salisbury's African Policy and the Heligoland offer of 1890', *English Historical Review*, LXXV, 1960, pp. 631-53.

A. J. P. Taylor's 'Prelude to Fashoda', *English Historical Review*, LXV, 1950, pp. 52–80; reprinted in *Rumours of Wars*, (London, 1952), pp. 81–113 is a detailed study of the part of the 1894 agreement dealing with the upper Nile. Little has been done on the part of the agreement concerning the Cape to Cairo corridor. Lois Raphael discusses the corridor through Ruanda-Urundi in *The Cape to Cairo Dream* (New York, 1937), which was based on evidence available in the 1930s. M. P. Hornik's use of the Austrian archives in 'The Anglo-Belgian Agreement of 12 May 1894', *English Historical Review*, LVII, April 1942, pp. 227-44 is especially valuable in discussing the role of the members of the Triple Alliance in the crisis.

The burden of searching newspapers is alleviated by the abundance of clippings which appear in the diplomatic files. *The Times* provides good commentary and translations from the German and Belgian presses, especially for the agreements of 1890 and 1894. The role of public opinion in the 1890 agreement is considered by Manfred Sell, *Das Deutsch-Englische Abkommen von 1890* (Berlin, 1926). Both 1890 and 1894 are discussed in Oron J. Hale, *Publicity and Diplomacy* (New York, 1940).

The broad outlines of the Kivu-Mfumbiro controversy can be followed through the following articles:

Dr. Wyneken, 'Deutsch-Ostafrika und Kongo', *Deutsche Kolonialzeitung*, XVI, August 1899, p. 281, September 1899, pp. 326–7, and October 1899, pp. 382–3.

Rudolf A. Hermann, 'Völkerrechtliche Betrachtungen über den Kiwu-Grenzstreit', *Deutsche Kolonialzeitung*, XVII, January 1900, pp. 24–25.

Brix Förster, 'Deutsch-Ostafrika, 1899–1901', *Globus*, LXXIX, 1901, pp. 233–5.

'Der sogenannte Mfumbiroberg und deutsch-englische Grenzfragen', *Globus*, LXXX, 1902, p. 17.

A. J. Wauters, 'La frontière orientale de notre colonie', *Mouvement Géographique*, XXVI, November 1909, pp. 535–8.

'La Conference de la frontière orientale du Congo belge', *Mouvement Géographique*, XVII, February 1910, pp. 106–7.

M. Moisel, 'Das neue Grenzabkommen zwischen Deutschland und Belgische-Kongo im Kiwusee-Gebiet', *Deutsche Kolonialzeitung*, XXVIII, September 1911, pp. 606–8.

C. Winkler, 'Die Regulierung der Nordwestgrenze von Deutsch-Ostafrika', *Deutsche Kolonialzeitung*, XXIX, March 1912, pp. 145–6.

'Die Wahrheit über den Kiwuseestreit', *Deutsche Kolonialzeitung*, XXXIII, August 1916, pp. 118–20. This article is misleading.

The most important journals giving background and opinion on the Kivu-Mfumbiro dispute are the semi-official *Deutsches Kolonialblatt*, the *Deutsche Kolonialzeitung*, the semi-official *Mouvement Géographique*, and the *Geographical Journal*.

The commentaries which appeared in the colonial journals, while grasping the points at issue between the governments, failed almost entirely to provide detailed documentation of what actually happened. Negotiations were secret; it was not until 1961 that British and Belgian documents of 1910 necessary for a complete account of the dispute became open to public inspection. In part because of this, in part because the Kivu-Mfumbiro controversy was simply forgotten, secondary sources are almost non-existent. The value of Arthur Hardinge's *A Diplomatist in Europe* (London, 1927) lies in its balanced remarks about Leopold II and Belgian politics rather than about the Kivu controversy. The Kivu dispute is only mentioned in the standard histories of the Congo; it is studied briefly in M. L. Stiers, *La frontière orientale du Congo belge* (Brussels, 1937), and P. Jentgen, *Les frontières du Ruanda-Urundi et le régime international de tutelle* (Brussels, 1957), both of which are based mainly on secondary sources. Paul van Vracem, 'Recherches historiques sur le Kivu', *Folia scientifica africae centralis*, March 1959, pp. 6–8, is a three-page summary of the Kivu entanglement apparently based on the Kivu district papers, which I have not had a chance to study. Especially valuable for the Belgian point of view is Pierre van Zuylen, *L'Echiquier Congolais* (Brussels, 1959).

Colonel Close gives a short and almost the only account in English of the Mfumbiro controversy in 'A 50 Years Retrospect', *Empire Survey Review*, II, July 1933, pp. 135–6. Sir John Gray has a penetrating discussion of Stanley's treaties in the *Uganda Journal*, 'Early Treaties in Uganda, 1888–1891', XII, 1948, pp. 25–42. J. M. Coote, a half century later, recounted the expedition 'organized and controlled by folk in London' in the *Uganda Journal*, 'The Kivu Mission, 1909–10', XX, September 1956, pp. 105–12. H. B. Thomas, who adds an interesting note to Coote's article (and cites additional bibliographical material) deals with the Kivu expedition briefly in chapter X of *A History of Uganda Land and Surveys* (written in collaboration with A. E. Spencer; Government Press, Uganda, 1938). This work deals thoroughly with the boundary commissions and the practical problems involved in the 'notoriously . . . difficult, expensive and laborious task'[1] of demarcating a boundary in unexplored, tropical country. E. M. Jack's *On the Congo Frontier* (London, 1914) is an intimate account of his experiences as British boundary commissioner in the Mfumbiro region.

II

The most novel sources used in this book are the documents of the German East Africa government concerning Ruanda-Urundi. They are well-preserved by the Belgian administration in Usumbura—probably one of the very few cases in all Africa where an administration has assumed adequate responsibility for German colonial documents. They are almost complete. There are approximately seventy volumes. Apart from the

[1] Lansdowne to Phipps, no. 72, 3 June 1902, F.O. 2/801.

annual reports, only about a dozen are of any great value—the volumes of correspondence and reports concerning administrative affairs (Verwaltungsangelegenheiten). Important questions found their way into these volumes. The other volumes for the most part are concerned with the land contracts of the missions. There are a few dossiers on economic development, health, forestry, and miscellaneous subjects. The documents for Ruanda are more nearly complete than the ones for Urundi.

The other main collection of unpublished documents used for the administrative section of this book is at the archives of the Entebbe Secretariat, Entebbe, Uganda, which contain complete files of the British administration in Kigezi. There are a few documents concerning the 'Urundi-Ruanda railway' at the Ministry of Railways and Harbours, Dar es Salaam, in a file marked 'Ruandabahn, XII, J,2'; these documents have been read by M. F. Hill in preparation for his *Permanent Way*, volume II, 'The Story of the Tanganyika Railways' (Nairobi, 1959). Ordinances of the German East Africa government were printed in the *Amtlicher Anzeiger für Deutsch-Ostafrika*, a collection of which may be found in the King George V Museum in Dar es Salaam.

In contrast to the volume of pre-First World War diplomatic history of Ruanda-Urundi, there has been little research on German colonial administration to serve as a background for a detailed study of the German administration in Ruanda-Urundi. In particular there is no adequate study of the administration of German East Africa—a problem that probably will remain unsolved until the German colonial records at the Potsdam Zentralarchiv are examined. (I was refused permission to study the documents at Potsdam.) Harry Rudin's *Germans in the Cameroons* (London, 1938) contains the best general discussion of German colonial administration. W. O. Henderson's *Studies in German Colonial History* (London, 1962) has a useful bibliography. M. E. Townsend's *Rise and Fall of Germany's Colonial Empire* (New York, 1930) is helpful only as general background reading.

To my knowledge Pierre Ryckmans is the only other person who has worked extensively with the German documents in Ruanda-Urundi. It was he who collected them and brought them to Usumbura.[2] His *Une page d'histoire coloniale* (Brussels, 1953), is accurate and perceptive; but it only deals with the relations of the German officers with the rulers of Urundi, an important but small part of the subject I have tried to cover. There is also an account of German rule in Urundi in Hans Meyer, *Die Barundi* (Leipzig, 1916 edition), which is of value in discussing Rundi politics and German plans for economic development of Urundi. His bibliography includes an extensive list of articles published by the knowledgeable Father van der Burgt. J. Vansina puts Urundi in the perspective of African history in 'Notes sur l'histoire du Burundi', *Aequatoria*, XXIV, 1961. The only other work worthy of special mention is *Historique et Chronologie du Ruanda* (Astrida, 1955), a slender volume compiled by various Belgian administrators which sketches the main outlines of the history of Ruanda. Although some of the facts and interpretations do not agree with the accounts in the German documents, it is the best guide to main events in Ruanda.

The exploration of Ruanda-Urundi produced rich narratives about the lakes, volcanoes, and peoples of the region in Oskar Baumann's *Durch Massailand zur Nilquelle* (Berlin, 1894); G. A. von Götzen's *Durch Afrika von Ost nach West* (Berlin, 1895); and the Duke Adolphus Frederick of Mecklenburg's *In the Heart of Africa* (English translation; London, 1910). Richard Kandt's *Caput Nili* (2 vols.; Berlin, 1919 edition)—'one of the most outstanding works in our German colonial literature'[3]—is a sensitive account of his early impressions of Ruanda as well as a record of his explorations.

E. Johanssen recounts his missionary experiences in *Ruanda— Kleine Anfänge, Grosse Aufgaben* (Bethel bei Bielefeld, 1912). Missionary reports appeared in *Gott Will Es!; Kreuz und Schwert; Afrika-Bote* (which has interesting illustrations); and *Nachrichten aus der Ostafrikansichen Mission*. There is an excellent collection of missionary sources at the Bethel-Mission, Bethel bei Bielefeld, Germany. The most important sources for missionary activity in Ruanda-Urundi are the unpublished documents of the Ruanda and Urundi Residencies; not only

---

[2] Cf. Pierre Ryckmans, 'La conquête politique', *Grands Lacs*, L, March 1936, p. 307; *Une page d'histoire coloniale*, p. 3.
[3] K. Roehl, 'Ruanda-Erinnerungen', *Koloniale Rundschau*, XXI, 1925, p. 289.

do they contain reports from the missionaries themselves, but also correspondence about subjects that the missionaries considered inappropriate to publish in their journals. As in the case of the contemporary articles appearing in the colonial press, the accounts in the missionary journals are less valuable as a source of information than as a means to judge the sensitivity of the German administration to public opinion. As the Gassldinger affair showed, a single article could have far reaching consequences. The Usumbura archive contains clippings from the missionary journals and the German colonial press, as well as from rare German East Africa publications such as the *Deutsch-Ostafrikanische Zeitung*. Roland Oliver's *Missionary Factor in East Africa* (London, 1952) is helpful background reading for missionary activity.

All research on the German era in Ruanda-Urundi is facilitated by the 201-page bibliography compiled by J. Clement: *Essai de Bibliographie du Ruanda-Urundi* (? Usumbura, 1959). This bibliography does not attempt to cover the pre-First World War diplomacy which affected Ruanda-Urundi; but on all other subjects, ranging from agriculture to zoology, it is definitive for practical purposes, and is probably the best bibliography on Ruanda-Urundi that will ever be compiled. It eliminates the need to try to mention all secondary works concerning various aspects of Ruanda-Urundi, and the two following lists are restricted to those works I have found expecially helpful.

Many German colonial writers touched on the subject of Ruanda-Urundi, but their accounts were often superficial. The following are some of the more significant:

Hans Meyer, *Auf Neuen Wegen durch Ruanda und Urundi* (Berlin, 1912).
K. Roehl, 'Die Socialen und Wirtschaftlichen Verhaltnisse Ruandas' *Koloniale Rundschau*, 1914, no. 5, pp. 270–87; no. 6, pp. 321–37.
H. Schnee, 'Ruanda', in *Deutsches Kolonial Lexicon* (3 vols.; Leipzig, 1920), III, p. 188.
J. M. van der Burgt, *Un grand peuple de l'Afrique Equatoriale* (Bois le Duc, Holland, 1903).
——, 'Land und Leute von Nord-Urundi', *Petermanns Mitteilungen*, 1912, p. 324.

Part of the following list is taken from the writings of

anthropologists, who have done by far the most research on Ruanda and Urundi:

Ethel M. Albert, 'Socio-Political Organization and Receptivity to Change: Some Differences between Ruanda and Urundi', *Southwestern Journal of Anthropology*, XVI, 1960, pp. 46–73.

Bernhard Ankermann, in *Das Eingeborenenrecht, Ostafrika* (E. Schultz-Ewerth and L. Adam, eds.; Stuttgart, 1929).

A. d'Arianoff, *Histoire des Bagesera, Souverains du Gisaka* (Brussels, 1952).

R. Bourgeois, *Banyarwanda et Barundi* (4 vols.; Brussels, 1953–8).

R. Borgerhoff, *Le Ruanda-Urundi* (Brussels, 1928).

A. Delacauw, 'Droit coutumier des Barundi', *Congo*, I, 1936, no. 3, pp. 332–57; no. 4, pp. 481–522.

F. Dufays, *Pages d'épopée africaine. Jours troublés* (Brussels, 1928).

J. Gorju, *Face au royaume hamite du Ruanda* (Brussels, 1938).

A. Jamoulle, 'Notre territoire à mandat: le Ruanda-Urundi', *Congo*, I, 1927, no. 3, pp. 477–96.

Alexis Kagame, 'Premiers contacts du Ruanda et de l'Occident', *Grands Lacs*, 1950, LXVI, no. 135, pp. 7–19. Kagame is one of the leading authorities on Ruanda. Further works by him are cited in the bibliographies of his books mentioned here.

——, *Les organisations socio-familiales de l'ancien Rwanda* (Brussels, 1955).

——, *La philosophie bantu-rwandaise de l'Etre* (Brussels, 1955).

——, *Histoire du Rwanda* (Leverville, 1958). A short, popular history of Ruanda.

——, *La notion de génération appliquée à la généalogie dynastique et à l'histoire du Rwanda des X-XI siécles à nos jours* (Brussels, 1959).

Louis de Lacger, *Ruanda* (2 vols.; Namur, 1940).

Jacques J. Macquet, *The Premise of Inequality in Ruanda* (London, 1961).

H. Meinhard, 'The Interlacustrine Bantu', 1947, typescript at the Institute of Social Anthropology, Oxford.

A. Pagès, *Un royaume hamite au centre de l'Afrique* (Brussels, 1933).

P. Ryckmans, 'L'organisation politique et sociale dans l'Urundi', *Revue Générale*, April 1921, pp. 460–84.

III

The military engagements fought in Ruanda-Urundi are discussed exhaustively in the official Belgian account, *Les campagnes coloniales belges, 1914–1918* (Ministère de la Defense

Nationale; 3 vols.; 1925–32); in a manuscript at the Bundes-archiv, Koblenz, by L. Boell entitled 'Der Feldzug in Ost-afrika', which was condensed into *Die Operationen in Ostafrika* (Hamburg, 1952); and in the official British account, *Military Operations in East Africa, 1914–1916* (2 vols.; based on a draft by Major H. FitzM. Stacke, and compiled by Lt.-Col. Charles Hordern; London, 1941). The second volume of the official British account has not been published. Of these three major works, the British account is the most analytical and is an excellent military history; but it only goes to 1916. Material for the second volume has been compiled at the War Office in London, but is not available for public inspection. Lt.-Col. H. Moyse-Bartlett used some of the sources collected for the second volume of the east African campaign[4] in his history of *The King's African Rifles* (Aldershot, Hants, 1956), but adds nothing new about Anglo-Belgian cooperation. It is a pity that the second volume has never been completed.

The following works give interesting insights into various aspects of Ruanda-Urundi and the First World War:

Beyens, *La Question Africaine*, (Brussels and Paris, 1918).
J. Buhrer, *L'Afrique Orientale Allemande et la guerre 1914–1918* (Paris, 1923).
A. Cayen, *Tabora* (Brussels, 1921).
P. Daye, *Avec les vainqueurs de Tabora* (Paris, 1918).
——, *Les conquêtes Africaines des Belges* (Paris, 1918).
——, *Trois ans de victoires belges en Afrique* (Brussels, 1920).
Sir Charles Lucas, ed., *The Empire at War* (5 vols.; London, 1921–26), IV.
A. Matagné, 'Des marches du Kivu jusqu'à Tabora', *Revue Nationale*, (Brussels) XXVII, September 1955, pp. 283–7. A summary of Olsen's career.
La Revue Coloniale Belge, I, no. 14, May 1946, pp. 3–7. Tombeur's reflections on the east African campaign.
Lt.-Gen. Baron Wahis, 'La participation belge à la conquête du Cameroun et de l'Afrique Orientale Allemande', *Congo*, April 1920, I, pp. 1–45.
Charles Stiénon, *La campagne Anglo-Belge* (Paris, 1917).
B. E. M. Weber, 'Influence des facteurs politiques sur la conduite de la guerre en Afrique Orientale Allemande', *Bulletin Belge des Sciences militaires*, February 1926, I, no. 2, pp. 174–90.

---

[4] Brigadier H. B. Latham in a letter to me of 19 March 1962.

Revealing accounts of the east African peace settlement can be found in O. Louwers, *La campagne africaine de la Belgique* (Brussels, 1921), and P. Hymans, *Mémoires* (2 vols.; Bruges, ?1957), and van Zuylen, *L'Echiquier Congolais*. The Milner papers (New College, Oxford) concerning the peace negotiations apparently have been returned to the British government. The van den Heuvel papers at the Archives Générales du Royaume, Brussels, are valuable for the general policy followed by the Belgian government during the African negotiations of 1919 and for background to the problem of the southern Congo bank. The full story of the Anglo-Belgian partition of east Africa in 1919, however, can be found only in other unpublished papers which I was kindly allowed to study for the preparation of the third part of this book; a condition attached to this generosity was that I would not reveal my source of information.

821621–s

NOTES

A. The most important Belgian and German documents for the years 1884–5 have been published and discussed in the article mentioned in footnote 1, 'Der Kiwusee-Grenzstreit mit dem Kongostaat'; a few more appear in Thomson's appendix, pp. 321–7.

In later years these documents were the subject of much commentary. Some of the most important unpublished documents in which discussion appears are: A. E. W. Clarke's memorandum of 8 October 1900, F.O. 2/800; I.D. to F.O., 23 December 1901, F.O. 2/800; Belgian memorandum, incl. in Phipps to Lansdowne, no. 36 Africa, 12 June 1902, F.O. 2/800; Dernburg to A.A., 24 October 1906, A.A. 3/1; 'Instruktion für den Wirklichen Legationsrat Dr. von Jacobs, geheim, 6 February 1908, A.A. 3/1; 'Note sur le territoire contesté de la Ruzizi et du Kivu', undated (1908), M.A.E. 1/38/5; Lindequist's memorandum of 21 October 1909, A.A. 3/3; 'Denkschrift über deutsch-ostafrikanisch-kongolesische Streitfragen', undated (1909), A.A. 3/3; Hardinge to Grey, no. 17 Africa confid., 11 February 1910, F.O. 367/174; Ebermaier to Dernburg, 21 February 1910, A.A. 3/4; 'Bericht über die in Brüssel geführten Verhandlungen behufs Abgrenzung des Nordwestens von Deutsch-Ostafrika', undated (1910), A.A. 3/6; 'Aufzeichnung über dem deutsch-belgischen Grenzstreit', undated (1910), A.A. 3/5; 'Exposé des Motivs', undated (1910), M.A.E. 1/38/4; 'Le malentendu entre l'Allemagne et la Belgique', undated (1910), M.A.E. 1/38/4.

See also: Dr. Wyneken, 'Deutsch-Ostafrika und der Kongostaat', *Deutsche Kolonialzeitung*, XVI, August 1899, p. 281, September 1899, pp. 326–7, and October 1899, pp. 382–3; Rudolf A. Hermann, 'Völkerrechtliche Betrachtungen über den Kiwu-Grenzstreit', Ibid., XVII, January 1900, pp. 24–25; ; Dr. Max Schlagintweit, 'Die Nordwestgrenze von Deutsch-Ostafrika', Ibid., XXV, January 1908, pp. 50–51; R. A. Hermann, 'Die Nordwestgrenze von Deutsch-Ostafrika', Ibid., XXV, February 1908, p. 143; Dr. Max Schlagintweit, 'Nochmals die Nordwestgrenze von Deutsch-Ostafrika', Ibid., XXV, April 1908, p. 295; A. J. Wauters, 'La frontière orientale de notre colonie', *Mouvement Géographique*, XXVI, November 1909, pp. 535–8; Alfred Zimmermann, 'Die Wahrheit über den Kivuseestreit', *Deutsche Kolonialzeitung*, XXXIII, August 1916, pp. 118–20.

B.

Tribes	Territory
1. Wanyankori	Ankole, Mpororo
2. Wahuma	Territory between the Ituri river
Bavira	and the Nyanza
Balegga	
3. Kitagwenda	Kitagwend, Unyapakada
4. Bakonju	Ukonju, Semliki valley
5. Basongora	Usongara
6. Bundussuma	Undussuma

The original treaties are in F.O. 2/139; copies are in F.O. 84/2081. The British Company wrote that the government 'may be pleased with as little delay as possible to declare a protectorate over the territories which have been ceded to the Company in virtue of the treaties'. British East Africa Company to F.O., 2 May 1890, F.O. 84/2081. See also Hertslet, I, pp. 374–8; *Accounts and Papers*, LVI, Africa no. 4, 1892; and the first annual report of the directors of the I.B.E.A. Company to the shareholders, cited in H. R. Fox Bourne, *The Other Side of the Emin Pasha Relief Expedition* (London, 1891), which describes how Stanley 'came into communication with the chiefs of many of the states through which he passed, and obtained from them the cession of their sovereign rights. . . . Stanley has patriotically transferred [them] to the company . . .' (p. 181). Neither Stanley's *Autobiography* (Dorothy Stanley, ed.; London, 1909), nor *In Darkest Africa* (2 vols.; London, 1890) reveal anything about the treaties.

C. Major Gibbons to Salisbury, 1 October 1900, F.O. 2/800.

Johnston wrote: 'Do we still aim at anything like direct communication between our territories in south and central Africa and those in the Nile basin? If so, there are two ways of effecting this end in the future. One is by looking forward to the eventual break-up of the Congo Free State and the attribution by Great Britain to itself of all the territory along the west coast of Tanganyika, and thence up to the Albert-Edward Nyanza. If this is the ambition we mean to hold in view to the extent of preventing this piece of territory being taken by Germany or France, then we can view with some degree of resignation the frontier of German East Africa being brought up to Lake Kivu and to the Ruzizi river. But if we are not prepared to anger Germany by interposing a strip of territory between her possessions on the east of Tanganyika and any ambition she may have of marching across the Congo Free State to the Atlantic, then I think we ought to stick out for a strip of territory to the north of Lake Tanganyika, past Lake Kivu and Mt. Mfumbiro to the south end of Albert Edward. The waters of Tanganyika being international, and our possessing the south end of it would give us a free highway from the Cape to Cairo by way of this strip connecting the north end of Tanganyika with the Uganda Protectorate. In such case we could view with equanimity a German empire stretching right across Africa from east to west (excepting the open water of Tanganyika). But I think it would be unfair to the interests of Great Britain that Germany should aim not only at the absorption of the greater part of the Congo Free State but also at the blocking of the land route between Uganda and the north end of Lake Tanganyika. Could we not arrive at some friendly and private understanding with her on this question?' Johnston to Brodrick, private, 27 August 1900, F.O. 2/800.

D. The activities of the boundary commissions are one of the few things which can be followed through published sources. Accounts appeared in the *Deutsches Kolonialblatt, Deutsche Kolonialzeitung, Mouvement Géographique, Globus, Mitteilungen aus den deutschen Schutzgebieten*, and several other geographical journals. There is no need to list all the articles appearing in these journals; most were merely duplications of commentaries which appeared in the *Kolonialblatt* or the *Mouvement Géographique*. The work of the commissions can be followed adequately through the following articles: *Kolonialblatt*, XI, November 1900, p. 864; XII, January 1901, p. 40; XII, 15 March 1901, p. 183; XII, April 1901, p. 232; XIII, May 1902, p. 194; XIII, August 1902, p. 335; XIII, August 1902, p. 363; *Mouvement Géographique*, XIX, June 1902, pp. 296-9, 307-8; XXI, April 1904, p. 199; XXI, October 1904, p. 488; XXIII, February 1906, pp. 49-52; XXIII, February 1906, pp. 95-99.

Since the Anglo-German boundary commission of 1902-4 did not visit the Mfumbiro region there is no reason to account for all its activities here. The reason why it did not fulfil its original instructions is only to be found in unpublished documents. See however, 'Extracts from Lt. Col. C. Delmé-Radcliffe's Typescript Diary Report on the Delimitation of the Anglo-German Boundary, Uganda, 1902-04', *Uganda Journal*, XI, March 1947, and his articles in the *Geographical Journal*, 'Surveys and Studies in Uganda', XXVI, November 1905, pp. 481-97, and December 1905, pp. 616-32. The Anglo-Congolese boundary commission of 1907 is similarly beyond the scope of this study, although it too was originally to have surveyed the Mfumbiro district. See Bright to C.O., confid., 28 October 1908, incl. in no. 38, C.O. to F.O., 8 December 1908, F.O. 403/403. The settlement of 1910 was dependent on the work of all three commissions, but the Congolese-German survey provided the information necessary to delimit Ruanda-Urundi.

The members of the various boundary commissions are listed in H. B. Thomas and A. E. Spencer, *A History of Uganda Land and Surveys*, chapter X (Government Press, Uganda, 1938).

E. The British obtained their information from Lt. Weiss, the surveyor of the Mecklenburg expedition. On 22 March 1908 Lt.-Col. Bright reported that he had discovered through a conversation with Weiss—who was 'unaware apparently that His Majesty's Government claim that [Mfumbiro] mountain region'—that

821621-s*

Weiss's mission had been to survey the Mfumbiro country, and that he had done this with the concurrence of the Congolese authorities. (Lt.-Col. Bright to F.O., secret, 22 March 1908, F.O. 403/403.)

Behrens, who had known Weiss on the Anglo-German boundary commission, saw him in Germany in July 1908; Behrens provided further information. Danckelmann, Behrens reported, was the one responsible for utilizing the Mecklenburg expedition to acquire surveys and reports of the economic value of the area; but Weiss and Mecklenburg, advocates of a 'very forward colonial policy', regarded Danckelmann's attitude as 'weak and wanting in firmness'. 'The Duke appears to interest himself in the subject, and expressed his intention of making certain that his most forward policy should prevail at the Colonial Office.' (Report by T. T. Behrens of 13 August 1908, F.O. 403/403. See also the memorandum of 9 June 1908 in A.A. 3/1. Cf. *Historique et Chronologie du Ruanda*, Astrida, 1955, p. 16.)

F. Ireland recounts the British withdrawal and Belgian advance: 'The whole mission evacuated Rubona on the 1st July 1909, marching 15 miles to Zenia stream. I stayed on Rubona sketching with an escort of Sikhs. I commenced sketching about 7:30 A.M. and saw the whole mission "safari" leave at 8 A.M. I remained sketching till 10:10 A.M. There was no one on Rubona when I left. On reaching Zenia camp I learnt in the evening that the political officer had that morning left two Soudanese privates, with a headmen, four porters, and a servant, behind to buy food the local natives were bringing in for sale. The headman had orders to remain half an hour and rejoin the mission "safari". He disobeyed these orders when I left, nor did I know anyone had been left behind, or I should have taken them on with me. Next morning, the 2nd July, early, one of the porters left at Rubona arrived at the mission camp at Zenia, and stated that after 12 noon the day before, Capt. Wangermée, with some 100 askaris, had most dishonestly broken his word and returned from Rutshuru. Seeing the two askaris and four porters, Captain Wangermée charged with his force and captured these British subjects. Though the local natives gave the headman ample warning of the Belgians' approach he and his party made no attempt to escape, having been assured by the political officer that the Belgians would not molest them. One porter, however, hid in the grass till nightfall, and escaped. He stated the Belgians were looting wholesale—a statement afterwards fully corroborated by the local natives. The Sikhs and Soudanese showed a very fine spirit in requesting permission to at once return and rescue their two comrades. They were persuaded to remain quiet till the political officer sent a letter of remonstrance. Capt. Wangermée's answer, when received, was obviously antedated two days, and was not dated from any place, though the bearer of it had seen it written 15 to 20 miles off Kigezi (the mission camp where the reply was awaited) on the date of delivery to the British political officer. His answer made no excuse for his behaviour, and was calculated to try and make one believe his civil superior was responsible for his return to disputed territory. As this officer had previously stated his civil superior was away, he was of course trying, by looting provisions and cattle, to remedy his ignorance of a considerable British force having been in his district for twelve days, and that posts had been formed by this force without his knowledge.' 'A Report of the Kivu Mission's Movements . . .', 5 July 1909, incl. 10 in no. 108, F.O. 403/411.

G. The Germans wanted the discussions to be held in Berlin. Hardinge commented: 'It is clear that they [the Germans] have some reason for wanting to negotiate at Berlin, but wish to lead us into supposing that they are making the proposal to oblige the Belgians. I do not like to hazard far-fetched suggestions, but you are aware that one of the elements which the Germans value in their proximity to the Congo State is the leverage which it gives them for bringing pressure here in Europe upon Belgium, and it is just possible, and would be quite consistent with the brutal tone of their last note to her, that they may have in view some concession or gain, commercial or other, to be obtained by them over here in return for a more conciliatory attitude in Africa, which would have the further advantage of shining in the eyes of the Belgian public by contrast to our own unyielding one; and if so, that they may prefer to continue to treat directly with Belgium side by side of course with the tripartite conference, through their own Foreign Office rather than through Count Wallwitz. The Belgians would naturally hail any indication of a disposition on the part of Germany to deal directly with them at Berlin. . . .' (Hardinge to Grey, no. 163—no. 150 Africa confid.—4 December 1909, F.O. 403/411; cf. Goschen to Hardinge, 4 December 1909, F.O. 367/129.)

The Germans, however, yielded to the British wish to have the conference in Brussels, where the British negotiations could be guided by Arthur Hardinge, who 'not only knows the subject thoroughly but has local knowledge'. (Langley's minute on Hardinge to Grey, no. 139 Africa confid., 4 December 1909, F.O. 367/129.)

H. 'The Belgians are, I believe, ready with a "proposition conciliante", but I shall be surprised if they do not regard the attitude of Germany as in the highest degree unconciliatory, or thank her for a concession which merely amounts to saying that she will not deprive them of more territory than she up to the present claimed. I pointed this out to Herr Ebermaier, and asked him whether, supposing the negotiations failed owing to the very unyielding position assumed by him, he would be prepared to submit his case to arbitration. Though he could not give a positive answer, he professed confidence that the Germans would win at arbitration, for the curiously Prussian reason that the Congo State and its successor Belgium as weak neutral powers, whose very existence depended upon the faith of treaties, were bound in their own interests to be peculiarly scrupulous—more so, he implied, than the masters of many legions—in observing the spirit as well as the letter of these instruments. He showed a certain reluctance to admit my contention that weak and great powers would be held by an arbitrator to be as equal in a public law suit as a poor and a wealthy citizen in a private one, and I look forward with some interest to his enunciating these Bismarckian doctrines in the conference, and to their effect upon the Belgian delegates.' Hardinge to Grey, no. 41 Africa confid., 12 March 1910, F.O. 367/174.

I. Subject to a satisfactory Congolese-German agreement and concession of British access to and commercial facilities on Lake Kivu. The boundary was to run to Karisimbi instead of Sabinyo (the Belgian suggestion); this would give Britain access to the highest mountain in the range. (18 April.) A few days later, van der Elst told Hardinge that the access to Kivu could be arranged, but that the change from Sabinyo to Karisimbi was a return to the original British position, since it cut off the Belgian post of Rutshuru from the villages on which it depended for its supplies. (21 April.) Hardinge explained the Belgian objections: 'The Belgian feeling is . . . a reluctance to avow to Parliament that Belgium has not only given all the fertile and populous portion of Mfumbiro save Rutshuru and the adjacent villages but has, in the dreary region of rock and lava left by us to her, surrendered its most conspicuous and interesting mountain peak.' (29 April.) Grey thought that since Karisimbi was composed of 50 square miles of all rock and lava that there was no point in causing the Belgians any more trouble simply because of the sentimental reason that it was the highest in the range. (2 May.) Crewe, however, was willing to yield Karisimbi only if it were clear that none of Coote's posts fell within 50 miles of it, and if this bargain were offered at the last moment, when all other outstanding points with the Belgians had been satisfactorily settled. (9 May.) Britain accordingly withdrew her claim to Karisimbi. Hardinge to Grey, no. 67 Africa confid., 18 April 1910; no. 71 Africa, 21 April; no. 77 Africa confid., 29 April; F.O. to C.O., 2 May; C.O. to F.O., 9 May; F.O. 367/175.

J. Schimmer argued that this was necessary because the 'S-Fonds' (*Selbstbewirtschaftungs-Fonds*) provided by the central government to the local authorities for administrative expenses were insufficient to cover the cost of construction. Apart from the 'S-Fonds' the Residencies in Ruanda and Urundi had several sources of local revenue, but they often had trouble balancing their budgets. The following figures indicate in German East Africa rupees the principal local revenues and expenditures for Urundi during the later years. The figures roughly approximate those in Ruanda.

Revenues

	1912	*1913*	*1914*
Hut and head taxes	5,560	600	1,000
Business taxes	3,469	6,100	4,500
Customs	372	540	—
Cattle and farming	6,420	6,750	5,300

Revenues

	1912	*1913*	*1914*
Beer tax	2,017	1,750	2,000
Hunting licences	445	200	200
Weapon licences	161	300	—
Judicial proceedings	2,719	3,200	3,500
Miscellaneous	2,015	500	500

Expenditures

Police force	—	20,293	31,000
Coloured personnel	3,430	4,112	3,698
Medical expenses	1,018	407	37
Schools	89	134	55
Building maintenance	803	2,380	300
Road construction	466	45	—
Rent	60	17	480
Agriculture	26	21	—
Office supplies	480	975	300
Freight, messages	2,517	3,742	830
District trips	3,133	3,057	530
Judicial proceedings	817	1,500	—
Miscellaneous	657	614	200

K. In both Ruanda and Urundi there was talk of building hospitals before the outbreak of the First World War. In Urundi there were great problems of public health, especially in the Tanganyika valley. 'Problems of health in the Tanganyika basin are *bad*', Langenn wrote in 1913. 'There is malaria, dysentery and sickness caused from worms throughout the whole year . . .' 'Dysentery is a plague in almost every native house in Usumbura, and malaria is a great danger for almost all Rundi who come down from the highlands. All the Europeans at the post have suffered more or less heavily from malaria despite precise preventive measures, and are almost all exhausted from the humid, hot climate. Two Europeans became ill with dysentery. . . . As far as the health of Europeans is concerned, the difference between Usumbura and the healthy highlands cannot be emphasized enough.' (Urundi Jahresbericht 1911.)

The German authorities regarded 'the combat against sleeping sickness as the most important responsibility'. A team of public health officials were assigned to devote their full time toward fighting the disease; in 1911, for example, there were four *Ärzte* and 10 *Sanitätsunteroffiziere*, who, 'through real, unceasing, and sacrificing work have made the road through the Ruzizi valley and the immediate neighbourhood around Usumbura from the northern end of the lake to the steamer-docks as well as the immediate region around the five camps, and the long bank along the Tanganyika, almost free of flies'. The work of the public health team included destroying flies and their breeding places, and reducing contagion of disease by medically treating those infected. In 1911 an average of 816 Africans a month were treated at the German posts, and 1,017 a month by the travelling team. While at Usumbura, the Resident found much of his time and energy spent on health; this was one of the main reasons why the Residency was moved to Kitega in 1912. The Urundi annual reports have the best descriptions of the battles against disease.

Inland the health conditions were more or less the same as in Ruanda: favourable. There were some cases of malaria, which was considered the most serious illness. Epidemics were infrequent; there were many cases of lung sicknesses, dysentery, skin diseases, and stomach troubles. Dysentery was perhaps the most common sickness apart from the lung illnesses, and was aggravated by unhygienic African toilet habits, which the Residents tried to correct by teaching the use of latrines. Another problem was diet; lack of proper nourishment was aggravated by bad beer. Gudovius regarded the main problem in public health as the 'carelessness and negligence' of the Africans in keeping their living quarters clean, and their indifference to preventive measures against infection. See Gesundheitsverhältnisse Ruanda, I V/C/41.

L. An instruction to the Residents of 15 June 1906 ran: 'Avoid if at all possible measures against tribal heads which could weaken their authority and their influence with the native tribal members; this relates especially to all degrading punishment.' Immediately before the outbreak of the First World War, the central government issued the following instruction to the Residents: 'If a Tutsi receives a thrashing it is degrading for him. Punishment by flogging should be given to Tutsi only in exceptional cases. A beaten Tutsi . . . will never forget the punishment.' (1 June 1914.)

Wintgens, Resident of Ruanda in 1914, replied that he seldom used flogging as punishment for Tutsi, but in some cases it was necessary and effective. Musinga himself, in fact, had occasionally asked the Resident to punish a disobedient Tutsi by thrashing. (Wintgens to Gouverneur, 28 July 1914, RU. IV I/D/34.)

Schimmer characteristically held a much stronger opinion. All other forms of punishment, he said, were ineffective: 'the Tutsi is accustomed to a hard school; whoever did not cooperate with Kissabo . . . had his hand hacked off. He finds it mild, and hardly degrading, if he receives a good flogging. That the Tutsi does not forget a flogging is desired; for then the purpose of the punishment is fulfilled.' (Schimmer to Gouverneur, 24 June 1914, UR. IV I/D/34.)

M. The government bought land in the immediate surroundings of the European settlements such as Usumbura, Kitega, Kigali; it was declared 'Crownland' (*Kronland*) which could then be sold to businesses or individuals. In 1910 in Ruanda 'Crownland' was sold from five to ten hellers a quadratmetre.

Schimmer wrote in August 1914: 'As far as Urundi is concerned, land alienation in large complexes is only concerned with missionaries; it will remain this way in the future also; there is no room for European planters and cattle rearers.' (Schimmer to Gouverneur, 1 August 1914, Erlasse, Verordungen in Grundstücksangelegenheiten, unnumbered.)

After the conclusion of the Kivu-Mfumbiro agreement of 1910, the military posts of Ischangi, Kisenyi, and Ruhengeri were abandoned by governmental decree of 22 July 1911. The XI Company retained a post at Kisenyi, but the town itself was placed under civil authority. A small customs post was maintained at Kisenyi, but did little business; in 1912 the total customs revenue was 276 marks for all of Ruanda. Ruhengeri was reoccupied shortly after its abandonment when the unrest in northern Ruanda increased.

N. Throughout German East Africa the officers were instructed to preserve their natural resources in the regions under their jurisdiction: in Ruanda-Urundi this instruction mainly concerned forests. Dr. Kandt wrote in 1910 that 'Ruanda is not poor in forests, as is often maintained, but the good regions are unfavourably divided'. Deforestation by the Hutu was considerable; but Kandt could not convince Musinga that this was a problem. Musinga had 'unsurpassable indolence' as far as forests were concerned; 'The forest was there already when we were born and it will still be there when we both die'. (Ruanda Jahresbericht 1909.) In 1911 the Rubengera district of Ruanda was declared 'forest reserve'. Until 1911 in Urundi the creation of forest reserves remained 'a pious wish'. In 1912 a 'Bururi' forest reserve was declared, and in 1913 Teza (Kibira); deforestation along mountains of the Ruzizi valley and in the Luwironza forest by Kitega was also forbidden.

O. Orts to Milner, 30 May 1919, with accompanying agreement and map. Milner wrote to Orts on 31 May:

'I am glad to find that we are now in agreement as to the proposition to be submitted to the Supreme Council with regard to the boundary between the Belgian and British spheres in that country, and that you accept the suggestion made in my letter of May 26th, that any part of German East Africa allotted to Belgium should be held on the same terms as apply to the part allotted to Great Britain.

'I note with satisfaction that you withdraw the demand for a pecuniary compensation to Belgium in respect of that part of the territory at present occupied by her, which, under the delimitation now proposed, she will have to evacuate. It would have been quite impossible for me to assent to such a proposal. On the other hand, I have always recognized that Belgium might claim to be indemnified for the cost of any permanent improvements effected in the territory hitherto occupied by her, but now to be transferred to Great Britain. You say, however, that you are willing to advise your government not to make any claim on this score or for any military expenses incurred by you in east Africa on British account, which have not yet been settled, provided we make no claim for similar expenses still unsettled, incurred by us on your account. Personally, I think it most desirable to get rid of these claims and counter claims, none of which can be of great amount, and while I cannot commit myself on the point without consulting the British Treasury and War Office, I will do my best to bring about an arrangement on the lines you suggest.

'I likewise agree with your proposal that the facilities of transit and transport to be accorded to Belgium through the east African territories under British control, about which we are in principle agreed—for I note that you regard my letter of May 26th as containing a fair interpretation of your demands under this head—should be settled by a Conference of expert representatives of both parties, to be held at an early date. The Conference in question would lay down the general lines of the contemplated arrangements which would have to be subsequently worked out in detail by the local authorities.

'As the understanding between us on the main points of discussion appears to be complete I have signed and herewith return to you the proposal. . . .'

INDEX

Aborigines Society, 252 nn. 7 and 8.
Agriculture and agricultural products, 109–10, 134, 151–2, 173–5, 257.
Aka boundary, 56 n. 8.
Akanjaru river, 104–6, 112, 165, 221.
Akidas, 129.
Albert, lake, 15–16, 32.
Alcohol regulations, 152.
Alexandra Nile, 104.
Allied and Associated Powers, 231, 236–7.
Allied Supreme Council, *see* Council.
Alvensleben, 34, 37, 42, 46, 81, 82 n. 1.
Anderson, Sir Percy, 92, 96, 96 n. 8; and the Anglo-German hinterland negotiations, 10 n. 8, 18, 18 n. 5, 19, 19 nn. 7 and 8, 20–22, 25 n. 5, 26 n. 3, 28, 28 n. 3; and the Anglo-Congolese negotiations of 1894, 31, 31 n. 8, 32, 32 n. 6, 33, 35, 39–40.
Anglo-Belgian cooperation in the First World War, 214–16, 216 n. 1, 222, 231.
Anglo-Belgian east African negotiations of 1919, *see* Milner-Orts negotiations.
Anglo-Belgian protocol of 1910, 91.
Anglo-Congolese agreement of 1894, 30, 32–33, 33 n. 8, 35, 37–38, 40, 41 n. 3, 49, 57, 72 n. 5, 73 n. 6, 81 n. 7, 83, 95, 97, 162; negotiations, 30–40.
Anglo-Congolese agreement of 1906, 73.
Anglo-Congolese boundary commission, 273 n. D.
Anglo-German agreement of 1909, 64–65, 71, 72 n. 6, 73–75, 75 n. 2, 77, 78 n. 9, 83, 85, 88–89, 95, 97; negotiations, 61–64.
Anglo-German boundary commission, 47–52, 55, 273 n. D.
Anglo-German east African boundary, 19, 53, 64, 259.
Anglo-German (Heligoland) agreement of 1890, 3–4, 11, 14, 16, 18, 26, 28, 30, 45, 49, 53, 55, 57, 62–63, 73 n. 6, 81 n. 7, 83–84, 84 n. 7, 96–97, 103, 161; negotiations, 17 n. 6, 18–29.
Anglo-German Mfumbiro conference of 1906, 53; 1908, 55–57, 97; 1909, 61–64, 87, 97.
Anglo-German protocol of 1906, 52–53; 1910, 91.
Anglo-Portuguese agreement of 1884, 233.

Angola, and the Paris Peace Conference, 233, 241, 243, 247.
Ankole, 11 n. 5, 69 n. 8, 213, 272 n. B.
Arab merchants, *see* Indian merchants.
Association Internationale du Congo, see International Association of the Congo.
'Astronomical' boundaries, 42, 46, 58, 80–81, 84, 93.
Atlantic Ocean, 4, 34, 207, 233–4, 244–5.
Austria-Hungary, 33.
Auswärtiges Amt, *see* Germany (Foreign Office).

Bafasoni, 111.
Baganda, agents in British Ruanda, 196–7.
Baha, 154.
Bahr el Gazal, 162
Bakonju, 272 n. B.
Balegga, 272 n. B.
Baletwa, 154.
Balfour, 254.
Bambutsa, 111.
Bami, *see* Mwami.
Banguelo, lake, 27 n. 8.
Bangura, 138, 138 n. 2.
Banjakarama, 132.
Banjiginja, 126.
Bansabugabo, 131, 134, 138.
Bantu, 107–8, 112, 143, 174, 194.
Barthelemy, Father, 123, 177.
Basongora, 272 n. B.
Bassebja, 148, 154–5, 157.
Bassompierre, de, 80 n. 4, 82, 253.
Bastien, 47, 59.
Batanga, 111.
Batare, 111.
Batware b'intebe, 110.
Baumann, Oskar, Urundi explorations, 41 n. 4, 103–4, 104 n. 6, 105.
Bavira, 272 n. B.
Bazobe, 154.
Beer, G. L., 252–3.
Beernaert, 46–47.
Behrens, T. T., 52, 55 n. 8, 61 nn. 9 and 1, 62, 80 n. 4, 87, 92, 274 n. E.
Belgian Colonial Ministry, *see* Belgium.
Belgian Foreign Ministry, *see* Belgium.
Belgian-German protocol of 1910, 91; 1911, 189.
Belgium (*see also* Congo State), 5 n. 4, 42, 64 n. 4; and the Kivu-Mfumbiro